Pearson

A new generation of literacy instruction

ReadyGEN

Grade 2 Classroom Library

The Grade 2 library includes 12 trade books, **25 copies each.** Please use this checklist to ensure that you have received each of the following trade books.

UNIT	MODULE	TITLE
1	A	Trouble in the Sandbox
1	B	Friends Around the World
2	A	Alexander, Who Used to Be Rich Last Sunday
2	B	Money Matters!
3	A	Theodore Roosevelt: The Adventurous President
3	B	Change Makers
4	A	The Earth Dragon Awakes
4	B	Disaster Alert!
5	A	John Chapman: Planter and Pioneer
5	B	Pioneers to the West
6	A	On Meadowview Street
6	A	68 Ways to Save the Planet Before Bedtime

PearsonSchool.com
800-848-9500

ISBN: 0328869732

PDF.0516.PC.KR.VK.

581L254

GRADE 2

Scaffolded Strategies
HANDBOOK

PEARSON

Glenview, Illinois • Boston, Massachusetts • Chandler, Arizona • Upper Saddle River, New Jersey

Acknowledgments of third-party content appear on page 495, which constitutes an extension of this copyright page.

ISBN-13: 978-0-328-85171-3
ISBN-10: 0-328-85171-X
12 19

Table of Contents

Part 1 Unlock the Text

Table of Contents

Part 2 Unlock the Writing

Scaffolded Lessons for the Performance-Based Assessments

Scaffolded Lessons for the Writing Types

Part 3 Routines and Activities

Reading Routines

Table of Contents

Part 4 Unlock Language Learning

Anchor Text, Supporting Text, and Writing

Language Routines and Resources

Acknowledgments

About This Book

What is the Scaffolded Strategies Handbook?

The *Scaffolded Strategies Handbook* is a valuable resource that provides support at the module level for all learners. As part of an integrated reading and writing program, this handbook works in tandem with each unit of the *ReadyGEN™ Teacher's Guide* to help you guide students as they read and write about the texts within each module. It provides models of scaffolded instruction, useful strategies, and practical routines that you can employ during reading and writing to support

- English language learners
- struggling readers
- students with disabilities
- accelerated learners

It is intended that these lessons be used during small-group time with students that you determine need additional scaffolded instruction for any of the ReadyGEN texts or writing activities. Refer to this handbook during planning to determine which lessons will provide the most focused scaffolds for your students. You may use any or all of the lessons or lesson parts as dictated by the needs of your students. Keep in mind that this handbook is meant not only for the classroom teacher, but can be used by any support person working with the diverse student population in your school.

Using the Scaffolded Strategies Handbook

Part 1 Unlock the Text

Within Part 1 of this handbook, titled Unlock the Text, every anchor and supporting text in the ReadyGEN program is supported by research-proven scaffolds and strategies. Each lesson is divided into three parts:

- **Prepare to Read** This portion of the lesson provides more intensive readiness before reading. Students preview the text, activate background knowledge, and are introduced to troublesome vocabulary.

- **Interact with Text** Here, students do close reading and focus on stumbling blocks in the text.

- **Express and Extend** This section allows students to react to the text by discussing and writing about their ideas.

With every student text, qualitative measures of text complexity, such as those determined by the Common Core Learning Standards, are identified:

- Levels of Meaning
- Structure
- Language Conventionality and Clarity
- Knowledge Demands

Each of the three lesson parts is divided to address all of these qualitative measures. These become customized access points for your specific student populations, allowing all students to access and make sense of complex texts.

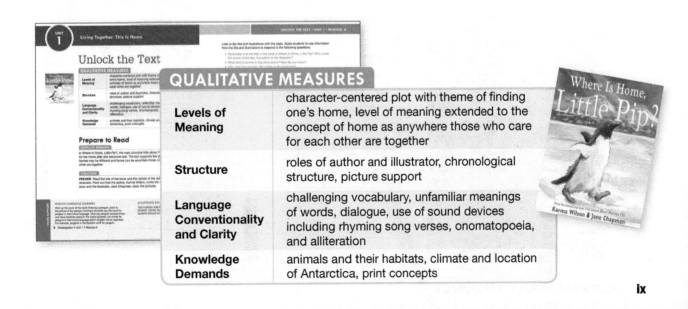

QUALITATIVE MEASURES	
Levels of Meaning	character-centered plot with theme of finding one's home, level of meaning extended to the concept of home as anywhere those who care for each other are together
Structure	roles of author and illustrator, chronological structure, picture support
Language Conventionality and Clarity	challenging vocabulary, unfamiliar meanings of words, dialogue, use of sound devices including rhyming song verses, onomatopoeia, and alliteration
Knowledge Demands	animals and their habitats, climate and location of Antarctica, print concepts

Part 2 Unlock the Writing

Part 2 of this handbook, titled Unlock the Writing, features two types of scaffolded writing lessons.

First, there are scaffolded lessons for each of the module-level Performance-Based Assessments in the core Teacher's Guide. Each lesson in the handbook walks students through the Performance-Based Assessment for that module, providing guidance with unlocking the task, breaking it apart, thinking through the process, and then evaluating their writing.

Next, there are scaffolded writing lessons that provide grade-appropriate support and guidelines for teaching each of the writing types required by the Common Core Learning Standards:

- Opinion Writing
- Informative/Explanatory Writing
- Narrative Writing

Each of these three lessons is divided into the tasks specific to the writing type. Instructional support is provided to help you introduce and model each task so that students will better understand the writing type and how to become proficient writers of each. There are ample opportunities for practice, including robust Deeper Practice activities.

As in Part 1, Unlock the Text lessons, the Unlock the Writing lessons provide specific scaffolded "notes" to support English language learners as well as both struggling and accelerated writers.

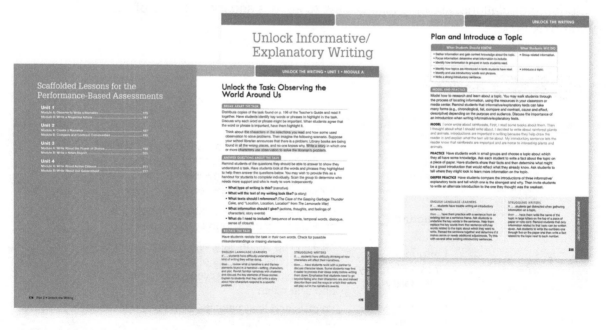

Part 3 Routines and Activities

Part 3 of the *Scaffolded Strategies Handbook* is a collection of routines and reproducible graphic organizers as well as engaging activities that you can use for support as you teach English Language Arts skills and address the Common Core Learning Standards. When appropriate, specific routines and activities are suggested and referred to in the lessons in Part 1 of this handbook.

You will find routines, many with accompanying graphic organizers, for teaching skills in

- Reading
- Writing
- Listening and Speaking
- Language, including Vocabulary and Conventions

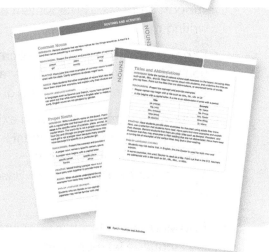

Part 3 also contains a variety of activities that provide extra scaffolded practice and instruction for language skills and vocabulary development, such as

- Noun and Pronoun Activities
- Verb Activities
- Adjective and Adverb Activities
- Sentence Activities
- Punctuation Activities
- Word Study Activities
- Vocabulary Activities and Games

This section of the handbook will be useful at any time during your teaching day. As you become familiar with the routines, graphic organizers, and activities, feel free to use them whenever they fit the needs of your students. Think of this section as a toolbox of ideas and suggestions to use with your struggling readers and writers. Turn to it often.

Using the Scaffolded Strategies Handbook

Part 4 Unlock Language Learning

Part 4 of the *Scaffolded Strategies Handbook* provides additional instruction for each Anchor Text selection and for each Supporting Text selection in the ReadyGEN program. Use these lessons to help English language learners construct meaning in the selections and explore vocabulary in order to develop mastery of reading, writing, and speaking.

Part 4 scaffolded support includes:

- **Build Background** Students explore important information needed to comprehend and enjoy each selection. Student pages provide practice and stimulate conversation.

- **Talk About Sentences** Students discover how good sentences are constructed. They learn to access key ideas by understanding the relationships between words and phrases in sentences.

- **Speak and Write About the Text** Students build academic language skills by asking and answering critical questions. Writing frames support students' development as they express ideas in specific writing modes.

- **Expand Understanding of Vocabulary** Students discover the generative nature of vocabulary and develop a curiosity about language as they gain an understanding of how words function in sentences.

- **Writing** Students benefit from extra scaffolding, including a student model, as they work toward addressing the Performance-Based Assessment writing prompt.

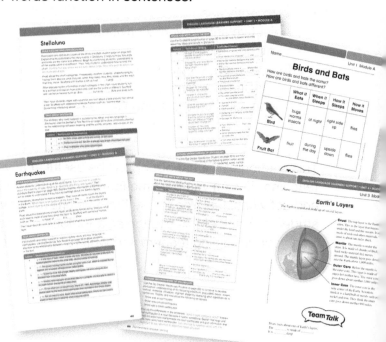

The following **Part 4** Routines provide English language learners with additional scaffolded instruction in reading, speaking, and listening.

- Dig Deeper Vocabulary
- Sentence Talk
- Clarifying Key Details
- Clarifying Information
- Reach an Agreement
- Text-Based Writing

PART 1

Unlock
the Text

Understanding Communities

TEXT SET

ANCHOR TEXT
Trouble at the Sandbox

SUPPORTING TEXT
Snowshoe Hare's
Winter Home

TEXT SET

ANCHOR TEXT
Friends Around the World

SUPPORTING TEXT
The House on
Maple Street

Cognates

Cognates are words that have similar spellings and meanings in two or more languages. Many words in English and Spanish share Greek or Latin roots, and many words in English came from French, which is closely connected to Spanish (and to Portuguese, Italian, and Romanian). Because of this, many literary, content, and academic process words in English (e.g., *gracious/gracioso; volcano/volcán; compare/comparar*) have recognizable Spanish cognates.

Making the connection to cognates permits students who are native Spanish speakers to understand the strong foundation they have in academic and literary English. These links between English and Spanish are also useful for native speakers of English and other languages because they help uncover basic underlying features of our language.

ANCHOR TEXT **Trouble at the Sandbox**

ENGLISH	SPANISH	ENGLISH	SPANISH
action	acción	plastic	plástico
blocked	bloqueó	probably	probablemente
bottle	botella	problem	problema
calm	calmado	really	realmente
camera	cámara	school	escuela
clearly	claramente	story	historia
front	frente	students	estudiantes
important	importante	using	usando
mining	minería	voice	voz
much	mucho	volcano	volcán
pile	pila		

SUPPORTING TEXT Snowshoe Hare's Winter Home

ENGLISH	SPANISH		ENGLISH	SPANISH
attention	atención		rock	roca
disappear	desaparecer		signal	señal
explore	explorar		tunnel	túnel
hibernate	hibernar			

These lists contain many, but not all, Spanish cognates from these selections.

Unlock the Text

Trouble at the Sandbox

By Phillip Simpson
Illustrated by Leigh Hedstrom

QUALITATIVE MEASURES

Levels of Meaning	accessible literal meaning about a group of younger children seeking a solution when older children steal their sandbox toys; more subtle theme about how members of a community should treat each other
Structure	simple chronological text structure in a single story line; events are clearly connected
Language Conventionality and Clarity	simple and complex sentences; occasional use of figurative language (*just to be on the safe side*); few domain-specific expressions (*Lights, Camera, Action!*) that may require direct instruction
Knowledge Demands	understanding of polite behavior, roles of teachers and students in a school setting

Prepare to Read

LEVELS OF MEANING

In *Trouble at the Sandbox,* Theo and his friends are playing in the school sandbox at recess when a group of older students take their toy trucks. Theo enlists the help of Ms. Lee, a teacher. Together, they learn that Mr. Park, another teacher, had asked the older boys to find toy trucks for a movie they are making in class. Mr. Park makes the leader of the older boys apologize for taking rather than asking, and he invites Theo and his friends to help with the movie. In the end, the leader of the older boys joins Theo and his friends at play in the sandbox.

MORE SUPPORT

ENGLISH LANGUAGE LEARNERS

Most of the vocabulary in *Trouble at the Sandbox* consists of common, familiar words. Encourage students to try reading each chapter independently and look up words they do not understand. Have students keep a list of the words they looked up, along with the definitions. Have students choose words from their lists and use each one in a sentence.

STRUGGLING READERS

Point out the illustrations on pp. 3, 9, and 20. Ask students to describe the settings and characters in the illustrations and compare them to settings and people in your school. Use students' answers to help them describe the setting and characters in the story.

STRUCTURE

PREVIEW Have students read the table of contents. Ask: How is this book organized? (It is broken up into chapters.) Explain the meaning of the Chapter 5 title, "Lights, Camera, Action!" (what a movie director says just before filming a scene). Then have students flip through the book and look at the illustrations. Ask: Where does this story take place? (at a school) Who are some of the characters in the story? (older and younger students, two teachers)

LANGUAGE CONVENTIONALITY AND CLARITY

PREVIEW VOCABULARY Use the Preview and Review Vocabulary Routine in Part 3 to assess what students know about the following words: *shade, shadow, scared, upset, breath, calm, searched, shrugged, sank, bravely, middle school, background, probably,* and *mumbled*.

DOMAIN-SPECIFIC VOCABULARY Use the Vocabulary Activities in Part 3 to pre-teach the following domain-specific vocabulary: *volcano, moat, staff room, quarry,* and *mining pit*. Explain that *staff room* is a place found in a school. The other words refer to structures a child could create in a sandbox.

COGNATES Use the list of Spanish cognates at the beginning of this module to guide your Spanish-speaking students as they read the selection.

KNOWLEDGE DEMANDS

ACTIVATE BACKGROUND KNOWLEDGE Have students review the rules for playground interactions at your school. Ask: What should you do if you want to use equipment someone else is using? How should you ask another student for something you want? What should you do if another student just takes something from you? Use the Quick Write and Share Routine in Part 3. You may also wish to explain that making a movie requires special equipment. Ask students to list items that are needed to make a movie.

Interact with Text

LEVELS OF MEANING

As you read *Trouble at the Sandbox,* assess students' understanding that Ben's behavior at the beginning of the book is hurtful and goes against the rules of the school community. Highlight the ways other characters in the book react to Ben taking the trucks. For example, in Chapter 2 Josh looks like he is going to cry, and in Chapter 5 Ms. Lee is angry.

> **If . . .** students have difficulty understanding how Ben's behavior affects those around him,
>
> **then . . .** use the Three-Column Chart Graphic Organizer Routine in Part 3 to support understanding. Label the columns *Theo, Ms. Lee,* and *Mr. Park,* and help students record how each character acts or feels in response to Ben taking the trucks.

Discuss why the characters' reactions show that taking the trucks is unacceptable.

STRUCTURE

Point out that the story is told in chronological order beginning with Theo and his friends playing in the sandbox on the first day. The writer does not name the days of the week during which the action takes place. However, he does use the sequence words *At lunchtime the next day* (p. 13) and *The next week* (p. 22) to indicate the passage of time.

> **If . . .** students have difficulty understanding the time periods during which the story takes place,
>
> **then . . .** use the Story Map A Graphic Organizer Routine in Part 3 to help students follow the story structure. At the top of the Beginning box, write *The First Day*. At the top of the Middle box, write *The Next Day*. At the top of the End box, write *The Next Week*.

Discuss how the sequence words in the story help readers understand the plot. Ask students what it would be like to read the book if the writer had left the words out.

ENGLISH LANGUAGE LEARNERS

To help students talk about the sequence of events in the story, provide them with a word bank of simple sequence words: *first, then, next, last, finally*. Model using the words in a brief retelling of the events in Chapter 1, then encourage students to use sequence words as often as possible in the discussion.

STRUGGLING READERS

To quickly assess understanding and promote oral and written language proficiency, use the Retell or Summarize Routine with Graphic Organizer in Part 3 with students. After students have read a section of text, have them turn to a partner and summarize it in a few sentences. Encourage partners to add one or two details to the summary.

LANGUAGE CONVENTIONALITY AND CLARITY

For the most part, the sentence structures in *Trouble at the Sandbox* are simple and easy to follow. However, many of the chapters contain a great deal of dialogue, which some students may find more challenging to read.

If . . . students have difficulty following sentences that include dialogue,

then . . . explain that quotation marks are used to indicate sentences spoken by the characters. Choose a sample of dialogue from the book and point out the punctuation. Then read the passage aloud with expression to help students understand the difference between dialogue and narration.

Choose additional dialogue passages and have students practice reading them aloud to consolidate their understanding of this sentence structure.

KNOWLEDGE DEMANDS

Students may not understand the illustration of the movie set on p. 17. Explain that the term *movie set* describes a place that has been created to be the setting of a scene in a movie. Point out that the set in the illustration consists of a scene that has been created on a tabletop with trucks, sand, and a painted background. Explain that the device on the left is a movie camera and the device on the right is a type of light that moviemakers use to cast a bright light onto a set.

ENGLISH LANGUAGE LEARNERS

Reading dialogue aloud can provide English learners with additional opportunities to improve their comprehension and reading fluency. Choose a short dialogue passage, such as a section of p. 21, and have pairs practice reading it aloud, taking turns reading the paragraphs. Have students go through the passage several times, until they can read it confidently.

MORE SUPPORT

Express and Extend

LEVELS OF MEANING

EXPRESS Explain that the theme of a story is the message or general idea that the author wants readers to understand. Authors do not always explicitly state the theme; often readers must infer it from the evidence in the text. Say: One theme of *Trouble at the Sandbox* is that people in a community should be polite and considerate to each other. I decided on this theme by comparing the beginning and the ending of the story. How do Theo and his friends feel after Ben takes the trucks the first time? **(angry, sad)** How do all the characters feel at the end of the story, after Ben speaks kindly to Theo? **(All the characters are happy.)**

> **If . . .** students have difficulty comparing and contrasting the events in the story,
>
> **then . . .** direct students' attention first to pp. 7–8 and have them look for words that describe emotion (*cry, upset*). Then have students reread p. 24 and look at Ben's expression in the illustration.

EXTEND Have students write a short paragraph recounting an event from their own lives that shows that people are happier when they work together or treat each other with consideration. In the last sentence, students should tell why their experience was similar to or different from Theo's.

STRUCTURE

EXPRESS Remind students that the events in *Trouble at the Sandbox* are told in chronological order. Say: The author tells us what happens first, then what happens next, and so on. What would happen if the author told the events in a different order? Have students discuss how readers would feel if, for example, the author started the story with Theo going to Ms. Lee, and then recounted what happened in the sandbox.

EXTEND Have students write a paragraph or short narrative telling what happens after Ben joins Theo and his friends in the sandbox. Tell them to recount at least three events in chronological order using sequence words. You may have students work independently or in pairs.

ENGLISH LANGUAGE LEARNERS

Allow students to listen to a recording of *Trouble at the Sandbox* while following along in the text. Hearing correct pronunciations and inflections for words and expressions used in the text may help students understand their meanings.

STRUGGLING READERS

Help students stay engaged with their reading by having them write questions they have about ideas in the text on sticky notes. When they have finished reading a section or chapter, have them revisit their notes to see if they can answer the questions.

EXPRESS Talk about Sentences and Words

Display and read aloud the following sentences from *Trouble at the Sandbox*.

"We'll see about *this*," she said. "Let's go."

"Some of your boys have been taking toys from my kids without asking," said Ms. Lee. "I don't think this is very fair *or* very nice."

Remind students that dialogue in text shows the words characters are speaking. Point out that these lines of dialogue have an extra feature—each has a word in italics. Reread the sentences aloud and ask students what was different about the way you read the italicized words. Discuss how adding emphasis to the words affects the meaning of each sentence. Note that in everyday speech, people sometimes put extra emphasis on the words they think are especially important. Explain that authors sometimes put dialogue words in italics so that the dialogue will sound like real speech in readers' minds.

TEAM TALK Have partners experiment with rereading the sentences and not emphasizing the italicized words or emphasizing different words. Ask them to discuss how the meanings of the sentences changed with the different emphases.

EXTEND Have students work in pairs to write a two- or three-sentence dialogue exchange between Ben and Theo, in which they argue over a truck. Tell them to underline a word in at least one sentence to show emphasis. Have partners read their exchanges aloud, using the appropriate emphasis.

EXPRESS Discuss what Ben did wrong when he took the trucks from Theo and his friends. Ask: What rules of good behavior did Ben break?

If . . . students have difficulty explaining why Ben was wrong to take the trucks in the way he did,

then . . . have them recall the earlier discussion about rules for considerate behavior at your school. Tell students to list the rules and give a thumbs-down for each one Ben broke.

EXTEND Have students reread p. 15. Tell them to imagine a different conversation, in which Ben follows the rules of polite behavior. Have students work in pairs to write and perform such a conversation.

ACCELERATED LEARNERS

Have students write a short scene that takes place between the end of Chapter 6 and the beginning of Chapter 7, in which Theo and his friends help make the movie. Remind students to recount events in time order and use sequence words.

Unlock the Text

QUALITATIVE MEASURES

Levels of Meaning	character-driven plot with unified theme resolved by end; changes over time
Structure	successive, parallel episodes
Language Conventionality and Clarity	multiple-meaning words; descriptive language
Knowledge Demands	differences of hibernation behaviors and habitats among common animal species; changing seasons

Snowshoe Hare's
Winter Home,
pp. 5–12

Prepare to Read

LEVELS OF MEANING

In *Snowshoe Hare's Winter Home,* the main purpose is to tell the story of Snowshoe Hare's first experience with saying goodbye to many of his forest friends as they prepare to hibernate or migrate to warmer places during the coming winter season. On a deeper level, it addresses changes over time and the importance of companionship.

STRUCTURE

PREVIEW Read aloud the title, author, and illustrator. Then examine the art. Say: This illustration shows the main character, Snowshoe Hare. What type of animal do you think Snowshoe Hare is? Reread the title, emphasizing the word *winter.* Ask: Based on the title and the illustration,

ENGLISH LANGUAGE LEARNERS

Help students expand their understanding of multiple-meaning words. Share labeled pictures that demonstrate the multiple meanings. For example, contrast an animal coat with the coat we wear. Use the words in sentences related to students' experiences.

STRUGGLING READERS

Some students might not be familiar with the different seasons or how the weather in each season differs. To help these students, display and label photos of each season, and have students describe what they see.

when does this story take place? (in the winter) Have students look at the illustrations in the selection. Ask:

- What animals do you see in the illustrations? (rabbits, a bear, a beaver, a fish, a turtle, a duck)
- Where does the story take place? (in a forest, where there are trees and water and where it snows)
- How do the illustrations change from the beginning to the end of the story? (The trees are barely covered with snow at the beginning; they're completely covered by the end.)
- What does this tell you? (Time is passing; winter is coming.)

LANGUAGE CONVENTIONALITY AND CLARITY

PREVIEW VOCABULARY Use the Preview and Review Vocabulary Routine in Part 3 to assess what students know about the following words: *den, exploring, lodge, coats, winter,* and *signal.* Note that *den, lodge,* and *coats* are multiple-meaning words. As students read, stop to make sure they understand which meanings are used within the context of this story.

CRITICAL VOCABULARY Use the Vocabulary Activities and Games in Part 3 to preteach domain-specific vocabulary words, such as *hibernate, hibernation, season, migrate,* and *migration.* Note that *migrate* and *migration* are not words used directly in the story, but they might be helpful to discuss in relation to the text.

COGNATES Use the list of Spanish cognates at the beginning of this module to guide your Spanish-speaking students as they read the selection.

KNOWLEDGE DEMANDS

ACTIVATE BACKGROUND KNOWLEDGE Ask students to share what they know about the four seasons. Draw a four-square box labeled *Spring, Summer, Fall,* and *Winter.* Ask students to tell what the weather is like in each season, and record their responses. Focus on the winter and spring seasons. Ask: What do the trees and land look like in winter? In spring? What challenges might animals face in winter? What might animals do in fall to prepare for winter? If students are unsure of how winter weather might affect animals, encourage them to think about how the different seasons affected the animal characters in *Snowshoe Hare's Winter Home.*

STRUGGLING READERS

To help students with the pronunciation of new vocabulary or multisyllabic words, point out which syllables are stressed. Some examples are *HI-ber-nate, hi-ber-NA-tion, SEA-son,* and *SIG-nal.* Have students gently tap the syllables of the word as they say it, tapping louder for stressed syllables.

Interact with Text

LEVELS OF MEANING

As you read *Snowshoe Hare's Winter Home,* periodically stop to assess students' understanding of the changes that occur when winter approaches and how those changes affect the characters. For example, after reading the first spread, ask: What does Bear say the signal is? (the cold air) What does the signal mean? (Winter is coming; it's time to hibernate.) What will Bear do? (sleep for the winter)

Have students find examples from the text that show changes in the seasons, and point out illustration details that support this.

If . . . students have difficulty understanding what happens when winter approaches and how the characters are affected,

then . . . use the Web Routine and Graphic Organizer in Part 3. Have students create a web for each character, with the character's name in the center. Then have them record in the outer ovals where each character goes for the winter and why. Make sure students understand that Snowshoe Hare doesn't go anywhere for the winter. He and the other hares stay in the forest.

STRUCTURE

As students read, assess their understanding of the story's repetitive structure. Say: Throughout the story, Snowshoe Hare meets different characters that are preparing for winter in some way. The characters all tell Snowshoe Hare about a certain signal and what the signal means to them. **Have students turn to p. 7 and reread the text. Point out that on this page, Snowshoe Hare meets Beaver. Ask:** What is Beaver's signal? (the snow flurries) What do the snow flurries signal to Beaver? (They signal that Beaver's pond will soon freeze over.) **Help students understand that the pond freezing over is a sign that winter is coming. Continue identifying each character's signal and what it means.**

If . . . students have difficulty identifying each character's signal and what it means,

then . . . use the Three-Column Chart Routine and Graphic Organizer in Part 3. Label the columns *Character, Signal,* and *What the Signal Means,* and help students identify and record this information.

ENGLISH LANGUAGE LEARNERS

Review with students what the word *signal* means in the context of this story. Provide students with examples of signals. For example, you might explain that the school bell is a signal that school is over.

STRUGGLING READERS

To make sure students understand what they are reading, use the Retell or Summarize Routine and Graphic Organizer in Part 3, and work with them to summarize or retell parts of the story. Have partners take turns reading a paragraph and retelling the information in their own words. Remind students to include details from the text in their retellings.

LANGUAGE CONVENTIONALITY AND CLARITY

The language of the story is direct and can be understood on a literal level. However, some students may have difficulty understanding the descriptive language.

Work with students to ensure they understand what the descriptive language means and why the author chose to use it. For example, if students have difficulty understanding a sentence such as "Something cold tickled Showshoe Hare on the nose," explain the use of the word *tickled* as a way to make the story interesting and colorful. Point out that the snowflakes can't really tickle Snowshoe Hare with fingers the way we tickle one another. By using the word *tickled,* the author is helping us feel what Snowshoe Hare is feeling.

Have students find similar examples of descriptive language in the story. Discuss each example, and talk about the sensory feeling each example illustrates.

KNOWLEDGE DEMANDS

The concept of a habitat may be unfamiliar to many students. Explain that a habitat is the natural environment in which an animal lives. Examine the illustrations in the text. Ask: In what kind of habitat do the fish and turtle live? What other animals live in this type of habitat? What is the habitat of the other animals in the story?

If . . . students have difficulty understanding animal habitats,

then . . . show pictures of a variety of habitats (forest, desert, ocean, and so on) and discuss the kinds of plants and animals that live in each habitat.

Guide students to use text and illustration evidence to describe the habitats of a bear, beaver, fish, turtle, duck, and hare.

STRUGGLING READERS

To help make the concept of a habitat more personal for students, point out that animals that live nearby, such as squirrels or birds, also have habitats. Encourage students to compare habitats in the text with habitats for familiar animal species.

MORE SUPPORT

Express and Extend

LEVELS OF MEANING

EXPRESS Lead a discussion about Snowshoe Hare's problem toward the end of the story. Ask: What is Snowshoe Hare's problem? (His friends have all left. He's sad. He can't or doesn't want to do the things they will do during the winter.) How do you think Snowshoe Hare feels as he says goodbye to his friends for the winter? How do their winter plans affect him? What happens to help solve his problem? (He meets other hares who explain that he doesn't need to find a new home for the winter. The hares are able to survive in the winter weather. Now Snowshoe Hare has friends to spend the winter with; he is happy that he is not alone.)

> If . . . students have difficulty understanding this problem and solution,
>
> then . . . talk about how Snowshoe Hare feels at the end of the story. Have them look at his expression in the last illustration. Snowshoe Hare's other "hare" friends have solved his problem.

EXTEND Have students write a sentence or short paragraph explaining how Snowshoe Hare solved his problem. Then have partners share their sentences with each other.

STRUCTURE

EXPRESS Review the structure of the story. Remind students that Snowshoe Hare hops through the forest talking to his friends one by one about what they're doing. Together, create a chart with the name of each animal character from the story. As a class, discuss each animal's winter behavior. Record a brief description under each name. Have students provide text evidence to support their responses.

EXTEND Remind students that each animal in the story has a signal that lets it know winter is coming. Have partners discuss what Snowshoe Hare's signal is. How did Snowshoe Hare and the other hares prepare for winter?

ENGLISH LANGUAGE LEARNERS

Give students examples of words and pictures describing various emotions, such as *happy, sad, disappointed, puzzled,* and *excited.* When the class is completing sentence frames to tell how Snowshoe Hare felt at the beginning and the end of the story, students can refer to these models.

STRUGGLING READERS

If students have difficulty completing the behavior chart, have them act out what each animal was doing when Snowshoe Hare stopped to talk. Have them discuss why that animal was doing what it was doing.

EXPRESS Talk about Sentences and Words

Read aloud the following sentences from the story.

> He looked up to see snowflakes tumbling and twirling. They carpeted the grassy clearing, coated the pine trees, and capped the rocks.

Ask: What does this passage mean? What do the words *tumbling* and *twirling* tell you about the snow? (The snow is falling and covering everything.) What other words could the author have used? *(falling, dropping)* Explain that descriptive language creates a picture in the reader's mind that helps the reader better understand what's happening. Then ask: What does the word *carpeted* mean? ("covered") Why do you think the author chose to use *carpeted*?

TEAM TALK Say: Turn to a partner and say the sentences again using simpler words for *tumbling, twirling,* and *carpeted.*

If . . . students need more support with understanding descriptive language,

then . . . revisit the illustrations. Point out specific examples where the snow is falling and covering the land like a carpet.

EXTEND Have students select and then illustrate another sentence from the text with descriptive language. Ask them to share why they selected the sentence and which words help create an image in the reader's mind.

EXPRESS Lead a discussion about hibernation. Ask: Do all of Snowshoe Hare's friends hibernate? Which animals hibernate? Which do not? Provide time for partners to revisit the text and make a list of animals that hibernate and those that do not.

If . . . students have difficulty concluding which animals hibernate,

then . . . remind them what *hibernation* means and guide them through the process of rereading the text to find which animals hibernate.

EXTEND The term *migrate* is not used in the story, but there is evidence of it in Duck's actions. Discuss what it means to migrate. Have students compare migration and hibernation. Then ask: Which animal in this story migrates? Where does it go? What words in the text support your answer?

ACCELERATED LEARNERS

Have students select an animal from the forest habitat to research. Ask students to find information about what it eats, where it lives, and how it behaves. Have them share their findings with the class.

MORE SUPPORT

Cognates

Cognates are words that have similar spellings and meanings in two or more languages. Many words in English and Spanish share Greek or Latin roots, and many words in English came from French, which is closely connected to Spanish (and to Portuguese, Italian, and Romanian). Because of this, many literary, content, and academic process words in English (e.g., *gracious/gracioso; volcano/volcán; compare/comparar*) have recognizable Spanish cognates.

Making the connection to cognates permits students who are native Spanish speakers to understand the strong foundation they have in academic and literary English. These links between English and Spanish are also useful for native speakers of English and other languages because they help uncover basic underlying features of our language.

ANCHOR TEXT Friends Around the World

ENGLISH	SPANISH	ENGLISH	SPANISH
animals	animales	hour	hora
apartment	apartamento	kangaroos	canguros
Arctic	Ártico	liberty	libertad
barbecue	barbacoa	million	millón
baseball	béisbol	motorcycle	motocicleta
boots	botas	museum	museo
caribou	caribú	ocean	océano
common	común	park	parque
competes	compite	protection	protección
dinosaur	dinosaurio	semester	semestre
doctor	doctor	skeleton	esqueleto
enormous	enorme	soup	sopa
especially	especialmente	sports	deportes
family	familia	stadium	estadio
famous	famosa	statue	estatua
favorite	favorito	surprise	sorpresa
football	fútbol	territory	territorio
fruit	fruta		

ANCHOR TEXT Friends Around the World (continued)

ENGLISH	SPANISH		ENGLISH	SPANISH
traditional	tradicional		vegetables	vegetales
train	tren		vendors	vendedores
uniform	uniforme			

SUPPORTING TEXT The House on Maple Street

ENGLISH	SPANISH		ENGLISH	SPANISH
admire	admirar		day	día
air	aire		family	familia
alarm	alarma		new	nuevo
animal	animal		rock	roca
automobile	automóvil		tepee	tipi
buffalo	búfalo		tunnel	túnel
California	California		visit	visitar
carpenter	carpintero			

These lists contain many, but not all, Spanish cognates from these selections.

Unlock the Text

QUALITATIVE MEASURES

Levels of Meaning	accessible literal series of letters between a girl named Isabel who lives in New York City and three e-pals from around the world: the Australian outback; northern Canada; and Ho Chi Minh City, Vietnam
Structure	text includes a brief introduction, letters from Isabel to each e-pal, and their responses, in a series of three exchanges; text features include photographs, captions, and a world map; text ends with a summative conclusion
Language Conventionality and Clarity	words from various cultures require direct instruction; geographical names may require specific support
Knowledge Demands	understanding that there are many and various countries in the world and the practice of writing letters to people you may have never met (e-pals)

Friends Around the World

WRITTEN BY ANA GALAN

Prepare to Read

LEVELS OF MEANING

Friends Around the World is an introduction followed by three exchanges of letters between a girl named Isabel and e-pals from three different places in the world. Through the letters, Isabel learns how the four of them are similar and different, and she compares and contrasts them in a closing paragraph. Photographs and captions illustrate the letters, and a world map shows the locations of all four children.

ENGLISH LANGUAGE LEARNERS

Explain that the word *letter* is a multiple-meaning word in English. A letter can be one symbol that is a unit of an alphabet, such as *A, B,* or *C.* A letter can also be a direct, personal written message addressed to someone else.

STRUGGLING READERS

Make sure students can pronounce the names of the four children: Isabel (IZ-uh-bel), Akiak (AYKEEAK), Dan (DAN), and Hau (HOW). Say them aloud together as you point to their photographs.

STRUCTURE

PREVIEW Read the introduction on page 4 aloud to students. Have them study the world map as you explain that this is a series of letters between Isabel and three pen pals. Explain that since the children are writing online, they are called *e-pals*. Isabel writes three different letters to her three e-pals, and they answer her. Ask: Which e-pal lives closest to Isabel? Where does this e-pal live? (Akiak lives closest to Isabel. He lives in Canada.)

LANGUAGE CONVENTIONALITY AND CLARITY

PREVIEW VOCABULARY Use the Preview and Review Vocabulary Routine in Part 3 to assess what students know about the following words: *exchange, subway, uniform, parka, outback, caribou, blizzard, barbecue,* and *common*.

COGNATES Use the list of Spanish cognates at the beginning of this module to guide your Spanish-speaking students as they read the selection.

DOMAIN-SPECIFIC VOCABULARY Use the Vocabulary Activities in Part 3 and a world map to pre-teach the following proper nouns and culturally-specific vocabulary: *Australia, Vietnam, Ho Chi Minh City, Arctic Circle, Inuit, Royal Flying Doctor Service, dragon fruit, dogsled, cricket,* and *museums*. Explain that the words that begin with capital letters name specific places, things, and people. The words that begin with lower case letters name things that are parts of communities.

KNOWLEDGE DEMANDS

ACTIVATE BACKGROUND KNOWLEDGE Explain that the children in *Friends Around the World* write letters to each other. Ask students to share their own experiences with letters. Bring in and show them a printed business letter, a handwritten friendly letter, and an e-mail message. Ask: Why do people write letters? (to send messages, to share information, to ask questions) How are these different kinds of letters alike? (One person writes them to another person. They begin with "Dear ___." They end with the name of the writer.) How are they different? (Two need stamps; one does not. Two use paper; one does not. One doesn't use a computer; two do.)

STRUGGLING READERS

Make sure that students understand that when these children exchange letters, they include photographs with captions. Use Isabel's letter on pages 6 and 7 to illustrate. Say and point: Isabel's letter is in this box on pages 6 and 7. She includes three photographs with her letter: one of the subway, one of the Statue of Liberty, and one of the Empire State Building. She writes a caption for each photograph to explain what the picture shows. Explain that each of the other letter-writers do the same: one letter, two or three photographs, and two or three captions.

MORE SUPPORT

Interact with Text

As you read *Friends Around the World,* assess students' understanding of the similarities and differences among the four children, their schools, the sports they enjoy, the foods they eat, how they travel, and the places they live. These details are located in the letters and reinforced and illustrated by the photographs and captions. As they read each letter, ask: What facts and details does this letter teach us about life in _____?

If . . . students have difficulty identifying these discrete facts and details,

then . . . use the Main Idea and Details Routine and Graphic Organizer in Part 3 to support understanding.

Point out that Isabel's first letter contains all three sentence types: statements, questions, and exclamations. Ask: Which sentences are statements? Which sentence asks a question? Which sentence is an exclamation? Suggest that good writers use all three types. Make sure that students observe and understand the dash in the sentence "Don't worry—there's an elevator!" Explain that a dash is a punctuation mark that indicates a pause or a break in thought.

STRUCTURE

Point out that the letters appear in order in time. Also, point out that Isabel's letters, on pages 6–7, 14–15, and 22–23, are addressed to all three of her e-pals. The other letters are addressed only to Isabel. Students can observe this in the "To" lines under the places in the colored bars above the letters. Also, point out that each letter begins with a greeting (the salutation). Each letter ends with a closing (such as "Your friend," "Yours truly," or "Talk to you soon!") followed by the writer's name (the signature). Explain that these are conventions, or customs, that most people follow when writing a letter. People have been using these conventions when writing letters for thousands of years.

Have students guess how much time passes between the letters. Explain that most letters include the dates on which they are written, but these letters do not. Since email can happen so quickly, the letters might have all been written in one day! Or several days could have passed between the various letters.

MORE SUPPORT

ENGLISH LANGUAGE LEARNERS

Ask students to make their own introductory boxes. Have them include their names, countries of origin, cities or towns, and the "type of place" they live in. Have them include a photograph of themselves and display their "introductions" in the classroom.

STRUGGLING READERS

If students struggle with the back-and-forth exchange among the letters, have them read all three of Isabel's letters, then all three written by Akiak, all three by Hau, and all three by Dan. It may give them a better opportunity to understand the children and places if they approach each person one by one.

LANGUAGE CONVENTIONALITY AND CLARITY

While much of the language will be clear and accessible to students, they may need extra support to understand words that are particular to other cultures.

If . . . students have difficulty understanding words from other cultures,

then . . . have them make a web for each using the Web with Graphic Organizer Routine.

You may want to begin by having students list words on the Three-Column Chart Graphic Organizer from Part 3. Help them rate each word as "Know," "Have Seen" or "Don't Know." In addition, remind students that they can find images on the Internet that illustrate these words. Help them find other pictures that illustrate words such as *subway, uniform, parka, outback, caribou, floods, blizzard, barbecue, dogsled,* and *cricket.* You can also have them draw their own pictures of these words. Let them have fun combining two of them. For example, what would a *blizzard* at a *barbecue* look like? Or a *caribou* attending a *cricket* game?

KNOWLEDGE DEMANDS

Some students may not be familiar with email. Use a computer to write a short letter from your class to someone else (another teacher, your school principal, or another administrator). Have them compose the letter together and use the style of the letters in this passage. Be sure to include a request to write back so that students will be able to see a reply. If possible, attach a photograph of a class activity with a short caption. Invite one of the students to "hit send." Print out the letter and display it in the classroom along with the reply when it arrives.

ENGLISH LANGUAGE LEARNERS

Make sure students can pronounce the specific proper names in the letters: *Australia, Vietnam, Ho Chi Minh City, Arctic Circle,* and *Inuit.* Invite them to repeat these words as you say them aloud, several times if necessary.

MORE SUPPORT

Express and Extend

EXPRESS Explain that this passage shows that the children have experiences that are both alike and different. They can compare two of the children by telling how their lives are alike. They can contrast two of the children by telling how their lives are different. Say: Isabel and Hau are alike in some ways and different in other ways. They are alike because they are both girls. They both live in big cities. Isabel is different from Hau because they speak different languages. They are different because Isabel rides a subway to school and Hau rides a motorcycle. Then, ask students to compare and contrast Isabel and either Akiak or Dan.

> **If . . .** students have difficulty listing and understanding similarities and differences between two children,
>
> **then . . .** have students use the Compare and Contrast Graphic Organizer and the Routine from Part 3 to record their observations.

EXTEND Have students use their skills to compare and contrast writing a letter with making a phone call. Ask: How would making phone calls be similar to writing these letters? How would it be different? What are the advantages of each way to communicate?

EXPRESS Point out that most of this passage is an exchange of letters. Take time to explore the word *exchange* with students. Model by saying: The verb *exchange* means "to give one thing and receive another." Isabel sent a letter to Akiak, Hau, and Dan, and then she received three letters in return. Isabel exchanged letters with her three new friends. Then, ask: Can you name other things that people exchange besides letters? (presents, greetings, one country's money for another)

> **If . . .** students have difficulty brainstorming things that can be exchanged,
>
> **then . . .** use the Web B Routine and Graphic Organizer in Part 3 with the word *exchange* in the middle of the web.

EXTEND Have students write letters to Isabel. Have them include specific details about their own lives, including where they live, how they get to school, what they like to eat, what sports they like to play, and what kind of building they live in. Remind them to include greetings, closings, and signatures.

ENGLISH LANGUAGE LEARNERS

Have students choose one photograph from the passage that appeals to them. Have them write one- or two-sentence descriptions of what they see in the photograph. Encourage them to use words about colors, sizes, and shapes.

STRUGGLING READERS

Help students compare and contrast by giving them categories to look for. Suggest these: Where They Live, How They Go to School, What They Do for Fun. Create a chart with these three column heads and a row for each of the children. Help students write a detail in each cell in the chart.

MORE SUPPORT

LANGUAGE CONVENTIONALITY AND CLARITY

EXPRESS Talk about Sentences and Words

Display and read aloud the following sentence from the paragraph that Isabel writes at the end of *Friends Around the World*.

> The weather is different in each country.

Point out that in this sentence, Isabel states a contrast because she writes about something that is different in each place. Say: When you point out a difference, you make a contrast. Ask students to find details about the weather in New York City, Vietnam, Australia, and Canada. Explain that when you add all these details up, you can see that the weather and seasons are not the same. Isabel read about the weather in each country and came up with this idea on her own.

TEAM TALK Have partners work in pairs and look at each other's shoes or shirts, hair or eyes. Have them observe three differences. Then, have each pair of students write a sentence about how one thing is different.

EXTEND At the end, Isabel writes, "I have learned so much from my new friends!" Remind students that the title of the story includes the word *Friends*. Have students explore their opinions about friendship as it is expressed in this story. Ask: Are these four children really friends? If so, what makes them friends? If not, why are they not friends? Encourage a class discussion about the topic of friendship and whether people can make friends with a person they have never met face to face.

KNOWLEDGE DEMANDS

EXPRESS Challenge students to write a letter to three imaginary children: Maria in Mexico City, Mexico; Vlad in Inta, Russia, and Yumi in Kōchi, Japan. First, use a world map to locate the three countries and cities. Then, have students initiate an exchange of letters modeled after Isabel's first letter.

If . . . students have difficulty thinking of words and phrases to include in their letters,

then . . . have them use the Three-Column Graphic Organizer to help them brainstorm details. Suggest that they label the columns "Fun Things to Do," "About My School," and "Weather."

EXTEND Organize groups of four students, as close to two girls and two boys in each group as possible. In each group, assign the "parts" of Isabel, Akiak, Hau, and Dan. Have students practice reading the three letters from their "character" aloud. Then, choose one person from each group to do a choral reading of all the letters in the order in which they appear in the text.

ACCELERATED LEARNERS

Invite students to choose one of the locations represented in this passage (Australia, Vietnam, Northern Canada) as the topic for a short report. Encourage them to use books or magazines from your library or information from an online resource. Have them choose details that show how the place is similar to and different from where they live. Encourage them to include at least one photograph or original drawing in their report. Also, encourage them to find and share a map of the country they choose.

Unlock the Text

QUALITATIVE MEASURES

Levels of Meaning	historical tracing of land use and inhabitants of a residential lot
Structure	narrative told in the third person; many shifts in time
Language Conventionality and Clarity	multiple-meaning words; some lengthy complex sentences
Knowledge Demands	social history of the United States from prehistory to present

ReadyGEN
Text Collection 2

The House on Maple Street, pp. 14–43

Prepare to Read

LEVELS OF MEANING

The House on Maple Street traces the history of a modern-day home back almost 300 years. While telling an entertaining story, this book details how land in the United States was settled and developed. On a deeper level, the illustrations portray the importance of family, which never changes over time.

STRUCTURE

PREVIEW Have students look at the pictures on pp. 14–15. Say: This story is called *The House on Maple Street.* What can you tell about the house from these pictures? (It is a brick house with a porch. A small family lives there.) Now have students flip through the other pictures in the book. Ask: Do most of the pictures show people from today or from long ago? (from long ago) Based on the title and what you see in the pictures, what do you think this story will be about?

ENGLISH LANGUAGE LEARNERS

Some students may have less knowledge about U.S. history than native English speakers. Spend extra time building these students' background knowledge of the events described in this story before reading each section of the text.

STRUGGLING READERS

Many students with reading difficulties have trouble decoding words that have complex vowel-sound spellings. Help students correctly pronounce words, such as *ablaze,* that include a silent *e,* and words with short *e* spelled *ea,* such as *arrowhead.*

LANGUAGE CONVENTIONALITY AND CLARITY

PREVIEW VOCABULARY Use the Preview and Review Vocabulary Routine from Part 3 to assess what students know about the following words: *deer, herd, buffalo, arrowhead, rabbits, fox, farm, owl, bricks.*

Preteach critical vocabulary words, such as *forest, spring, ablaze, tepees, hunter, wagon train, wagon trail, paved, carpenters,* and *masons.* Focus on providing prior-knowledge connections to each word. For example, say: When I saw the forest fire on the news, it looked like the entire town was ablaze.

COGNATES Use the list of Spanish cognates at the beginning of this module to guide your Spanish-speaking students as they read the selection.

KNOWLEDGE DEMANDS

ACTIVATE BACKGROUND KNOWLEDGE Use the Quick Write and Share Routine in Part 3 and ask: Who do you think lived where we live hundreds of years ago? What did the land look like? Do you think this country has always had neighborhoods like the ones we live in today? Before students get started, model an example of using prior knowledge to make an educated guess about how the United States looked hundreds of years ago. For example, say: I read a book about Native Americans who lived here before this country was called the United States. They lived in tepees instead of houses, and they had to move around a lot. They hunted buffalo for food and had to follow the herds wherever they went.

Interact with Text

LEVELS OF MEANING

As you read *The House on Maple Street,* periodically assess students' level of understanding of the author's purpose. Ask students to examine the illustrations and text to understand the author's purpose. Help students identify examples from *The House on Maple Street* that help show that although the text is fiction, its purpose is to provide information about the history of the land on which the house stands. For example point out the following text on p. 26: "A wagon train passed by heading for California. The settlers stopped beside the stream for a night. But they dreamed of gold and places far away and were gone the next morning." Help students understand how this passage provides a history of the land.

STRUCTURE

As students read, pause to assess their understanding of the story's structure. Have students examine the illustrations. Ask: How far back in time does the story go? (about 300 years) What evidence in the text and illustrations helps you understand the changes in time? Model locating text and illustration evidence to support student responses. For example, the following phrases indicate a shift in time: *three hundred years ago, one day, the next spring, stayed for a whole summer, for a long time, soon after, now.* Point out to students the circular nature of the story and how it begins with the modern family, goes back in time, and ends again with the modern family.

> **If . . .** students have difficulty understanding the shifts in time throughout the story,
>
> **then . . .** use the Time Line Routine and Graphic Organizer in Part 3. Work with students to complete the time line, starting with the first chronological event and ending with the present-day children finding the arrowhead.

LANGUAGE CONVENTIONALITY AND CLARITY

This story includes some multiple-meaning words that may confuse students, such as *rose* and *banks*.

If . . . students have difficulty understanding the meaning of a word,

then . . . help them use context clues to clarify the word's meaning.

For example, read aloud the following sentence on p. 29: He pulled up the tree stumps left from the fire and planted his crops. Ask: What do you think *left* means in this sentence? Does it mean "the side opposite the right," or does it mean "not used up"? Substitute both meanings in place of *left* in the sentence, and have students tell which one makes sense. Use the Analyze Multiple-Meaning Words Routine in Part 3 to provide additional support.

KNOWLEDGE DEMANDS

Explain that this story spans about 300 years. Use the Two-Column Chart Routine and Graphic Organizer in Part 3. Label the chart with the headings *Past* and *Present*. Examine the illustrations and ask students to note details from the images that belong in each column. Ask: What clues tell you this illustration is about the present time? (modern clothes; jeans; house is brick) What clues tell you the illustration is about the past? (open fields; buffalo; Native Americans)

If . . . students have difficulty understanding the clues,

then . . . point out details in an illustration, and ask students if the picture shows something they see today, such as the wild herd of buffalo or a covered wagon.

Express and Extend

LEVELS OF MEANING

EXPRESS Help students recall the characteristics of informational and entertaining text. Then ask for examples from *The House on Maple Street* that show its purpose is to provide information to readers.

If . . . students have difficulty identifying historical references,

then . . . remind students that informational text gives true statements about real people, places, and things. Show students an example of a true statement in the selection, such as, "The buffalo moved on, searching for new grass, and the people packed up their tepees and followed." Then have students find more examples.

EXTEND Tell students that most texts have one main purpose but can also have other purposes. Ask: Is *The House on Maple Street* entertaining? When is it entertaining? (when it tells about how the arrowhead was lost and found by different children) Is this story informational? When is it informational? (when it tells about the settlers and the wagon train)

Have students create a T-chart with the headings *Entertaining* and *Informational*. Have them write their ideas about the story that fit under each heading. Then have students share their ideas with a partner.

STRUCTURE

EXPRESS Point out to students that the narrator telling the story is not involved in the story. The narrator is telling the story about other people. Explain that this is called a third-person narrator. Read aloud the first sentence on p. 15. Ask: If the narrator is not involved in the story, did any of the events happen to him or her? How do you know the narrator is talking about someone else? Remind students to use text evidence to support their responses.

EXTEND Have small groups discuss how having a third-person narrator affects the story. Would readers be able to know about so many different people in different times if the story had been told by Chrissy or Jenny? Why or why not? Ask volunteers to share their responses with the class.

MORE SUPPORT

ENGLISH LANGUAGE LEARNERS

The detailed illustrations will help students understand the text. Point out the correspondence between text and illustrations. For example, the text on p. 27 begins, "Other wagons came . . ." and the picture shows covered wagons.

STRUGGLING READERS

If students are having trouble with vocabulary acquisition, point out visual representations of the words in the illustrations to provide support. Use prompts such as: Point to the ___. Is this a ___? Find the ___.

LANGUAGE CONVENTIONALITY AND CLARITY

EXPRESS Talk about Sentences and Words

Display the following sentence from *The House on Maple Street* and read it aloud.

> For a while there was a trickle of water in the spring when the snow melted, but weeds and dirt filled in the bed, until hardly anyone remembered a stream had ever been there.

Ask: What does the word *spring* mean in this sentence? Does it mean "a metal coil," "to jump," or "a place where water comes up from the ground"? (a place where water comes up from the ground) How do you know? (The sentence says *there was a trickle of water in the spring*.)

To help students understand lengthy, complex sentences such as the one above, you may wish to use the Sentence Activities in Part 3.

TEAM TALK Have partners work together to write a sentence using the word *spring*. Tell them the sentence should use a different meaning for this word than the story does. Have partners share their sentence with the class.

EXTEND Have partners work together to brainstorm other words that have multiple meanings. Encourage students to look through the text for other examples. Have students write a sentence using one of the words.

KNOWLEDGE DEMANDS

EXPRESS Ask students to compare the lifestyle of Native Americans, early settlers, and modern-day people. Review the illustrations together. Ask: Even though times have changed in the story, what has stayed the same about the people? (families) Why do you think families have not changed over time? (Family members will always be important to each other, even when other things change.)

> **If . . .** students have difficulty understanding the importance of family history,
>
> **then . . .** guide them through the process of examining the illustrations to find support for the questions.

EXTEND Have students think about their own family and illustrate what they and their surroundings might look like ten years from now. Ask students to label the names of family members and write a sentence or two explaining what's happened.

ACCELERATED LEARNERS

Invite students to find out more about the history of the town in which they live. Have them work together to create a poster with facts and photos from their research. Display the poster in the classroom.

MORE SUPPORT

UNIT 2

Making Decisions

TEXT SET

ANCHOR TEXT
Alexander, Who Used to
Be Rich Last Sunday

SUPPORTING TEXT
A Chair for My Mother

TEXT SET

ANCHOR TEXT
Money Matters!

SUPPORTING TEXT
I Wanna Iguana

Cognates

Cognates are words that have similar spellings and meanings in two or more languages. Many words in English and Spanish share Greek or Latin roots, and many words in English came from French, which is closely connected to Spanish (and to Portuguese, Italian, and Romanian). Because of this, many literary, content, and academic process words in English (e.g., *gracious/gracioso; volcano/volcán; compare/comparar*) have recognizable Spanish cognates.

Making the connection to cognates permits students who are native Spanish speakers to understand the strong foundation they have in academic and literary English. These links between English and Spanish are also useful for native speakers of English and other languages because they help uncover basic underlying features of our language.

ANCHOR TEXT **Alexander, Who Used to Be Rich Last Sunday**

ENGLISH	SPANISH	ENGLISH	SPANISH
absolutely	absolutamente	garden	jardín
accident	accidente	hour	hora
air	aire	magic	mágico
bottles	botellas	market	mercado
bus	autobús	perfect	perfecto
cents	centavos	plants	plantas
chocolate	chocolate	purple	púrpura
diamonds	diamantes	rest	resto
dollars	dólares	rich	rico
especially	especialmente	telephone	teléfono
garage	garaje	visit	visitar

SUPPORTING TEXT A Chair for My Mother

ENGLISH	SPANISH	ENGLISH	SPANISH
apartment	apartamento	paint	pintar
bananas	bananas	peel	pelar
bank	banco	pizza	pizza
bills	billetes	potatoes	patatas
bus	autobús	roses	rosas
cat	gato	sandals	sandalias
count	contar	sofa	sofá
curtains	cortinas	soup	sopa
family	familia	tomatoes	tomates
mama	mamá	tulips	tulipanes

These lists contain many, but not all, Spanish cognates from these selections.

Unlock the Text

QUALITATIVE MEASURES

Levels of Meaning	to show what happens when people do not spend their money wisely; to differentiate between wants and needs
Structure	events related in a circular fashion, changing from present to past and back to present; illustrations show what happens in the text
Language Conventionality and Clarity	repetitive phrases; idioms; figurative language
Knowledge Demands	spending and saving money

Prepare to Read

LEVELS OF MEANING

Alexander, Who Used to Be Rich Last Sunday starts with a boy, Alexander, who receives a dollar from his grandparents when they come to visit. The story shows how he foolishly spends his money and ends up with useless items.

STRUCTURE

PREVIEW Have students look at the title page and illustrations. Then ask the following questions:

- Who is the main character? How can you tell? (The boy with the number one on his shirt. We know this because he is in every illustration.)
- On many pages, there is a coin with wings. What do you think that means? (The picture shows us how much money Alexander is losing.)

ENGLISH LANGUAGE LEARNERS

Display various coins, and discuss their values and different words to talk about them. For example, explain that a penny is one cent, a nickel is five cents, a dime is ten cents, and so on. Display pictures of the coins and their various names in a prominent place in the classroom.

STRUGGLING READERS

Before reading, guide students to use related words to understand unfamiliar terms. For example, write *stoop* on a chart. Write words related to a stoop, such as *stairs, house,* and *porch.* Discuss the relationship to the original term.

- Look at the thought bubble on page 9. What is Alexander thinking about? (all the things he will do with his money)
- Look at Alexander and the things he bought. Do you think he's happy with what he bought? (No, he looks upset.)

LANGUAGE CONVENTIONALITY AND CLARITY

PREVIEW VOCABULARY Use the Preview and Review Vocabulary Routine in Part 3 to assess what students know about words such as the following: *tokens, rent, downtown, stoop, walkie-talkie, ratty, rich, especially, fined, accident.*

ANALYZE IDIOMS AND EXPRESSIONS The following are idioms and expressions in *Alexander, Who Used to Be Rich Last Sunday* that might be confusing to students: *buy a new face, a dollar tree, positively saving money, ratty and mean.* Explain and discuss the figurative meaning of each, and have students work together to draw pictures of the literal meaning.

COGNATES Use the list of Spanish cognates at the beginning of this module to guide your Spanish-speaking students as they read the selection.

KNOWLEDGE DEMANDS

ACTIVATE BACKGROUND KNOWLEDGE Ask students the following questions to see what they know about spending and saving money. Ask: Why do people save money? What is something important to spend money on? What is something you should not spend money on?

After giving students time to write a one-sentence response to each question, have students share their responses with the class. Record and discuss any similarities between their responses.

Interact with Text

As you read, check and make sure students understand exactly how Alexander is spending and losing his money.

> If . . . students have difficulty understanding how Alexander is spending and losing his money,
>
> then . . . have students complete a T-chart labeled *Amount Spent* and *How It Was Spent.*

For example, Alexander made a bet with his mom and lost, so he had to pay fifteen cents. Under the *Amount Spent* column, students would write *fifteen cents,* and under the *How It Was Spent* column, they would write *made a bet with his mom.* There are a few times where we do not see how much Alexander loses or spends. Tell students to focus on examples that show how much money Alexander spent or lost.

STRUCTURE

At points in the story, verb tenses change to show events that happened in the past. In this story, we see how events in the past led Alexander to spend all of his money.

> If . . . students have difficulty identifying events in the past,
>
> then . . . discuss word clues that students can use to determine when each event happens and identify examples of past-tense words.

For example, the text on p. 21 reads, "Last Sunday, when I used to be rich, by accident I flushed three cents down the toilet." Point out that *Last Sunday* is a time clue that tells readers when the event occurred. Read the page aloud, and help students identify other words that show events that happened in the past *(used to, flushed, fell, walked, tried).* Ask students what they notice about most of the words. (They end in *-ed*.) Use the Verb Activities in Part 3 to provide students with additional support as needed.

ENGLISH LANGUAGE LEARNERS

Use the pictures to start a discussion on literal versus figurative meaning. For example, one picture shows Alexander digging a hole in the yard. He is using his dollar like a seed and hoping the seed will grow into a dollar tree.

STRUGGLING READERS

Students sometimes work so hard to decode text that they lose track of the meaning of the text. Provide opportunities for multiple readings of the text—the first time for decoding and subsequent times for comprehension and nuances.

LANGUAGE CONVENTIONALITY AND CLARITY

This book includes informal and figurative language.

If . . . students have difficulty with informal language, sarcasm, and expressions,

then . . . break down each confusing sentence and help students make connections to the text.

For example, students might have difficulty understanding the following sentence on p. 13: "Anthony told me to use the dollar to go downtown to a store and buy a new face. Anthony stinks." Read the sentence aloud and ask students the following questions to help them understand the figurative meaning. Ask: What does the picture show? Was Anthony making an honest suggestion when he told Alexander to "buy a new face"? Alexander says, "Anthony stinks." Does Anthony smell bad?

Ask students what they think Anthony meant. Guide them to understand that Anthony is teasing Alexander, and Alexander is angry with Anthony when he says that he "stinks."

Discuss other sentences that may be difficult for students to understand, such as "Anthony said when I'm 199 I still won't have enough money for a walkie-talkie," and "Nick said I'm too dumb to be let loose."

KNOWLEDGE DEMANDS

As you read *Alexander, Who Used to Be Rich Last Sunday,* assess whether students understand how Alexander spends his money over time.

If . . . students have difficulty understanding that Alexander is spending his money foolishly,

then . . . use a T-chart to examine what Alexander spends his money on and how much he spends.

Label the chart with the headings *Item* and *Amount.* After recording each item and its cost, break students into pairs and assign them an item from the list. Have them decide whether it was a good use of Alexander's money and write a sentence explaining why.

Express and Extend

LEVELS OF MEANING

EXPRESS Explain that Alexander's power to spend his own money on whatever he wants impairs his decision-making process. Reread the section in which Alexander goes to Cathy's garage sale. Ask: Do you think Alexander really needed the candle, teddy bear, or deck of cards, or did he just want them?

> If . . . students do not understand the difference between *want* and *need,*
>
> then . . . define the words *want* and *need,* and help students create a short list of items they want (chocolate, a football, toys) versus items they need (shoes or school supplies). As a class, decide in which category they would place the items Alexander bought.

EXTEND At various times in the text, we see there is something that Alexander really does want to save up for: a walkie-talkie. Have students work in pairs to identify places in the text (either words or pictures) that illustrate that Alexander really wants to save up for a walkie-talkie. Then have students compare their findings with another pair.

STRUCTURE

EXPRESS Point out to students that the story has a circular structure. It starts in the present, then tells about the past, and ends in the present. Guide students in understanding that the ending is also the starting point of the story.

> If . . . students have difficulty understanding the order of events in the story,
>
> then . . . remind them that in much of the story, Alexander is telling about things that happened the week before. Remind students that Alexander uses past-tense verbs when telling about the past. Examine examples from the text, and have students complete the Story Map A Graphic Organizer in Part 3 to show the order of events in the story.

EXTEND List three sentences from the book that are in past tense. Have students rewrite the sentences in present tense. Be aware that some verbs may have irregular forms that may make it difficult for students to conjugate them into other tenses.

MORE SUPPORT

ENGLISH LANGUAGE LEARNERS

Not all students read with an internal voice that allows them to understand why certain phrases and expressions are funny. Read aloud idiomatic and sarcastic language so students can hear how it is supposed to sound.

STRUGGLING READERS

Because some students often take longer to finish a book, they may miss out on extension activities. Be sure to provide all learners with opportunities for active and creative extensions to enrich their understanding of the text.

LANGUAGE CONVENTIONALITY AND CLARITY

EXPRESS Talk about Sentences and Words

Display and read aloud the following sentence with students. Afterward, ask the questions listed below.

I absolutely positively was saving the rest of my money.

Ask: What does the phrase *absolutely positively* mean? (It means that someone is definitely going to do something.) The words *absolutely* and *positively* have similar meanings. Why did the author use them both? (to add emphasis) What does the phrase *the rest of* imply? (It implies that Alexander has part of what he started with. Here he is referring to what money he has left after he has lost and spent some of it.)

TEAM TALK Have students work with a partner to rewrite the sentence, replacing *absolutely positively* and *the rest of.* Have partners share their sentences in small groups.

EXTEND Have students discuss a time they had to talk themselves into doing something they really did not want to do. Ask students to write examples of what they said to themselves. Have students share their examples with a partner.

KNOWLEDGE DEMANDS

EXPRESS Have students compare Alexander's feelings before and after he spends his money. Focus on the feeling of remorse that often comes when something is gone that cannot be regained.

If . . . students are unable to compare Alexander's feelings before and after spending his money,

then . . . help students find evidence in the text and illustrations that shows the comparisons.

EXTEND Have students choose one item in the story that Alexander was unhappy with (such as the gum, cards, or bear). Have them reread the section that discusses the item and write down a few sentences showing why Alexander was unhappy with his purchase. Provide time for students to share their statements.

ACCELERATED LEARNERS

Ask students to write a few sentences telling what they think Alexander should have done with his money. If they like the items that Alexander bought, they should write a few sentences explaining why those were good purchases.

Unlock the Text

QUALITATIVE MEASURES

Levels of Meaning	character-driven plot reveals love among family members
Structure	events related out of chronological order, using present and past tense
Language Conventionality and Clarity	complex sentences; pronouns; quotation marks
Knowledge Demands	overcoming obstacles; working toward a goal

A Chair for My Mother, pp. 51–80

Prepare to Read

LEVELS OF MEANING

A Chair for My Mother is the story of a young girl who helps save money for a chair after a fire destroys her family's home. Illustrations complement the text and help students understand a family's affection for one another and the sequence of events.

STRUCTURE

PREVIEW Read aloud the title, and have students preview the pictures in the story. Ask: Who do you think the main characters are in this story? (a girl, her mother, and her grandmother) Look at the jar on page 54. What is in the jar? (coins, money) Now look at other pictures with the jar in them. What do you notice? (The jar has more coins in it.) Based on the title and what you see in the pictures, what do you think this story will be about?

MORE SUPPORT

ENGLISH LANGUAGE LEARNERS

The variety of characters in *A Chair for My Mother* can be difficult for students to keep track of. Help students by creating a simple family tree that shows how the main characters are related to each other. Add other names as characters are introduced.

STRUGGLING READERS

When discussing new vocabulary, be sure to include practice with pronunciation. Point out to students which syllables are stressed in a word. Have them gently tap the syllables of the word on their desk as they say it, tapping louder for stressed syllables.

LANGUAGE CONVENTIONALITY AND CLARITY

PREVIEW VOCABULARY Use the Preview and Review Vocabulary Routine in Part 3 to assess what students know about the following words: *waitress, tips, coins, bargain, savings, charcoal, spoiled, ashes, wrappers, boost, sandals, pumps, block.* You can also use the Vocabulary Activities in Part 3 to preteach critical vocabulary.

COGNATES Use the list of Spanish cognates at the beginning of this module to guide your Spanish-speaking students as they read the selection.

KNOWLEDGE DEMANDS

ACTIVATE BACKGROUND KNOWLEDGE Use the Quick Write and Share Routine in Part 3 to assess what students know about saving money. Ask: Have you or someone in your family ever saved money to buy something? What did you want to buy? Was it something you wanted or something you needed?

Before students get started, model describing an experience you have had with saving money. For example, say: When I was about six years old, I really wanted a pair of cowboy boots. My mom said I would have to pay for them myself, so I started saving my money. I saved my money in a big jar and would often dump out the money and count it. When I finally had enough money, we went to the store to buy the boots. I'll never forget those neat cowboy boots!

Interact with Text

LEVELS OF MEANING

As you read *A Chair for My Mother,* assess students' understanding of how the characters save money.

If . . . students have trouble identifying how the characters save money,

then . . . use the Three-Column Chart Routine and Graphic Organizer in Part 3. Have students label the columns *Little Girl, Mother,* and *Grandmother.*

Read aloud pp. 53, 55, and 57. After each page, pause and allow students time to write down one way the little girl, mother, or grandmother saves money. When students have completed their charts, lead a discussion about how the characters worked together toward a common goal. **Ask:** Do you think the family would have saved enough money to buy the chair if only one member had been saving money? Why or why not?

STRUCTURE

As students read, assess their understanding of the story's use of present and past tense.

If . . . students have difficulty understanding when the narrator is speaking about the past or the present,

then . . . model for students how to close read p. 59 to identify past- and present-tense words.

After each sentence, stop and ask students to help you identify the verbs. Then, look at the verbs and ask students if the verbs are in the past or present tense. Discuss similar characteristics of present-tense words and past-tense words. For more practice, use the Verbs for Past, Present, and Future Activity in Part 3.

ENGLISH LANGUAGE LEARNERS

Point out irregular past- and present-tense verbs used in the text, such as *stood/stand, brought/ bring,* and *took/take.* Create a class chart for students to refer to.

STRUGGLING READERS

Help students understand past and present by writing past- and present-tense verbs from the text on cards, such as *clap/clapped, count/counted,* and so on. Display word pairs and say: Today I ___. Yesterday I ___. Have students indicate which verb to use in each sentence.

LANGUAGE CONVENTIONALITY AND CLARITY

Students may need support to understand the complex sentences used in *A Chair for My Mother.*

If . . . students have difficulty breaking down and understanding complex sentences,

then . . . have students examine each part of a sentence separately and then determine the relationship between the parts.

Read aloud this sentence: Whenever she gets a good bargain on tomatoes or bananas or something she buys, she puts by the savings and they go into the jar.

Start with the beginning of the sentence. Ask: Who is the *she* that the narrator is talking about? (Grandma) What does it mean to get a *good bargain*? (Getting a good bargain refers to buying something on sale or for a lesser amount than normal.) What does the narrator mean when she says that Grandma *puts by the savings*? (She takes the money she saves and puts it into the savings jar.)

Discuss how the two parts are related by asking the following questions: What does Grandma do first? (She gets the bargain.) Then what does she do? (She puts the money away.)

KNOWLEDGE DEMANDS

Aid students in understanding why the family needs to buy a new chair. Reread p. 59 and ask: What happened to the family's old chairs and sofa? (They burned in a fire.) Have students reread p. 63. Ask: When Mama and the little girl see their house on fire, what do they worry about? How can you tell? Guide students in understanding that the family members are more concerned about each other than they are about their possessions.

ENGLISH LANGUAGE LEARNERS

When students are reading complex sentences, encourage them to cover the clause after the comma and determine the meaning of the first part. Then have them do the same to examine the second part before thinking about how the parts are related.

Express and Extend

LEVELS OF MEANING

EXPRESS Working to overcome obstacles is a prominent theme in *A Chair for My Mother.* Tell students that an obstacle is something that makes it difficult for a person to do something. Have students work in pairs to identify the obstacle the characters faced and what they did to overcome it.

> If . . . students have trouble identifying the obstacle and how the characters overcome it,
>
> then . . . have students work in pairs to fill out a T-chart showing how the characters overcome their obstacle (the fire).

Give pairs a T-chart with the headings *Effects of the Fire* and *Character Actions.* Flip through the illustrations and point out that the obstacle is the fire. Have pairs look at the pages and list the effects of the fire under *Effects of the Fire* (loss of their home, loss of their furniture, loss of their food). Then, have them list how the characters overcame those effects under *Character Actions.* (They lived with their family; received furniture from neighbors; and received pizza, cake, and ice cream from neighbors.)

EXTEND Although the main characters get a place to live, food, and things for their house, they still don't have a big armchair or a sofa. Have students work alone or in pairs to identify parts in the text that tell why having a big armchair is so important for the main characters.

STRUCTURE

EXPRESS Reread with students the text on pp. 57–59. Point out the following verbs on p. 57: *sit, likes, has, gets, puts.* Discuss with students whether these verbs tell about the present, past, or future. Then have partners look at the verbs on p. 59. Have them identify two or three verbs and explain whether they tell about the past, present, or future. Encourage partners to share their lists and responses with the class.

EXTEND Divide students into small groups, and assign them a page. Have the groups reread the page and find other words and phrases that identify the past or present. Some examples are: *while we count, we sit, Grandma sits, often she has, whenever she gets.* Create a large T-chart on chart paper with the headings *Present* and *Past.* Invite students to write their phrases under the correct heading. Review the completed chart together.

ENGLISH LANGUAGE LEARNERS

Provide opportunities for students to record themselves reading the text. Then have them follow along in the text as they listen to themselves reading.

STRUGGLING READERS

Before students share with others, provide time for them to review their answers. This will allow students to become more comfortable with their response and give them time to change it prior to sharing with other students.

EXPRESS Talk about Sentences and Words

Display and read aloud the following sentence from *A Chair for My Mother.*

"You are all the kindest people," she said, "and we thank you very, very much."

Ask: Why are there markings around some of the words? (Those markings are called quotation marks. They show us that a character in the story is saying those words.) Who is saying the words inside the quotation marks? (Grandma) Who is Grandma referring to when she says *we*? (the mother, the little girl, and herself) Who is Grandma referring to when she says *you*? (the neighbors who brought the main characters food and items for their apartment)

TEAM TALK Have students turn to a partner and discuss how they know who the pronouns *you* and *we* refer to just by reading that sentence.

> If . . . students need more support in understanding pronouns,
> then . . . use the Pronoun Activities in Part 3.

EXTEND Provide students with sentences, such as: Grandma and I ate apples. Then, have them decide what pronouns they could use to replace the nouns. In this sentence, they could replace *Grandma* with *She* or *Grandma and I* with *We*.

EXPRESS Have students write a few sentences and draw a picture of something they learned about overcoming obstacles from *A Chair for My Mother.* Have small groups discuss what they learned.

> If . . . students have difficulty writing sentences to show what they learned about overcoming obstacles,
> then . . . provide a few sentence starters such as: Overcoming obstacles is ___ because ___.

EXTEND Have students write a summary of what they learned from their group discussion.

ACCELERATED LEARNERS

Ask students to decide what their favorite piece of furniture is in their own home. Have them write three sentences showing the steps they would take to replace it if something were to happen to it.

Cognates

Cognates are words that have similar spellings and meanings in two or more languages. Many words in English and Spanish share Greek or Latin roots, and many words in English came from French, which is closely connected to Spanish (and to Portuguese, Italian, and Romanian). Because of this, many literary, content, and academic process words in English (e.g., *gracious/gracioso; volcano/volcán; compare/comparar*) have recognizable Spanish cognates.

Making the connection to cognates permits students who are native Spanish speakers to understand the strong foundation they have in academic and literary English. These links between English and Spanish are also useful for native speakers of English and other languages because they help uncover basic underlying features of our language.

ANCHOR TEXT **Money Matters!**

ENGLISH	SPANISH	ENGLISH	SPANISH
bank	banco	markets	mercados
bracelets	brazaletes	ordinary	ordinario
collectors	coleccionistas	paper	papel
company	compañía	philanthropist	filántropo
cost	costo	plastic	plástico
credit	crédito	precious	precioso
crime	crimen	probably	probablemente
decisions	decisiones	projects	proyectos
deposit	depósito	respectable	respetable
economists	economistas	role	rol
electronic	electrónico	salary	salario
government	gobierno	salt	sal
grains	granos	transactions	transacciones
illegal	ilegal	value	valor
interest	interés	yogurt	yogur

SUPPORTING TEXT **I Wanna Iguana**

ENGLISH	SPANISH	ENGLISH	SPANISH
baby	bebé	lesson	lección
class	clase	mature	maduro
compassionate	compasivo	probably	probablemente
decide	decidir	reptile	reptil
exactly	exactamente	space	espacio
financial	financiero	spaghetti	espagueti
hamsters	hámsteres	tarantulas	tarántulas
iguana	iguana	trophies	trofeos

These lists contain many, but not all, Spanish cognates from these selections.

Unlock the Text

QUALITATIVE MEASURES

Levels of Meaning	basic financial terms and concepts; some abstract concepts relating to money and economics
Structure	chapters presented as self-contained two-page spreads; main topics in chapter titles; photos with captions; table of contents; some information presented in tables
Language Conventionality and Clarity	short, simple sentences with some domain-specific words
Knowledge Demands	introduction of economic principles: trade and the origin of money; forms of money; earning, budgeting, saving, and spending money

Money Matters!

WRITTEN BY NIKKI TATE

Prepare to Read

LEVELS OF MEANING

Money Matters! has two main purposes. The first is to inform readers about basic economic principles underlying the use of money—why it exists and how it is exchanged. The second is to teach readers how to make wise decisions about spending and saving their own money.

STRUCTURE

PREVIEW Read the title *Money Matters!* Ask: Can you tell what this book is about just by reading the title? (yes) Let's preview the pages to see if we can get an even better idea of what the book is about. **Have students preview the table of contents. Say:** The table of contents mentions money several times. It also has words such as *trade, banks,* and *save*. What do you think some of the chapters will be about? (Possible response: how

ENGLISH LANGUAGE LEARNERS

As students are introduced to new vocabulary words, use the words in sentences related to their lives. For example, ask: Will you be *spending* any money today? What will you buy? How could you *earn* some money?

STRUGGLING READERS

Students may have difficulty understanding the more abstract concepts in the text, such as bartering and credit. Before they begin reading, remind them that they can use the photographs to help them better understand the concepts.

to save and spend money) Have students page through the book and look at the photos, captions, and tables. Ask: Do all the photos show money? (no) What types of things do they show? (Possible responses: things money can buy, people using money) Do you think this book is a made-up story or an informational text? (informational) What makes you think that? (The photos show things in the real world. The tables give factual information.)

LANGUAGE CONVENTIONALITY AND CLARITY

PREVIEW VOCABULARY Use the Preview and Review Vocabulary Routine in Part 3 to assess what students know about the following words: *spending, earn, amount, valuable, bought, borrow, skills, chores, services,* and *measures.*

COGNATES Use the list of Spanish cognates at the beginning of this module to guide Spanish-speaking students as they read the selection.

DOMAIN-SPECIFIC VOCABULARY Use the Vocabulary Activities in Part 3 to pre-teach the following domain-specific vocabulary: *currency, exchange, transactions, income, budgeting, salary,* and *wage.* Explain that these words are all associated with earning, saving, and spending money.

KNOWLEDGE DEMANDS

ACTIVATE BACKGROUND KNOWLEDGE Explain that *Money Matters!* explores several aspects of the topic of money. Say: We'll learn why people use money and when money was invented. We'll also talk about how you can make smart decisions about your own money. Ask students to share what they know about personal finance. Use the Quick Write and Share Routine in Part 3. Ask: What are some ways that you get money? What do you do with your money? How do you spend it? When do you save it?

STRUGGLING READERS

Provide extra support for students who struggle to interpret the information in tables. Walk students through the first few items in a column. For example, on page 20, say: A dozen eggs cost 39 cents in India. A dozen eggs cost $1.80 in Hong Kong. A dozen eggs cost $3.39 in Russia. In which country would you pay the most for eggs? Help students understand what items each table is comparing.

Interact with Text

LEVELS OF MEANING

During reading, pause to ensure students are grasping the abstract concepts. Break the concepts into smaller steps and illustrate them with examples from real life. For example, read pp. 18–19 with students. Then discuss how credit and debit cards work.

If . . . students have difficulty understanding how one borrows money with a credit card,

then . . . narrate a recent credit-card purchase you made, step by step. You may use the Steps in a Process Routine and Graphic Organizer in Part 3 to outline the process: you swiped the card at the store, the bank paid the merchant for your purchase, the bank sent you a bill, you paid the bill.

Follow up by comparing and contrasting the process for using a debit card.

STRUCTURE

As students read, point out the chapter titles as a way to understand the "big ideas" of each chapter. Explain that some chapter titles in *Money Matters!* refer to one aspect of the big idea as a way to introduce the idea and get readers interested. For example, read the chapter title on p. 14 ("Making Paper Money") aloud and have students look at the photos and captions. Ask them what this chapter will be about.

Point out to students that the captions tell more about the photos, but they also provide additional details about the big ideas. For example, the photo on p. 14 shows what Chinese paper money looked like. Remind students to look at the photos and read the captions along with the main text.

If . . . students have difficulty relating the chapter title to the big idea of the chapter,

then . . . read aloud the first paragraph and point out the connection between the Chinese laws about paper money and the title "Making Paper Money."

Follow up by asking students to think of other titles for the chapter that would more explicitly state the big idea. You may wish to follow a similar process for "Borrowing Money" (pp. 18–19) and "How Much Is That Loaf of Bread?" (pp. 20–21).

ENGLISH LANGUAGE LEARNERS

To help students internalize vocabulary and concepts, provide scenarios, such as shopping, saving, or budgeting, to act out. Encourage students to use specific vocabulary words in their role play.

STRUGGLING READERS

To help students track the key concepts in *Money Matters!*, create a four-column chart with the following questions as headings: *Why did people start using money? What forms of money do people use? How can I be smart about my money? How important is money to me?* As they read, have students note details that can help them answer each question.

Money Matters! contains several domain-specific words that are essential to understanding the topic. As you read, stop periodically to assess students' grasp of domain-specific words and model strategies for understanding them. For example, if students do not understand the word *currency* on p. 8, model using the context to guess the meaning: This chapter is about trading. I think currency is something people trade. Then model looking up the word in a dictionary to confirm its meaning. As you read further, encourage students to use context clues to guess word meanings.

If . . . students have difficulty understanding domain-specific vocabulary,

then . . . determine on a case-by-case basis whether to have students try guessing the words from context before looking them up or to define the words yourself.

You may follow up by challenging students to think of synonyms for some of the domain-specific words you encounter.

KNOWLEDGE DEMANDS

Students may have heard about credit and debit cards, but since they are young, they may not be sure how they are different. Explain that using a credit card is one way of borrowing money. A bank allows people to spend money using the credit card, but that money must be paid back. If it is not paid back on time, fees may be charged. A debit card is a way to use money from your own bank account without carrying cash or checks. Explain that people need to keep track of the money they spend.

ENGLISH LANGUAGE LEARNERS

Have students work in pairs or small groups and use a jigsaw strategy to achieve a deeper understanding of each chapter. Assign each student in the group one section of the chapter to read carefully. Encourage students to read their sections more than once and use any strategies they have learned to decode the words. Then have students explain the content of their section to the others in the group.

MORE SUPPORT

Express and Extend

EXPRESS Point out that *value* is one of the important themes of *Money Matters!* Say: The value of a thing is what it is worth to you. The book says that value is not only about money. **Ask:** How do people decide which things are worth more money than others? How do you decide what things have value to you?

If . . . students have difficulty thinking of items of relative value,

then . . . prompt them with lists of examples from the book and personal experiences, such as gold, a cow, beads, a house, a TV, a vacation, a pet, time to play with friends.

EXTEND Have students list three items that have value to them. If possible, have students ask their parents or someone at home to estimate the value of each item in terms of money. If that is not possible, tell students to guess the monetary value. Have students write a sentence telling whether the items with personal value were also the items with a higher monetary value.

STRUCTURE

EXPRESS Have partners select a chapter and write a sentence that summarizes its main idea. Remind students that they can refer to the chapter titles for clues about the "big ideas."

If . . . students have difficulty writing a sentence that summarizes the main idea,

then . . . use the Main Idea and Details Routine and Graphic Organizer in Part 3 to support understanding.

EXTEND Ask: What is the most interesting detail you learned from this book? Have students write a sentence that answers the question. Then have them write another sentence that tells what they can do with this new knowledge. For example, some students may say that they will create a plan for saving money toward something they want to buy. Have students share their answers with the group.

MORE SUPPORT

ENGLISH LANGUAGE LEARNERS

Allow students to preview comprehension questions that you will be asking about the text. Then have them work with a partner to find the answers. Giving students this head start with the questions will help them participate in class discussions later.

STRUGGLING READERS

Have students use the charts they created in the Interact with Text section to help them formulate answers to the questions about main ideas.

LANGUAGE CONVENTIONALITY AND CLARITY

EXPRESS Talk about Sentences and Words

Display and read aloud the following sentences from *Money Matters!.*

> It is very important that people keep track of what they spend with a credit card. If not, they could be spending more than they can pay back.

> A budget is a plan. It helps you save and spend your money sensibly.

Point out that these sentences are in two different chapters, "Borrowing Money" and "Budgeting." The author brings up that it is important to keep track of the money you spend twice in the book.

TEAM TALK Have partners discuss what the author means by "save and spend your money sensibly." After the pairs have conversed, ask volunteers to share their ideas with the class.

EXTEND Have students imagine they are a parent giving their child advice about saving and spending money. Tell them to write two or three sentences telling the child how to save and spend money.

KNOWLEDGE DEMANDS

EXPRESS Have small groups discuss why saving is an important part of budgeting.

If . . . students have difficulty determining why saving is important,

then . . . review pp. 28–31. Ask: What does saving help you do? (afford something you need or want in the future)

EXTEND Have students think of some things they would like to have or do. Then ask them to write a sentence or two telling how saving could help them achieve their goals.

ACCELERATED LEARNERS

Have students work together to brainstorm a list of needs and wants for their classroom. Then invite them to create a plan for earning and saving money toward one need and one want. Have them share their plan with the class.

MORE SUPPORT

Unlock the Text

QUALITATIVE MEASURES

Levels of Meaning	character-driven plot; use of persuasion; explicit purpose
Structure	chronological narrative told through a series of letters; argument and counterargument
Language Conventionality and Clarity	mainly simple and compound sentences with familiar vocabulary; some idioms and slang
Knowledge Demands	persuasion through reasoning, compromise, and negotiation; responsible pet ownership

ReadyGEN
Text Collection 2

I Wanna Iguana, pp. 81–95

Prepare to Read

LEVELS OF MEANING

On the surface, *I Wanna Iguana* is a humorous exchange between a boy and his mother. However, another purpose of this playful story is to introduce readers to important ideas, such as how to earn a privilege, take responsibility, be considerate of others, and present a convincing argument.

STRUCTURE

PREVIEW Read the title and preview the letter format. Explain that the story is told through a series of letters between a boy named Alex and his mom. Display p. 84. Point out that the text has two different fonts. Explain that one font is used for the letters from Alex to Mom, and another font is used for the letters from Mom to Alex. Next, point out and name the heading, body, closing, and signature. Draw students' attention to the commas in the letters and discuss their purpose.

ENGLISH LANGUAGE LEARNERS

To help students participate in the Activate Background Knowledge activity, explain to students what *persuade* means. Provide examples of persuasion, and have students use *persuade* in a sentence of their own.

STRUGGLING READERS

Some students may not be familiar with iguanas. Provide these students with photos of iguanas, and explain that they are a type of reptile. Help them understand that some people keep these reptiles as house pets.

LANGUAGE CONVENTIONALITY AND CLARITY

PREVIEW VOCABULARY Use the Preview and Review Vocabulary Routine in Part 3 to assess what students know about words, such as *iguana, sensitive, compassionate, hamsters, adorable, tarantulas, pet, cage, concerned, lonely, tricks,* and *wizard.* Preteach critical vocabulary, such as *doubt, mature, reptile, trial basis, responsible, allowance,* and *financial.*

CONTRACTIONS This selection uses many contractions. Use the Contractions Activity in Part 3 to help students identify contractions and understand how they are used. Create a contractions chart to record contractions from the selection.

COGNATES Use the list of Spanish cognates at the beginning of this module to guide your Spanish-speaking students as they read the selection.

KNOWLEDGE DEMANDS

ACTIVATE BACKGROUND KNOWLEDGE Ask students to share what they know about the art of persuasion. Use the Quick Write and Share Routine in Part 3 and ask: What does it mean to persuade? Have you ever persuaded your parents to let you do something? How did you persuade them?

Before students get started, model recalling a time you persuaded your parents to let you do something. For example, say: One time a friend asked me to walk to school with him. I had never walked to school without my mom before, and she was unsure if she should let me go with a friend instead of her. I persuaded her that we were mature enough to walk on our own by promising that we would look both ways before crossing streets and that we would walk straight to school, without talking to any strangers. In the end, I convinced her!

Interact with Text

LEVELS OF MEANING

As you read *I Wanna Iguana,* assess students' understanding of persuasive techniques. For example, on p. 82 Alex presents his first reason why Mom should let him have the iguana: "If I don't take it, he goes to Stinky and Stinky's dog, Lurch, will eat it."

Alex also uses the persuasive technique of asking a question that prompts the person being persuaded to agree with the logic of the argument. He asks, "You don't want that to happen, do you?" The question is also designed to appeal to his mom's emotions, because she wouldn't want to be responsible for any harm to the iguana.

> **If . . .** students have difficulty understanding the art of persuasion,
>
> **then . . .** read Alex's letters on pp. 92 and 93.

Point out that in these letters Alex promises to be responsible and to pay for the iguana's food in the hopes his mom will let him take the iguana.

STRUCTURE

As students read, assess their understanding of the story's use of letters as a format for the text. Guide students to see each of Alex's letters as an argument and each of Mom's letters as a counterargument. Explain that an argument tries to convince someone of something, and a counterargument rebuts the argument. Then ask: What does Alex hope his letters will convince his mother to do? (He hopes his letters will convince Mom to change her mind about letting him take home the iguana.)

After students read each of Alex's letters, ask: What does Alex say to try to convince Mom to change her mind? After each of Mom's letters, ask: Did Alex's letter persuade Mom to let him have the iguana? Help students identify the reasons Mom gives for not letting Alex have the iguana. After students read p. 93, ask: What do you notice about the text on this page? (There is one letter, but then Alex and Mom talk face to face.)

ENGLISH LANGUAGE LEARNERS

Some students might not be familiar with having a house pet. Provide these students with examples of common house pets, such as dogs, cats, birds, hamsters, iguanas, and so on. Explain the different responsibilities of owning a pet, such as feeding it.

STRUGGLING READERS

Almost all of the letters have a different closing. Help students understand how each closing relates to the content of the letter. For example, on p. 84, Alex says in his letter that iguanas are cute. He then closes his letter with "Your adorable son."

LANGUAGE CONVENTIONALITY AND CLARITY

As you read *I Wanna Iguana,* help students analyze examples of figurative language and slang to determine their meaning. On p. 83, for example, point out the idiom *Nice try, though.* Explain that an idiom is an expression that means something slightly different from what the meanings of its individual words may suggest. Discuss how to use context to help understand its meaning. Say: In this letter, Mom is responding to Alex's letter on page 82. Reread Alex's letter. What did Alex try to do in his letter? (He tried to convince Mom to let him have the iguana.) Did he succeed? (no) Mom calls his attempt a "nice try." If something is nice, is it more likely to be good or bad? (good) So, what do you think Mom means when she says "nice try"? (You made a good attempt at convincing me.) Use the Analyze Idioms and Expressions Routine in Part 3 to provide additional support.

KNOWLEDGE DEMANDS

Some cultural references may be particularly challenging for students because they have no framework on which to base understanding.

If . . . students are confused by the reference to Godzilla,

then . . . suggest ways they might find out who or what Godzilla is.

Ask: What are some ways that we can find out who or what Godzilla is? (Ask a friend or an adult; use the Internet.) How can we use context clues to get enough information about Godzilla to understand the text? Guide students to use context clues to gather that Godzilla is ugly. Ask: If the iguana is uglier than Godzilla, is Godzilla more likely to be a little ugly or really ugly? (really ugly)

Express and Extend

LEVELS OF MEANING

EXPRESS Have pairs of students choose one of Alex's letters from *I Wanna Iguana* to show their understanding of persuasion. In groups of four, have each set of partners explain the reasons and details Alex uses to support his opinion that he should be able to take Mikey's iguana.

> **If . . .** students have difficulty identifying the reasons Alex provides,
> **then . . .** call students' attention to specific reasons in the text.

For example, reread Alex's letter on p. 85. Ask: Why does Alex think the iguana wouldn't be a problem for Mom? (She would never have to see it, because Alex would keep the iguana in a cage in his room.) Do you think this is a good reason for Mom to let Alex have the iguana? Why or why not?

EXTEND Have students think of something they want but do not need. Ask them to write a persuasive, friendly letter to an adult who can help them get what they want. Tell them the letter should include reasons and details that support their opinion. Have students trade their letters with a partner to evaluate. Have partners tell whether they think the letter is persuasive and why.

STRUCTURE

EXPRESS Reread the story with students, and help them identify the point at which Mom decides to let Alex have the iguana. Ask: What finally causes Mom to let Alex have the iguana? (Alex says he would clean his room and the iguana's cage, and he would pay for the iguana's food with his allowance.)

EXTEND Recall the basic purpose and structure of a thank-you note. Then have partners work together to write one set of letters between Alex and Mom. Tell them that Alex's letter is a thank-you note to Mom for letting him have the iguana, and Mom's letter is a response to Alex's thank-you note. Provide time for partners to read their notes within small groups.

MORE SUPPORT

ENGLISH LANGUAGE LEARNERS

Support students' participation in discussions by displaying sentence starters, such as: Alex says he will ___. Alex says he is ___. Provide word choices, such as *responsible, tidy, feed,* or *mature,* for completing the sentences.

STRUGGLING READERS

Provide support as students write their letters. For example, make sure students' letters have an opening, body, and closing. Review with them where they should use commas.

EXPRESS Talk about Sentences and Words

Display and read the following letter from p. 91 of *I Wanna Iguana*:

Dear Alex,
Let's say I let you have the iguana on a trial basis. What exactly would you do to take care of it?
Love,
Mom

Remind students that an idiom is a phrase with a meaning other than the basic meanings of its words. Point out the phrase *Let's say.* Explain that it is an example of an idiom, because it does not really mean "let us say" something; it means "let's pretend for a moment that this is true." Then point out the expression *trial basis*. Explain that a trial basis is a period for trying something out. Ask: What is Mom considering allowing Alex to do on a trial basis? (have the iguana) What would that mean? (She would have to see if he could take care of it like he promised.) What would happen if the trial failed? (She would not let him keep the iguana.)

TEAM TALK Have students turn to a partner and use *trial basis* in a sentence of their own.

EXTEND Have students choose something, such as an instrument or a pet, that they would like to talk their parents into letting them have on a trial basis. Then have them write a list of things they would have to do in order to keep their chosen item or pet. Have students share their lists with a partner.

EXPRESS Discuss the meaning of this sentence: "Remember what happened when you took home the class fish?" To guide meaning, ask: If it is a class fish, to whom does it probably belong? (the class) What do you think happens to the fish when school is out? (The classroom teacher or a student probably takes it home for the summer.)

EXTEND Have students write a few sentences telling what they know about class pets and whether they would ever consider being responsible for one. Ask: What would you need to know in order to be the class pet's caretaker? Have students read their sentences aloud. List students' ideas about caring for pets on a class chart.

ACCELERATED LEARNERS

Have students choose the letter they felt was most persuasive and write a sentence or two telling why. Provide time for students to share their opinions and reasons.

MORE SUPPORT

Building Ideas

TEXT SET

ANCHOR TEXT
Theodore Roosevelt: The
Adventurous President

SUPPORTING TEXT
Marching with Aunt Susan

TEXT SET

ANCHOR TEXT
Change Makers

SUPPORTING TEXT
City Green

Cognates

Cognates are words that have similar spellings and meanings in two or more languages. Many words in English and Spanish share Greek or Latin roots, and many words in English came from French, which is closely connected to Spanish (and to Portuguese, Italian, and Romanian). Because of this, many literary, content, and academic process words in English (e.g., *gracious/gracioso; volcano/volcán; compare/comparar*) have recognizable Spanish cognates.

Making the connection to cognates permits students who are native Spanish speakers to understand the strong foundation they have in academic and literary English. These links between English and Spanish are also useful for native speakers of English and other languages because they help uncover basic underlying features of our language.

ANCHOR TEXT Theodore Roosevelt: The Adventurous President

ENGLISH	SPANISH	ENGLISH	SPANISH
active	activo	extinct	extinto
adventure	aventura	fortunate	afortunado
animals	animales	gallop	galopar
asthma	asma	governor	gobernador
battle	batalla	group	grupo
buffalo	búfalo	ideas	ideas
canal	canal	illegal	ilegal
candidate	candidato	insects	insectos
conservationist	conservacionista	island	isla
creatures	criaturas	jungle	jungla
different	diferente	leaders	líderes
direction	dirección	mines	minas
elected	elegido	monopoly	monopolio
excellent	excelente	mountain	montaña
experts	expertos	nation	nación
explorers	exploradores	naturalist	naturalista
explosion	explosión	nature	naturaleza
		operate	operar

ANCHOR TEXT Theodore Roosevelt: The Adventurous President (continued)

ENGLISH	SPANISH	ENGLISH	SPANISH
parks	parques	stomach	estómago
party	partido	study	estudiar
politics	política	surprise	sorpresa
president	presidente	terrible	terrible
promise	prometer	tragedy	tragedia
proverb	proverbio	tropical	tropical
scientist	científico	unusual	inusual

SUPPORTING TEXT Marching with Aunt Susan

ENGLISH	SPANISH	ENGLISH	SPANISH
adult	adulto	inspire	inspirar
bicycle	bicicleta	justice	justicia
campaign	campaña	mount	montar
decide	decidir	pedal	pedalear
decision	decisión	prepare	preparar
election	elección	public	público
equal	igual	referendum	referéndum
exercise	ejercicio	roses	rosas
family	familia	suffrage	sufragio
government	gobierno	tea	té
honor	honor	votes	votos
imagine	imaginar		

These lists contain many, but not all, Spanish cognates from these selections.

Unlock the Text

QUALITATIVE MEASURES

Levels of Meaning	biography with detailed information about a broad range of subjects; themes of fairness and courage
Structure	chronological (excluding first chapter); photos with captions; sidebars with fun facts; time line
Language Conventionality and Clarity	multiple-meaning words; using root words; implications
Knowledge Demands	conserving nature

Prepare to Read

LEVELS OF MEANING

Theodore Roosevelt: The Adventurous President is a biography with fairly detailed information about Roosevelt's experiences, such as family life, travels, and political life. The book aims to tell the story of Roosevelt's life and explore the concepts of being fair and standing up for one's beliefs.

STRUCTURE

PREVIEW Have students preview the text by reading the title of the book and the chapter titles on the table of contents page and looking at the pictures. Ask: Based on the title of the book and chapter titles, what kind of book do you think this will be? (a biography) What do biographies usually tell us? (They tell about a person's life and are written by someone other than that person.) What do you notice about the pictures? (They are in black and white and many have captions.) Do the pictures look old or new? What does this tell you about the biography? (They look old. The biography is about someone who lived a long time ago.)

ENGLISH LANGUAGE LEARNERS

Display the time line on p. 44 in a prominent place in the classroom. Review with students the purpose of a time line. When students begin reading, refer to the time line to help them keep track of important events in Roosevelt's life and the order in which they occur.

STRUGGLING READERS

Students may have trouble keeping track of Roosevelt's family members since they go by a variety of different names. As students read, help them create a simple family tree that shows the relationship of each family member to Roosevelt and lists all the names each person has.

Point out the various text features in the book, such as the captions, map, sidebars, subheads, and time line.

LANGUAGE CONVENTIONALITY AND CLARITY

PREVIEW VOCABULARY Use the Preview and Review Vocabulary Routine in Part 3 to assess what students know about the following words: *asthma, candidate, government, politician, chief, conservationists, elected, reporters, assassinated, monopoly, progressive, canal,* and *governor.* You can also use the Vocabulary Activities in Part 3 to preteach critical vocabulary words.

MULTIPLE-MEANING WORDS Many words in the text have different meanings based on the context. For example, the meanings of *strike, party,* and *run* differ from their commonly used definitions. Point these words out to students as you read. Use the Analyze Multiple-Meaning Words Routine in Part 3 to provide support.

COGNATES Use the list of Spanish cognates at the beginning of this module to guide your Spanish-speaking students as they read the selection.

KNOWLEDGE DEMANDS

ACTIVATE BACKGROUND KNOWLEDGE Ask students to share what they know about conservation. Use the Quick Write and Share Routine in Part 3 and ask: Why is it important to protect nature? How can people protect nature?

Before students begin, briefly explain conservation with the following example: Nature is the plants and animals in the world around us. It is important to protect, or conserve, nature so plants and animals are not lost forever. We can protect the natural environment by being responsible about the way we interact with nature and by taking simple steps to conserve and use resources wisely, such as recycling and turning off the faucet when it's not in use.

Explain to students that in *Theodore Roosevelt: The Adventurous President,* the author discusses the ways Roosevelt tried to protect nature. The term the author uses when she talks about protecting nature is *conservation*.

Interact with Text

LEVELS OF MEANING

An important theme throughout the selection is Theodore Roosevelt's fairness. Discuss what it means to be fair by using the Web Graphic Organizer in Part 3. Write *fair* in the center oval. Then have students brainstorm examples of fairness, and record their responses in the outer ovals. Then, help students identify and list what Roosevelt did that was fair. Use a web for Roosevelt if needed.

If . . . students have trouble identifying Roosevelt's acts of fairness,

then . . . give pairs the Two-Column Chart Graphic Organizer in Part 3 with the headings *Action* and *Why It Was Fair.* Assign students one of the following pages or sets of pages to reread and analyze Roosevelt's actions: 21, 28, 29–30.

Model the activity using the paragraph starting on p. 12. Read the paragraph aloud, and then under *Action* write *passed laws about government jobs.* Under *Why It Was Fair,* write *Teddy's law allowed anyone who worked hard to get a job in the government. Before his law, you had to know someone in order to get a job.*

STRUCTURE

Assign students one of the sidebars, and have them use the Venn Diagram Graphic Organizer in Part 3 to record important information from the text and the sidebar. Then, have them record in the middle any facts that appear in both the text and sidebar. Afterward, students should write a sentence or two saying whether the sidebar supports information from the text.

If . . . students have difficulty deciding whether a sidebar supports information from the text,

then . . . work as a class to summarize and analyze the sidebar on p. 33.

Reread the paragraphs under the section heading "Teddy's Great Plans" on p. 32. As a class, summarize the information from the text and record the summary on the board. Organize students into small groups, and have them read the sidebar at the end of the section and summarize the information. Then, let students decide whether the sidebar supports information from the paragraphs they just read.

ENGLISH LANGUAGE LEARNERS

Have students write unfamiliar words and phrases on index cards. After working with them to define a word, have students record on the index card the sentence in the biography that uses the word as well as the word's definition.

STRUGGLING READERS

Some students may struggle to summarize information from the text or from the sidebars. Use the Retell or Summarize Routine and Graphic Organizer in Part 3 to provide additional support.

LANGUAGE CONVENTIONALITY AND CLARITY

Demonstrate how identifying and defining root words in a confusing term can help students understand the term.

For example, point out the word *progressive* on p. 36, and read it aloud. Ask students if any part of the word looks familiar to them. If students are having trouble, write the word on the board, and underline the word *progress* in *progressive*. Ask students if they can define the word *progress,* or share the definition with them. Point out that *progressive* means relating to progress." Afterward, use the word in a sentence of your own, and display it on the board. For example: *Having a cell phone in the 1980s was very progressive, but now almost everyone has a cell phone.* Discuss why the word *progressive* makes sense in your sentence, and then have students write sentences of their own to share with a partner or the class.

KNOWLEDGE DEMANDS

At various times in the text, the author refers to Roosevelt's love of nature and shows how it led him to become a famous conservationist.

If . . . students have trouble understanding how Roosevelt's love of nature led him to become a conservationist,

then . . . use the Cause and Effect Routine and Graphic Organizer in Part 3 to help students organize information.

For example, assign one of the following sections for students to reread: "A Sickly Kid," "Animals Everywhere," or "A Conservationist Is Born." Students should identify an action that led Roosevelt to become a famous conservationist and record it on their graphic organizer.

Express and Extend

EXPRESS Fairness is an obvious theme in this selection. However, courage is an equally important theme that students may have difficulty identifying in some instances.

If . . . students have difficulty identifying examples of courage in the selection,

then . . . do a close reading of the examples of Roosevelt's courage using the second and third paragraphs on p. 9, the first two paragraphs on p. 21, or the text on pp. 29–30 about the miners on strike. Ask: What does it mean to have courage? How were these acts courageous?

EXTEND Have students think about the ways in which Roosevelt's behavior and beliefs made him different from others. Have students list examples from the text that show how Roosevelt was different from other politicians. Have partners share their examples.

STRUCTURE

EXPRESS Assign small groups one chapter. Use the Main Idea and Details Routine and Graphic Organizer in Part 3 to identify the main idea and important details about Theodore Roosevelt's life.

If . . . students have difficulty identifying the main idea of a chapter,

then . . . assign pairs one section in a chapter to analyze, using the Main Idea and Details Graphic Organizer. Afterward, have the pairs share the information from their organizers. Record the information on the board, and use it to guide the class in creating a summary for the entire chapter.

EXTEND Have students review the text and make a list of Roosevelt's major achievements. Ask: Which do you think was the most important achievement and why? Provide the sentence starter: I think Roosevelt's most interesting or important achievement was _____ because _____. Tell students to use text evidence to support their opinion. Have students read their sentences to the class and determine which achievement is the most popular.

ENGLISH LANGUAGE LEARNERS

Allow students to use sticky notes to flag difficult or unfamiliar words and sentences as they read. Afterward, have students work together to clarify misunderstandings and explain how they were able to reach their answers.

STRUGGLING READERS

Some students may need additional practice summarizing information from the text. Have these students work in groups at the end of each chapter to summarize what they have read. Remind them that they can use this strategy when they read other biographies.

MORE SUPPORT

LANGUAGE CONVENTIONALITY AND CLARITY

EXPRESS Talk about Sentences and Words

Display the following sentence from *Theodore Roosevelt: The Adventurous President,* and read it aloud.

> He seemed too small for the rugged western life.

Ask: What is the pronoun in this sentence? *(he)* Who does *he* refer to? (Teddy Roosevelt) What does the phrase *too small* mean? ("not big enough") What does *rugged* mean? ("tough" or "difficult") Have students discuss what is being implied about small people in the sentence. Ask: Why would a small person not be able to handle a rugged, or tough, environment?

TEAM TALK Have partners find other descriptive sentences that imply something about a person and read them to each other.

EXTEND Tell students the word *too* signals a description. In this case, Roosevelt's size is described as being too small to fit with rugged western life. Have students write comparisons of their own using the sentence frame: ___ is too ___ for ___. For example: *The soup is too hot for my little brother.* Have students read their sentences to a partner. Have partners identify what the word *too* is describing.

KNOWLEDGE DEMANDS

EXPRESS Have small groups discuss what they learned about conservation.

If . . . students have difficulty talking about conservationists' beliefs,

then . . . provide examples from the text that support Roosevelt's efforts to preserve and protect the natural environment, and ask students how those examples help protect the environment. For example, you might ask: How does creating national parks protect the environment?

EXTEND Have students work in small groups to research a national park, such as Theodore Roosevelt National Park or Yellowstone National Park, which are highlighted on pp. 30–31. Have students do a brief presentation in which they give two reasons why the land protected in the preserve is important.

ACCELERATED LEARNERS

Make copies of the time line from the back of the book. Have students add to the time line two important things that Roosevelt did. Provide students with age-appropriate websites or texts for their search.

Unlock the Text

QUALITATIVE MEASURES

ReadyGEN
Text Collection 2

Levels of Meaning	historical fiction focused on discrimination against women and the fight for women's suffrage
Structure	chronological narrative with dialogue; illustrations
Language Conventionality and Clarity	unfamiliar words; complex sentence structure in song lyrics; word choices on signs
Knowledge Demands	women's suffrage; gender roles

Marching with
Aunt Susan,
pp. 103–135

Prepare to Read

LEVELS OF MEANING

In *Marching with Aunt Susan,* there are two levels of meaning. One purpose of the text is to introduce Susan B. Anthony and the fight for women's suffrage. A further purpose is to explore the issues of discrimination and gender roles as experienced by a young girl.

STRUCTURE

PREVIEW Have students preview the book and note anything that sparks their attention. Then ask students questions about what they previewed. Ask: Is there dialogue in this story? (yes) How do you know? (quotation marks) How do you know who is speaking when reading dialogue? (I look for clues in the text, such as *she said.*) What do the illustrations tell you about the story's setting? (Based on what the characters are wearing, the story took place a long time ago.)

ENGLISH LANGUAGE LEARNERS

Explain to students that they can understand the meaning of unfamiliar words by reading the words and sentences around them. Point out that in some cases, the illustrations can also help them understand a word's meaning.

STRUGGLING READERS

Help students keep track of story events by showing them how to take notes as they read. Tell them to record the most important events and ideas on each page of the story. As they read, they can refer back to their notes for support.

PREVIEW VOCABULARY Use the Preview and Review Vocabulary Routine in Part 3 to assess what students know about the following words: *rally, auditorium, government, headquarters, freedom, rights, suffrage, election,* and *campaigns.* Use each word in a sentence. Then assign students one word each, and have them write a sentence of their own using the word. Have students read their sentence aloud to the group.

COGNATES Use the list of Spanish cognates at the beginning of this module to guide your Spanish-speaking students as they read the selection.

ACTIVATE BACKGROUND KNOWLEDGE Ask students to share what they know about the right to vote. Use the Quick Write and Share Routine in Part 3 and ask: Did everyone always have the right to vote? Why do you think it is important to vote?

Before students begin writing, model by describing what you know about voting and why is it important to you. For example, say: Today, everyone over the age of eighteen can vote in the United States. It wasn't always that way. There was a time when my grandmother couldn't vote. Today, voting is the right of every citizen. It is also a responsibility. When we vote, we choose people we believe will represent us in the government.

Give students examples of people that citizens vote for today, such as presidents, senators, or governors. Explain that voting booths are sometimes set up in local libraries and schools. Ask whether students have noticed these booths, and discuss why they are used.

Interact with Text

As you read *Marching with Aunt Susan,* periodically assess students' level of understanding of discrimination.

If . . . students have difficulty identifying discrimination against women,

then . . . read examples of discrimination in the selection, and ask students why what was said or done is not right.

For example, call students' attention to the dialogue on p. 105. Ask students to think about what Bessie's father and brothers say about what girls can do. Point out the text evidence, beginning with the sentence, "Strenuous exercise is not for girls . . ." Explain that this way of thinking is not fair and is discriminatory, because it means Bessie cannot do something because she is a girl.

STRUCTURE

As you read, make sure students understand how to read the dialogue. They should be able to identify who says certain parts of the dialogue or text.

If . . . students have difficulty identifying the speaker of dialogue,

then . . . have students act out the dialogue.

For example, have students read aloud the scene between Bessie and her mother on p. 106. Have students work together in groups of three. Assign each student in the group a role: narrator, Bessie, and Mama. Alternatively, you might assign the scene on p. 113, again assigning each student in the group a role. Provide time for students to gain fluency by practicing their lines in groups before presenting to the class. Have students share how they decided who speaks when. You might ask: How did you know Bessie was supposed to say that line? How did you know what parts the narrator was supposed to say? Tell students to use the illustrations to help them understand the text.

If . . . students have difficulty making connections between the text and the illustrations,

then . . . have students reread the text. Give pairs of students the Two-Column Chart Graphic Organizer in Part 3 with the headings *Text* and *Illustration.* Under the *Text* heading, they should list details from the text. Under the *Illustration* heading, they should describe what is in the illustrations. Afterward, students should discuss what the illustrations and text have in common.

MORE SUPPORT

ENGLISH LANGUAGE LEARNERS

Students may incorrectly associate the term *suffrage* with *suffer*. Print pictures of a voting ballot and a bandage. Write the terms *suffrage* and *suffer* on cards. Explain that *suffer* means "to endure pain." Place the card next to the picture of the bandage. Then repeat the process for *suffrage.*

STRUGGLING READERS

When students are working in groups, make sure to provide sentence starters to help them organize their thoughts into a conversation. Provide sentence starters such as: I think that ___. I disagree because ____. I agree because ___.

LANGUAGE CONVENTIONALITY AND CLARITY

This story includes words that might be unfamiliar to students.

> If . . . students have difficulty with unfamiliar words,
> then . . . explain the meaning of the words, and have students use them in sentences.

For example, students may have difficulty with the word *crabby* in the following sentence: "She looks like a crabby old lady." Explain that *crabby* is used to describe someone who is bad-tempered. Then have students use the word in a sentence.

Students may have particular difficulty with understanding the lyrics on p. 120. Review each line of the lyrics with them. Help students rewrite the lyrics in words they understand. For example, "Our country now from thee, claim we our liberty, in freedom's name" may be rewritten as *Now we claim our liberty from you in freedom's name.* Afterward, discuss what the song means.

KNOWLEDGE DEMANDS

Marching with Aunt Susan explores the different expectations for men and women during the nineteenth century.

> If . . . students have difficulty understanding the different gender roles of the nineteenth century,
> then . . . assign students a two-page spread, and have them identify examples of things men and women were expected to do during that time in history.

For example, ask students to identify things boys and girls were expected to do (or not do). Use a T-chart with the headings *Boys* and *Girls* to record examples. Guide students to cite evidence from the text to support their responses.

MORE SUPPORT

Express and Extend

LEVELS OF MEANING

EXPRESS Use the Have a Discussion Routine in Part 3. Have small groups discuss *Marching with Aunt Susan*. Provide chart paper for each group. Then have them create a list of the three most important things they learned about the suffrage movement or Susan B. Anthony.

Model an example, such as: I read that Susan B. Anthony fought for women's rights for fifty years. On my list, I will write down *Susan B. Anthony fought for women's rights for fifty years.*

> **If . . .** students have difficulty determining the most important ideas from *Marching with Aunt Susan,*
>
> **then . . .** reread the text aloud. Pause after each page and model how to identify important ideas or information regarding the suffrage movement or Susan B. Anthony.

EXTEND Use the Venn Diagram Routine and Graphic Organizer in Part 3. Have partners compare girls' and women's lives today with their lives during the late nineteenth century. Ask students to point out specific examples from the text to support their comparisons.

STRUCTURE

EXPRESS Divide the text into three sections (beginning, middle, and end), and support small groups as they use the Story Map A Graphic Organizer to identify and summarize what happens during each section. Point out that the story is written in chronological order.

> **If . . .** students have difficulty completing the organizer,
>
> **then . . .** have students work in small groups to summarize one event from the story. Afterward, have students share their events and then work as a class to put the events in the correct order.

EXTEND Bessie's mother says, "Aunt Susan says that a bicycle gives a woman freedom." Given that at the end of the story women are still not allowed to vote, have students decide why the book ends with Bessie's mother riding a bicycle. Have students complete the following sentence frame: Voting gives women ___, and riding a bicycle gives women ___. Then have students explain their thinking.

MORE SUPPORT

ENGLISH LANGUAGE LEARNERS

Help students summarize the story by using the words *suffrage, campaign,* and *vote*. Review the meaning of each term.

STRUGGLING READERS

Ask questions about the themes of the text, such as: How was Bessie's home life different from Rita's? Why did Bessie give all her coins to Susan B. Anthony? Model locating the information in the text and responding to the questions.

LANGUAGE CONVENTIONALITY AND CLARITY

EXPRESS Talk about Sentences and Words

Display and read aloud the following passage from *Marching with Aunt Susan.*

**REMEMBER YOUR DAUGHTERS—
VOTE YES ON REFERENDUM #6**

I couldn't tell if I got more pats on the head or grumbles from the men walking by.

Ask: What was happening while Bessie was standing with the sign? (Some men were patting her on the head and some were grumbling.) Why did some of the men pat her on the head? (They thought she was sweet.) Why did some men grumble? (They didn't think women should have the right to vote.) Why are the words above in dark print? (They are in dark print because they are on the sign; no one is saying them.)

TEAM TALK Have partners focus on the words from the sign and discuss why the sign asks people to "remember your daughters." Ask: Would it make sense if the sign said, "Remember your sons"? Why or why not?

EXTEND Have student pairs look at other sections of the text, such as the song lyrics or conversations the girls overheard from the women, and discuss how and why the author set those sections of text apart from the rest.

KNOWLEDGE DEMANDS

EXPRESS Have students find and list examples from the text to support the following statements: I think Bessie's father will vote *yes.* I think Rita's father will vote *no.*

If . . . students have difficulty supporting the above statements,

then . . . model how to find examples from the text to support one of the statements, and then have students work in small groups to find examples to support the other statement.

EXTEND Given what they've read in the text, have students write a list giving three reasons someone might vote against women's suffrage. Have students discuss their ideas in small groups.

ACCELERATED LEARNERS

Have students research another prominent woman in the fight for suffrage, such as Elizabeth Cady Stanton, Lucretia Mott, or Sojourner Truth. Ask students to present their findings to the whole group.

MORE SUPPORT

Cognates

Cognates are words that have similar spellings and meanings in two or more languages. Many words in English and Spanish share Greek or Latin roots, and many words in English came from French, which is closely connected to Spanish (and to Portuguese, Italian, and Romanian). Because of this, many literary, content, and academic process words in English (e.g., *gracious/gracioso; volcano/volcán; compare/comparar*) have recognizable Spanish cognates.

Making the connection to cognates permits students who are native Spanish speakers to understand the strong foundation they have in academic and literary English. These links between English and Spanish are also useful for native speakers of English and other languages because they help uncover basic underlying features of our language.

ANCHOR TEXT **Change Makers**

ENGLISH	SPANISH	ENGLISH	SPANISH
action	acción	fruits	frutas
adults	adultos	future	futuro
animals	animales	generator	generador
art	arte	habitat	hábitat
battery	batería	hurricane	huracán
capital	capital	ingredient	ingrediente
cell phone	teléfono celular	invent	inventar
charge	cargar	inventor	inventor
climate	clima	machines	máquinas
community	comunidad	mural	mural
computers	computadoras	number	número
continues	continúa	ocean	océano
creative	creativo	orangutan	orangután
destroyed	destruido	palm	palmera
different	diferente	plans	planes
disaster	desastre	plants	plantas
electricity	electricidad	population	población
electronic	electrónico	problem	problema
energy	energía	product	producto
extinct	extinto	project	proyecto
family	familia	rescue	rescate
foundation	fundación	shampoo	champú

ANCHOR TEXT **Change Makers (continued)**

ENGLISH	SPANISH	ENGLISH	SPANISH
solar panels	paneles solares	vegetables	vegetales
solve	resolver	victims	víctimas
types	tipos		

SUPPORTING TEXT **City Green**

ENGLISH	SPANISH	ENGLISH	SPANISH
coffee	café	mama	mamá
color	color	notes	notas
copies	copias	papers	papeles
decide	decidir	park	parque
dollar	dólar	petition	petición
flower	flor	program	programa
garden	jardín	simple	simple
group	grupo	tomato	tomate
list	lista		

These lists contain many, but not all, Spanish cognates from these selections.

Unlock the Text

QUALITATIVE MEASURES

Levels of Meaning	accessible information about kids making the world a better place, including three specific examples of "change makers" and descriptions of community projects that involve young people
Structure	text includes Contents, introduction, three 6-page features about specific young people and their work, 6 pages about community actions, 4-steps to changing the world, and a glossary
Language Conventionality and Clarity	some higher-level words and statistical data may require direct instruction; geographical names may require specific support
Knowledge Demands	understanding of West African cultures, orangutans and rain forests, hurricanes, community gardens, and murals

Prepare to Read

LEVELS OF MEANING

Change Makers offers many examples of young people who work hard on various projects that help change the world for the better. These projects include recycling materials to generate electricity in Sierra Leone, protecting the habitats of endangered orangutans in Sumatra, collecting supplies for families hit by disasters, community gardens, and murals. The last pages suggest a four-step process for making the world a better place. The text includes a contents page and a glossary and index.

STRUCTURE

PREVIEW Read pages 4 and 5 aloud to students. Ask them to copy the equation on page 4: Ideas + Action = Change. Explain that they will read

MORE SUPPORT

ENGLISH LANGUAGE LEARNERS

Explain that the word *change* is a multiple-meaning word in English. As a verb, it means "to make or become different." As a noun, it names the act of making or becoming different. Ask: Which definition is used in the title of this text? (the act of making something different)

STRUGGLING READERS

Preview the parts of the text and make sure struggling readers understand that the parts all contribute to the whole text. The parts are: title page, contents page, introduction, the community projects, the Four Steps, and the glossary and index.

many examples that illustrate this equation. Ask: What is the difference between an idea and an action? (An idea is not real; it is in your mind. An action is something that a person does.) What do you think of when you hear the word *change*? Use the Web with Graphic Organizer Routine in Part 3 to record students' responses.

LANGUAGE CONVENTIONALITY AND CLARITY

PREVIEW VOCABULARY Use the Preview and Review Vocabulary Routine in Part 3 to assess what students know about the following words: *community, inventor, creative, products, donated, healthy, harvest, projects, champions,* and *solve*.

COGNATES Use the list of Spanish cognates at the beginning of this module to guide your Spanish-speaking students as they read the selection.

DOMAIN-SPECIFIC VOCABULARY Use the Vocabulary Activities in Part 3 and a world map to pre-teach the following nouns: *generator, windmill, solar power, rain forest, United Nations, environment,* and *mural*. Explain that two of these nouns name places (*rain forest, environment*) and the others name things. Tell students that the text will contain many proper nouns that name people and places.

KNOWLEDGE DEMANDS

ACTIVATE BACKGROUND KNOWLEDGE Focus students on the word *creative* as it is used in the question in the first paragraph: *Are you creative and smart?* Explain that the word *creative* comes from the word *create* which means "to make something new." Ask: What are some things that kids create? (a meal, a painting, a book, a mess, a song, a garden, a drawing, a story, a joke, a game) List responses so that everyone can see them. Then, suggest that they will read about many examples in this text of kids being *creative*.

STRUGGLING READERS

Help students understand that the writer of this text tries hard to make her readers feel like she is talking to them. Say and point: Look at the heading on the first page. The writer is addressing you directly with the word *you*. Even though she is writing about people all over the world, she is really writing to you. She does this when she writes, "What Can You Do?" on pages 11, 17, and 23. She also does it when she asks, "Did You Know?" on pages 15 and 21. Challenge students to scan the text for other examples of the writer addressing the reader directly by using *you* or *your*. (pages 28, 29, 30 and 31)

Interact with Text

LEVELS OF MEANING

As you read *Change Makers*, call students' attention to the "Fact File" features on pages 6, 7, 12, 13, 18, 19, 26, 27, and 29. Explain that these features contain specific facts about people, their ages, and locations. Some of them contain maps that show where people live. Others contain photographs and "Facts." Ask: What is a fact? (a piece of real information that is true for everyone) Is every sentence in this text a fact? If not, can you point to a sentence that is not a fact? (*Be creative like Kelvin!* on page 11; *Write a letter to that company.* on page 17)

> **If . . .** students have difficulty identifying facts,
>
> **then . . .** ask "Is this sentence or detail something that can be measured, located, or is true for everyone?

Explain that the "What Can You Do?" features on pages 11, 17, and 23 and the four steps on pages 30–31 contain sentences that are commands. Some commands are very short: *Work hard!* Others are longer: *Follow these four steps to make the world a better place*. Commands tell the reader what to do.

STRUCTURE

Focus a discussion on the three narratives embedded in the text (the one about Kelvin Doe on pages 6–10, the one about Madison Vorva and Rhiannon Tomtishen on pages 12–16, and the one about Zach Banner on pages 18–22). Each narrative has a beginning, middle, and end. For each of these narratives, students can use the Story Map A Graphic Organizer in Part 3 to keep track of each story's beginning, middle, and end.

You might also help students see the similarities and differences between two of the narratives by using the Story Comparison Routine and Graphic Organizer in Part 3. Help them understand that the stories and the people they are about are alike because of the ideas they illustrate but different in terms of their specific details.

ENGLISH LANGUAGE LEARNERS

Explain that the author of this text uses the word *kids* to mean "young people," even though the word literally means "young goats." The word is used in this text as slang, or in an informal way.

STRUGGLING READERS

This is a good opportunity to review using a Venn diagram. Choose two of the subjects (Kelvin, Madison and Rhiannon, and Zach) and use the names as labels for the two circles. Through discussion, help students fill in the three parts of the Venn diagram.

LANGUAGE CONVENTIONALITY AND CLARITY

While much of the language will be clear and accessible to students, they may need extra support to understand the statistical information in the "Did You Know?" and "Fact Files" features.

If . . . students have difficulty understanding mathematical concepts,

then . . . use graphic representations such as pie charts, pictographs, or comparisons to help them understand.

To help students understand certain unknown concrete words, such as *community, inventor, harvest, champion,* and *mural,* use the Three-Column Chart Graphic Organizer from Part 3. Help them label the three columns "Know," "Have Seen" or "Don't Know." Have students write each of the words in one of the three columns. In addition, remind students that they can find images on the Internet that illustrate these words. You can also have them draw their own pictures of these words.

KNOWLEDGE DEMANDS

Some students may not be familiar with the places mentioned in this passage. Use a world map to help students locate Sierra Leone, Sumatra, Borneo, and the United Kingdom. Use a map of the United States to help them locate Michigan, New York City (the location of the United Nations), Arkansas, Florida, Louisiana, Mississippi, and California. Ask: Which place is closest to us? Which place is farthest away?

ENGLISH LANGUAGE LEARNERS

Focus attention on the mural made by students in Miami, described on page 27. Have students use the Internet to find an example of a mural from their native country. Give them an opportunity to share and describe the murals to the rest of the class.

Express and Extend

EXPRESS Help students recognize that another way the writer engages readers is to ask questions. Say: From the very beginning, this writer asks a lot of questions. She begins with three important questions in the first paragraph. What are they? (Are you creative and smart? Do you work hard? Do you ever give up?) Then, help them recognize that the writer also expresses strong feelings with exclamations. Say: On page 5, the writer uses the first of several exclamations. She is expressing a strong feeling in this sentence. Sentences like this end in exclamation points. Ask: Can you find another exclamation in the text? (*Kelvin had an idea to help the lights stay on!* on page 7; *Zach got enough supplies to fill 27 trucks!* on page 18)

> **If . . .** students have difficulty recognizing the three type of sentences (statements, questions, and exclamations),
>
> **then . . .** have them use the Three-Column Chart and Graphic Organizer and Routine from Part 3 to list examples from the passage of each type.

EXTEND Have students choose one of the questions in the first paragraph of the text and write 3–5 sentences that answer it. Encourage them to include an example or story from their life as part of their answers. Have them use each of the three sentence types in their answers.

EXPRESS Lead a discussion about the adage, "A picture is worth a thousand words." First, write the adage on the board and ask: What does this sentence mean to you? (It means that a big idea that might take many words to express can sometimes be expressed with a single still image.) Choose one of the photographs from the text as an example. Encourage students to study the photograph closely and to list all of the many details that they see. For example, if you choose the photograph on page 4, guide students to observe the mountains in the background, the city building and streets, the yellow watering bucket, and other details. Then ask: What smells, sounds, textures, and tastes does this photograph make you imagine when you look at it? (smell of fresh air, crunch of rocky soil under shoes, scratchy twigs and smooth leaves, taste of cold water)

EXTEND Have students, or pairs of students, choose another photograph from the text and list as many details as they possibly can, using both observation and imagination.

ENGLISH LANGUAGE LEARNERS

Remind students of the five senses: sight, sound, smell, taste, and touch. Explain that good writers and good illustrators use all five senses to communicate to readers.

STRUGGLING READERS

Point out that the author provides pictures of each of the young people she refers to. Ask: Why do you think the author included these pictures? (The pictures help us remember that these really are young people that made such big changes.)

LANGUAGE CONVENTIONALITY AND CLARITY

EXPRESS Talk about Sentences and Words

Display and read aloud the following sentence from the first paragraph under the heading "Community Gardens."

Around the world, people are planting gardens and trees in their communities.

Point out that to write a strong paragraph, the writer repeats words to reinforce the main idea and to make connections among the details. Say: Notice how many times the writer uses the words *community* and *garden* in this part of the text. She also uses related words such as *food, seeds,* and *plant.* Point out that since the concept of community is so important throughout the text, the author uses the word *community* often. Help students recognize words related to *community* such as *neighborhoods, neighbors, families,* and *school.*

TEAM TALK Have partners work in pairs to choose another key word the author uses frequently, such as *idea, action, work, help,* or *change*. Then, ask them to go back and find related words.

EXTEND Ask students to write a description of a community project that has happened, or that could happen, in your school. Ask: What idea started the project? What kind of hard work will it require? What problem will it solve? As they write their descriptions, remind them to repeat the most important words.

KNOWLEDGE DEMANDS

EXPRESS Using the Internet, help students locate the community garden nearest you. Share photographs. Gather information about the garden. Find photographs. Try to find out something about its history. Perhaps there was a young person who helped start the garden or one who works there now. If so, discuss that person's role. Help the class write a collective letter to the garden asking for printed materials and more information.

If . . . students need help organizing what they discover about the garden,

then . . . have them use the Web Graphic Organizer in Part 3 with the name of the garden in the center.

EXTEND Have students write a letter to one of the young people in the text. Ask them to include their ideas about the person and questions they'd like that person to answer. Have them include in their letters something about themselves that they have in common with the person they've chosen.

ACCELERATED LEARNERS

Challenge students to learn more about the two kinds of orangutans, building on the information offered on p. 13. Prompt them with questions such as: How big are orangutans? Where do orangutans live? What do they eat? How long do they live? How do they spend their days? How intelligent are they? Students will be interested to know that orangutans are among the smartest and creative of all primates, just like the young people described in this text!

Unlock the Text

City Green, pp. 136–165

QUALITATIVE MEASURES

Levels of Meaning	realistic fiction about transformation and community; character development
Structure	chronological structure; illustrations help tell the story
Language Conventionality and Clarity	informal language; contractions; dialogue; figurative language
Knowledge Demands	city neighborhoods; community gardens; renting property

Prepare to Read

LEVELS OF MEANING

City Green is about a community that turns an ugly, abandoned lot into a beautiful garden. On another level, the story shows how cooperating on a project takes hard work and brings even the most reluctant community members together.

STRUCTURE

PREVIEW Read aloud the title of the story, and have students flip through the pages. Tell students to look carefully at the pictures, because the pictures play an important role in this story. They provide readers with important information about the story that the words do not. Together with students, examine the pictures in the book. Ask: Who do you think will be the main character? (the girl) Who will be another important character? (the lonely old man on the stoop) Where does the story take place? (in a city neighborhood) What do you predict the story will be about? (It will be about a group of neighbors who get together to make a garden. The old man and the girl become friends.)

ENGLISH LANGUAGE LEARNERS

Tell students that the word *stoop* has more than one meaning in English. Act out the meaning of a person stooping over. Then point out the picture of the old man on the stoop in the story. Model sentences for each meaning of the word. Have partners use the word in their own sentences.

STRUGGLING READERS

For students who do not have any knowledge of gardening or gardens in general, provide photos of different types of gardens. Ask students to describe what they see.

PREVIEW VOCABULARY Use the Preview and Review Vocabulary Routine in Part 3 to assess what students know about the following words: *lot, wrecking ball, stoop, rubble, rent, neighbors, petition, marigold, junk, raised bed, sour.* Discuss with students the meanings of these words as you relate them to a community garden.

INFORMAL LANGUAGE The author uses informal dialogue throughout the story. The speakers often use incomplete sentences, contractions, and double negatives, such as: "I'm not helpin' nobody." Explain that the reason the author uses this informal language is to show how the people in the neighborhood talk to each other. Help students identify examples of these sentences as you read.

COGNATES Use the list of Spanish cognates at the beginning of this module to guide your Spanish-speaking students as they read.

KNOWLEDGE DEMANDS

ACTIVATE BACKGROUND KNOWLEDGE Ask students to share what they know about gardening or gardens in general. Then ask them to describe any known community gardens in their own town or city.

Before students get started, model an example of planting a garden. For example, say: In the spring, when all danger of frost is over, I like to plant a garden in my yard. I usually plant the garden with my neighbor. We plant flowers and vegetables. My favorite flowers are petunias. My neighbor's favorite flowers are daisies. I love it when the flowers bloom later in the summer and when I can pick the vegetables to eat.

Interact with Text

LEVELS OF MEANING

As you read *City Green,* periodically stop to assess students' level of understanding of how members of the community come together to build the garden.

If . . . students have difficulty identifying the community members who help build the garden,

then . . . have students look for specific details in the text.

Use the Web Routine and Graphic Organizer in Part 3. Have students write the word *Garden* in the center oval. Stop after each two-page spread and have students write in each outer oval something that was contributed to the garden and the name of the community member who contributed it. Remind students that not all contributions are actual items. Some people contribute their time and labor.

STRUCTURE

The events in this story occur in chronological order. Point out to students that the author uses time-order words to help readers follow the events. For example, the words *then, the next week, Saturday morning, today,* and *after* help readers know when things happen. Have students make a list of other time-order words and phrases in the story as they read.

If . . . students are confused by the flashback on p. 138,

then . . . explain that at this point in the story, Marcy is sharing a memory so that readers know the history of the empty lot. Then point out the word *now* on p. 140, and explain that this indicates to readers that Marcy is talking about the present, not the past.

ENGLISH LANGUAGE LEARNERS

As new characters are introduced in the story, have students take time to write down their names, a fact or description about them, and how they relate to the main characters in the story.

STRUGGLING READERS

Retelling is a useful technique for monitoring students' reading comprehension. For example, ask students to retell or reconstruct what they read on p. 141. Ask them to read the page silently, orally, or both. After students have finished reading, ask them to retell the page.

LANGUAGE CONVENTIONALITY AND CLARITY

The narrator of the story is a little girl, Marcy, who lives in an inner city neighborhood. The author writes in the way the girl would speak. As a result, the language is informal. For example, the sentence "Every single day" has no verb.

If . . . students have difficulty understanding some of the informal language,

then . . . use the Word Order and Complete Sentences Activities in Part 3. Together, identify informal language in the text. Discuss why each example does not meet the criteria for formal English. Model revising the sentences into formal English.

In addition to informal language, students may have difficulty interpreting some of the figurative language in the text. For example, *hard as nails* means "tough." Other examples are *quick as a wink* and *sour grapes.* Define the terms as they appear in the text, and then have students draw a picture to help remember the meaning of the term or phrase. Allow students to share and compare their pictures.

KNOWLEDGE DEMANDS

Students might have difficulty understanding why the community members have to rent the lot from the city or what it means to rent something. Read aloud the following sentence on p. 142: "You can't dig more dirt than that. This lot is city property." Explain to students that when a lot is city property, it means that the city owns it. In order for someone to build something on a lot owned by the city, that person must buy or rent the lot from the city. Ask: Do you know what it means to rent something? Explain that when you rent something, you pay money to use it. Guide students in understanding that the community members pay the city in return for use of the lot.

Express and Extend

LEVELS OF MEANING

EXPRESS Discuss with students how Old Man Hammer changes throughout the story. Ask: Do you think Marcy and the garden helped Old Man Hammer change? Why or why not?

> If . . . students have trouble identifying how and why Old Man Hammer changes from the beginning of the story to the end,
>
> then . . . have them look for details in the pictures of Old Man Hammer and in the text that show how he changed.

For example, point out the pictures on pp. 142, 147, 159, 163, and 165. Ask: Based on what you see in the pictures, can you tell if Old Man Hammer changed from the beginning to the end of the story? Then work with students to identify text evidence. For example, on p. 142 Old Man Hammer refers to the lot as "good for nothin'." On p. 162, he refers to the lot as "nothin' but good." Discuss with students how these details show a change in the character.

EXTEND Point out to students that Old Man Hammer isn't the only thing that changes in the story: the lot changes too. Have students write a description of the lot before and after the garden. Have partners exchange and compare their descriptions.

STRUCTURE

EXPRESS Assign pairs of students a picture of the lot from different points in the story. Have them work together to write a two- to three-sentence caption for the picture.

> If . . . students have difficulty writing their captions,
>
> then . . . give pairs the Three-Column Chart Graphic Organizer in Part 3 with the headings *Colors, People/Animals,* and *Things.* Have students write what they see in the appropriate column. Students can use their completed charts to help them write a caption.

EXTEND Assign each student a character from the story, and have students write a two- to three-sentence description of the character based on the illustrations in the selection. Have students read their description to a partner without naming the character. Have the partner identify the character being described.

MORE SUPPORT

ENGLISH LANGUAGE LEARNERS

Write the words *sad, happy, mad, surprised, tired,* and *hopeful.* Ask students to demonstrate a facial expression for each term. Ask: What is Old Man Hammer feeling? What clues in the illustrations tell you?

STRUGGLING READERS

Provide students with a list of descriptive words to use as they write about the lot. For example, you might provide them with the words *ugly, empty, bare, lush, beautiful, welcoming,* and *colorful.*

LANGUAGE CONVENTIONALITY AND CLARITY

EXPRESS Talk about Sentences and Words

Display and read aloud the following sentences from the story that contain contractions, underlining the contractions for students.

"I'm not signin' nothin'," he says. "And nothin' is what's gonna happen."

Ask: Why are there quotations around certain words? (They show that someone is talking.) What does *nothin' is what's gonna happen* mean? (It means that nothing is going to happen.)

TEAM TALK Have partners identify the words in the above sentences that are contractions versus the other words with apostrophes. Have them write out the contractions they see. For example, *I'm* would be written as *I am*.

> **If . . .** students are having trouble identifying which words are contractions,
>
> **then . . .** use the Contractions Activity in Part 3 to help students understand the contractions.

EXTEND Have students use a T-chart labeled *Contractions* and *Not Contractions* to categorize examples of words that use apostrophes in the text. Have partners compare their charts and identify the letter that is missing in each contraction.

KNOWLEDGE DEMANDS

EXPRESS Explain that authors will often vary the way their characters speak to show something about their characters' personalities. Choose a character in the story who speaks at various times. Ask students what the character's way of speaking shows about him or her. Does the language make the story more interesting to read? Why or why not?

EXTEND Rewrite some of the dialogue in the story in formal English and display it in the classroom. Ask students to read the revision and to decide which version of the story they like better. Have them write two to three sentences supporting their opinion.

ACCELERATED LEARNERS

Have students write on a sentence strip one sentence from *City Green* that uses a contraction, leaving a blank space where the contraction belongs. Have students exchange strips and say the sentence aloud. Explore additional contractions that make sense in the sentence.

Facing Challenges and Change

TEXT SET

ANCHOR TEXT
The Earth Dragon Awakes

SUPPORTING TEXT
Seek the Sun

TEXT SET

ANCHOR TEXT
Disaster Alert!

SUPPORTING TEXT
Danger! Earthquakes

Cognates

Cognates are words that have similar spellings and meanings in two or more languages. Many words in English and Spanish share Greek or Latin roots, and many words in English came from French, which is closely connected to Spanish (and to Portuguese, Italian, and Romanian). Because of this, many literary, content, and academic process words in English (e.g., *gracious/gracioso; volcano/volcán; compare/comparar*) have recognizable Spanish cognates.

Making the connection to cognates permits students who are native Spanish speakers to understand the strong foundation they have in academic and literary English. These links between English and Spanish are also useful for native speakers of English and other languages because they help uncover basic underlying features of our language.

ANCHOR TEXT **The Earth Dragon Awakes**

ENGLISH	SPANISH	ENGLISH	SPANISH
abandon	abandonar	fraud	fraude
air	aire	hero	héroe
animals	animales	honor	honrar
antique	antigüedad	hospital	hospital
avenue	avenida	hotels	hoteles
bank	banco	instruments	instrumentos
brigade	brigada	invisible	invisibles
calms	calmar	list	lista
camp	acampar	manuscripts	manuscritos
carnival	carnaval	megaphone	megáfono
chimney	chimenea	memorize	memorizar
cistern	cisterna	moment	momento
collapse	colapsar	monster	monstruo
collection	colección	muscle	músculo
column	columna	obediently	obedientemente
destruction	destrucción	oceans	océanos
dialect	dialecto	operator	operador
dollars	dólares	pirates	piratas
dozen	docena	pistol	pistola
dynamite	dinamita	police	policía
escape	escapar	possessions	posesiones
estimates	estimar	protest	protestar
explosion	explosión	rats	ratas
family	familia	ruins	ruinas

ANCHOR TEXT **The Earth Dragon Awakes (continued)**

ENGLISH	SPANISH	ENGLISH	SPANISH
secret	secreto	triumph	triunfo
structures	estructuras	tunnel	túnel
temperature	temperatura	violently	violentamente
transform	transformar		

SUPPORTING TEXT **Seek the Sun**

ENGLISH	SPANISH	ENGLISH	SPANISH
dragon	dragón	plants	plantas
fortune	fortuna	sandal	sandalia
fruit	fruta	temple	templo
machines	máquinas	tourists	turistas
park	parque	visit	visitar

These lists contain many, but not all, Spanish cognates from these selections.

Unlock the Text

QUALITATIVE MEASURES

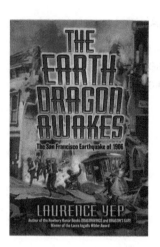

Levels of Meaning	event-driven plot with deepening character development; themes of heroism; factual earthquake information
Structure	chapters; chronological order with cause-and-effect elements; shifts between narrative and informational content
Language Conventionality and Clarity	figurative language; content-specific vocabulary
Knowledge Demands	earthquakes; the effects of natural disasters; immigrant life

Prepare to Read

LEVELS OF MEANING

The Earth Dragon Awakes is a story about how two families are affected by the Great Earthquake of 1906. Although it is a fictional narrative, it is based on a real natural disaster, and it includes factual information about the science of earthquakes.

STRUCTURE

PREVIEW Prior to reading, have students flip through the pages of the book and discuss what they notice about the organization of information in the story. Ask: How are the chapters of the story divided? (like a journal with times of day, dates, and locations) What does this tell you about the structure of the story? (The events of the story are told in time order.) Why are the locations included in these chapter titles? (The location descriptions help the reader to keep track of which family he or she is reading about and where the family has traveled.)

ENGLISH LANGUAGE LEARNERS

Students may need extra support to understand scientific terms in this text. Support understanding by creating a word wall with words related to plate tectonics and earthquakes. Use video clips or pictures as additional support when introducing the words.

STRUGGLING READERS

Have students work in groups to create a vocabulary list that categorizes the words. Ask students to think about the criteria they would use to group unfamiliar words. For example, they may choose to group words about earthquakes, firefighting, or San Francisco.

LANGUAGE CONVENTIONALITY AND CLARITY

PREVIEW VOCABULARY Use the Preview and Review Vocabulary Routine in Part 3 to assess what students know about words such as the following: *tenement*, *earthquake*, *plates*, *tremor*, *fault*, *core*, *aftershock*, *mains*, *cisterns*. Use the words in sentences that relate to the context of the reading. Reinforce comprehension by relating the words to students' experiences. You can also use the Vocabulary Activities and Games in Part 3 to preteach critical vocabulary words.

COGNATES Use the list of Spanish cognates at the beginning of this module to guide your Spanish-speaking students as they read the text.

KNOWLEDGE DEMANDS

ACTIVATE BACKGROUND KNOWLEDGE Ask students to share what they know about earthquakes. Use the Quick Write and Share Routine in Part 3 and ask: What are earthquakes? What happens during an earthquake?

Before students get started, model describing what you know about earthquakes using an example, such as: When I was young, I visited Catalina Island in California for vacation. The whole island smelled like seaweed. It was very unpleasant. A friendly store clerk told me there had been an earthquake just a few days before I had arrived there. It shook beneath the water and stirred up all the seaweed from the bottom of the bay. It was a small earthquake, so there was no damage to the island. It could have been much worse.

MORE SUPPORT

Interact with Text

LEVELS OF MEANING

Toward the beginning of *The Earth Dragon Awakes,* the reader learns about Henry's family and Chin's family. Distribute the Venn Diagram Graphic Organizer in Part 3. Have students discuss the similarities and differences between the two families and record their responses in the graphic organizer. Afterward, ask: What do these details tell us about the lifestyles of the two families? Make sure students support their responses with evidence from the text. For example, students might respond by saying they know Henry's family is wealthy because the parents have hired staff to help in their home.

If . . . students have trouble understanding how the text demonstrates the main characters' lifestyles,

then . . . have them use the Web Graphic Organizer in Part 3 to record details about one of the families. After recording the details in the ovals, students should work in pairs to decide what those details show about the lifestyle of Henry's or Chin's family. Have students repeat this activity with the other family.

STRUCTURE

Students may have difficulty following the text, since the narrative content alternates with the informational content. Have students complete the following activity to analyze the purpose of the text's structure.

Have students use a T-chart and label one column *Narrative* and the other *Informational.* Have small groups revisit a section of the narrative text and take notes in the chart and then do the same with a section of the informational text. Afterward, have students decide whether the informational text helps them better understand the narrative text. Ask: Does the informational text help you understand what's going on in the narrative? Why do you think the author included the informational text?

ENGLISH LANGUAGE LEARNERS

To help students identify and distinguish between causes and effects, remind them that some causes have multiple effects, and some effects have multiple causes.

STRUGGLING READERS

To help students keep track of format shifts, have them create a time line. On the time line, include the date and time of the section and the main event that occurs.

MORE SUPPORT

LANGUAGE CONVENTIONALITY AND CLARITY

The following activity will help students analyze the figurative language used in *The Earth Dragon Awakes* with the Analyze Idioms and Expressions Routine in Part 3.

Read and display an example of figurative language from the text such as, "It [the fire] is chewing on houses and skyscrapers. The other [fire] feasts on warehouses in the east." Ask students: How can a fire "chew" and "feast" if it doesn't have teeth? (The fire is burning more and more buildings, so it is consuming them similar to the way a person eats food.) If needed, explain by saying: The fire is being compared to a monster because it is big and scary. The buildings are being compared to food because when the fire moves over them, it looks like the fire is eating them. Afterward, assign pairs other examples of figurative language and have them decide what is being compared.

KNOWLEDGE DEMANDS

To help students understand the effects of a natural disaster on the characters, have them reread portions of the text that show how the earthquake affected either Chin's or Henry's family. Ask them to record their findings in the Cause and Effect Graphic Organizer in Part 3 and share them with the class. Make sure the causes students record are specific. For example, instead of writing *earthquake* in all of the boxes, they should write *the fire* or *the gas leak.*

If . . . students have difficulty deciding what to put in the Cause boxes,

then . . . give them a list of possible causes to choose from. Make sure the list you provide includes more than three causes so that students can make their own decisions.

MORE SUPPORT

Express and Extend

EXPRESS At the beginning of the selection, Henry and Chin think their fathers are boring, and the boys instead favor "real heroes" like the cowboy in the penny novels. Have students fill out the Three-Column Chart Graphic Organizer in Part 3 to show the differences among Chin's and Henry's fathers and the hero in the penny novels, using evidence from the text for support. Afterward, ask: Do Chin and Henry's opinions of their fathers change at the end of the story, or do they stay the same? Why do you think so?

EXTEND Have students write a paragraph telling whether they think Henry's father and Chin's father are brave. Have them support their opinions with evidence from the text. Encourage students to use vocabulary from the selection in their paragraphs. Have partners share their ideas.

EXPRESS Have students reread two sections of either Henry's story or Chin's story. Ask: Can either Henry's or Chin's story stand alone, or do they need to be together to make sense? Students should support their answers with evidence from the text. If students say the stories need to be together simply because Chin references Henry and Henry references Chin, follow up by asking: If those references were taken out, could either character's story stand alone?

EXTEND Ask students: Why do you think the author included both Henry's and Chin's stories? Have them write their responses and share them with the class.

ENGLISH LANGUAGE LEARNERS

The large amount of figurative language in the text can be overwhelming for students who are unfamiliar with the English language. After reading passages heavy in figurative language, stop and review each example with students to make sure they understand what is being described.

STRUGGLING READERS

To analyze characters on a deeper level, as a class create a web graphic organizer for each character. Tell students to add details as they learn more about a character.

MORE SUPPORT

LANGUAGE CONVENTIONALITY AND CLARITY

EXPRESS Talk about Sentences and Words

Display the following excerpt from *The Earth Dragon Awakes.* Read it aloud with students.

> Higher and higher the Ham and Egg fire grows. It rears up like a giant monster. A tongue of flame licks its fiery mouth.

Ask: How is the fire like a monster? (It is scary.) What does it mean to "rear up?" (to throw one's head backward) We know that a fire cannot really be a monster rearing its head, so what is the fire actually doing? (It is getting taller and spreading.) What does the phrase *a tongue of flame* refer to? (part of the flames that moves like a tongue licking at the air) Does the fire actually lick its mouth? (No, the fire is being compared to a monster licking its mouth because it is hungry.)

TEAM TALK Practice using figurative language by having students choose something else to compare to the fire and share it with a partner. Remind them to give reasons they chose to compare the fire with their new object. A response could be: I compared the fire with an angry horse, because when horses are angry they run around just like the fire is "running" over California.

> If . . . students have trouble making a new comparison,
>
> then . . . give them a list of options to choose from, such as puppy, warrior, and spider. Then, have students tell which comparison they think would work best and why.

EXTEND Have students write a paragraph explaining the effect of figurative language on the story. Ask: Which expression with figurative language made the most sense to you and why? Would the story be as interesting or as informative if it did not have figurative language? Why or why not?

KNOWLEDGE DEMANDS

EXPRESS Have students work in small groups to locate details in the text about Chinese immigrants. After those details have been recorded, have students review details about Henry's life. Then, have students discuss why Chin and Henry live so differently.

> If . . . students have difficulty finding details about Chinese immigrants or Henry's family,
>
> then . . . have them refer to the Venn diagram they created earlier in the lesson for clues.

EXTEND Have students write a letter from Chin to his mother in China with details about life in Chinatown before the Great Earthquake and Fire.

ACCELERATED LEARNERS

Have partners take on the role of Chin or Henry and interview each other about their experiences, using evidence from the text. The interviewer should ask questions regarding the character's most frightening experience, how he felt during and after the earthquake, and how he felt when he left his home.

MORE SUPPORT

Unlock the Text

QUALITATIVE MEASURES

Levels of Meaning	event-driven plot; theme of community members working together; inspired by real-life events
Structure	events told in chronological order; cause-and-effect and problem-and-solution structures; illustrations
Language Conventionality and Clarity	culture-specific vocabulary; comparisons
Knowledge Demands	life in Japan; how laws are changed

Seek the Sun, pp. 5–11

Prepare to Read

LEVELS OF MEANING

Seek the Sun is a story about a shoemaker and his wife who, along with their neighbors, are affected by the construction of a tall office building in their city. A deeper level of meaning suggests that the people who live in a community need to work together to change laws and protect their rights.

STRUCTURE

PREVIEW Have students look at the title of the text and the pictures. Ask: Based only on the illustrations, what do you think happens in this story? (A tall building casts a shadow on a neighborhood; people talk to a judge; and people sit outside.) What might be the main problem in this story? (the tall building) How do you think the problem will be solved? (The people go to a judge.)

ENGLISH LANGUAGE LEARNERS

Help students clarify word meanings by drawing a picture that represents each word. Then have them draw a non-example picture. Provide sentence frames for students to discuss their drawings: This is a ___. This is not a ___ because ___.

STRUGGLING READERS

Students need a variety of strategies and multiple exposures to deepen their knowledge of vocabulary, so plan to quickly review words each day in a different and meaningful way.

LANGUAGE CONVENTIONALITY AND CLARITY

PREVIEW VOCABULARY Use the Preview and Review Vocabulary Routine in Part 3 to assess what students know about words such as the following: *seek*, *shade*, *tend*, *precious*, *fierce*, *gust*, *prosper*, *fortune*, *rights*.

DOMAIN-SPECIFIC VOCABULARY Help students understand the following domain-specific words by providing examples and non-examples of each word: *tatami*, *bonsai*, *judge*, *citizen*, *temple*, *ordered*, *ruled*, *law*, *courthouse*. For example, say: A courthouse is a place where people go to enforce the law. A courthouse is not a store or an office. Have students explain why a courthouse is different from each non-example. You can also use the Vocabulary Activities and Games in Part 3 to preteach the domain-specific vocabulary.

COGNATES Use the list of Spanish cognates at the beginning of this module to guide your Spanish-speaking students as they read the text.

KNOWLEDGE DEMANDS

ACTIVATE BACKGROUND KNOWLEDGE Explain that a fortune is a prediction about what will happen in the future. Display and read aloud two fortunes that are central to the story: "Seek the sun each day," and "Light will fill an empty space." Tell students that the fortunes in the story are read by the sandalmaker and his wife and are connected to the problems the characters face. Use the Quick Write and Share Routine in Part 3 and ask: What do the two fortunes have in common? What clues do you think they give about what will happen in the story?

Interact with Text

LEVELS OF MEANING

Help students understand the importance of community members working together by rereading the people's complaints on pp. 7–8. Remind students to use the text for support. Ask: How was each community member affected by the tall building? (sandalmaker's wife: her house is cold, her clothes don't dry, the bed quilts are smelly, the mats are moldy; sandalmaker: his shop is dark; tatami maker: his straw cannot dry; tofu maker: her cart blows away) Why is it important that all of the community members share their complaints? (It makes their case stronger for the judge.)

If . . . students have trouble identifying each of the complaints,

then . . . provide them with the Web Graphic Organizer in Part 3 with the center oval labeled *Community Complaints.* Make sure there are enough ovals for students to record the name and complaint(s) of each person in a separate oval. Tell students that each oval must be filled with the name of the community member and at least one complaint from that person about the tall building.

STRUCTURE

Have students use the Cause and Effect Graphic Organizer in Part 3 to record causes and effects from the story as they read. For example, the sandalmaker and his wife say the building casts a shadow on their home, which makes their house dark and cold. For this example, students should write *the building* in the Cause box and *the sandalmaker's house was dark and cold* in the Effect box.

If . . . students have trouble understanding what the effects are,

then . . . explain that one cause can have more than one effect. Refer students back to their Web graphic organizers and help them understand that each oval represents one effect caused by the tall building. Have students use their web graphic organizers to help them complete their cause and effect graphic organizer.

MORE SUPPORT

ENGLISH LANGUAGE LEARNERS

Point out to students that, in the context of this story, the word *maker* means "a person who is responsible for creating a particular object to sell for money." Therefore, a tofu maker is someone who makes tofu and then sells it to earn money.

STRUGGLING READERS

Remind students to refer to the illustrations in the text to help them understand what is happening or what is being described. Have students describe one illustration to a partner, and then have partners decide what part of the text the illustration is describing.

LANGUAGE CONVENTIONALITY AND CLARITY

Read aloud the paragraph near the bottom of p. 10 that begins with "The next day...," as well as the following paragraph that continues on p. 11 and ends with "...has come true!" Then say: The sandalmaker tells his wife that the fortune has come true after he sees the park. How is the park like a light that fills an empty space? Have students work in pairs to brainstorm and record their responses before sharing them with the class. Their responses should be at least two sentences long.

If . . . students have difficulty understanding how the park is like a light that fills an empty space,

then . . . display and provide students with the Web Graphic Organizer from Part 3 with the word *light* in the center, and help students fill it out.

Ask: What words do you associate with the word *light*? Model an example by putting the word *happy* in a surrounding oval. Say: When it's light outside, I am happy because like sunny days. Have students work with a partner to fill in the remaining ovals. Then, have students share their responses and record them on the web graphic organizer displayed for the class. Ask: What do you know about parks? What do parks have in common with the words and feelings we associate with the word *light*? An example response might be: A park is a place that makes people happy, just like light makes people happy.

KNOWLEDGE DEMANDS

Help students understand the role of the judge in the story by using the Problem and Solution Graphic Organizer in Part 3. Ask students to locate the section of the story relating to the judge to help them fill out the organizer.

If . . . students have difficulty identifying the problem or the solution,

then . . . have them refer back to their web graphic organizers, on which they recorded community complaints, and their cause and effect graphic rganizers. Have students use the information on these two graphic organizers to help them determine the problem. Then ask: Is the judge part of the problem or the solution? What does he do to help the members of the community?

Express and Extend

LEVELS OF MEANING

EXPRESS To help students understand the connections between the story and the real-life event that inspired it, have partners reread the text box at the end of the story. Ask them to write and share a few sentences explaining the similarities between the story and the real-life event.

EXTEND Have students share why they think the author chose to include this information at the end of the story. Ask: Why is it important to know that this story was inspired by something that actually happened? Would the story be better or worse without this information? Explain your response.

STRUCTURE

EXPRESS Remind students that the order in which events happen is critical to understanding how a problem is solved. Have students explain how the order of events in this story leads to the solution of the characters' problem.

If . . . students have difficulty explaining the order of events that led to the problem being solved,

then . . . have them use the Story Map B Graphic Organizer in Part 3 to list the events in the story that led to the law requiring that "sunlight shine in a family's living room for a certain number of hours each day."

EXTEND Have students reread the conclusion of the story. Have partners discuss the following questions: Do you think the judge's ruling was fair? Why or why not? Should he have been more or less strict? Students should support their opinion with evidence from the text in at least three sentences.

ENGLISH LANGUAGE LEARNERS

Remind students that some words in the text are specific to Japanese culture. Because of this, some of these words do not have English translations. Encourage any students who speak Japanese to share their knowledge of the language with the class.

STRUGGLING READERS

Students may struggle to understand why there are not restrictions everywhere on how tall buildings may be. Discuss with students that every city and town has different rules and laws.

LANGUAGE CONVENTIONALITY AND CLARITY

EXPRESS Talk about Sentences and Words

Display the following excerpt from *Seek the Sun.* Read it aloud with students to decode the meaning. Have students use the text as support for their answers.

"You would think a dragon had moved into the neighborhood!" he cried.

Ask: Why does the author use quotation marks? (to show that the words in quotation marks are being spoken aloud by a character) Why is there an exclamation mark at the end of the quotation? (The speaker is saying something in a loud voice. He is exclaiming.) What is a dragon being compared to? (the tall building)

TEAM TALK Have students turn to a partner and decide why the tall building might be compared to a dragon.

If . . . students are unsure why the author made this comparison,

then . . . have them use the Venn Diagram Graphic Organizer in Part 3 with the labels *Dragon* and *Tall Building.* Have them list characteristics of each in the respective circles and then list the ways they are similar in the center of the diagram.

EXTEND Have pairs of students think of a different object that could be compared to the tall building in the story. Have them write a sentence or two that compares the tall building to the object. Have partners share their ideas with the class.

KNOWLEDGE DEMANDS

EXPRESS Have students work together and decide which community members might be involved in the story if it took place in the United States. Ask: If the story were set in the United States, do you think there would be a tofu maker or tatami maker? Why or why not? What type of community members might be included in the story?

EXTEND Have students discuss a problem that has happened, or might happen, in their neighborhood and how people worked, or might work, together to solve it. Then have students write a summary of the discussion.

ACCELERATED LEARNERS

Have groups of students rewrite and then act out the scene in the courthouse. Students should act as the community members who have complaints and as the builders of the tall building, and one should act as the judge. Have both sides present their view of the situation. Then have the judge give his or her ruling.

Cognates

Cognates are words that have similar spellings and meanings in two or more languages. Many words in English and Spanish share Greek or Latin roots, and many words in English came from French, which is closely connected to Spanish (and to Portuguese, Italian, and Romanian). Because of this, many literary, content, and academic process words in English (e.g., *gracious/gracioso; volcano/volcán; compare/comparar*) have recognizable Spanish cognates.

Making the connection to cognates permits students who are native Spanish speakers to understand the strong foundation they have in academic and literary English. These links between English and Spanish are also useful for native speakers of English and other languages because they help uncover basic underlying features of our language.

ANCHOR TEXT Disaster Alert!

ENGLISH	SPANISH	ENGLISH	SPANISH
active	activo	meteorologists	meteorólogos
air	aire	military pilots	pilotos militares
coast	costa	million	millón
current	corriente	porous	poroso
disaster	desastre	pressure	presión
dissolves	disuelve	protective	protector
electricians	electricistas	rescue	rescatar
emergency	emergencia	rock	roca
eruptions	erupciones	solar system	sistema solar
extinct	extinto	temperature	temperatura
habitat	hábitat	tornado	tornado
humidity	humedad	violent	violento
lava	lava	volcano	volcán
magma	magma	volcanologists	vulcanólogos

SUPPORTING TEXT Danger! Earthquakes

ENGLISH	SPANISH
central	central
collapse	colapsar
destroy	destruir
different	diferente
exactly	exactamente
future	futuro
Italy	Italia
lines	líneas
magnitude	magnitud
million	millón
minute	minuto

ENGLISH	SPANISH
move	moverse
natural disaster	desastre natural
Pacific	Pacífico
parts	partes
reduce	reducir
Richter scale	escala de Richter
rocks	rocas
scientists	científicos
valley	valle
violent	violento
zones	zonas

These lists contain many, but not all, Spanish cognates from these selections.

Unlock the Text

QUALITATIVE MEASURES

Levels of Meaning	accessible, visually supported information about five types of natural disasters: tornadoes, floods, sinkholes, volcanoes, and bushfires
Structure	text includes contents, either 4 or 6 pages about each type of disaster; each part includes descriptions and definitions, facts about specific events, job profiles, fact features, and tips about how to survive
Language Conventionality and Clarity	some higher-level weather- and geography-related terms may require direct instruction; geographical names may require specific support
Knowledge Demands	understanding of emergency situations and workers, weather, and world geography

Prepare to Read

LEVELS OF MEANING

Disaster Alert! describes five kinds of natural disasters. For each kind, the text offers definitions and descriptions, real life examples, facts, job profiles, and survival tips. The text combines lively headings, prose paragraphs, and bulleted lists. Visuals include photographs, maps, and illustrations. A glossary defines ten unfamiliar words.

STRUCTURE

PREVIEW Focus students' attention on the Contents on page 3. Read each word, emphasizing each syllable, and have students repeat each one. For each word, ask: Who knows what this word names? Then ask:

MORE SUPPORT

ENGLISH LANGUAGE LEARNERS

Make sure students understand the words *warn* and *danger*. Explain that people give other people warnings when there is *danger* at hand. Point out that the warnings in this passage are about dangerous weather.

STRUGGLING READERS

Explain that the writer uses many different ways to communicate information about each of the five disasters. For example, each part begins with an introductory question, such as "What is a Tornado?" on p. 4. Help find other features in the text that contain useful tips or advice.

How are these things alike? (They are all bad events. They are all disasters. They all happen in nature. They are dangerous. They can hurt or kill people.) Have students write the word *disaster* and say it aloud. Say: A disaster is a sudden natural event that causes great damage and destruction and can cause the loss of lives. These are five different kinds of disasters. Use the Web Graphic Organizer in Part 3 to show that these are five examples of disasters.

LANGUAGE CONVENTIONALITY AND CLARITY

PREVIEW VOCABULARY Use the Preview and Review Vocabulary Routine in Part 3 to assess what students know about the following words: *rotating, violent, alerts, electrical, collapse, explore, pressure, extreme* and *shelters.*

COGNATES Use the list of Spanish cognates at the beginning of this module to guide your Spanish-speaking students as they read the selection.

DOMAIN-SPECIFIC VOCABULARY Use the Vocabulary Activities in Part 3 to pre-teach the following nouns: *humidity, coastal, battery, magma, trenches.* Tell students that the text will also contain many proper nouns that name specific places around the world.

KNOWLEDGE DEMANDS

ACTIVATE BACKGROUND KNOWLEDGE Help students understand that one way that writers teach readers about disasters is to use words that help us picture people, places, or things. Read the first paragraph aloud. Ask: In the first sentence, what does the word *rotating* tell you about? (thunderstorms) What do the words *warm, dry* and *cold* describe? (the air) What does the word violent describe? (storm) Say: The words *rotating, warm, dry, cold,* and *violent* are adjectives. Adjectives help us picture how people or things look, sound, smell, taste, or feel. Adjectives usually come before the nouns they describe. Then, explain that they will read many adjectives in this text that describe all kinds of people, places, and things, such as *burning* trees, *lost* dogs, and *loud* noises.

STRUGGLING READERS

Explain that weather disasters happen all over the country and the world. Preview the place names throughout the text by pointing to them on a United States or world map. Say each place name aloud and have students repeat. Use a United States map to say and point to: Joplin, Missouri (p. 5); Oklahoma City, Oklahoma (p. 9); Rocksprings, Texas (p. 17); Clermont, Florida (p. 19); and Hawaii (p. 23). Use a world map to say and point to: Tewkesbury, England (p. 11); Beijing, China (p. 17); Belize (p. 20); Japan (p. 25); Iceland (pp. 24 and 26); and Victoria and Melbourne, Australia (pp. 29 and 31).

Interact with Text

As you read *Disaster Alert!*, call students' attention to the three "How to Survive" features on pages 9, 13, and 24. Explain that these features contain instructions or directions that are addressed to "you," the reader. Say: These instructions are written as commands. Commands are sentences that tell readers what to do. This may be a good opportunity to discuss what would happen if a disaster occurred during the school day. Ask: What would we do, as a school community, if a tornado struck? If a flash flood happened? If a fire broke out? It also might be a good time to invite a firefighter or another first responder to visit your classroom and provide some firsthand information.

If . . . students need support to answer these questions,

then . . . use the Ask and Answer Questions Routine in Part 3 to record both questions and responses.

STRUCTURE

Since this text is highly visual, encourage students to choose one of the most important photographs as the subject for a deep discussion. Ask: What is happening in this photograph? What sentence in the text does the photograph illustrate? For example, the photograph on pages 10 and 11 shows people in cars and trucks escaping a flooded street. The low shrubs look like they are floating in water. Some of the people are wearing bright orange life jackets. The cars' and trucks' wheels are deep in water. Everyone's pant legs are rolled up. The people seem, however, to be safe and cooperative. The sentence in the text that the photograph illustrates is: "The water spills into streets and houses."

After you do a deep reading of one photograph as a group, invite students to choose another photograph to analyze on their own. Give them the opportunity to share their observations with each other.

MORE SUPPORT

ENGLISH LANGUAGE LEARNERS

Some English Language Learners may be uncomfortable responding to questions in front of the class. To encourage participation and confidence, allow time for them to work with a partner to attain fluency before speaking to the class.

STRUGGLING READERS

Focus students' attention on the EF scale at the bottom of pp. 6 and 7. Discuss the ways the six kinds of tornadoes are different? (wind speeds, EF numbers, amount of damage, the illustrations, the descriptions, the colors) Ask: What kind of tornado hit Joplin, Missouri? (an EF5)

LANGUAGE CONVENTIONALITY AND CLARITY

While much of the language will be clear and accessible to students, they may need extra support to understand the statistical information in the "Real Life" and "Did You Know" features (e.g., 50,000 homes, $99 million, 70% of the Earth's surface, 35,000 feet, 3,500 firefighters, 2,200 degrees). They also may need to be reminded about the planets in the Solar System noted on page 23.

> **If . . .** students have difficulty understanding the relative dates of the "Real Life" disasters,
>
> **then . . .** have students use the Time Line Graphic Organizer in Part 3 to organize the five events from pages 5, 11, 19, 26, and 29.

KNOWLEDGE DEMANDS

To avoid focusing on the negative aspects of the content (damage, death, and destruction) and focusing instead on the positive (saving lives, rescue, and prediction), call students' attention to the various jobs that are described in the text: meteorologists (p. 6), storm chasers (p. 7), emergency workers (pp. 8 and 19), electricians (p. 15), volcanologists (p. 27), and firefighters (pp. 29–30). Ask: If you had to choose one of these jobs, which one would you choose? Why? Help them understand that each of these jobs requires special education and skills. You can use the Three-Column Chart Graphic Organizer in Part 3 to organize details about one or several of the jobs under the headings Training, Skills, and Equipment.

ENGLISH LANGUAGE LEARNERS

Remind students that the suffix -ist is added to many words in English to turn actions or subjects into people who do that action or study that subject. For example, in this text, a meteorologist is a person who studies meteorology (or weather). A volcanologist is a person who studies volcanoes. Ask: What does a dentist do? An artist? A scientist?

Express and Extend

EXPRESS Help students recognize that water plays many roles in this text. There are references to flood water, drinking water, and water that fights fires. Challenge students to skim the text to see how many times they see the word *water*. Encourage them to find and notice related words, too (such as *ice, snow, flood, riverbanks, overflow*). Say: Water plays many different roles in this text. What are some of them? Focus attention on the sentence on page 11, "There was no drinking water for seventeen days." Use this opportunity to talk about the many health benefits of drinking clean water every day.

> If . . . you want to record students observations of water-related words,
>
> then . . . use the Web Graphic Organizer from Part 3 to track and record their observations.

EXTEND Have students write paragraphs that answer this question: How do I use water? Encourage them to see that all human beings need water to live and use water in many other ways, too. Have them illustrate their paragraphs with drawings that show one way they use water.

EXPRESS Focus attention on the three illustrations on page 16: "How Is a Sinkhole Formed?" Explain that these three pictures and their captions show three steps in a process: what happens first, second, and last over time. Show students the word *sequence*. Have them pronounce it out loud and write it down. Say: Sometimes things happen all at once, but most of the time, things take time to happen. They have a beginning, middle, and end. Big events, such as natural disasters, are really made up of many smaller events. For example, sinkholes are formed in three steps. Each step leads to the next step. This is called a sequence. Point out that this is not the case with the illustration on pages 6 and 7. These pictures do not describe a sequence of events. Instead, they show a scale used to measure tornadoes. They are not steps in a process. They are not a sequence.

EXTEND Have students choose another sequence from the text and create three drawings with captions to show the steps. They might choose the three steps for cleaning up after a flood (pages 14–15), the three steps in forming a volcano (page 22), or the three steps in the Black Saturday Bushfire (page 29).

ENGLISH LANGUAGE LEARNERS

Focus attention on the concepts *beginning, middle,* and *end*. Then, offer other words that describe sequences: 1, 2, and 3; first, next, last; spring, summer, fall, winter; morning, afternoon, evening.

STRUGGLING READERS

Because the five parts of this text are distinct and self-contained, you may use any one (or two, three, or four) of them without the others. You might also assign small groups of students to read each part and report to the whole group about what they have read.

LANGUAGE CONVENTIONALITY AND CLARITY

EXPRESS Talk about Sentences and Words

Display and read aloud the following sentences from page 5 of *Disaster Alert!*

> Tornadoes are dangerous because they move very fast. The average speed of a tornado moving along the ground is 30 miles per hour. Wind inside a tornado can reach speeds of more than 200 miles per hour.

Point out that the first sentence here is a general statement based on facts. The second and third sentences are the facts that support the general statement. Say: The facts "30 miles per hour" and "200 miles per hour" support the ideas "dangerous" and "move very fast." Explain that throughout this text, the writer gives the reader ideas and then supports those ideas with facts. Facts can be statistics, examples, definitions, or other kinds of details.

TEAM TALK Have partners work in pairs to find other ideas in the text that are supported by facts, statistics, details, and examples. Have them use the Main Ideas and Details Graphic Organizer in Part 3 to record their observations.

EXTEND Ask students to write about a time in which they faced a dangerous situation. Remind them to use all five senses to describe their experiences. Suggest that their first sentence be an idea. Their other sentences should be facts and examples to support it.

KNOWLEDGE DEMANDS

EXPRESS Using an Internet search engine, help students find a news article about a natural disaster that happened near you in the last year. Use the words *who, what, when, where, why,* and *how* to prompt questions about the disaster that the article will likely answer. Find and study photographs that will support their understanding. Ask students to think about and discuss ways in which people can best survive this kind of disaster in the future.

> If . . . students need help organizing what they discover about the disaster,
> then . . . have them use the Web Graphic Organizer in Part 3 with the name and date of the disaster in the center.

EXTEND Have students use details from the text to make a list of supplies and equipment that people should keep in their homes to help them survive disasters.

ACCELERATED LEARNERS

Challenge students to create a two- or four-page spread about a natural disaster that is not covered in this text. For example, they might choose avalanches, mudslides, earthquakes, hurricanes, or lightning strikes. Have them create and include a "Real Life" feature, a "Job Profile" and a "How to Survive" feature. Have them design their pages to match the style of *Disaster Alert!*

MORE SUPPORT

Unlock the Text

QUALITATIVE MEASURES

Levels of Meaning	informational text about earthquakes (including causes and safety, plus examples of specific earthquakes)
Structure	photographs; maps; no table of contents, index, or captions
Language Conventionality and Clarity	domain-specific vocabulary; dates and figures
Knowledge Demands	basic understanding of earthquakes; Mercalli and Richter scales

ReadyGEN
Text Collection 2

Danger! Earthquakes,
pp. 12–43

Prepare to Read

LEVELS OF MEANING

Danger! Earthquakes is an informational text about earthquakes, including what they are, what causes them, how scientists measure them, how to remain safe during them, and facts about specific earthquakes.

STRUCTURE

PREVIEW Ask students to look at the photographs and maps. Ask: Based on the pictures, what do you think this book is about? (the damage caused by earthquakes) What might the maps tell us that the pictures don't? (where earthquakes are most likely to happen) What clues do the pictures give you about the type of damage earthquakes can cause? (They can cause buildings to collapse and can damage roads.)

ENGLISH LANGUAGE LEARNERS

Remind students that even though the word *quake* is a verb, it is also a commonly used abbreviation for the word *earthquake*. Help students identify when *quake* is used as a verb and when it is used as an abbreviation.

STRUGGLING READERS

While the photographs provided demonstrate what can happen during an earthquake, they don't always help students unlock complex ideas in the text. When the photographs cannot be use as aids, assist comprehension by providing graphic organizers o encouraging students to do paired repeated readings.

PREVIEW VOCABULARY Use the Preview and Review Vocabulary Routine in Part 3 to assess what students know about the following words: *level, damage, disaster, wreck, destroy, scale, measure, recorded, collapse.*

DOMAIN-SPECIFIC VOCABULARY Use the Vocabulary Activities and Games in Part 3 to help students with the following domain-specific words: *magnitude, crust, fault zones, mantle, plates, grind.*

COGNATES Use the list of Spanish cognates at the beginning of this module to guide your Spanish-speaking students as they read the text.

KNOWLEDGE DEMANDS

ACTIVATE BACKGROUND KNOWLEDGE Use the Quick Write and Share Routine in Part 3 to activate students' background knowledge of earthquakes. Ask: What do you know about earthquakes? Where do they often occur? Remind students to use materials from previous readings, such as completed graphic organizers, to help them complete this activity.

ENGLISH LANGUAGE LEARNERS

Some students may have trouble visualizing what an earthquake looks or feels like. Find videos from news channels or geography Web sites that show how buildings shake during an earthquake.

Interact with Text

LEVELS OF MEANING

While *Danger! Earthquakes* provides general information about earthquakes, it also looks more closely at earthquakes in California, Alaska, and Mexico City. Provide students with the Three-Column Chart Graphic Organizer in Part 3, and have them record three facts about each earthquake. Then have students write 3–5 sentences that explain the differences among the three earthquakes.

If . . . students have trouble comparing and contrasting the three earthquakes,

then . . . give students the Venn Diagram Graphic Organizer in Part 3 with the names of two of the locations, such as Mexico City and California, and have them complete the Venn diagram using the information from their three-column chart.

STRUCTURE

Use the following activity to help students understand how the photographs or maps support information in the text.

Provide students with the Venn Diagram Graphic Organizer in Part 3, and have them label one circle *Printed Text* and the other *Photograph or Map.* Assign students a page from the text, and have them record information about the printed text and the photograph or map in the appropriate circles before recording the similarities between the two in the middle of the graphic organizer. Afterward, have students work together, using their Venn diagrams, to answer the following question: How does the information in the photograph or map relate to the printed text?

ENGLISH LANGUAGE LEARNERS

Even though English Language Learners have difficulty with words, their knowledge of numbers may be on par with, or even exceed, their peers. When possible, allow students to utilize this strength by having them use numbers when explaining and comparing the earthquakes.

STRUGGLING READERS

When possible, allow students to choose which graphic organizer they would like to use when completing an activity. This encourages students to take responsibility for using the materials that help them learn best, which will allow them to become more independent learners.

LANGUAGE CONVENTIONALITY AND CLARITY

To help students comprehend difficult, domain-specific language, have them work in small groups to draw a diagram of Earth. The diagram should show the geological parts that cause earthquakes, such as the mantle, plates, and fault zones. (Provide students with at least three terms from the domain-specific vocabulary list.) Then have students label the parts of the diagram and write a one-sentence explanation of each part. Afterward, have groups present their diagram to the class.

> If . . . students are unsure of how to draw particular geological parts that cause an earthquake,
>
> then . . . provide them with a premade diagram that shows each of the parts, and ask them to label the parts. Check their labels before having them complete the rest of the activity.

KNOWLEDGE DEMANDS

Have students complete either the Venn Diagram Graphic Organizer or the Two-Column Chart Graphic Organizer in Part 3 by recording information about the Mercalli and Richter scales. After they have recorded at least three facts about each scale, have students write sentences that compare and contrast the two scales.

Express and Extend

EXPRESS Have students reread p. 41. Provide them with the Steps in a Process Graphic Organizer in Part 3, and have them write the steps they would need to take to be safe during an earthquake.

EXTEND Have students create a small safety poster, using the text for support. The poster should include a picture or student drawing and give step-by-step instructions for how to stay safe during an earthquake at school. Display the posters, and invite students to read them to the class.

EXPRESS Point out that *Danger! Earthquakes* lacks both a table of contents and section headings to separate the topics. Assign students a group of pages. Have them reread the pages and then create an appropriate section heading for those pages. Tell them that the section heading must give readers a hint about what that section discusses. After students create a section heading, they should write 2–3 sentences explaining how their heading accurately previews their section of text.

> If . . . students have difficulty thinking of an appropriate section heading,
>
> then . . . provide students with the Main Idea and Details Graphic Organizer in Part 3. Have them determine the main idea of the section to create their heading. Afterward, they should write 2–3 sentences that explain why the heading they chose is the best fit for their section of text.

EXTEND Have students create a table of contents for the text. Remind students that in order to complete this activity, they will have to create section headings for the rest of the text and include the page number for the start of each section. Have partners use each other's table of contents to locate sections in the book.

ENGLISH LANGUAGE LEARNERS

When referring to different text features, try to show examples from texts that students have read in class. This will help them remember not only what the features look like but how they function in a familiar text. They can then use that knowledge to help them with future texts.

STRUGGLING READERS

Some students may have difficulty finding information because they are unsure of how to skim for information. As students read, give them sticky notes labeled with topics to flag pages accordingly. Topics may include what causes earthquakes, how scientists measure earthquakes, and what to do if you're in an earthquake.

LANGUAGE CONVENTIONALITY AND CLARITY

EXPRESS Talk about Sentences and Words

Display and read aloud the following sentences from *Danger! Earthquakes*:

> In 1811, an 8+ quake shook the Mississippi valley. It caused church bells to ring in Boston, nearly 1,000 miles away.

Point out that many of the sentences in the text contain dates and facts in the form of numbers. Ask: What does *1811* refer to? (the year) What does *8+* refer to? (a measurement of the earthquake) How do you know what the number *1,000* represents? (distance in miles, according to the label after the number) Have students rewrite the sentence using *one thousand* in place of *1,000*.

TEAM TALK Have partners compare the two sentences and determine which sentence is easier to read.

EXTEND Have students find three other examples of facts with numeric figures in the text. Have them rewrite the sentences using words in place of the numerals. Then have students write a sentence stating whether they think the sentences should be written with words or numerals.

KNOWLEDGE DEMANDS

EXPRESS Have students review the section of text that discusses common geographic locations of earthquakes. Then have them write about why they think earthquakes seem to occur in the same parts of the world. Have them use at least one example from the text to support their opinion.

EXTEND Have students write a letter that they would send to a family member if he or she were planning to travel to one of the locations discussed in the text. In the letter, they should explain the things they learned from the text, warn their family member about the dangers of earthquakes in that area, and explain how he or she can use caution in the event of an earthquake during the trip. Invite students to share their letters with the class.

ACCELERATED LEARNERS

Have students create a three-page book about earthquakes. Students should explain how earthquakes occur, give an example of a destructive earthquake not discussed in the text, and tell how to stay safe in the event of an earthquake in their home. Each page should be accompanied by an illustration.

Pioneering New Ideas and New Worlds

TEXT SET

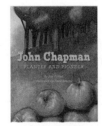

ANCHOR TEXT
John Chapman: Planter
and Pioneer

SUPPORTING TEXT
Johnny Appleseed

TEXT SET

ANCHOR TEXT
Pioneers to the West

SUPPORTING TEXT
Going West

Cognates

Cognates are words that have similar spellings and meanings in two or more languages. Many words in English and Spanish share Greek or Latin roots, and many words in English came from French, which is closely connected to Spanish (and to Portuguese, Italian, and Romanian). Because of this, many literary, content, and academic process words in English (e.g., *gracious/gracioso; volcano/volcán; compare/comparar*) have recognizable Spanish cognates.

Making the connection to cognates permits students who are native Spanish speakers to understand the strong foundation they have in academic and literary English. These links between English and Spanish are also useful for native speakers of English and other languages because they help uncover basic underlying features of our language.

ANCHOR TEXT John Chapman: Planter and Pioneer

ENGLISH	SPANISH	ENGLISH	SPANISH
animals	animales	nation	nación
cider	sidra	pile	pila
coffee	café	plant	plantar
colony	colonia	plants	plantas
creatures	criaturas	protect	proteger
energy	energía	relax	relajarse
family	familia	sack	saco
frontier	frontera	simple	simple
fruit	fruta	states	estados
hero	héroe	story	historia
legend	leyenda	vegetables	vegetales
miles	millas	venomous	venenosas
mosquitoes	mosquitos	visitors	visitantes

SUPPORTING TEXT Johnny Appleseed

ENGLISH	SPANISH
frontier	frontera
plant	plantar
stories	historias

These lists contain many, but not all, Spanish cognates from these selections.

Unlock the Text

QUALITATIVE MEASURES

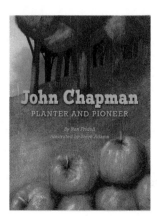

Levels of Meaning	accessible, visually supported informational text about John Chapman, a.k.a. Johnny Appleseed, including anecdotes, opinions, and reasons that he is famous, beloved, and the subject of legend
Structure	text is mostly chronological, organized under five headings
Language Conventionality and Clarity	some historical and agricultural words may need special instruction
Knowledge Demands	understanding of apples and trees and the concept of living in the "great outdoors"

Prepare to Read

LEVELS OF MEANING

John Chapman: Planter and Pioneer describes the man who became famous as the legendary Johnny Appleseed. The first section compares John Chapman to the newly formed United States. "At Home Outdoors" describes his habits. The third section focuses on planting apple trees. "A Simple Life" describes his interactions with others. "A Legend is Born" describes some of the exaggerated stories about him. Lively, colorful illustrations on every page support understanding.

STRUCTURE

PREVIEW Display the pairs of words *wild/wilderness* and *seed/seedling* for students to see, pronounce, and copy. Say: See how the short words, *wild* and *seed*, are contained inside the longer words? These short words

ENGLISH LANGUAGE LEARNERS

Call students' attention to pp. 4-5 and how the illustrator makes John look like one of the trees. Find the words, "Out here a young man like me can stretch and grow" on p. 4. Have students stand up and stretch their arms and hands upward as if they were trees.

STRUGGLING READERS

The writer uses many different kinds of sentences on pp. 4 and 5. Ask students to point to examples of a question, an exclamation, a quotation, and italics (to express thoughts). As you continue to read, have them notice the different kinds of sentences the writer uses to give information about John.

are root words. The longer words grow from them. **Explain that a wilderness is a big place that is still wild. A wilderness does not contain houses, schools, or businesses. Explain that a seedling is a small plant that grows from a seed. Explain that both pairs of words will be important in this passage. Use the KWL Chart Graphic Organizer in Part 3 to keep track of what students already know about these words and what they may want to learn.**

PREVIEW VOCABULARY Use the Preview and Review Vocabulary Routine in Part 3 to assess what students know about the following words: *tangled, amazed, visitors, clever, tattered, thankful,* and *legend.*

COGNATES Use the list of Spanish cognates at the beginning of this module to guide your Spanish-speaking students as they read the selection.

DOMAIN-SPECIFIC VOCABULARY Use the Vocabulary Activities in Part 3 to pre-teach the following words: *nation, apple cider, venomous,* and *superman.*

ACTIVATE BACKGROUND KNOWLEDGE Make sure students understand the relationship between apple seeds, apple trees, and apples. Bring in an apple and pass it around for students to touch and observe. Then, slice the apple open to expose and extract the tiny seeds. Use the words *skin, stem,* and *core* to describe its parts. Say: If a person plants one of these tiny seeds in dirt and gives it water and sunshine, it might sprout a tiny seedling. It takes about three years for a small tree to grow and to bear its first fruit. When it is about eight years old, the tree can grow 20 feet tall and produce hundreds of apples. Apple trees have been grown all over the world for thousands of years. **Students might be interested to learn that apple trees have the longest life spans of any fruit trees. Most live as long as eighty years! One tree in England is said to be over 200 years old (but perhaps this, like Johnny Appleseed, is a legend).**

STRUGGLING READERS

Focus students' attention on the illustration on pp. 14 and 15 in which John Chapman is planting a tiny apple seed. Read the last paragraph on p. 15 aloud as students look at the illustration. Point out the verbs that show the steps of planting: *went out, found, dug, placed,* and *pushed.* Explain that this simple act of planting is the most important detail in the passage. As the title suggests, Chapman was a planter (a person who plants).

MORE SUPPORT

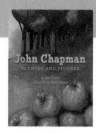

Interact with Text

As you read *John Chapman: Planter and Pioneer,* help students understand that the information in the last part, "A Legend is Born," is different from the information in the parts before it. This part includes "the stories that made Johnny sound like a hero." Say: The stories described in this part are not true. They are not based on facts. The writer suggests this when he writes, "Could that really happen? Or does it sound too good to be true?" The answer is probably it sounds too good to be true. Point out the author's statements on p. 27: "These stories may not all be true. But they show what people thought of Johnny Appleseed." Take this opportunity to explain the difference between a fact (something that is true for everyone) and an opinion (what people think about a person or thing). Explain that information about John Chapman includes both facts and opinions. For example, the name "John Chapman" is a fact. The name "Johnny Appleseed" reflects people's opinions of him.

If . . . students need support to understand what makes someone a legend,

then . . . have students use the Web Graphic Organizer in Part 3 to record the various stories about Johnny Appleseed with the word "Legend" in the center of the web.

STRUCTURE

As you read *John Chapman: Planter and Pioneer,* help students see and understand that each of the five parts has its own heading (on pp. 3, 7, 11, 17, and 24). Each part also has its own beginning, middle, and end. As you encounter each part, say: What is this part about? How does it fit into the whole text? What is the most important detail in this part? Suggest that each part introduces new ideas to readers. For example, "From Apples to 'Appleseed'" introduces the idea of apple cider and cider presses. It also introduces the idea that John planted trees on the edge of civilization to welcome the settlers when they arrived.

ENGLISH LANGUAGE LEARNERS

Many of the legends described in the last part of this text involve animals. Have students list all of the animals named in the text (bears, owl, mosquitoes, wolf, bird, horses, snakes, cows). Allow them to share the names of these animals from their native languages.

STRUGGLING READERS

Focus students' attention on the second paragraph on p. 7 and the contrast of "home" and "homeless." Remind them that the suffix *-less* means "without" in English, so a homeless person is without a home (i.e., does not have a home). Ask: What would a treeless farm be like? A starless sky? A shoeless person?

LANGUAGE CONVENTIONALITY AND CLARITY

This writer uses the word *And* to begin sentences and to connect details in the text. Say: Look at the way the writer begins two paragraphs with the word *And* on page 4. He does this to join one paragraph to the next and to connect one idea to the next idea. The sentence "And so he would stay right there" connects to the word *wilderness* in the sentence before. The sentence "And that is what John did" connects to the sentence "I will plant apple trees" in the paragraph before. Ask students to find other examples of *And* at the beginning of sentences (pp. 6, 8, 11, 19, 21, 26, 28, and 31). Suggest that this word propels the sentences forward and gives the writing a casual, friendly tone, as if someone is sharing this information aloud.

If . . . students have difficulty understanding how conjunctions link ideas,

then . . . use the Compound Sentences and Commas Activity in Part 3 to model how to use conjunctions to link ideas. Modify the activity to guide students to see how the author used conjunctions in a familiar, or casual, tone in separate sentences, instead of linking sentences.

KNOWLEDGE DEMANDS

Focus students' attention on the idea of money introduced on pp. 20 and 21. Ask: How did John Chapman earn his money? (He owned lots of land.) What did he do with his money? (We do not find out. We only learn that he didn't buy a big house or stop working.) Point out that these are facts that readers learn from the text. Then ask: Why do you think John chose not to buy a house or stop working? As students offer and discuss answers to this question, point out that their ideas are not facts but opinions. Not everyone agrees with opinions. Suggest that opinions often grow from facts.

ENGLISH LANGUAGE LEARNERS

Point out that when Johnny says, "Well, no thanks" to someone who offered him a warm bed, he means "No, thank you." Invite students to share translations of "Thank you" in other languages. Invite students to discuss what the writer means when he states that Johnny felt that a person "should be thankful for whatever you had." Explain that *thankful* means "full of thanks."

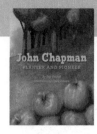

Express and Extend

EXPRESS Encourage a discussion of the idea of hero as it applies to John Chapman on p. 24. Say: The writer states that the stories told about Johnny made him sound like a hero. What is a hero? (a person who helps other people, shows great courage, or does great deeds) Is being a hero a matter of fact or opinion? (opinion) What is the difference between a hero and a superman (p. 28)? (A superman can do things that normal humans cannot do; a hero is a normal human.) Make sure students know that a woman can be heroic, too. The noun *heroine* names a female hero.

> If . . . you want students to record ways in which John Chapman was heroic,
>
> then . . . use the Web Graphic Organizers from Part 3 to track and record their observations.

EXTEND Have students write paragraphs about people that they know or know of that they consider heroic. How is the person like John Chapman? How is the person different? Make sure they include specific reasons for their choices. Give them the opportunity to share their choices and reasons with the whole group.

EXPRESS Focus attention on the illustrations throughout the text by asking questions such as: Which illustrations happen at night? (pp. 6–7, 8–9, 22–23, 26–27) Which one shows a cider press? (pp. 12–13) What is John wearing on his head on page 10 and why? (It looks like a frying pan. Maybe it shows that he can cook anytime and anywhere.) Which illustration shows John doing something superhuman? What is he doing? (On pp. 28–29, he is jumping "so high that it takes him a whole day to come back to earth.") What are the children doing on page 30? (They are reading a book about Johnny Appleseed sitting beside the trunk of a huge tree.)

EXTEND Have students choose one illustration from the text that they especially like. Ask them to write short paragraphs describing what is happening in the illustration. Have them include the reasons they chose this illustration in their paragraphs.

ENGLISH LANGUAGE LEARNERS

Encourage students to share examples of heroes or heroines from their native cultures. Ask them to share how the heroes or heroines are like John Chapman and how they are different from him. Have them draw pictures of them and write short captions to share with the class.

STRUGGLING READERS

Point out the words *stronger, kinder,* and *smarter* on p. 31. Explain that the suffix *-er,* when added to an adjective in English, means "more than someone or something else." These words mean that Johnny Appleseed was more stron more kind, and more smart than other people. Ask student: what the adjectives mean in the phrases *bigger tree, bright star,* and *smaller creature.*

EXPRESS Talk about Sentences and Words

Display and read aloud the following sentences from p. 19 of *John Chapman: Planter and Pioneer.*

> Everyone agreed that Johnny was a clever man. This Johnny Appleseed knew right where new settlers wanted to live. And those apple trees were oh so pretty! No wonder people settled down to stay. People also liked Johnny for his energy. Was there ever a man who worked harder?

Remind students that an opinion is an idea or feeling that someone has about a subject that may not be the same for everyone. Opinions are based on facts, but they are not facts. Say: These sentences include three opinions about Johnny Appleseed: that he was clever, that the apple trees were "oh so pretty," and that he worked harder than anyone else. These are the writer's feelings or opinions. They are not facts that are true for everyone. Direct students to the two sentences on p. 32. Ask: Which sentence is a fact? Which is an opinion? Why?

TEAM TALK Have partners work in pairs to write one sentence that is a fact about Johnny Appleseed and one sentence that is an opinion about him. Have them share their sentences with the whole group.

EXTEND Ask students to express their opinions about this passage. Prompt with this question: Did you like this story? Why or why not? Help them see that words such as *funny, interesting, colorful,* or *entertaining* express opinions. To support these opinions, they need to give reasons based on the story itself.

EXPRESS Focus students' attention on the word *Pioneer* in the title. Remind them that a pioneer might be among the first people to explore or settle a new country or area. A pioneer might also be a person who discovers or applies a new idea or experience. Ask: What are some different ways in which John Chapman was a pioneer?

If . . . students need help organizing their thoughts about pioneers,

then . . . have them use the Web Graphic Organizer in Part 3 with the word Pioneer in the center.

EXTEND Encourage students to picture themselves as pioneers. Where would you explore? What would you do? What might you discover? How would your discoveries benefit other people? Have them write short descriptions of their exploits and include illustrations with captions.

ACCELERATED LEARNERS

Challenge students to find out more about apple growing today. Encourage them to make informative visuals to illustrate information they discover. For example, they might make pictographs about the top ten apple producing states or illustrations of the top ten apple varieties. They might find information about a local apple orchard. You might even invite a local grower to your classroom to give a talk. The website of the US Apple Association is a good source of information and ideas.

Unlock the Text

Levels of Meaning	explicit, informational biography detailing the life of John Chapman
Structure	illustrations and captions aid in comprehending the main text; time line provides visual representation of events
Language Conventionality and Clarity	domain-specific vocabulary defined in context and pictures; past-tense and present-tense verbs
Knowledge Demands	general knowledge of pioneer life; general knowledge of U.S. geography in pioneer times

Johnny Appleseed,
pp. 50–69

Prepare to Read

LEVELS OF MEANING

Johnny Appleseed is a biography about the life of John Chapman, commonly known as Johnny Appleseed. This nonfiction text provides factual information related to Chapman's life and his travels. This selection offers comparable information to the text *John Chapman: Planter and Pioneer.*

STRUCTURE

PREVIEW Have students preview the text focusing on photographs, illustrations, and text features. Ask: What do you notice when looking at the pictures? (There are both photographs and illustrations.) What other text features are provided in this selection? (picture captions and a time line) Recall the text *John Chapman: Planter and Pioneer* and compare the information learned from that text to the text features you have previewed

---

ENGLISH LANGUAGE LEARNERS

When possible, provide visual aids to help students understand the meaning of unfamiliar words or phrases, such as *frontier*, *orchard*, *cider mill*, and *settler*. This will support students' retention of the words. Post visual aids on walls for easy reference as students read the text.

STRUGGLING READERS

Allow students multiple and varied ways to interact with new vocabulary. After previewing the words, have students choose a word and then draw a picture of it, act it out, or use the word in a sentence. Have partners guess the word based on the drawing or action or determine the definition from the sentence.

in this selection. What can you predict regarding the ways in which this selection will be the same as or different from *John Chapman: Planter and Pioneer?* (Both texts provide information about Johnny Appleseed. Based on the time line, real photographs, and picture captions, this selection appears to be more factual.)

LANGUAGE CONVENTIONALITY AND CLARITY

PREVIEW VOCABULARY Use the Preview and Review Vocabulary Routine in Part 3 to assess what students know about the following words: *time line, frontier, settlers, west, collected, cider mill, pressing, orchard, nickname, gravesite.* Review vocabulary from the previous selection, *John Chapman: Planter and Pioneer,* using the Vocabulary Activities and Games in Part 3 to compare related vocabulary in this selection.

COGNATES Use the list of Spanish cognates at the beginning of this module to guide your Spanish-speaking students as they read the selection.

KNOWLEDGE DEMANDS

ACTIVATE BACKGROUND KNOWLEDGE Use the Quick Write and Share Routine in Part 3 and have students share what they remember about *John Chapman: Planter and Pioneer.* Ask: What is John Chapman remembered for? What facts about his life did you learn? What are some things about him that are legends? Explain that this selection will focus more on the factual information about John Chapman than on the legend.

Interact with Text

LEVELS OF MEANING

While reading the biography, guide students to understand that the text is solely about John Chapman and his actions. Ask: Whom does the text tell us about? (John Chapman) Does the text tell what other people were doing at the time? (no) What is the purpose of the text? (to inform the reader about John Chapman's life) What is a biography? (a text about a person's life)

STRUCTURE

As students read, assess their understanding of the time line along the bottom of each page.

If . . . students have difficulty understanding why the author included a time line,

then . . . have students identify the information on the time line on each spread and compare it with the accompanying text.

Ask: What information does the time line provide? (dates and short summaries of events that took place during John Chapman's life) How does the time line change from page to page? (New dates and summaries are added when John moves to a new place. All of the previous information remains on the time line.) Why do you think the author chose to include the time line? (to provide a quick way to find information in the text)

MORE SUPPORT

ENGLISH LANGUAGE LEARNERS

As you read, point out on a map the locations noted in the text to provide for students a visual representation of John's travels. Review the directional markings on a map compass to clarify the meaning of *traveling west*. Occasionally trace John's route on the map with your finger as you read.

STRUGGLING READERS

If students struggle to see how the time line relates to the text, guide them in finding the information in the text that matches the information on the time line. Reread the time line and have students find the years in the text. Then have students read the sentence that refers to each year to see how it relates to the time line.

LANGUAGE CONVENTIONALITY AND CLARITY

Much of the domain-specific vocabulary, such as *frontier*, *cider mill*, and *orchard,* is defined in context as well as through the pictures. As you read, clarify students' understanding while encouraging independence by asking guided questions about text features and activating background knowledge from the previous related selection, *John Chapman: Planter and Pioneer*. For example, while reading pp. 56–67, say: The text tells us that John collected apple seeds from nearby cider mills. How can we determine what a cider mill is? What does the author provide to help us understand this term? Have we discussed anything similar to this recently? (The picture caption indicates that the people are pressing apples to make cider.)

KNOWLEDGE DEMANDS

Remind students of the lifestyle differences between John Chapman's time and today. Have students recall information from *John Chapman: Planter and Pioneer* about the way that John chose to live. Refer students to the pictures in *Johnny Appleseed* for comparison. For example, when reading pp. 54–55, point to the photograph and ask: Does this road look similar to or different from roads today? How did people travel from place to place in the late 1700s and early 1800s?

Clarify students' understanding of John's travels as well as of his encounters with settlers who were also traveling west. As you read the text, trace John's route on a United States map or, if possible, provide students with a map of the United States from the time in which John Chapman lived. Point out that the western portion of our country was still not fully explored and that many people were heading west to settle the land and build new homes.

Express and Extend

LEVELS OF MEANING

EXPRESS Revisit the purpose of *John Chapman: Planter and Pioneer* and compare it with the purpose of *Johnny Appleseed*. Discuss the different ways in which information is presented in each selection. *John Chapman: Planter and Pioneer* relates the legend of John Chapman, whereas *Johnny Appleseed* gives more factual information about the man. Use the Venn Diagram Graphic Organizer in Part 3 to compare the two selections.

> **If . . .** students have difficulty recalling the purpose of *John Chapman: Planter and Pioneer,*
>
> **then . . .** review *John Chapman: Planter and Pioneer* and use the Main Idea and Details Graphic Organizer in Part 3 to review the purpose of the text.

EXTEND Further students' understanding of biographies by providing additional biographies of notable Americans from the school or classroom library for students to read. Then, have students write a paragraph summarizing the most interesting facts they learned about the individual they read about. Have partners share their paragraphs.

STRUCTURE

EXPRESS Use the Retell or Summarize Graphic Organizer in Part 3 to guide small groups in retelling details from the text, including details that are conveyed only through the illustrations and photographs. Compare the details provided in *Johnny Appleseed* with those in *John Chapman: Planter and Pioneer.* Ask: How does the information conveyed in this text compare with the information provided in *John Chapman: Planter and Pioneer?*

> **If . . .** students have difficulty recalling details from the illustrations in both texts,
>
> **then . . .** take a picture walk through both texts with students, making sure to point out elements of the photographs and illustrations.

EXTEND Have students look at the photograph on the last spread of the text and describe what they see. Say: John Chapman's grave marker says, "He lived for others." Based on what you have learned from both *John Chapman: Planter and Pioneer* and *Johnny Appleseed,* what does this mean? Have students write a paragraph describing the meaning of this sentence, citing evidence from both texts. Have students share their ideas with the class.

ENGLISH LANGUAGE LEARNERS

Remind students to review both selections when comparing information between the texts. Have students review the pictures to recall information. Also, allow students to use previously made graphic organizers as reference tools.

STRUGGLING READERS

Review the Verb Activities in Part 3 with students who struggle to differentiate among past, present, and future tense. Provide theme-related oral sentences, such as *I plant seeds, I planted seeds, I will plant seeds,* and help students identify the tense of each verb.

LANGUAGE CONVENTIONALITY AND CLARITY

EXPRESS Talk about Sentences and Words

Display the following sentences from p. 55 of *Johnny Appleseed* and read it aloud:

Around 1794, John left his home. He started walking west.

Discuss the sentences and identify the verbs in each. Ask: In what verb tense is this passage written: past, present, or future? (past) How do you know? (The word *left* is the past-tense form of *leave*, which indicates that something has already happened. The ending *-ed* in the word *started* is another clue for past-tense verbs.) Have students look at the time line on the bottom of p. 54 and ask: What is the verb tense of the word *travels* on the time line? (present) Why do you suppose the author used two different verb tenses?

TEAM TALK Have partners discuss why the author chose to write the main text in past tense and the time line in present tense. (The text is discussing events that already happened. The time line is being constructed as the text progresses and describes an event that is happening at the time listed.)

EXTEND Have students rewrite the time line using the past tense. Have partners compare their time lines.

KNOWLEDGE DEMANDS

EXPRESS Have small groups discuss how knowledge of life in America in the 1700s and 1800s helped them better understand the life of John Chapman in both *John Chapman: Planter and Pioneer* and *Johnny Appleseed*. Ask: How did learning about the importance of apples and John's mode of transportation contribute to your understanding of the text?

If . . . students have difficulty understanding the role these concepts played in John Chapman's life,

then . . . have students cite evidence from both texts that tell why John was willing to walk such distances to share apples. Ask students: What did pioneers use apples for? How did John get from one location to the next? Guide students to understand that apples were a vital resource for both food and drink and that the way in which John traveled was different from the way in which people travel across states today.

EXTEND Have small groups write a paragraph about why it was important for settlers to have food that would last through the winter. Remind them to use what they know about the pioneers. Have groups share their ideas with the class.

ACCELERATED LEARNERS

Have students compile information learned in both *John Chapman: Planter and Pioneer* and *Johnny Appleseed* to write an explanatory paragraph about the life and legend of John Chapman. Students should cite evidence from both texts, including dates and locations, as well as differentiate fact from speculation.

MORE SUPPORT

Cognates

Cognates are words that have similar spellings and meanings in two or more languages. Many words in English and Spanish share Greek or Latin roots, and many words in English came from French, which is closely connected to Spanish (and to Portuguese, Italian, and Romanian). Because of this, many literary, content, and academic process words in English (e.g., *gracious/gracioso; volcano/volcán; compare/comparar*) have recognizable Spanish cognates.

Making the connection to cognates permits students who are native Spanish speakers to understand the strong foundation they have in academic and literary English. These links between English and Spanish are also useful for native speakers of English and other languages because they help uncover basic underlying features of our language.

ANCHOR TEXT Pioneers to the West

ENGLISH	SPANISH	ENGLISH	SPANISH
adventure	aventura	migration	migración
Americans	americanos	miner	minero
Atlantic Ocean	océano Atlántico	Mormons	mormones
camps	campamentos	October	octubre
canyon	cañón	offer	ofrecer
Christianity	cristianismo	oppportunity	oportunidad
decoration	decoración	organize	organizar
describe	describir	Pacific Ocean	océano Pacífico
experiences	experiencias	person	persona
familes	familias	photograph	fotografía
fortune	fortuna	poem	poema
imagination	imaginación	popular	popular
inspector	inspector	reservation	reservación
inspired	inspirada	territory	territorio
May	mayo		

SUPPORTING TEXT Going West

ENGLISH	SPANISH		ENGLISH	SPANISH
animals	animales		flowers	flores
bacon	beicon		garden	jardín
Bible	Biblia		piano	piano
chimney	chimenea		potatoes	patatas
constant	constante		rifle	rifle
cross	cruzar		visitors	visitantes

These lists contain many, but not all, Spanish cognates from these selections.

Unlock the Text

QUALITATIVE MEASURES

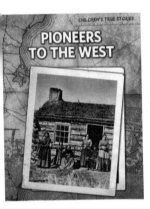

Levels of Meaning	nonfiction accounts of real people faced with challenges while settling in the West
Structure	broken into chapters with additional information provided in text boxes
Language Conventionality and Clarity	academic language presented with definitions in context
Knowledge Demands	understanding of U.S. history and geography (territories and Native American tribes)

Prepare to Read

LEVELS OF MEANING

Pioneers to the West is an informational text about real people who traveled west across the United States to find new opportunities and start new lives. The main purpose of the text is to present historic information.

STRUCTURE

PREVIEW Before reading, walk students through the table of contents at the beginning of the book. Ask: What observations can you make about how this book is structured, based on the chapter titles? (The chapters are divided by geographic location and by years. They are in chronological order.) Tell students to read the text boxes on the contents page. Ask: Based on the descriptions in the text boxes, what do you think you will learn about? Is the information the author included in these text boxes helpful? If so, how?

ENGLISH LANGUAGE LEARNERS

As you examine the table of contents, have students ask questions they would like the text to answer. Record their questions in the left column of a T-chart. Periodically revisit the questions and record the answers in the right column.

STRUGGLING READERS

To help students utilize the text features, display or make a photocopy of the contents page, which includes a description of each text feature in the book. Students can use this as they read without having to flip back to the contents page.

PREVIEW VOCABULARY Use the Preview and Review Vocabulary Routine in Part 3 to assess what students know about the following words: *migration*, *migrant*, *settlers*, *pioneers*, *territories*, *tribes*, *planting*, and *harvesting*.

Use the words in sentences that relate to the context of the selection and in sentences that relate to contexts outside of the classroom. Use the Vocabulary Activities and Games in Part 3 to provide additional practice with the vocabulary words in meaningful contexts.

COGNATES Use the list of Spanish cognates at the beginning of this module to guide your Spanish-speaking students as they read the selection.

KNOWLEDGE DEMANDS

ACTIVATE BACKGROUND KNOWLEDGE Ask students to share what they know about the geography of the western United States. Have them share what they know about how and why many Americans traveled to the West in the 1800s. Though there are maps in the text, display a large map of the United States to address any confusion regarding geography. Use the Quick Write and Share Routine in Part 3 and ask: How do you think people traveled across the country to the West before there were cars or airplanes? What do you know about pioneers or pioneer life? What do you think the hardest part of traveling across the country in the 1800s was? Why?

Before students get started, model describing what you know about pioneers in the West: I visited St. Louis once and learned that it was the starting point for many wagon trains going west in the 1800s. I know that people wanted to go to California to find work and gold, but the journey was very, very hard. There were no cars, so people traveled in wagons. I think the most difficult part of traveling across the country in the 1800s was probably trying to cross over mountain ranges in a wagon.

Interact with Text

LEVELS OF MEANING

As you read *Pioneers to the West,* periodically stop to assess students' level of understanding. Have them create either a web or a T-chart graphic organizer to help them keep track of the challenges each person in the text faced. If you choose to have students use the web organizer, they should write one person's name in the center oval. In the outer ovals, students should record notes about the challenges the person faced as well as notes regarding what happened to him or her while traveling west. If you choose to have students use the T-chart, they should write in the left column the names of the people, and record in the right column notes about the challenges each person faced.

STRUCTURE

Remind students that asking and answering questions as they read can help them better understand a text. Help students relate the information in the text boxes to the people and events in the main text. Have students work in groups to ask and answer questions about the different kinds of text boxes and the author's purpose for including each one.

For example, in the first chapter, the author includes an excerpt from a famous poet in a text box labeled "On the Scene." The contents page tells readers that the On the Scene boxes provide eyewitness accounts of migrations in the migrant's own words. Students should ask and answer questions about Walt Whitman's personal experience as a migrant and about why the author chose to include this text box in the selection. Ask: How does the information in the text box relate to the main text? Use the Ask and Answer Questions Routine in Part 3 if needed.

ENGLISH LANGUAGE LEARNERS

To help students understand the rhythm in poetry, read or play an audio clip of "Pioneers! O Pioneers!" to model the intonation. Reread the poem, line by line, and have students echo your reading.

STRUGGLING READERS

Help students answer the question posed by the author after the Walt Whitman excerpt on p. 5. Point out important words in the poem and discuss their meanings. Then have students synthesize that information to make a guess about the type o person Whitman was talking about.

LANGUAGE CONVENTIONALITY AND CLARITY

Pioneers to the West includes many words that may be unfamiliar to students but that are defined in context. Have small groups work together to determine how they can best use context clues to confirm or self-correct their understanding of any unfamiliar words in the text.

If . . . students have difficulty defining words using context clues,

then . . . walk the class through a think aloud in which you use context clues to determine the meaning of a word.

For example, show students this sentence: "[Mormons] first settled in western Illinois, but conflicts with their neighbors made them head west." Ask students if they can tell from the context what the word *conflicts* might mean. Model a think aloud for the class as you ask questions that will lead you to understanding what the word *conflicts* means. Say: I'm not sure what *conflicts* means. I can look at the surrounding words and sentences for clues to its meaning. I know from reading the sentence that conflicts are things Mormons had with their neighbors, so it must be a noun. Conflicts are what made the Mormons head west, which means they are probably negative things. I think conflicts are problems or arguments. I will look the word up in a dictionary to check the meaning. Model looking up the word *conflicts* in a dictionary. Read aloud the dictionary definition.

KNOWLEDGE DEMANDS

To help students connect the information in the text features with the information in the main text, have groups of students write a summary for each chapter. Assign a chapter to each group and have them write a short summary that will serve as a reminder of the most important information presented in the chapter. Provide time for groups to present their information to the class.

If . . . students have trouble determining the most important information in a chapter,

then . . . provide them with a printed copy of their chapter, and have them underline or highlight important information. If providing a printed copy is not an option, have students record on paper important information they find. Before they highlight or record, they should ask themselves if the information helps them understand the person's journey west. If not, they should not make a note of it.

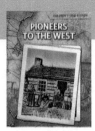

Express and Extend

LEVELS OF MEANING

EXPRESS The purpose of this selection is to show how people faced challenges as they moved west in search of new opportunities. Have students use the Sequence of Events Graphic Organizer in Part 3 to track one person's journey west.

EXTEND Tell students to use the text evidence they included in their graphic organizers to write a short essay about one of the profiles in this selection. Have each student choose one person depicted in the selection and retell his or her story in the first person in a problem-and-solution essay.

> If . . . students have difficulty identifying problems and solutions,
> then . . . use the Problem and Solution Routine and Graphic Organizer in Part 3.

STRUCTURE

EXPRESS Remind students that one On the Scene text box in this selection contains a first-person account. Ask students to explain why this text box is included in the selection. Have them discuss which text features most help them understand the selection.

EXTEND Have students work in small groups to write an On the Scene box for the section about George Staples. Remind them that their boxed text should be short and written in the first person, from George's point of view. Have the groups share their writing with the class. Then, as a class, discuss how the On the Scene boxes contribute to the main text.

ENGLISH LANGUAGE LEARNERS

Some students may struggle to identify and write common types of context clues. Provide these students with an example of each of the following types of context clues: synonym, antonym, example, and explanation. Students can refer to these examples during discussion and writing.

STRUGGLING READERS

Students may have trouble getting started on their profiles about George Staples. Remind them of the keys to writing in the first person. Make sure they understand to use the pronouns *I*, *me*, and *mine*, as well as draw examples from the text.

LANGUAGE CONVENTIONALITY AND CLARITY

EXPRESS Talk about Sentences and Words

Display and read aloud the following excerpt from *Pioneers to the West*:

> In 1845 a U.S. magazine writer said it was his country's "Manifest Destiny," or fate, to stretch from the Atlantic Ocean to the Pacific Ocean. By the end of the 1800s, that dream came true, as western lands were settled and turned into new U.S. states.

Point out how the author defines the term "Manifest Destiny" by including a definition of the term in the sentence. Explain that the author uses commas around the definition to set it off. Discuss the author's purpose in including this kind of context clue. Ask: Why does the author choose to provide the definition of the term "Manifest Destiny" in the body of the text instead of including the term in the glossary?

TEAM TALK Remind students that some common types of context clues include synonym clues, antonym clues, example clues, and explanation clues. Have partners rewrite the first sentence in the excerpt above, replacing the explanation clue with another kind of context clue.

EXTEND Have students locate an unfamiliar word in the selection that is defined in the glossary. Have them rewrite the sentence to include a context clue. Have students share their sentence in small groups. Ask group members to determine whether the clue is a synonym, antonym, example, or explanation.

KNOWLEDGE DEMANDS

EXPRESS Have students work in small groups to create visual aids, using the chapter summaries they produced in a previous activity. The visual aids can be in the form of posters, maps, or diagrams. Tell students that their visual aids should make the important information, places, and events clear.

EXTEND Have each group write and perform a short oral essay about their chapter. Groups should explain their visual aids, as well as identify the main problems the person profiled in their chapter faced while traveling west.

ACCELERATED LEARNERS

Have students write a fictional story about a family traveling west from Missouri. The story should include facts they learned from the selection as well as troubles the family may encounter. They can choose to write the story as a first- or third-person narrative.

MORE SUPPORT

Unlock the Text

QUALITATIVE MEASURES

Levels of Meaning	narrative text that chronicles a girl's move out west in the 1800s; provides information about U.S. history
Structure	narrative told in chronological order; problems and solutions throughout
Language Conventionality and Clarity	commas, semicolons, and colons; domain-specific vocabulary (agricultural terms) defined in context
Knowledge Demands	basic knowledge of early settlers

Going West, pp. 70–117

Prepare to Read

LEVELS OF MEANING

Going West is a story about a young girl in the 1800s traveling with her family to start a new life in the West. The main purpose of this story is to tell how and why families chose to move west in the 1800s.

STRUCTURE

PREVIEW Have students do a picture walk of the illustrations in *Going West*. Use the Story Predictions Routine and Graphic Organizer in Part 3. Have students complete the first two columns of the graphic organizer. Ask: Based only on the title and illustrations, what do you think will happen in this story? (A family will travel and then build a house and farm.) What might be a main problem in this story? What in the pictures

ENGLISH LANGUAGE LEARNERS

Students who have difficulty understanding new vocabulary will benefit from creating their own picture cards for each word. They can write the word and definition on one side of the card and draw their illustration on the other side.

STRUGGLING READERS

If students need help getting started on their Quick Write and Share, provide them with these sentence frames: I think people move because ___. Some troubles I think people have when moving are ___. If I were moving, I would be afraid ___.

makes you think that? As students read the story, have them return to the graphic organizer to complete the last column, using evidence from the text.

LANGUAGE CONVENTIONALITY AND CLARITY

PREVIEW VOCABULARY Use the Preview and Review Vocabulary Routine in Part 3 to assess what students know about the following words: *farm*, *grow*, *planting*, *prairie*, *stable*, *soil*, *plowing*, *seeds*, and *sprouting*.

Use the words in sentences that relate to the context of the reading and in sentences that relate to situations outside of the classroom. Reinforce comprehension by relating the words to students' own experiences. Provide visual representations of the words when possible.

COGNATES Use the list of Spanish cognates at the beginning of this module to guide your Spanish-speaking students as they read the selection.

KNOWLEDGE DEMANDS

ACTIVATE BACKGROUND KNOWLEDGE Ask students to share what they know about moving to a new place. Use the Quick Write and Share Routine in Part 3 and ask: Why do people move to new places? What new opportunities might people find in new places? What do you think the scariest or most difficult part of moving would be? Why do you think that? Has your family ever made a big move? If so, what changed? What stayed the same?

Before students get started, model describing what you know about moving to a new place: My great-grandparents left their home in Sicily to start a new life in the United States of America. They were told that there was money to be made and work to be done in the new land, so they packed up what they could carry and left everything else behind. They had to meet new people and learn a new language. They were very brave.

Interact with Text

LEVELS OF MEANING

Ask students to work in small groups to determine the author's purpose. Ask students: What purpose might the author have had for writing this story? (to inform readers about the settlers) Have students use the Web Graphic Organizer in Part 3 to record details from the text that tell about life during the 1800s in America. Examples may include the following: few or no neighbors; vast grassland; winters with little food; scarce supply of food, such as bacon, flour, and sugar; Indians visiting; traveling by covered wagon; building their own cabin with a dirt floor.

STRUCTURE

Have students use the Sequence of Events Graphic Organizer in Part 3 to recall major events in the story. Remind them to cite specific examples from the text to support their responses. Ask: How does using a graphic organizer help you understand the order in which events happened? What other kind of organizer do you think might help you understand the sequence of events? (a time line)

If . . . students have difficulty following the sequence of events,

then . . . explain that the author uses the changing seasons to show the passage of time. Point out that the family begins the journey and finds a place to settle in the spring, survives a hailstorm during the hot summer and snowstorms during the frigid winter, and eventually plants new crops the following spring.

MORE SUPPORT

ENGLISH LANGUAGE LEARNERS

Have students record time-order words as they encounter them in the text. Students should record the time-order words and tell whether they indicate that something happened in the past, present, or future. Students will use these lists for future writing activities.

STRUGGLING READERS

To help students understand how time passes, review the four seasons with students. Ask volunteers to describe the weather in spring, summer, fall, and winter where they live and to tell things that happen during each season. Then have them discuss how each season might have affected pioneer travelers.

LANGUAGE CONVENTIONALITY AND CLARITY

Students may have difficulty understanding the use of commas, semicolons, and colons to separate ideas. Ask students to state the purpose of commas (to separate clauses or items in a sentence). Then briefly introduce semicolons and colons as another way to show a pause or separation between clauses or ideas.

Display and highlight the semicolons and colon in the sentence on p. 73, in which the narrator tells who the members of her family are. "There were five of us: Papa and Mama; me, Hannah, just turned seven; my little brother Jake; and Rebecca, a fat baby with yellow curls."

Ask students to think about strategies they can use to determine the meaning of complex sentences such as this one. Then have groups work together to rewrite the sentence in smaller parts. For example, students might revise the sentence to say: "There were five of us: Mama, Papa, Jake, Rebecca, and me. My name is Hannah. I am seven years old. Jake is my little brother. Rebecca is a fat baby with yellow curls."

If . . . students have difficulty rewriting the sentence,

then . . . use the Sentence Activities in Part 3 to provide students with practice identifying and writing simple, complex, and compound sentences.

KNOWLEDGE DEMANDS

Have students compare and contrast Hannah's story with one of the profiles they read in *Pioneers to the West* in a two- to three-paragraph essay. Make sure students understand that although Hannah is a fictional character, the experiences she has in the story could have happened in real life.

If . . . students have difficulty comparing and contrasting the two stories,

then . . . have them use the Venn Diagram Graphic Organizer in Part 3 to help them visualize how the two stories are similar and different.

For example, remind students of the story of George Staples, the boy whose family left him with the Sioux people because he was too sick to finish the trip west. George and Hannah both traveled to the West with their families to find a new home. Hannah and her family had to cross a deep river and endure some harsh weather. George fell ill and had to stay behind. Hannah was probably lonely because she had no neighbors. George was probably lonely because he and his neighbors spoke different languages. Both Hannah and George faced challenges, but their stories eventually had happy endings.

Express and Extend

LEVELS OF MEANING

EXPRESS The narrator in this story describes how the house Hannah's family builds on the prairie is transformed from a lonely, empty house to a place that feels like home. To better understand the deeper meaning of *home*, have students flip through the pages of the book and scan for the words *house* and *home*. Help them understand that when Hannah uses the term *home* at the beginning of the story, she is referring to the home her family left behind. The house Hannah's family built was only a shelter at first. It was a place where they slept, but it didn't feel like home. Eventually the new house started to feel like home. Help students understand that the people who visited the house, the neighbors who moved in next door, and the time the family spent together in the house helped make the house feel like more than a shelter—it made it feel like home.

EXTEND Have students write a paragraph that describes their home. Ask them to describe the building they live in, including the neighborhood. Then ask them to describe the things about where they live that make it feel like home. Tell them to relate these things to the things that made Hannah's house feel like home. Have partners share their writing.

STRUCTURE

EXPRESS Explain that some stories have more than one structure. While this story is told in sequential order, there are also multiple problems and solutions described. Have students work in small groups to explore strategies they can use to identify problems and solutions in a text. For example, students can look at their sequence of events graphic organizers to find the events that created problems (crossing the river) and their solutions (the horses swimming across the river with the wagon).

If . . . students have difficulty identifying the problems and solutions,

then . . . use the Problem and Solution Routine and Graphic Organizer in Part 3.

EXTEND Have students write a paragraph that tells about some of the problems early settlers faced during their move west and how the settlers solved those problems. Have them include evidence from both this story and previous selections. Have students share their writing in small groups.

ENGLISH LANGUAGE LEARNERS

To help students organize their problem-and-solution paragraphs, provide them with the following sentence frames: When ___ happened, the family was in danger; but then ___ happened. One of the family's major problems was ___. They addressed this by ___.

STRUGGLING READERS

Some students may struggle with rewriting the sentence that contains the list. To help these students, use the Sentence Activities in Part 3.

LANGUAGE CONVENTIONALITY AND CLARITY

EXPRESS Talk about Sentences and Words

Display the following excerpt from *Going West*. Read it aloud.

And then Papa came back. He brought flour and bacon and six sheep that he traded for one of the horses and a surprise: real white sugar.

Ask students to reread this excerpt aloud. Tell them that because the list is not in the typical list order, the second sentence can be a little confusing. Say: The author doesn't use commas between the items in the list. What does the author use instead? (the word *and* and a colon) Do you think the meaning of this sentence would be clearer if the author had used commas instead of the word *and* and a colon? Why or why not?

TEAM TALK Have partners count how many things Papa brought back with him and tell how they would rewrite the second sentence to make it clearer.

EXTEND Have students rewrite the second sentence in a way that is most clear to them. Have them create an illustration to show Papa coming back with the supplies. Have students share their sentence and illustration with the class.

KNOWLEDGE DEMANDS

EXPRESS Ask students to use what they know about this period in American history to make inferences about how Hannah and her family felt when the Indians came to visit. Have students find text evidence that shows how the characters respond to events in the story. Ask: How do you think Hannah and Jake feel when the Indians come to visit? (afraid) What in the text tells you this? (Jake hides under the bed, and Hannah trembles with fright.) How does Mama respond to the same event? (She bakes donuts and shares food with her visitors.) What do you think the children learned from watching Mama's behavior when the Indians came? (They saw that she was calm and treated the visitors respectfully so that they would treat her and her family the same way.) Why was this an important lesson? (They would likely encounter other native people and strangers in the West.)

EXTEND Using both this text and previous selections, have students create a how-to guide for moving to the West in the 1800s. Have them include problems and solutions relating to farming, encountering native people, and traveling in wagons. Have students trade their guide with a partner to read.

ACCELERATED LEARNERS

Have students expand on their how-to guide to include a list of supplies settlers will need. Their lists should explain why each item is important and when settlers might need to use each item.

Changing the World

TEXT SET

ANCHOR TEXT
68 Ways to Save the
Planet Before Bedtime

SUPPORTING TEXT
On Meadowview Street

TEXT SET

ANCHOR TEXT
Alfred Nobel

SUPPORTING TEXT
A Picture Book of
Eleanor Roosevelt

Cognates

Cognates are words that have similar spellings and meanings in two or more languages. Many words in English and Spanish share Greek or Latin roots, and many words in English came from French, which is closely connected to Spanish (and to Portuguese, Italian, and Romanian). Because of this, many literary, content, and academic process words in English (e.g., *gracious/gracioso; volcano/volcán; compare/comparar*) have recognizable Spanish cognates.

Making the connection to cognates permits students who are native Spanish speakers to understand the strong foundation they have in academic and literary English. These links between English and Spanish are also useful for native speakers of English and other languages because they help uncover basic underlying features of our language.

ANCHOR TEXT **68 Ways to Save the Planet Before Bedtime**

ENGLISH	SPANISH	ENGLISH	SPANISH
activity	actividad	important	importante
adult	adulto	impossible	imposible
air	aire	insects	insectos
aluminum	aluminio	message	mensaje
animals	animales	monsters	monstruos
area	área	mountain	montaña
atmosphere	atmósfera	oxygen	oxígeno
button	botón	paper	papel
carbon dioxide	dióxido de carbono	planet	planeta
causes	causa	plants	plantas
celebrate	celebrar	plastic	plástico
chemicals	químicos	pollution	polución
completely	completamente	possible	posible
computers	computadoras	problem	problema
effect	efecto	produces	produce
electricity	electricidad	reason	razón
energy	energía	recycle	recicla
extreme	extremas	reduce	reduce
fossil	fósil	refrigerator	refrigerador
fruit	fruta	seconds	segundos
gas	gas	superheroes	superhéroes
group	grupo	sweater	suéter
human	humano	symbols	símbolos
idea	idea	temperature	temperatura

SUPPORTING TEXT On Meadowview Street

ENGLISH	SPANISH		ENGLISH	SPANISH
admire	admirar		flower	flor
caverns	cavernas		garden	jardín
colors	colores		idea	idea
creatures	criaturas		insects	insectos
decide	decidir		perfect	perfecto
different	diferentes		plants	plantas
explore	explorar		plastic	plástico
family	familia		salamander	salamandra

These lists contain many, but not all, Spanish cognates from these selections.

Unlock the Text

QUALITATIVE MEASURES

Levels of Meaning	information with introductory problem ("global warming") followed by 68 suggestions, highly visual, about how a young person can take action to address the problem
Structure	Contents, then 2-page introduction followed by 68 distinct and discrete independent units of text, and glossary. Some are one-page, others are clusters of six. "Fast Fact" and "Top Tip" features throughout.
Language Conventionality and Clarity	Two-page introduction is scientific in tone; suggestions are written as imperative sentences; text includes lively diagrams, illustrations, and headings
Knowledge Demands	understanding of global warming and the planet as an environment

Prepare to Read

LEVELS OF MEANING

68 Ways to Save the Planet Before Bedtime begins with the definition and explanation of the problem of global warming, including an illustration. The even-numbered pages 4–20 introduce larger ideas with "Fast Facts" and "Top Tips." The odd-numbered pages 5–19 offer six or seven additional suggestions related to the information on the even pages. Despite the fact that the "ways" are organized in clusters by topic, all suggestions stand on their own. Beyond pages 2–3, students can read the ideas in any order.

ENGLISH LANGUAGE LEARNERS

Although S.O.S. is not an abbreviation, some people remember it by thinking that it stands for "Save Our Ship." Of course, this is only in English. Ask students to translate "Save Our Ship" into other languages. For example, in Spanish it would be SNB (*salvar a nuestro barco*).

STRUGGLING READERS

Point out that this writer asks a lot of questions. Ask students to find the seven questions on the first two pages. Read the questions aloud. Suggest that questions make the reader feel like they are an active part of the text. Point out the question about a question on page 23.

STRUCTURE

PREVIEW Point to the abbreviation S.O.S. Say: S.O.S. is a code used in radio signals. People use it all over the world to tell others that they are in distress or danger. Why do you think the writer uses this code in the first heading of this passage? (because Earth is in danger because of what humans are doing to it) Point to the three bullets on page 2. Explain that these are three effects of global warming. Make sure students understand the technical terms *temperature, sea levels,* and *fossil fuels.* Explain that global warming is the big problem that this passage is about. The writer will offer 68 ways that each person can help solve the problem.

LANGUAGE CONVENTIONALITY AND CLARITY

PREVIEW VOCABULARY Use the Preview and Review Vocabulary Routine in Part 3 to assess what students know about the following words: *resources, litter, waste, switch, reduce, produce, reuse,* and *reason.*

COGNATES Use the list of Spanish cognates at the beginning of this module to guide your Spanish-speaking students as they read the selection.

DOMAIN-SPECIFIC VOCABULARY Use the Vocabulary Activities in Part 3 to pre-teach the following words: *atmosphere, charity, devices, landfills, recycle,* and *pollution.*

KNOWLEDGE DEMANDS

ACTIVATE BACKGROUND KNOWLEDGE Point to the illustration of a spider on page 5 and the spider web on pages 4 and 5. Ask students to share their own experiences and feelings about spiders and spider webs. Ask questions such as: Have you ever seen a spider? Where? When? What did it look like? How big was it? Did it make you feel afraid? Why or why not? Point out the food chain diagram on page 4 and explain that spiders are an important part of a natural circle that includes birds and other insects, such as flies. Without spiders, the plants and animals mentioned in the circle would be put in danger. Point out that the illustration shows three aspects of spiders: eight legs, big eyes, and the ability to spin of to make their webs.

STRUGGLING READERS

Help students understand that when the writer places "ways" on one page, they are alike in some way. Challenge them to name the way the six "ways" on page 5 are alike. (They are all about nature: animals, plants, and outdoor areas.) Students can make similar observations about the clusters on the subsequent odd-numbered pages.

MORE SUPPORT

Interact with Text

As you read *68 Ways to Save the Planet Before Bedtime*, help students understand that the writer includes a lot of facts about nature and our habits along with the suggestions. Say: Some of the facts are in the Fast Fact features such as the one on page 5. These facts are things you might learn in school. The writer wants you to learn facts as well as learn about things you can do to help the planet. Remind students that facts are true for everyone. Opinions, on the other hand, may not be true for everyone. For example, on page 6, the sentence "The cotton has to go from the field to the mill and then to the factory to be made into a T-shirt" is a fact. It is true for everyone and cannot be argued with. On the other hand, the sentence, "Wear fewer clothes, and save the world!" expresses an opinion. Someone could argue against it. It may not be true for everyone.

If . . . students need support to distinguish between facts and opinions,

then . . . use the Tell What You Think Routine in Part 3 to explore how writers share their opinions.

STRUCTURE

As you read *68 Ways to Save the Planet Before Bedtime*, focus students' attention on the 68 headings. Some headings are simple statements, such as "Put on a hat." Others are intended to make the reader curious, such as "In place." Challenge students to go on a heading scavenger hunt to find examples such as these: Can you find a heading that tells you *not* to do something? ("Start a 'no-TV day'" on page 11 or "Don't drop it" on page 5) Can you find a heading that is an exclamation? ("Clean up!" on page 5 or "Celebrate!" on page 21) Can you find a heading that is puzzling until you read the whole box? ("Think fast" on page 11 or "Double it" on page 19) When students find the heading you've suggested, have them read the idea aloud.

MORE SUPPORT

ENGLISH LANGUAGE LEARNERS

Focus attention on headings that repeat initial consonant sounds (i.e. use alliteration). For example, point out "Poster power" on page 11. Exaggerate the alliteration as you say it aloud. Students can find examples and read them aloud.

STRUGGLING READERS

Make sure students understand that sometimes the writer refers to other suggestions in a tip. For example, on page 5, the last line of "Watch it!" refers to two other ideas on the same page. On pages 11, 13, and 22, the writer uses arrows to point to ideas that are related in some way to what is on the page.

LANGUAGE CONVENTIONALITY AND CLARITY

Most of the 68 ways are written using imperative sentences. Say: There are four kinds of sentences in English. Most sentences are statements that say that something is true. Other sentences ask questions. Some sentences exclaim! A fourth kind of sentence is a command. Commands give readers directions. They tell readers to do something. This writer uses commands in many of the ideas. Commands begin with verbs. Then, choose an idea that is written as a command, such as "Use the leg of old jeans as door draft stoppers." Explain that the subject of a command is "you" even though the word does not appear in the sentence. Challenge students to find other examples of commands.

If . . . students have difficulty understanding commands,

then . . . use the Type of Sentences: Commands Activity in Part 3 to further their understanding.

KNOWLEDGE DEMANDS

Focus students' attention on the idea of waste on page 12. Say: When people waste something, they use it carelessly or they use more than they need. What are some things that people waste? (paper, cans, bottles, food, time) Then, focus attention on the three words *Reduce, Reuse*, and *Recycle*, and make sure students understand what each word means. Explain that in two of these words, the prefix *re-* means "to do something again." Say: To reuse means "to use something again for the same purpose." To recycle means "to put something into a container so that it will be collected and used to make new things." *Reduce* simply means "to make something smaller, less, or fewer."

ENGLISH LANGUAGE LEARNERS

Explore other words that use the prefix *re-* to mean "to do something again." Ask students what happens when someone *rereads* a favorite book. What happens when an instant *replay* occurs in a football game? What happens when students *review* a lesson?

Express and Extend

EXPRESS Use idea 66 on page 21 to encourage students to look back at all of the ideas and group them. Explain that grouping ideas in these different ways is called categorizing, or putting single things into groups according to what they have in common. Say: There are many ways to put these ideas into groups. For example, idea 66 asks you to decide which of the ideas listed in the book can be done at school. Here are some other ways to group the suggestions: Which ones can be done outdoors? Which ones cost money? Which ones require help from an adult? Which ones involve organizing a project?

> **If . . .** you want students to record the categories and the ideas that belong to them,
>
> **then . . .** use the Three-Column Chart Graphic Organizer from Part 3 to track and record their observations.

EXTEND Have students think of their own category to organize the ideas. For example, they might choose Things You Can Do Alone or Things that Require Other People.

EXPRESS Focus attention on the word *save*. Ask: Can one person really "save the world" by doing these simple things? Explain that the writer clearly believes that tiny steps taken by many individuals will make a huge difference in the future of the whole planet. The phrase "one small step at a time" on page 3 shows that the writer believes that a long journey (saving the planet) begins with a single step (What can I do?) Ask: What does it mean to save something? (to keep it safe, to rescue it, to store it up for future use) What other things can a person save? (an animal, money, a document on the computer)

EXTEND Encourage students to share a time where they saved something. Maybe it was a plant that needed water or a pet their family adopted. Ask: Is saving something always a good thing? Encourage discussion and broad thinking about this concept.

ENGLISH LANGUAGE LEARNERS

Lead a choral reading of the story on p. 22 that begins "One day a *cavewoman* . . ." (Help them understand *cavewoman* and *Presto!* if needed.) Have them repeat the reading several times, adding more drama and expression each time.

STRUGGLING READERS

Point out that the phrase "save the world" (or "saving the world") appears on all of the one-page ideas. Repeating key words is one way to make writing fit together into one whole passage. Ask them to name and find other key words that repeat (*recycle, waste, less, heat*).

LANGUAGE CONVENTIONALITY AND CLARITY

EXPRESS Talk about Sentences and Words

Display and read aloud the following sentence from page 16 of *68 Ways to Save the Planet Before Bedtime.*

> Bikes are way better than cars, for loads of reasons. The main reason is that they don't let out greenhouse gases. Oh, and they don't get stuck in traffic jams either! A bike can take you practically anywhere.

Point out that the writer states an opinion in the first sentence. Say: Words like *way better* signal that the writer is expressing an opinion, not a fact. This sentence is not true for everyone. The writer supports his opinion with three reasons: 1. Bikes don't let out greenhouse gases, 2. Bikes don't get stuck in traffic jams, and 3. Bikes can take you practically anywhere. Explain that this is a very common pattern in writing: stating an opinion and then supporting the opinion with three reasons.

TEAM TALK Have partners work in pairs to choose two ideas that they found most helpful or interesting. Have them support their choices by giving two or three reasons for each one.

EXTEND Ask students to express their opinions about this selection. Help them see that words such as *fun, lively, colorful,* or *entertaining* express opinions. To support these opinions, they need to give reasons and examples from the text.

KNOWLEDGE DEMANDS

EXPRESS After reading the passage, refocus students' attention on the problem of global warming as it is described on pages 2 and 3. Ask: Which ideas do you think are the best solutions to the problem of global warming? Remind them that the answer to this question is their opinion. They should be able to support their opinions with reasons.

> **If . . .** students need help organizing their thoughts about which ideas are best,
>
> **then . . .** have them use the Main Ideas and Details Graphic Organizer in Part 3 to organize their choices and reasons.

EXTEND Encourage students to think of one more way they might help solve the problem of global warming. Have them write a heading and then describe the action in 1–3 sentences, using the same style as the other suggestions in the book. Have them illustrate their idea.

ACCELERATED LEARNERS

Challenge students to find out how your school heats and/or cools its indoor environment. Does it depend on fossil fuels such as coal, oil, or gas? If so, what does your school do to make sure it does not waste energy or fuel? If possible, invite someone from your school's maintenance department to come in and speak to your class. Ask them what their department is doing to save energy costs and to prevent global warming "one step at a time."

68 Ways to Save the Planet Before Bedtime   **163**

Unlock the Text

QUALITATIVE MEASURES

Levels of Meaning	explicit tale of a young girl who creates a meadow in her yard; implicit lesson of leading by example to make a difference
Structure	chronological sequence of events; variety of text placement; detailed illustrations contribute to understanding of text; labels
Language Conventionality and Clarity	dialogue; possessive nouns
Knowledge Demands	suburban neighborhoods; lawns; wildflowers and meadows; wildlife

Henry Cole

Prepare to Read

LEVELS OF MEANING

On Meadowview Street tells the tale of a young girl who cares for and transforms her suburban lawn into a meadow that provides a home for many creatures. An implicit message is that even young children can make a difference in the world around them.

STRUCTURE

PREVIEW Have students preview the title and illustrations in *On Meadowview Street* to formulate a prediction of what the story will be about. Ask: What clues tell the setting of this story? (The illustrations show a suburban neighborhood. The title and the first illustration tell us the name of the street.) Can you identify some of the main characters of the story based on the pictures? (a girl and her father) What can you predict

ENGLISH LANGUAGE LEARNERS

Make a word wall of terms related to meadows. Provide pictures or samples of flowers and seeds to show students. Also show pictures of meadows along with insects, birds, and other creatures that live in meadows.

STRUGGLING READERS

Some students may have difficulty grasping the vivid details presented in the story. As students read, take time to help them visualize passages that contain sensory details, such as this one: "In no time there were birds and insects everywhere, around the tree and zipping among the flowers."

about the story? (With some help from her father, the girl will grow a large meadow in her yard.)

PREVIEW VOCABULARY Use the Preview and Review Vocabulary Routine in Part 3 to assess what students know about the following words: *meadow, blossom, mower, halt, pleaded, wildflower, preserve, wren, admired, lugged, ledges, caverns, creatures.*

COGNATES Use the list of Spanish cognates at the beginning of this module to guide your Spanish-speaking students as they read the selection.

KNOWLEDGE DEMANDS

ACTIVATE BACKGROUND KNOWLEDGE There are many interesting topics addressed in this story. Use the Quick Write and Share Routine in Part 3 to assess what students know about the following topics: suburban neighborhoods, lawns, wildflowers, meadows, wildlife. **Ask:** What do lawns usually look like in suburban neighborhoods? Where do wildflowers typically grow? What types of creatures can you find in a meadow?

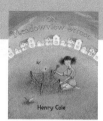

Interact with Text

As you read *On Meadowview Street,* periodically stop to assess students' understanding of the order of events.

> **If . . .** students have difficulty understanding the order Caroline follows when creating the meadow,
>
> **then . . .** use the Sequence of Events Routine and Graphic Organizer in Part 3 to help students understand how Caroline creates a meadow in her yard.

Ask questions to guide students' thought process, such as: What does Caroline notice after asking her dad to mow around the wildflower? (More wildflowers began to grow.) What happens after more wildflowers start to grow in the lawn? (Caroline plants a tree, builds a birdhouse, and constructs a pond in her yard.) Complete the graphic organizer together, and then review the events.

STRUCTURE

The text in this selection is placed in varying positions throughout the book. As students read, have them be mindful of the flow of the text. Remind them of the proper order of reading from left to right, and from top to bottom. Have them use their fingers to point to each chunk of text as they read. Tell them if something doesn't make sense as they read, they should check that they are reading the text in the correct order.

ENGLISH LANGUAGE LEARNERS

Use the illustration for each event to help students understand what is happening. Begin by asking students to identify what the characters in the picture are doing. Then have them compare what they learned from the illustration to the surrounding text on the page.

STRUGGLING READERS

Grouping words by category is helpful for remembering new words. As a class, compile a list of words in the text that relate to meadows and wildlife, such as *wildflower*, *bird nest*, *maple tree*, and *wren*. Use pp. 28–29 as a starting point to gather words. Invite students to suggest a sentence for each of the chosen words.

As students read, periodically stop to assess their understanding of the story's dialogue. Point out the use of quotation marks in the story. Have students explain how quotation marks are used in the story.

If . . . students have difficulty understanding dialogue within the story,

then . . . have students look at passages with quotation marks and identify who is speaking.

For example, display and read aloud the following sentences:

"Daddy!" Caroline pleaded. "Couldn't you mow around my flower?"
"Hmph," he said, thinking, *Well, that's less mowing for me!*

Ask: What does Caroline's father say? ("Hmph") How do you know? (There are quotation marks around his response.) How does the author show that a character is thinking about something, rather than saying it out loud? (He uses italics, such as in, *Well, that's less mowing for me!*)

Some students may be confused by the concept of wildflowers. Explain to students that wildflowers are different from flowers that people typically plant in gardens. Wildflowers are plants that grow naturally in an open area, often without being planted by humans. Ask: Is Caroline busily planting the wildflowers in her yard? (No, they are naturally growing there.)

MORE SUPPORT

Henry Cole

Express and Extend

EXPRESS The concept of taking initiative is a main theme in this story. By creating a beautiful meadow in her backyard, Caroline inspires her neighbors to stop mowing their lawns and allow nature to take over. Caroline's mission may have begun out of curiosity and caring for one little flower, but it quickly turned into an environmental movement to create a beautiful space that people and wildlife can share. Use the Cause and Effect Routine and Graphic Organizer in Part 3 with students to record Caroline's actions and the resulting effects. Discuss how certain events prompt Caroline to do certain things. For example, when Caroline notices that her yard is very hot, she plants a maple tree to provide shade.

EXTEND Have students consider ways that children in other communities can introduce more nature and wildlife into their lives. For example, children living in a city might plant a small window garden or work in a community garden. Have small groups create a list of ideas to share with the class.

STRUCTURE

EXPRESS Have small groups discuss how the varying placement of the text coordinates with the illustrations. Ask: Does the placement of the text relate to the illustrations? How do you know? How do the illustrations contribute to the understanding of the text? What is the purpose of the labels?

EXTEND Have students write a fictitious article for the Meadowview newspaper about the girl who created a meadow in her yard. Articles should include a title, a description of the sequence of events as they happened, a summary of Caroline's achievement, and an illustration that coordinates with one part of the text. Have students share their articles with a partner. Have partners identify how the illustration complements the text.

ENGLISH LANGUAGE LEARNERS

Remind students that we form the possessive of most singular nouns by adding an apostrophe and s. We form the possessive of most plural nouns by adding an apostrophe only. Write examples on the board using students' names. For example, [Maria's] bike; [Henry's] soccer ball; all the boys' backpacks.

STRUGGLING READERS

Provide sentence frames to assist students in contributing to group discussions. For example, This illustration relates to the text by ___. The illustration helps me understand this page because ___.

MORE SUPPORT

EXPRESS Talk about Sentences and Words

Display the following passage from *On Meadowview Street,* and read it aloud with students:

> The more Caroline and her family worked on their yard, the more it changed. It was now a home to many things. And soon, the Jacksons' yard changed. And the Smiths'. And the Sotos'.

Explain to students that this passage contains possessive nouns. A possessive noun is a noun that shows ownership. Apostrophes are often used to show possession. For example, "the Jacksons' yard changed." The apostrophe shows that the yard belongs to the Jacksons. And because *Jacksons* is plural, we place the apostrophe after the *s.* Have students identify the other possessive nouns in the passage. Use the Noun Activities in Part 3 for additional practice, if needed.

TEAM TALK Have partners reread the passage and determine what belongs to the Smiths and what belongs to the Sotos. There is an apostrophe after their names, but there is no word to indicate what belongs to them. Explain that the writer is *implying* that their yards changed as well.

EXTEND Have students find other examples of possessive nouns in the text and determine the owner and the object that is possessed.

EXPRESS Have students synthesize what they have learned about creating a wildflower meadow in a three-paragraph essay.

> If . . . students have difficulty determining what to include in three paragraphs,
>
> then . . . provide sentence frames to help students formulate their paragraphs: Meadows need ___ to grow. ___ are found in meadows. A ___ is an animal that lives in a meadow.

Have students use one of these three sentences as a main idea for each of their three paragraphs. They should then expand on the topic by adding additional information about what meadows need, which plants are found in meadows, and the types of animals that live in meadows. Remind them to refer to the selection for support.

EXTEND Have students create a public awareness poster explaining how neighborhoods can create their own meadows. Students should include evidence from the text, as well as any additional information that they can find. Have students share their poster with the class.

ACCELERATED LEARNERS

Have students use the Story Comparison Graphic Organizer in Part 3 as a guide in comparing Caroline's actions to those of other characters in stories they've read. Have students write a paragraph, citing evidence from both texts, telling how the two are similar.

MORE SUPPORT

Cognates

Cognates are words that have similar spellings and meanings in two or more languages. Many words in English and Spanish share Greek or Latin roots, and many words in English came from French, which is closely connected to Spanish (and to Portuguese, Italian, and Romanian). Because of this, many literary, content, and academic process words in English (e.g., *gracious/gracioso; volcano/volcán; compare/comparar*) have recognizable Spanish cognates.

Making the connection to cognates permits students who are native Spanish speakers to understand the strong foundation they have in academic and literary English. These links between English and Spanish are also useful for native speakers of English and other languages because they help uncover basic underlying features of our language.

ANCHOR TEXT Alfred Nobel: The Man Behind the Peace Prize

ENGLISH	SPANISH	ENGLISH	SPANISH
announcement	anuncio	literature	literatura
art	arte	medicine	medicina
attack	ataque	obituary	obituario
chemistry	química	organizations	organizaciones
create	crear	physics	física
different	diferentes	physiology	fisiología
dynamite	dinamita	poetry	poesía
equal	igual	problems	problemas
escape	escapar	proved	probar
experimented	experimentar	science	ciencias
exploded	explotar	services	servicios
explosions	explosiones	solve	resolver
famous	famoso	special	especial
individuals	individuos	tragedy	tragedia
invention	invención		

SUPPORTING TEXT A Picture Book of Eleanor Roosevelt

ENGLISH	SPANISH		ENGLISH	SPANISH
admire	admirar		October	octubre
attacked	atacadas		others	otros
attention	atención		polio	polio
detailed	detallados		political	políticas
devotion	devoción		popular	popular
differences	diferencias		president	presidente
distant	distante		public	público
elected	elegido		pure	puro
enter	entrar		reports	reportes
importance	importancia		representative	representante
important	importante		retire	retirar
infant	infante		revolution	revolución
interested	interesados		serious	seria
leaders	líderes		servants	sirvientes
millions	millones		strict	estrictas
mines	minas		students	estudiantes
minorities	minorías		United Nations	Naciones Unidas
November	noviembre			

These lists contain many, but not all, Spanish cognates from these selections.

Unlock the Text

QUALITATIVE MEASURES

Levels of Meaning	biography of Alfred Nobel, the Swedish inventor of dynamite and the founder of the Nobel Peace Prize; themes of generosity and promoting peace
Structure	information presented in chronological order; detailed illustrations
Language Conventionality and Clarity	vocabulary acquisition; scientific terms
Knowledge Demands	inventions; lab experiments and safety precautions; Nobel Foundation/Nobel Peace Prize

ReadyGEN
Text Collection 2

Alfred Nobel: The Man Behind the Peace Prize, pp. 123–151

Prepare to Read

LEVELS OF MEANING

Alfred Nobel: The Man Behind the Peace Prize is a biography of Alfred Nobel, the Swedish inventor who is best known for inventing dynamite. He intended for his invention to be used to create safer methods of bridge and road construction and was dismayed when people began using dynamite as a military weapon. This book takes readers through key events in Nobel's life that led to his creation of the Nobel Peace Prize.

STRUCTURE

PREVIEW Have students preview the text by reading the title and looking at the illustrations. Ask: Based on the title and what you see in the illustrations, what do you think this book will be about? (Alfred Nobel's life) Explain that this selection is a biography. Ask: What do biographies usually tell us? (They tell about a person's life.) What can you tell about Alfred Nobel by looking at the illustrations?

ENGLISH LANGUAGE LEARNERS

Have students do a picture walk through the text, pausing on each page to tell you or a partner what they think is happening in the illustration. Tell them to remember their predictions as they read to see if the text confirms them.

STRUGGLING READERS

Help students with underdeveloped vocabularies improve their reading comprehension by helping them create a set of picture cards to use while reading. Make cards for the vocabulary words, as well as any other terms that may be difficult for your students. Include the words, the definitions, and an illustration for each word.

LANGUAGE CONVENTIONALITY AND CLARITY

PREVIEW VOCABULARY Use the Preview and Review Vocabulary Routine in Part 3 to assess what students know about the following words: *peace*, *ignite*, *gunpowder*, *blasting cap*, *tragedy*, *dynamite*, *obituary*, *services*, *pleased*, *wealthy*, *rendered*, *physics*, *physiology*, *literature*, and *legacy*.

COGNATES Use the list of Spanish cognates at the beginning of this module to guide your Spanish-speaking students as they read the selection.

KNOWLEDGE DEMANDS

ACTIVATE BACKGROUND KNOWLEDGE Ask students if they have ever heard of Alfred Nobel. Then ask if they have heard of the Nobel Peace Prize. To help students gain confidence before reading and to ensure that everyone has some foundational understanding of the text, read aloud p. 130. Then ask: What do you learn about Alfred Nobel on this page? (He has a brother. He makes and sells something called blasting oil.) What did Alfred want people to use blasting oil for? (to build roads, railways, bridges, ports, and towns) Reread the title of the book aloud for students. Ask: What do you think blasting oil has to do with the Peace Prize?

Interact with Text

As you read *Alfred Nobel: The Man Behind the Peace Prize,* periodically stop to assess students' level of understanding of how Nobel invented dynamite.

> **If . . .** students have difficulty understanding Nobel's invention,
>
> **then . . .** have students reread the text on p. 136, which describes the process of igniting nitroglycerin in a way that is safer for workers.

Have students look at the illustration of Nobel's notebook on p. 136 as they read the text. Explain how Nobel created blasting oil and how his method of containing explosives in a bottle and using a blasting cap made it safer for construction workers to handle.

STRUCTURE

As students read, periodically stop to assess their understanding of the chronological features in the biography. Use the Time Line Routine and Graphic Organizer in Part 3 to record the key events in Alfred Nobel's life.

Start by drawing students' attention to the passage that tells how Nobel loved literature and poetry as much as science and chemistry. Explain that Nobel decided science would be the best profession to pursue because he could make money. Then discuss the events that led to Nobel inventing blasting oil and then dynamite. (Nobel and his brother make and sell blasting oil. Emil and other people die in an explosion. Nobel works to create a safer product. Nobel invents dynamite. Nobel becomes famous and wealthy. People use dynamite to harm others, not to help others.) Have students record these events in chronological order on the time line. In lieu of dates, have students number the events.

> **If . . .** students have difficulty recording events on the time line,
>
> **then . . .** work with them to identify time-order words and phrases in the text, such as *not long after*, *one day*, *two years after*, and *one morning*.

ENGLISH LANGUAGE LEARNERS

Display a chart of time-order words for students to use as a reference. Periodically review the words and talk about what they mean. Tell students to look for these words when they read to help them understand the order of events.

STRUGGLING READERS

When reading, pause after a key event in Nobel's life to make sure students understand and remember what happened. Ask students to summarize what has happened. Remind students to use this strategy when reading independently.

MORE SUPPORT

LANGUAGE CONVENTIONALITY AND CLARITY

This story uses a number of scientific terms and science-related words.

If . . . students have difficulty understanding and remembering these words,

then . . . create a list of scientific terms and science-related words that are found in the text, such as *nitroglycerin, dynamite, gunpowder, chemistry*, and *rods*.

Have students look up in print or online dictionaries the unfamiliar terms. Next to each word on the list, write a definition for or draw a picture of the word. Display this list in the classroom for students to refer to as they read. Explain that knowing the meaning of these terms will help them better understand the text.

KNOWLEDGE DEMANDS

Students may not have experience with reading about science and chemistry. Have students discuss the dangers of working with science materials and the necessary safety precautions a person should take when performing a science experiment at school. Then, have them locate places in the text where Alfred Nobel discusses safety in science and chemistry. Have them create a T-chart with the labels *Our Lab Safety Rules* and *Alfred's Lab Safety,* and record these rules and text examples in the appropriate columns.

ENGLISH LANGUAGE LEARNERS

Help students assess their knowledge of rich, expressive vocabulary words by providing the following statements for them to use as they read: 1. I do not know the word; 2. I have seen this word before. I think I know what the word means; 3. I have used this word before. I can say it in a sentence; 4. I can explain this word to someone else.

MORE SUPPORT

Express and Extend

LEVELS OF MEANING

EXPRESS Generosity and promoting peace are themes in this selection. Have students discuss how Alfred Nobel wanted his invention to be used (to better society) and how it was ultimately used (as a destructive device). Ask: How did Alfred Nobel feel about the way people used his invention? Tell students to cite text evidence when giving their responses. Point out that people started to associate Nobel's name with destruction. Nobel was concerned about how the world would remember him, especially after reading the erroneous obituary. Ask: How did the way people used Nobel's invention lead him to create the Nobel Peace Prize?

> If . . . students have difficulty identifying the theme of this story,
>
> then . . . do a close reading of p. 142 and ask: How would you feel if you invented something to help people only to find out that it was being used to hurt people? Do you think that experience might motivate you to create something that would promote peace? Why or why not?

EXTEND Have students write a paragraph telling whether they think Alfred Nobel would be happy with his legacy. Have partners exchange their writing and discuss their ideas.

STRUCTURE

EXPRESS Choose two important illustrations in the text that add meaning to the main idea and theme of the selection. Ask students what details the illustrations show that the main text does not. Have them share in small groups.

EXTEND Have students each write three sentences giving their opinion about what they think were Alfred Nobel's most important contributions to society. Students should cite text evidence in their writing. Have students create an illustration or collage to accompany their answers. Students can share their opinions and illustrations in small groups.

MORE SUPPORT

ENGLISH LANGUAGE LEARNERS

Students may have difficulty organizing their thoughts before writing. Provide students with copies of three graphic organizers. Have students form small brainstorming groups to decide which graphic organizer will help them with each writing assignment. Emphasize that what works for one student may not work for another.

STRUGGLING READERS

Students may need additional structure for writing assignments. Provide the following sentence frames for their opinion sentences: Alfred Nobel valued ___. Alfred Nobel did not like ___. I think Alfred Nobel's most important contribution was ___. I think this because ___

LANGUAGE CONVENTIONALITY AND CLARITY

EXPRESS **Talk about Sentences and Words**

Display the following passage from *Alfred Nobel: The Man Behind the Peace Prize*. Read it aloud with students.

> So on that very day, Alfred Nobel, the man who loved literature and poetry and the art of discovery, left a legacy to be remembered for always—as the man who founded what became known throughout the world as The Nobel Prizes.

Ask: What does the word *legacy* mean? ("something handed down from a predecessor or from the past") Do you think that Alfred Nobel would be happy to know that people think about these prestigious prizes when they hear his name, rather than think of him as the inventor of dynamite? Why or why not?

TEAM TALK Have students work in small groups to discuss how Alfred Nobel felt upon discovering his own obituary and the steps he took to change the world's perception of his values.

EXTEND Have students write a short paragraph describing the legacy that they would like to leave in the world. Have students explain what lessons they learned from reading about Alfred Nobel. Help students brainstorm altruistic virtues or actions they would take to make the world a better place. Ask student volunteers to share their paragraphs with the class.

KNOWLEDGE DEMANDS

EXPRESS Have students work in small groups to discuss what they learned about Alfred Nobel and the Nobel Prizes. Have them create a list of qualities that a person or organization should have in order to receive a Nobel Peace Prize.

EXTEND The list of Nobel Peace Prize winners ends with the 2008 winner. Provide students with books or online resources, and ask them to make a list of the Nobel Peace Prize recipients since 2009. Have them write a paragraph that describes something that all of the recipients have in common, besides winning the Nobel Peace Prize.

If . . . students have difficulty writing their paragraphs,

then . . . provide them with copies of the Web Graphic Organizer from Part 3. As students research the recipients, have them take notes about each person's life, career, accomplishments, and so on. When students are ready to write their paragraphs, they can use their webs to look for similarities among the recipients.

ACCELERATED LEARNERS

Have students think of one invention, accomplishment, or service they think is deserving of a Nobel Prize, in any category. Tell them the idea does not need to be something they can actually make or do—it just needs to be a great idea. Then have them write a persuasive paragraph about why this idea is deserving of the prize.

MORE SUPPORT

Alfred Nobel **177**

Unlock the Text

QUALITATIVE MEASURES

Levels of Meaning	biography focused on the life of First Lady Eleanor Roosevelt; Eleanor's character traits and contributions; U.S. history
Structure	biography; illustrations; chronological order
Language Conventionality and Clarity	vocabulary acquisition; political terminology
Knowledge Demands	presidential duties; role of the first lady

ReadyGEN
Text Collection 2

A Picture Book of
Eleanor Roosevelt,
pp. 153–183

Prepare to Read

LEVELS OF MEANING

A Picture Book of Eleanor Roosevelt tells in chronological order the life
story of First Lady Eleanor Roosevelt. It includes historical events in U.S.
history, as well as personal events in Eleanor's life.

STRUCTURE

PREVIEW Have students preview the selection and take note of anything
that stands out in the illustrations. Ask: What do you notice about the
illustrations in the story? (They begin with Eleanor as a young girl and
then show her as an adult.) Based on the illustration on pages 170 and
171, what do you think Eleanor did as an adult? (I see red, white, and blue
banners, so I think she did something patriotic.) What type of selection do
you think this will be? Why?

MORE SUPPORT

ENGLISH LANGUAGE LEARNERS

Use photos, illustrations, or video clips to help
students understand some of the vocabulary
words. Then have students take turns using the
words in sentences. Have students share their
sentences with the group.

STRUGGLING READERS

Have students create a vocabulary journal for this
selection. Have them record vocabulary words with
illustrations or brief definitions. During reading,
students can record predictions, summaries, and
lingering questions in the journal.

LANGUAGE CONVENTIONALITY AND CLARITY

PREVIEW VOCABULARY Use the Preview and Review Vocabulary Routine in Part 3 to assess what students know about the following words and phrases: *president, servants, campaign, polio, political, first lady, Great Depression, minorities, women's rights, mourned, representative,* and *human rights.*

COGNATES Use the list of Spanish cognates at the beginning of this module to guide your Spanish-speaking students as they read the selection.

KNOWLEDGE DEMANDS

ACTIVATE BACKGROUND KNOWLEDGE Ask students to share what they know about the roles of president and first lady of the United States. Use the Quick Write and Share Routine in Part 3 and ask: What are some key responsibilities of the president of the United States? What roles does the first lady of the United States have? Can you name the current president and first lady? What other first ladies can you name? What did they do for the country?

Interact with Text

LEVELS OF MEANING

As you read *A Picture Book of Eleanor Roosevelt,* periodically stop to assess students' understanding of Eleanor's character.

Discuss each example of Eleanor's bravery in the narrative. Lead students to understand that these acts of bravery show that Eleanor was a strong, determined woman who had empathy for others because of her own experiences. For example, call students' attention to pp. 154–156. Discuss with students how Eleanor must have felt when she was orphaned and how it would feel to be nicknamed "Granny" as a child.

STRUCTURE

Explain that biographies typically follow a chronological order. As students read, periodically stop to assess their understanding of the chronology of the text.

If . . . students struggle to follow the chronological order,

then . . . use the Time Line Routine and Graphic Organizer in Part 3. Have students record on the time line events that occurred in Eleanor's life.

For example, have students find dates within the text and record them on their time lines. Then have them write one short sentence detailing the event that happened on that date. Students may wish to create small illustrations that help them remember the event, such as an American flag for 1932 when FDR was elected president.

ENGLISH LANGUAGE LEARNERS

Some expressions in the text may be confusing for students, such as *lost their jobs* or *campaign for public office.* Use the Analyze Idioms and Expressions Routine in Part 3 to provide more practice for students as they internalize specific expressions and phrases.

STRUGGLING READERS

Students may need help describing Eleanor's character traits. Create a web graphic organizer with Eleanor Roosevelt in the center. Invite students to suggest words that describe Eleanor to complete the web. Have students refer to the selection for ideas.

LANGUAGE CONVENTIONALITY AND CLARITY

This selection includes political terms that students may have difficulty understanding.

If . . . students need additional help understanding these terms,

then . . . have them place a sticky note in the text near unfamiliar political terms.

Students can work in groups to define these terms based on experience and context clues. Have groups explain the meanings to the class, and have them use the terms in sentences.

For example, students may have difficulty with the following sentence on p. 168: "Eleanor helped Franklin campaign for public office." Ask students if they have ever heard the word *campaign* used around election time. Explain that *campaign* is a term for a series of activities designed to achieve a certain goal, in this case, to win an election—a political campaign.

KNOWLEDGE DEMANDS

Have small groups discuss *A Picture Book of Eleanor Roosevelt.* Then have them create a brief presentation about one period of Eleanor's life—her childhood and young adult life, her time as a first lady, or her time after living in the White House.

For their presentations, have students include any trouble Eleanor faced, how she overcame it, and the goals she had. Tell students to include illustrations or other visuals to make the presentation more interesting.

Express and Extend

LEVELS OF MEANING

EXPRESS Biographies are based on historical facts and records. Although the reader gets some insight into Eleanor's personality, another focus of the story is on how she fought for the rights of others. Lead a discussion on Eleanor's contributions to those in need and her motivations for helping others. Ask: Whom did Eleanor aim to help? How do you know this? What did she do to help these people?

EXTEND Using a T-chart graphic organizer titled *Eleanor's Contributions,* place events in U.S. history in the left column (the Great Depression, the bombing of Pearl Harbor, or the formation of the United Nations). In the right column, have students write a short description of Eleanor's contribution to each event. Have partners share their ideas.

STRUCTURE

EXPRESS Have small groups use the Story Map A Graphic Organizer in Part 3 to summarize what happens during the beginning, middle, and end of *A Picture Book of Eleanor Roosevelt.* Remind students to think about the most important events that took place in the story and then summarize those events, rather than telling every detail.

If . . . students have difficulty completing the story map,

then . . . help them identify major events that happened during Eleanor's childhood, her early married years, and as first lady.

EXTEND Have students write an opinion paragraph about the event in Eleanor's life they think was most significant. Tell students there are no right or wrong answers, but they must justify their opinion with reasons and support from the text. Have students share their writing in small groups.

MORE SUPPORT

ENGLISH LANGUAGE LEARNERS

Help students summarize the story by having them complete the following sentence frames: Eleanor was taught the importance of helping others by ___. This was a lesson she took seriously in her role as ___.

STRUGGLING READERS

Have a group discussion with students about the themes of the story. Ask questions, such as the following: What are some of the ways Eleanor showed kindness? How did Eleanor exhibit her leadership qualities? Can you find an example of Eleanor's personal strength?

EXPRESS Talk about Sentences and Words

Display the following sentences from *A Picture Book of Eleanor Roosevelt.* Read it aloud with students.

> Eleanor didn't wait to do things. Her motto was, "Tomorrow is now."

Discuss the meaning of the sentences with students. Ask: What is a motto? (a short phrase that tells the beliefs of a person or group) What does the motto "Tomorrow is now" mean? (It means you shouldn't wait to do something important.)

TEAM TALK Have partners reread the sentences and discuss how they can apply Eleanor's motto to their own lives.

EXTEND Have students create a motto of their own. Tell them to think about their ideals and values and come up with a motto that would help them be better members of society. Have students write their motto on a sheet of paper and then display it in the classroom.

KNOWLEDGE DEMANDS

EXPRESS Have partners discuss what they learned about the life of Eleanor Roosevelt. Have them decide on the three most important facts about Eleanor that they would want to tell their families. Record their ideas.

EXTEND This story about Eleanor Roosevelt presents a positive message about service to one's country. It details Eleanor's determination to succeed in the face of difficulty. Have students write a short paragraph about how Eleanor's story is an inspiration to them. Have partners share their paragraphs.

ACCELERATED LEARNERS

Have students research another woman in politics. Explain that they can research another first lady or any other woman involved in politics. If needed, provide students with a list of possible women to research. Students should research the position the woman held or holds, what her responsibilities in that position were or are, and whether any other woman has ever held that same position. Tell students to write about how the woman is similar to and different from Eleanor Roosevelt.

Unlock the Writing

Part 2 Unlock the Writing

Scaffolded Lessons for the Performance-Based Assessments

Unlock the Task: Write A New Story

Distribute copies of the task found on page 146 of the Teacher's Guide. Read the task together. Guide students to identify important key words or phrases to highlight in the task that can help them better understand what to do and how to do it. Have students highlight the agreed-upon key words and phrases.

> Write a narrative in which you write a new story using the characters from *Trouble at the Sandbox*. You may draw or describe the characters and setting. You will write a short sequence of events with a beginning, middle, and end. Use signal words to show sequence of events.

ANSWER QUESTIONS ABOUT THE TASK

Remind students of the questions they should be able to answer in order to demonstrate their understanding of the task. Display the questions for all to see. Tell students to look at the words and phrases they highlighted to help them answer the questions listed below. As students become familiar with this process, you may provide the questions as a handout for students to complete individually. Monitor students to determine who needs more support and who is ready to work independently.

- **What type of writing is this?** (narrative)
- **What will the text of my writing look like?** (a new story from *Trouble at the Sandbox*)
- **What text should I reference?** *(Trouble at the Sandbox)*
- **What details should I give?** (descriptions of the characters and setting; descriptions of the actions, thoughts, and feelings of the characters in the story)
- **What do I need to include?** (sequence of events with a beginning, middle, and end; signal words)

RESTATE THE TASK

Have students restate the task in their own words. Check for possible misunderstandings or missing elements.

ENGLISH LANGUAGE LEARNERS

If . . . students do not yet understand the difference between a story and an event,

then . . . explain that an event is a particular occurrence that happens in a story, and that a story consists of a series of events as well as the setting and characters involved in the events. Review stories students have read and identify examples that are made up of several events.

STRUGGLING WRITERS

If . . . students are confused and disorganized when figuring out how to approach this writing task,

then . . . guide students in selecting a line from the story that suggests something is about to happen, or a part of the story they wish had happened differently. Once students have chosen a line, have students think about what they think will happen next, or what they wish would have happened instead. Suggest the use of a graphic organizer to keep track of the setting, characters, and events as students brainstorm.

Prepare to Write

DETERMINE FOCUS

Once students clearly understand the writing task, have them review *Trouble at the Sandbox*. Have students use the Contents page to help them locate and skim their favorite parts instead of spending time flipping through the book page by page. Suggest that students place sticky notes next to illustrations or paragraphs that they might want to set their story after. Encourage students to flag several ideas quickly so they have several possibilities from which to choose.

Have students review the parts of the story they have flagged and decide what their new event will be about. Remind them that they should decide which characters from the story they will use and that their new story should follow logically from what has happened before. Remind them to identify whose point of view the story will be told from and be sure they stay with that character throughout.

GATHER IDEAS

Once students have decided on the event they want to write about, have them put together ideas for their narratives. Remind them that their scene should have a clear beginning, middle, and ending. Model how to use the Story Map A Graphic Organizer in Part 3 to plan a narrative. In the *Beginning* box write details about the setting and characters to open the story. In the *Middle* box write events to answer the question *What is happening in the story?* In the *End* box write a possible ending for the scene to answer *How does the story end?* Have students then write their own ideas into the boxes of the graphic organizer to plan their stories.

Remind students that their story should use characters from *Trouble at the Sandbox,* and should make sense with what has already happened. Note that they should be able to point to details and evidence in the text to explain why the events in their new story would be likely to happen.

ACCELERATED WRITERS

If . . . students are trying to include too many events in their story,

then . . . help them focus on which events would be the most interesting and important to include. Have them write their event ideas on note cards and then try arranging the events in different sequences, pulling out cards that seem to describe weaker or less interesting events, until students are satisfied with the order.

TALK IT THROUGH

Encourage students to talk through their narratives with a partner to help them get their ideas together. Students may benefit from modeling these prewriting conversations or reviewing some questions the writer might ask a listener.

Questions a Writer Might Ask

- What is the setting of this narrative?
- What happens during the beginning, middle, and end of this story?
- From which point of view is your story being told?
- How do the characters think and feel about these events?
- What do the characters do or say?
- What other details might be useful to know about the events in this scene and the characters' thoughts, feelings, and actions?
- How well could you picture the setting?
- How well could you follow the sequence of events?
- What might be missing?
- Is there anything that I should leave out?

Encourage students to also formulate questions of their own.

GET ORGANIZED

Have students think about the feedback they received when talking through their story idea with a partner. Remind them that using that feedback to organize their narratives will save them time and effort when writing and rewriting.

Have students finalize the order of the events they will narrate, making sure they have an interesting beginning, a middle event, and a sense of closure at the end. Next have students check how well they know what their characters will think, feel, do, and say during this scene. Remind them to include only the most relevant details about the setting, characters, and events.

ENGLISH LANGUAGE LEARNERS

If . . . students struggle to write ideas in their graphic organizers,

then . . . have them draw pictures in each box to visualize their story before writing. Then pair students and have them examine the pictures together, pooling their vocabulary to share possibilities for words and phrases that could describe what should be written in each box.

STRUGGLING WRITERS

If . . . students have difficulty coming up with what their characters might think, do, and say,

then . . . have them think about what they have learned about one of the characters in *Trouble at the Sandbox*, and use this knowledge to pretend to be this character. Tell them to ask themselves how they (as the character) might react to the first event in their story and write some notes about this reaction. Have them continue to come up with potential reactions for the other events they think they might include in their stories and make notes about what the character would say or do.

Write

Work with students to create a chart that describes the elements of a narrative. Remind them that they must include the setting, characters, and plot events. Creating a chart such as the one shown below can be especially helpful for struggling writers. Invite students to give examples for each row in the chart. This chart may also be used to assess student understanding.

Element	Definition	Example
Beginning	• Starts with an interesting moment or action to catch the reader's attention • Introduces the main character • Establishes the setting	It was hot in the sandbox. *Really* hot. It didn't matter, though. Theo was with his friends Izzy and Josh. . . . Theo and his friends spent every lunch time in the sandbox.
Middle	• Reveals the problem facing the character • Includes descriptions that tell about the main character's actions • Includes details and dialogue that tell what the main character feels or is thinking • Uses signal words to clarify the sequence of events	"Ms. Lee, Ms. Lee, there are these boys and they've. . ." Theo began. Ms. Lee held up one hand to stop him. "Theo," she said with her soft voice. "Take a deep breath and calm down first. Then you can tell me the whole story."
End	• Includes details and dialogue that tell what the main character feels, does, or is thinking • Uses signal words to clarify the sequence of events • Ends with an event that concludes the action	Then Ben smiled. "That looks like fun," he said. Theo smiled back at him. "It is," he said. "I thought you guys could use a hand," Ben said. Theo picked up one of the trucks and handed it to him. "We need some sand moved over there," Theo said, pointing to a corner. Ben nodded and started loading the truck. They all got to work. They had lots to do if this volcano was going to be better than the last.

MONITOR AND SUPPORT

ENGLISH LANGUAGE LEARNERS

If . . . students have difficulty thinking of vocabulary to use to tell about their character,

then . . . provide them with simple frames to complete to explain what their character thinks, feels, and says. For example: [Character] thought ___. [Character] felt ___. [Character] said ___.

STRUGGLING WRITERS

If . . . students struggle to use signal words to indicate the sequence of events,

then . . . remind them of the different kinds of signal words they could use, such as words that tell time and words that tell order. Have them review their writing with a partner and look for places where they might clarify what is happening by adding words that tell when things happen (*that morning, sooner, later*) and in what order (*first, next, then, finally*).

Look Closely

LOOK AT CONVENTIONS

SENTENCES Remind students that they have worked on writing simple sentences, which include a subject and a verb. Review examples of simple sentences in the text and have students look back over their writing to locate examples of simple sentences they have written, revising these sentences as necessary if they are lacking either a subject or a verb.

NOUNS Review that nouns name people, places, and things, and that proper nouns name specific people, places, and things and must begin with a capital letter. Encourage students to check their narratives to make sure that they have used *the* and *a/an* before each noun and that they have correctly spelled and used singular, plural, irregular plural, and collective nouns.

PRONOUNS Review that a subject pronoun takes the place of a noun that is the subject of a sentence, an object pronoun takes the place of a noun that is not used as a subject, and a reflexive pronoun refers back to a subject pronoun. Advise students to review their writing to make sure their reflexive pronouns correctly match the subject pronouns to which they refer and that they have replaced nouns with the correct pronouns.

LOOK AT CRAFT

SENTENCES Explain that students can make their narratives more interesting to read by including some description of events that happened in the past. Add that they must be careful to use only present-tense verbs to talk about things happening now and past-tense verbs to talk about things that happened in the past. Have students check their writing to make sure they have used correct verb tenses throughout.

SIGNAL WORDS Remind students that writers use signal words to tell the reader the order in which events happen. Have students highlight temporal words they have used in their narratives and check for places where they could add other temporal words to make the sequence of events clearer. Tell them to use a variety of these words and point out good examples from the texts as models whenever possible.

ENGLISH LANGUAGE LEARNERS

If . . . students have difficulty remembering how to use subject, object, and reflexive pronouns properly,

then . . . write sets of matching subject, object, and reflexive pronouns on separate note cards (*I/me/myself, he/him/himself, she/her/herself*). Provide student pairs with sentence frames and have them practice placing the cards into the sentences to use the different pronouns to complete each sentence. Tell students to read each finished sentence aloud to practice hearing these pronouns used correctly in context.

STRUGGLING WRITERS

If . . . students continue to write incomplete sentences,

then . . . remind them that a complete simple sentence must contain both a subject and a verb. Have them reread sample simple sentences from their writing and circle subjects in red and verbs in blue. Tell them to add a subject or a verb to any sentence that is missing either of these parts.

Name_____

Title_____

Write A New Story Writing Checklist

❏ Did I start with an interesting event?

❏ Did I describe the setting?

❏ Did I use information from *Trouble at the Sandbox*?

❏ Did I include descriptions of the characters' actions and words?

❏ Did I include details that tell about my characters' thoughts and feelings?

❏ Did I include a clear beginning, middle, and ending?

❏ Did I organize my sequence of events in logical order?

❏ Did I use words and phrases to signal the order of events? Example:

_____

❏ Did I use nouns and pronouns correctly? Example:

_____

❏ Did I use past and present verb tenses correctly?

❏ Did I include a strong ending?

❏ Did I review my work for correct capitalization, punctuation, and spelling?

❏ (Optional) Did I use a computer to write the final version of my story?

Unlock the Task: Compare and Contrast Communities

Distribute copies of the task found on page 286 of the Teacher's Guide. Read the task together. Guide students to identify important key words or phrases to highlight in the task to help them better understand what to do and how to do it. Have students highlight the agreed-upon key words and phrases.

Write a compare-and-contrast paragraph about two communities from *Friends Around the World.* Introduce the communities and include at least one fact about how each community is the same and how each community is different. Provide a closing sentence.

Display or distribute the questions students should be able to answer to demonstrate their understanding of the task. Have students review the highlighted words and phrases to help them answer the questions. Monitor students to see who needs more support and who is ready to work independently.

- **What type of writing is this?** (informative)
- **What will the text of my writing look like?** (sentences that describe how two communities are alike and different)
- **What text should I reference?** (*Friends Around the World*)
- **What information should I give?** (details about Isabel's community and the community the other e-pal lives in, include information about the e-pal, their school, and their community)

Have students restate the task in their own words. Check for possible misunderstandings or missing elements.

ENGLISH LANGUAGE LEARNERS

If . . . students are unclear about the meaning of *compare and contrast,*

then . . . explain that to compare and contrast means to tell how two things are alike and how they are different. Have students think about a cat and a dog. Two ways that they are alike are they both can be pets and they both have four legs. Two ways that they are different are that cats purr and dogs bark.

STRUGGLING WRITERS

If . . . students have difficulty distinguishing between the various parts of this task,

then . . . have children review the communities the e-pals in *Friends Around the World* live in and choose which one they would like to compare to Isabel's community. Next, have students use a T-chart graphic organizer to record details about each community. Finally, have students identify the ways the communities are alike and different.

Prepare to Write

Once students understand the writing task, have them review the selection and consider which of the other communities they are most interested in comparing to Isabel's community. Students should list one or two of the other communities that they might like to write about. Have them write down one or two reasons for choosing each one.

Next, have students go back over their ideas and decide which other community they want to use in their paragraph.

Determine with students who the audience of the task will be. Then discuss how their paragraph will help the reader better understand what life is like for children in the two communities. How are the communities alike? How are they different?

GATHER IDEAS

Once students have determined which community they will compare to Isabel's, tell them to read the letters each one wrote in *Friends Around the World*. They can use the Two-Column Chart with Graphic Organizer in Part 3 to record the information they collect. Have them write New York City at the top of the left column and the name of their chosen community in the top of the right column. Then have them record details on how the communities are alike and how they are different.

Remind students that they need to take the information from the graphic organizer and begin to write their paragraph. Remind them to include the name of the community they are talking about as often as possible so that the reader is not confused. If time permits, help students use the Internet to find more information about the countries the e-pals are from.

ACCELERATED WRITERS

If . . . students want to select another e-pal and compare that community with Isabel's and their first choice,

then . . . suggest that they look at their graphic organizers again and add the ways that the new community is alike and different from the first two. Work with students to see if they can make a statement about school life in each of the communities.

TALK IT THROUGH

Encourage students to talk through their planned paragraphs with a partner to help them get their ideas together. Students may benefit from modeling these prewriting conversations or reviewing some questions the writer might ask a listener.

Questions a Writer Might Ask

- Which community will I compare to Isabel's?
- What details do I need to include about each community?
- What things can I compare and contrast?
- Did I include any details that do not fit my paragraph?
- Could I include any additional details to make my paragraph stronger?

Encourage students to also formulate questions of their own.

GET ORGANIZED

Have students think about the feedback they received when talking through the topic with a partner. Remind them that using this feedback to organize their explanatory text will save them time and effort when writing and rewriting.

Have students go back over their ideas and decide which ones will best inform a reader about ways the communities are alike and different. Suggest that they return to the task and review the bullet points to be sure they have completed each part of the task. Students might use the Two-Column Chart Graphic Organizer in Part 3 to organize the information they plan to use to compare the two communities.

ENGLISH LANGUAGE LEARNERS

If . . . students have difficulty understanding some of the terms used in *Friends Around the World,*

then . . . remind them use the Glossary at the end of the story to review the definition of each term. Find the e-pal letter that uses each of the terms. Pronounce each term for students and ask them to repeat the term aloud.

STRUGGLING WRITERS

If . . . students are struggling with how to begin choosing which experiences to compare and contrast,

then . . . have them look at the first letter from each e-pal, and find how each child gets to school. Discuss this with students and ask them to identify whether this is one way the e-pals' experiences are alike or different.

Write

Work with students to create a chart that describes the elements of an explanatory text. Remind them that their explanation should focus on one topic, providing facts and details that will help a reader understand new things about this topic. Creating a chart such as the one shown below can be especially helpful for struggling writers. Invite students to give examples for each row in the chart. This chart may also be used to assess student understanding.

Element	Definition	Example
Title	• Catches the attention of the reader	New York City and Ho Chi Mihn city
Introduction	• Introduces the topic • Uses details to help a reader understand what the writer will explain	Today my teacher, Miss Thomson, gave us a great surprise. We will exchange emails, letters, and pictures with our new friends from around the world!
Body	• Describes the topic • Provides facts and supporting details that explain the topic • Uses definitions to tell the meaning of difficult vocabulary words	I live in New York City, in the United States of America. I live on the 14th floor of a big apartment building. Don't worry - there's an elevator! I take the subway to school with my mom. The subway is an underground train.
Conclusion	• Gives the writing a sense of closure	We have lots of things in common too. We all have to do school work, and we all like to have fun. There are exciting things to do in all four places. I can't wait to learn more about other kids from all over the world!

ENGLISH LANGUAGE LEARNERS

If . . . students are stuggling with comparisons,

then . . . help them choose one thing to compare from two pen pal letters, such as how the children get to school. Have them talk about the different ways. Then ask if the ways they get to school are alike or different from one another.

STRUGGLING WRITERS

If . . . students are intimidated by the task,

then . . . have them start by looking at Isabel's letters. Help students make a list of the things Isabel does in New York City, such as how she gets to school and what activities she likes.

Look Closely

SENTENCES WITH ADVERBS AND ADJECTIVES Remind students that they have worked recently on writing sentences that use adjectives and adverbs to describe things more precisely. Remind students that adjectives describe nouns—people, places, and things—and might tell size, color, or how many. Then review how adverbs tell how, where, or when something is done. Find examples in *Friends Around the World* of sentences that use adjectives and adverbs to explain information. Students can use these sentences as models for their own writing. Work with students as needed to check that they have used adjectives and adverbs correctly in their own sentences.

CONTRACTIONS Have students recall what they learned about using contractions correctly. Encourage students to review their writing to make sure they have deleted letters and placed apostrophes correctly when writing a contraction.

SENTENCES Explain that strong explanatory writing begins with introductory sentences that introduce the topic. Then students should have several sentences that explain or provide supporting details about the topic. Finally, they will end with concluding sentences that bring the text to a close. Tell students to review their work to make sure they have included all three of these types of sentences.

TEMPORAL WORDS Have students recall how writers use temporal words to help readers understand when events happen. Encourage students to look to see how they have used temporal words in their expository texts to describe or explain the time at which their scene is taking place or to clarify a sequence of events. Tell them to search for opportunities to use temporal words and phrases. Point out model examples from *Friends Around the World* as necessary.

ENGLISH LANGUAGE LEARNERS

If . . . students place adjectives in the wrong part of a sentence,

then . . . review how adjectives should be placed before the noun they describe, not after it. Provide students with note cards with nouns and adjectives written on them and tell students to practice placing the adjective cards in front of the noun cards and reading aloud the descriptions they make each time.

STRUGGLING WRITERS

If . . . students struggle to add adverbs to their sentences,

then . . . have them pick a sentence they would like to revise, identify the verb, and then ask themselves if there is any additional information they could supply to their reader about how this action is done, when it is done, or where it is done.

Name_____

Title_____

Compare and Contrast Communities Writing Checklist

❏ Did I introduce the topic clearly?

❏ Did I clearly identify the two communities I am comparing?

❏ Did I give examples of ways the communities are alike and different?

❏ Did I use facts and details from the book *Friends Around the World*?

❏ Did I use words and phrases when needed to explain the kind of things the e-pals did in their communities?

❏ Did I use adjectives to describe things? Example:

_____

❏ Did I use adverbs to describe actions? Example:

_____

❏ Did I use contractions correctly? Example:

_____

❏ Did I include a strong ending?

❏ Did I review my work for correct capitalization, punctuation, and spelling?

Unlock the Task: Write About a Decision

Distribute copies of the task found on page 146 of the Teacher's Guide and read it together. Have students suggest important key words or phrases to highlight in the task that will help them understand how to complete it. Have students highlight the agreed-upon key words and phrases.

> Think about the characters in the texts you read and the decisions they made. Write your own story about a character who makes a decision about money. Include a beginning, middle, and end, and at least two events. Use words such as *first, next, then,* and *in the end* to tell the order of events. Add details about the thoughts and feelings of the character. Include a sentence that wraps up your story.

Display or distribute the questions students should be able to answer to demonstrate their understanding of the task. Students should refer to what they highlighted in the task to help them answer the questions.

- **What type of writing is this?** (narrative)
- **What will the text of my writing look like?** (a story told in sequence)
- **What texts should I reference?** (*Alexander, Who Used to Be Rich Last Sunday* and *A Chair for My Mother*)
- **What details should I give?** (the thoughts and feelings of a character who needs to make a decision about money)
- **What do I need to include?** (a short sequence of events that includes action; linking words; details that tell thoughts and feelings; an ending to the story)

Have students restate the task in their own words. Check for possible misunderstandings or missing elements.

ENGLISH LANGUAGE LEARNERS

If . . . students have difficulty coming up with English words to name a need or a want,

then . . . review how needs are things people must have to live, while wants are just things that people would like to have. Provide students with a two-column chart and have them draw examples of things people need in one column and examples of things people might want in the second column. Then work with students to label their drawings.

STRUGGLING WRITERS

If . . . students have difficulty keeping track of all the parts required by this writing task,

then . . . work through the task together, pulling out different things students must do and helping them to reword each requirement and record it as part of a to-do list. For example, they must introduce the character, identify the decision he or she will make, explain whether this is a need or a want (and why), and describe why he or she makes this decision.

Prepare to Write

Once students clearly understand the writing task, have them review the selections *Alexander, Who Used to Be Rich Last Sunday* or *A Chair for My Mother.* Have students record ideas for plot events and character thoughts, feelings, and actions that they might want to use when developing their own characters and narratives. Some students may benefit from putting sticky notes next to sentences or on pictures that spark ideas.

Have students review their ideas and decide which will be most helpful when determining what will happen to their character. Remind students that they must determine the following three things: who the character is, what decision the character will make about money, and whether the character will be successful or not in the end. Remind students that they should also know whether the purchase is a need or a want and begin to think about how the character might go about trying to get the money needed to purchase it. If students have difficulty deciding whether the character will be able to afford the purchase, have them decide whether they find it more interesting to write about the character being successful or not.

GATHER IDEAS

Have students put together ideas for their narratives. Students can use a web graphic organizer to organize ideas about who their character is, writing the character's name in the center and what the character thinks, feels, or does in the outer ovals. Encourage students to record ideas about different ways to communicate information about their character, such as through straight description or through dialogue. Similarly, students can use the Story Map A Graphic Organizer in Part 3 to record their ideas in order from the beginning, middle, and ending of their stories. As students record their ideas, they should determine who their audience will be and how to express their character appropriately.

Discuss how students can use details from the two selections as models, but how as much as possible, students should be creative and adapt these models to write their own, unique stories starring a character of their own invention who experiences new events.

ACCELERATED WRITERS

If . . . students quickly write a narrative with a rapid, straightforward solution to the character's problem,

then . . . suggest that they develop the middle of their stories using a more sophisticated structure, such as multiple unsuccessful attempts to get the money, followed by a successful attempt and the purchase of the item. Note that they could also begin their narrative with an event that happens in the middle of the sequence of events and then use past tense verbs to talk about what happened before this point to mirror the sequence of events in *A Chair for My Mother.* Provide them with more complex sequence charts to use for planning out the order of events.

Encourage students to talk through their narrative with a partner to help them get their ideas together. Students may benefit from modeling these prewriting conversations or reviewing some questions the writer might ask a listener.

Questions a Writer Might Ask

- What are the main events?
- What does the main character do because of these events and why does he or she do these things?
- How does the main character think and feel about these events?
- What details and descriptions are most important?
- What details would be good to know about the character's thoughts, feelings, and actions?
- How well can the sequence of events be followed?
- What might be missing from the story?
- Was there anything that was misleading in the story that should be left out?

Encourage students to also formulate questions of their own.

GET ORGANIZED

Have students think about the feedback they received when talking through the narrative with a partner. Remind them that using this feedback to organize their narrative will save them time and effort when writing and rewriting.

Have students finalize the order of the events that they will narrate, including which event will serve as a strong beginning, which events will make up the middle of the story, and which will provide a strong ending. Then have students determine how well they know their main character and decide which details about this character's thoughts, feelings, and actions they will include during each event in their narrative. Remind them to include only the most relevant details about this character and his or her life.

ENGLISH LANGUAGE LEARNERS

If . . . students have difficulty coming up with words to tell how their character thinks and feels,

then . . . have them use a two-column chart to list the main events they will narrate in one column and then draw pictures of their character reacting to each event in the second column. Then have partners discuss each other's pictures and pool their vocabulary to come up with words and phrases to use to describe each reaction.

STRUGGLING WRITERS

If . . . students have difficulty planning the order of the events,

then . . . provide them with extra support by having them write each event on a separate note card. Then ask students to experiment with arranging the note cards in different orders, thinking about which order makes the most sense and/or makes the story more exciting to read. Remind them also to keep verb tenses in mind to make sure they use past- and present-tense verbs properly.

Write

Work with students to create a chart that describes the elements of a narrative. Remind them that the narrative should have a beginning, middle, and end. Note that they should also include detailed information about their character and setting. Creating a chart such as the one below can be especially helpful for struggling writers. Invite students to give examples for each row in the chart. This chart may also be used to assess student understanding.

Element	Definition	Example
Title	• Catches attention • Hints at story's theme	Five Dollars by Friday Ava Needs New Boots!
Beginning	• Introduces the main character • Establishes the setting • Introduces the main problem and what the character wants • Describes the character's thoughts, feelings, and actions	Splish! Ava wiggled her toes and frowned as cold water soaked her sock. She loved to jump in rain puddles. Unfortunately, she had a hole in the bottom of her left boot. Mom had said she would buy Ava a new pair of plain boots. If Ava wanted a fancy silver pair with sparkles, though, she would have to save up the money by herself.
Middle	• Uses temporal words to tell about a sequence of events • Includes descriptions that tell about the main character's actions • Includes details that tell what the main character feels or is thinking	Monday morning Ava went to water Mrs. Gomez's garden. Mrs. Gomez had said she would pay Ava two dollars to water the plants once. Ava let the hose run and run. Maybe Mrs. Gomez would pay Ava four dollars if Ava watered each plant twice… Tuesday morning, Ava tried a new job. Perhaps she would have more luck walking Mr. Chiao's dog.
End	• Includes details to tell what the main character feels, does, or is thinking • Uses temporal words to signal the end of the story • Ends with an event that provides a sense of closure	"That's a lot of money you have saved, Ava," Dad said. "Are you sure you want to spend it on boots?" Ava smiled. She was sure. And every time she wore the boots, she would remember how hard she had worked to earn them!

ENGLISH LANGUAGE LEARNERS

If . . . students struggle to think of words to use to clarify what their main character needs and why this character needs it,

then . . . provide them with sentence frames they can use to write the first draft of their narrative, such as: ___ needed ___ because ___. ___ wanted a ___ so that he/she could ___. If ___ had a/ an ___, he/she would be able to ___. Remind students to read each sentence frame aloud after they have completed it to make sure that it makes sense.

STRUGGLING WRITERS

If . . . students lack the stamina to write the whole narrative from start to finish,

then . . . have them work on it in parts, writing a draft of each piece separately and then joining all of the pieces together with temporal words and phrases. Have students use the Story Map B Graphic Organizer in Part 3 to write a sentence for each part of the story in each of the boxes (characters, setting, events). Then have students order their sentences in their writing. Encourage students to add additional sentences to enhance their story and to ensure there are no missing pieces.

Look Closely

SENTENCES Remind students that a simple sentence tells a complete thought and is made up of a subject and a predicate that always has a verb. A compound subject is a sentence with two or more subjects. A compound predicate is a sentence with two or more verbs. Use examples from the texts to show that compound subjects and compound predicates portray more complicated descriptions about a character or event. Encourage students to add variety to their writing by mixing short, simple sentences with longer sentences using compound subjects or compound predicates.

POSSESSIVES Focus attention on how to use singular and plural possessives and possessive pronouns. Have students review their narratives to make sure that they have used apostrophes correctly when forming each singular or plural possessive. Have them confirm that each possessive pronoun matches the subject with which it is paired.

VERB TENSES Remind students of the proper use of past- and present-tense verbs. Have students identify the tense in the scenes they are narrating. Have students confirm that they have used the correct verb tenses in each case.

LOOK AT CRAFT

SENTENCES Students' sentences should work together to recount the events that make up their narratives and provide detailed information about the main character. They should use adjectives to make their descriptions of the character's thoughts and feelings more interesting and add adverbs to clarify how, when, and where the actions performed are done.

LINKING WORDS Review temporal words and phrases and point out examples from the texts that show variety in their use. Note that some make more sense when used in the beginning, in the middle, or at the end of a narrative. Have students review the temporal words they have used and check for opportunities to edit or add to their writing. Point out examples from the texts that demonstrate variety of temporal words and phrases.

ENGLISH LANGUAGE LEARNERS

If . . . students struggle with possessive pronouns in English,

then . . . provide them with a list of sentences that could use possessive pronouns but do not. For example: The hat that belonged to him was on the table. Have students practice crossing out the phrase that could be replaced by a possessive pronoun and rewriting the sentence to use this possessive pronoun. (His hat was on the table.)

STRUGGLING WRITERS

If . . . students have trouble forming compound subjects and compound predicates correctly,

then . . . remind them that in a compound subject, both subjects must be performing the same action, while in a compound predicate, one subject is performing two different actions. Note that if two things are performing two different actions, the writer should write a compound sentence instead. Then help students review their writing to look for sentences that could logically be combined to form compound subjects, compound predicates, or whole sentences.

Name_____

Title_____

Write About a Decision Writing Checklist

❑ Did I start with an interesting opening scene?

❑ Did I introduce my main character and describe what the decision about spending money will be?

❑ Did I use details inspired by *Alexander, Who Used to Be Rich Last Sunday* or *A Chair for My Mother*?

❑ Did I include details that tell about my main character's thoughts and feelings?

❑ Did I include a clear beginning, middle, and ending?

❑ Did I use temporal words and phrases when needed to signal the order of events? Example:

_____

❑ Did I use singular and plural possessive nouns correctly? Example:

_____

❑ Did I use possessive pronouns correctly? Example:

_____

❑ Did I include a strong ending that concludes the action and provides the reader with a sense of closure?

❑ Did I review my work for correct capitalization, punctuation, and spelling?

Unlock the Task: Write an Opinion

BREAK APART THE TASK

Distribute copies of the task found on page 286 of the Teacher's Guide and read it together. Have students suggest important key words or phrases to highlight in the task that will help them understand how to complete it. Have students highlight the agreed-upon key words and phrases.

> Use the information from *Money Matters!* and the persuasive writing examples from the story *I Wanna Iguana* to do this task. Write an opinion piece about something you want. Before writing, make a list of reasons why you want this and why you should have it.

ANSWER QUESTIONS ABOUT THE TASK

Display or distribute the questions students should be able to answer to demonstrate their understanding of the task. Students should refer to what they highlighted in the task to help them answer the questions.

- **What type of writing is this?** (opinion)
- **What will the text of my writing look like?** (an opinion piece)
- **What texts should I reference?** (*Money Matters!* and *I Wanna Iguana*)
- **What information should I give?** (a statement telling what I want and why I should have it; supporting reasons)
- **What do I need to include?** (an introduction to my want, linking words that connect my opinions and reasons)

RESTATE THE TASK

Have students restate the task in their own words. Check for possible misunderstandings or missing elements.

ENGLISH LANGUAGE LEARNERS

If . . . students have difficulty restating the task in their own words,

then . . . have partners use the previously highlighted words and their answers from the questions answered about the task to complete the following sentence frames: I want to buy a/an (object). I will use (narrative; informative; opinion) style writing to tell the reader ___. I will remember to include ___ in my writing.

STRUGGLING WRITERS

If . . . students are focusing on just one thing to buy,

then . . . have them make a list of any number of things that they would like to buy. Have them give a reason why they would buy each item. Then help them narrow down their choices to the one item they need or want the most.

Prepare to Write

Once students clearly understand the task, have them review the selections *Money Matters!* and *I Wanna Iguana.* Have students record interesting ideas about what they might want to buy, and how they might be able to provide reasons for having this thing. Some students may benefit from putting sticky notes next to sentences or on headings, pictures, or captions that provide them with inspiration.

Next have students narrow their focus by picking which of their wants they will write about. Prompt them to pick something about which they are truly passionate so that they will be motivated to think of many good reasons they should have this thing. If students have difficulty choosing between two wants, tell them to consider how many reasons they can think of to support an argument for why they should have each thing and then pick the want for which they have a stronger argument.

Have students put together ideas for their opinion piece by following the directions from the third sentence of the task. Have students use a T-Chart. Ask them to label the left column *Why I Want It,* and the right column *Why I Should Have it*. Under *Why I Want It*, students should list reasons describing the attributes of the object that cause them to want the object, for example: It is unique. Under *Why I Should Have It*, students should list reasons detailing what they could do if they had the object. Have students complete the following sentence frame to guide them as needed in recording reasons in the second column: If I had this object I would ___.

Remind students to consider their audience when offering reasons to support their need for this item. You may want to have students come up with a plan for how they will work to get the item they want. This will help to further persuade the reader that they should have it.

ACCELERATED WRITERS

If . . . students want to strengthen their argument in favor of their opinion,

then . . . suggest that as they decide which facts and key details might be best to use, they think ahead in order to address how the reader might argue against their supporting reasons. Suggest they use a three-column chart to list their reasons in the first column, how a reader might argue against each reason in the second column, and what students could say to persuade the reader to convert to their opinion in the third column.

TALK IT THROUGH

Encourage students to talk through their opinion piece with a partner to help them get their ideas together. Students may benefit from modeling these prewriting conversations or reviewing some questions the writer might ask a listener.

Questions a Writer Might Ask

- What do I want to have?
- Which reasons and explanations best support my opinion?
- In what ways does my opinion need more support?
- How could my reasons be rearranged in a stronger or more logical order?
- Where could I add linking words to clarify how my reasons connect with my opinion?
- What might be missing?
- Was there anything that should have been left out?

Encourage students to also formulate questions of their own.

GET ORGANIZED

Have students think about the feedback they received when talking through the topic with a partner. Remind them that using this feedback to organize their opinion piece will save them time and effort when writing and rewriting.

Have students decide which reasons and explanations they will use to support their opinion, as well as the order in which they will present these reasons. Then have students consider what linking words and phrases they can use to connect their opinion with the reasons that support it. Remind them to check that all of the facts and details they are using relate to and support their opinion and that they are including only the strongest supporting reasons, particularly the ones identified by their partner as being the most persuasive.

ENGLISH LANGUAGE LEARNERS

If . . . students need help using content-specific vocabulary properly when figuring out their opinion and gathering details for writing their supporting reasons,

then . . . review what they have learned about the meaning of terms such as *budget, earn, valuable,* and *borrow.* Help students write a definition for each word and, when applicable, sketch a picture to help them remember how the word is used.

STRUGGLING WRITERS

If . . . students have difficulty listing reasons they should have the object,

then . . . prompt them by asking questions such as, What would this thing be used for? How would this object make me or someone else happier? How much would it cost?

MONITOR AND SUPPORT

Write

Work with students to create a chart that describes the elements of an opinion statement. Remind them that they must include an opinion statement, reasons and evidence, and a conclusion. Creating a chart such as the one shown below can be especially helpful for struggling writers. Invite students to give examples for each row in the chart. This chart may also be used to assess student understanding.

Element	Definition	Example
Opinion Statement	• Catches attention • Introduces the main topic • States opinion clearly	It is important for every child to learn how to be responsible. That is why I think I should get a puppy. If I had a puppy to take care of, I would become better at doing all of my chores.
Reasons and evidence	• Provides reasons that support the writer's opinion • Uses linking words to connect reasons to the opinion	I know that I would have to buy many things for my puppy. It would need food, a bed, and some toys. But I also know that I can set a budget and make a plan. This would help me to save my allowance to be able to buy these things. What are some problems my parents might have with a puppy? My mom will want to know where it can play. We have a small backyard, but I will walk it to the park each day for exercise.
Conclusion	• Gives readers a short summary of the opinion • Restates why the reader should agree with this opinion • Ends with concluding statement that gives the writing a sense of closure	I can prove that I am responsible enough to take care of a puppy. Why? Because I am responsible enough to make a plan now for how to take care of it. And because I can answer any reason someone might have for why I should not get a puppy.

ENGLISH LANGUAGE LEARNERS

If . . . students struggle to articulate their reasons for why they want something or why they should have it,

then . . . offer them support by providing them with sentence frames. For example: I want a ___ so that I can ___. I should have a ___ because it would help me ___.

STRUGGLING WRITERS

If . . . students need to provide stronger reasons to support their opinions,

then . . . pair students and have them read each other's writing. Have partners flag text evidence that they can tell is supporting the writer's opinion and then rate how good each reason is. Then have partners work together to figure out ways to reword reasons to make them more persuasive.

Look Closely

SENTENCES Review simple and compound sentences. Recall that simple sentences have one clause made up of both a subject and a predicate, while compound sentences have two independent clauses joined by a comma and a conjunction such as *and* or *but*. Point out examples from the texts for students to use as models for writing their own simple or compound sentences. Have students share examples of both sentence types from their own writing.

COMMAS IN A LIST Review how to use commas to separate items in a list. Note that such commas should be used when students are listing details to support an opinion. Have students review their writing to confirm that they have used commas correctly when listing more than two things.

COMMA USAGE WITH ADJECTIVES Focus attention on using commas to separate two or more adjectives. Discuss how adjectives describe the reasons the author is offering to support his or her opinion, and suggest that students check back through their writing to confirm that they have punctuated all adjectives correctly. Identify and display examples from the texts as needed.

SENTENCES Point out that variety in sentence structure creates interesting writing. Too many short, simple sentences sound choppy, and it is often hard to follow a string of compound sentences. Have students check their writing for places where they can use commas and conjunctions to combine related short, simple sentences into longer ones or places where they can break apart a long compound sentence into two shorter sentences.

ADVERBS AND ADJECTIVES Have students recall how adverbs and adjectives make their writing more precise and interesting to read. Have them reexamine their writing to identify places where they can expand their sentences by adding adverbs and adjectives to make their reasons more descriptive and exact. Remind them to check that they have used a variety of different adverbs and adjectives instead of the same ones over and over again.

ENGLISH LANGUAGE LEARNERS

If . . . students struggle to remember how to use linking words correctly to join their reasons and opinions,

then . . . have students record potential linking words to use on index cards with short descriptions or illustrations of times when it would be good to use each one. For example, they might use *between* when writing about choosing one thing over another; *because* to explain why to do something; *as you know* to emphasize that their audience probably agrees with the upcoming reason; and *also, and, as well,* or *too* to provide an additional reason.

STRUGGLING WRITERS

If . . . students have difficulty checking that they have crafted their compound sentences correctly,

then . . . tell students that the two sentences joining to make a compound sentence are like two objects balancing on a scale, with the comma and conjunction in the middle. Point out the subject and predicate on each side of a sample sentence. Have partners circle the subjects in blue and the predicates in red, making sure there is at least one of each color circle on each side of the comma and conjunction.

Name_____

Title_____

Write an Opinion Writing Checklist

❏ Did I fully introduce my want?

❏ Did I clearly state my opinion about why I should have this want in the beginning?

❏ Did I use *Money Matters!* and *I Wanna Iguana* as models?

❏ Did I include several reasons that support my opinion?

❏ Did I organize my reasons in a logical order?

❏ Did I use linking words and phrases when needed to connect my opinion and reasons? Example:

_____

❏ Did I use commas correctly? Example:

_____

❏ Did I use both simple and compound sentences to discuss my opinion? Examples:

_____

❏ Did I include a strong concluding statement that provides the reader with a sense of closure?

❏ Did I review my work for correct capitalization, punctuation, and spelling?

❏ (Optional) Did I type my opinion and ask my teacher to help me add a photo or drawing of what I want?

Unlock the Task: Write a Biographical Sketch

BREAK APART THE TASK

Distribute copies of the task found on page 146 of the Teacher's Guide and read it together. Have students identify and discuss important key words or phrases to highlight in the task.

> In this unit, you have read about people who have made important contributions to the United States. Look back at *Theodore Roosevelt: The Adventurous President* as you research another American who did something special to help our country.
> Focus your research on the contributions he or she made to our country. Conduct shared research with a small group. Write three questions and answers that are found during shared research. Write three paragraphs that state your questions and answers. Use appropriate question words, such as *what, when,* and *why.*

ANSWER QUESTIONS ABOUT THE TASK

Display and read aloud the following questions. Help students answer them.

- **What type of writing is this?** (informative/explanatory)
- **What will the text of my writing look like?** (three questions and three answers in three paragraphs)
- **What texts should I reference?** (*Theodore Roosevelt;* other texts)
- **What information should I give?** (facts and key details that answer my questions and tell about an important person in American history)
- **What do I need to include?** (question words; research related to everyday life, big ideas, and contributions to our country)

RESTATE THE TASK

Have students restate the task. Check for misunderstandings.

ENGLISH LANGUAGE LEARNERS

If . . . students have difficulty understanding how a biographical sketch differs from a full biography,

then . . . discuss how a biography covers all or most of a subject's life, while their biographical sketches should present focused information about one topic related to their subject's life— how he or she was a big idea thinker who contributed to the country. Add that their three questions should all relate to this main topic. Bring in samples of texts that use a question-and-answer format to provide students with models.

STRUGGLING WRITERS

If . . . students are overwhelmed by the task of selecting a person to research and figuring out questions to ask,

then . . . offer them a list of potential research subjects. Have students narrow their decision by answering questions such as: What makes them an important historical figure? What were some of their big ideas? What important actions did they take? How did their actions change our country?

Prepare to Write

Once students clearly understand the writing task, have them review the quote from *Theodore Roosevelt: The Adventurous President* and consider the relationship between a "big idea thinker" and someone who has made great contributions to our country. Provide groups with a list of historical figures from American history and resources such as social studies textbooks or age-appropriate biographies to find people about whom they might want to learn more. As they come across interesting and important figures, they should use sticky notes to mark paragraphs, photos, time lines, and other text features that might spark ideas for questions or evidence to explain why this figure is significant.

Once groups have a few ideas about the people they might want to research, have students narrow their focus by settling on one person in particular and then each brainstorming which three questions to ask about this person. Students might start with four or five questions and narrow them down as they get further into the research process and find out how much information is available to answer each question. Remind students that these questions need to be specific, not general, and that they should consider the audience of their sketch presentation when preparing their questions and answers.

GATHER IDEAS

Once students are ready to start researching, have them decide which sources will be best to find information about their chosen person. Consider collaborating with the school librarian or technology specialist to support students in locating proper research tools in both print and digital formats.

When students begin to conduct their actual research, remind them that they can use glossaries, indexes, and Contents pages to help them locate the parts of a book that most directly cover their topic. Students might use note cards or sticky notes to record or mark specific text details that can be used to answer each of their questions. Tell students that they should keep track of the sources they use so that they can identify where they have found each bit of information to be able to cite it correctly.

ACCELERATED WRITERS

If . . . students want to add more detail to the answers of their questions,

then . . . guide students to find sources that provide direct quotes from their person. Have students read the quotations to determine if any can be included in the answers to their questions, or perhaps inspire them to ask more elaborate questions.

Encourage students to talk through their questions and answers with a partner to help them get their ideas together. Students may benefit from modeling these prewriting conversations or reviewing some questions the writer might ask a listener.

Questions a Writer Might Ask

- What three questions am I asking about my person?
- Do I use an appropriate question word with each of my questions?
- What facts or details best support the answer for each question?
- Do I describe how this person contributed to our country?
- What other research can be done to better support my answers?
- What might be missing?
- Is there anything that I should leave out?

Encourage students to also formulate questions of their own.

GET ORGANIZED

Tell students to think about the feedback they received when talking through their questions and answers with a partner. Remind them that using this feedback to organize their questions and answers will save them time and effort when writing and rewriting. Suggest that they use a graphic organizer, such as a three-column chart, to organize the facts and details they will use to answer each question. Students can record the text evidence they plan to use to answer each question in its own column.

Review with students how to build ideas by taking what they have learned from reading multiple texts and putting this knowledge together in a new way to answer a question. Point out that they may have to connect historical events mentioned in different texts. Emphasize that each paragraph should begin with the clearly stated question and continue with the strongest facts and details to answer this question.

ENGLISH LANGUAGE LEARNERS

If . . . students have difficulty thinking of the words needed to write an answer to each question,

then . . . have students review the vocabulary from the unit, as well as any vocabulary notebooks or glossaries they have created during the unit. Students should use strategies learned from the Preview and Review Vocabulary Routine or the Vocabulary Activities in Part 3 to guide their use of vocabulary in their writing.

STRUGGLING WRITERS

If . . . students are not using quality text evidence to support their answers,

then . . . briefly discuss which sources might offer better quality information—for example, a biography contains more accurate facts than a piece of historical fiction would, since historical fiction might include made-up characters and actions. Suggest that students list the facts they plan to use and make tally marks next to each to confirm that they have found at least two good sources to support each fact.

MONITOR AND SUPPORT

Write

Work with students to create a chart that describes the elements to include in each question and answer. Remind them that the answer must address all points raised by the question. Creating a chart such as the one below can be especially helpful for struggling writers. Invite students to give examples for each row in the chart. This chart may also be used to assess student understanding.

Element	Definition	Example
Question	• Clearly stated • Begins with a question word such as *Who, What, When,* or *Why* • Ends with a question mark	What did President Thomas Jefferson do that had a great effect on our country?
Answer	• Uses facts from research • Uses details and descriptions from research • Defines difficult or unfamiliar terms • Answers question thoroughly	In 1803, Jefferson said yes to the Louisiana Purchase. The United States spent $15 million dollars to buy the land France owned west of the Mississippi River. The United States now had twice as much land as it had before this purchase. More importantly, it controlled the Mississippi River and the port of New Orleans, which was a very important trade center. Because of him, the United States spread all the way to the Pacific Ocean, and many goods and people still pass through the port of New Orleans today.

ENGLISH LANGUAGE LEARNERS

If . . . students struggle to paraphrase text from their research,

then . . . review how they should not copy the text word for word, but instead put it into their own words. Work with students to identify words they can replace with synonyms. Then have students use these synonyms to explain aloud what they think they want to say. Help them write down their explanations and check to make sure they have truly put the ideas in their own words.

STRUGGLING WRITERS

If . . . students have difficulty keeping the information related to each question and answer organized,

then . . . have students review their first paragraph with a colored pen or pencil. Tell them to underline the question and draw a double line under its question word. Then tell them to circle each fact or detail in the paragraph that helps to answer this question. Have them repeat this task with different colors for the second and third paragraphs. Then have them go back and move any evidence that is placed in the wrong paragraph and delete any sentences that were never marked at all.

Look Closely

LOOK AT CONVENTIONS

SENTENCES Review the concept of using adjectives and adverbs to expand simple and compound sentences. Point out examples from the text of sentences that are more interesting to read because they use adjectives and adverbs. Have students use these examples as models for expanding some of their own sentences by adding adjectives and adverbs.

COMMON NOUNS Review that common nouns name general people, places, and things and should not be capitalized. Have students review their writing to confirm that they have begun each common noun with a lowercase letter.

PROPER NOUNS Recall that proper nouns name specific people or places and should be capitalized. Note that many names and places will be mentioned in a biographical sketch. Have students review their writing to confirm that they have capitalized all proper nouns correctly. Identify and display examples from the text as needed.

LOOK AT CRAFT

SENTENCES Review the proper format for question-and-answer writing. The topic sentence states the question the writer will be answering. The supporting sentences use facts, details, and definitions to answer the question. Finally the conclusion sentence wraps up the topic and provides a sense of closure. Have students confirm the inclusion of these types of sentences in each of their paragraphs.

ADVERBS AND ADJECTIVES Recall that a variety of adverbs and adjectives make writing more precise and interesting to read. Have students reexamine their writing to check that they have used adverbs to tell more about how, where, and why an action was done and that that they have used adjectives to make their descriptions of nouns more detailed. Remind them to check that they have used a variety of different adverbs and adjectives instead of the same words over and over again. As necessary, point out examples from the text as models.

ENGLISH LANGUAGE LEARNERS

If . . . students need more practice with proper and common nouns,

then . . . provide students with a short sentence written using common nouns, such as *The girl traveled to the city*. Discuss why *girl* and *city* are common nouns that should not be capitalized. Then work with students to rewrite the sentence with capitalized proper nouns— *Emma traveled to Boston*. Provide students with additional sentences with which they can practice rewriting sentences to change common nouns to proper ones and vice versa.

STRUGGLING WRITERS

If . . . students struggle to remember how to use adjectives and adverbs properly,

then . . . remind them that adjectives tell more about a noun, while adverbs tell more about verbs, adjectives, and other adverbs. Provide students with short sentences and simple adverbs and adjectives written on note cards and have students practice adding at least one adjective and one adverb to each sentence.

Name_____

Title_____

Write a Biographical Sketch Writing Checklist

❏ Did I clearly state each question?

❏ Did I begin each question with a good question word?

❏ Did I use facts and details from my research to answer each question?

❏ Do I have at least two reliable sources for each bit of information I included?

❏ Did I organize my ideas so that each question and its answer are in their own paragraph?

❏ Did I use adjectives and adverbs correctly? Example:

_____

❏ Did I capitalize or not capitalize proper and common nouns correctly? Example:

_____

❏ Did I review my work for correct capitalization, punctuation, and spelling?

❏ (Optional) Did I research my important person online, find and include online images of the person doing something important, and type my biographical sketch?

Unlock the Task: Design a Park

Distribute copies of the task found on page 286 of the Teacher's Guide and read it together. Have students suggest important key words or phrases to highlight in the task that help them understand how to complete this task. Have them highlight the agreed-upon key words and phrases.

In this unit, you have read texts about people who have made a difference in their communities. Refer back to the texts *Change Makers* and *City Green* as you write about a park that you would like to create for your city or town. Design a park and explain how the park will benefit your community. Write about the qualities and characteristics of your park. Write about how the park will benefit your community. Illustrate your newly designed park.

ANSWER QUESTIONS ABOUT THE TASK

Display or distribute the questions students should be able to answer to demonstrate their understanding of the task. Students should use what they highlighted to help them answer the questions.

- **What type of writing is this?** (informative/explanatory)
- **What will the text of my writing look like?** (explanatory text about a park)
- **What texts should I reference?** (*Change Makers; City Green*)
- **What information should I give?** (qualities and characteristics of my park; how my park will benefit the community)
- **What do I need to include?** (park plan; facts and details that explain information)

RESTATE THE TASK

Have students restate the task in their own words. Check for possible misunderstandings or missing elements.

ENGLISH LANGUAGE LEARNERS

If . . . students are unclear about the meaning of the word *benefit* and how it is being used in this task,

then . . . provide them with some simple synonyms or explanations, such as "help to do something" or "give good things to." Explain that a park that benefits a community gives people in the community a place to do things that they were not able to do before, such as plant a garden.

STRUGGLING WRITERS

If . . . students become overwhelmed by the amount of work needed to complete this task,

then . . . help them break it into smaller parts and complete it in small chunks spread out over a period of time. Suggest that students attack one bullet point at a time, such as first drawing a park. Remind them that they can go back and revise their park if they come up with new ideas during a later part that would affect something they have already drawn or written.

Prepare to Write

Once students clearly understand the task, have them think about the community gardens described on pages 25 and 26 of *Change Makers*, and the garden that was planted in the empty lot in *City Green*. Students should flip through the pages and take notes about anything that sparks ideas about features they might want to include as part of their parks.

Next, have students recall what they have learned from selections in the unit, as well as any other related texts, about how people use parks and gardens and how creating parks and gardens can change life in a community. Tell them to make a list of possible features they might want to include in their park design and to begin to think about how each feature might affect the lives of people living in the community.

Finally, have students focus their thinking by putting together a list of questions that they can ask themselves as they plan each part of their park. For example— What is this feature? Where would it fit best in my park? How would it make people's lives better? How should people use it? What should people not do with it?

GATHER IDEAS

Once students have put together a list of features for their park plans, they can return to the texts to collect specific facts and details to help them finalize their design for each feature. Although students will be writing an explanatory text, they will need to state their opinion about why this park will benefit the community. Therefore, students need to gather facts and details that will support the statements they plan to make about their park design, and think about words and phrases they can use to convey their point of view about the topic. Remind students of the importance of considering who their audience is when choosing the tone of their writing. Encourage them to consider cause-and-effect relationships and to locate details in the text about how each feature will change life in their community. Note that each feature can be thought of as the cause, and how people will benefit from it can be thought of as the effect.

ACCELERATED WRITERS

If . . . students are overly enthusiastic about their park and quickly complete their list of beneficial characteristics,

then . . . have students expand upon their drawing with text features such as labels, text boxes, and maps. Suggest that students consider creating a brochure for their park that includes an idea to raise money for the purpose of building the park.

TALK IT THROUGH

Encourage students to talk through their park plan with a partner to help them get their ideas together. Students may benefit from modeling these prewriting conversations or reviewing some questions the writer might ask a listener.

Questions a Writer Might Ask

- What are the main features of my park?
- What qualities and characteristics of my park do I describe?
- What other facts and details should I include to explain the features of my park more clearly to my audience?
- How will my park benefit the community?
- What reasons and evidence do I use to support this view?
- What else should I include?
- Is there anything that should be left out?

Encourage students to also formulate questions of their own.

GET ORGANIZED

Have students think about the feedback they received when talking through their park plan with a partner. Remind them that using this feedback to organize their explanatory text will save them time and effort when writing and rewriting.

Point out that the task itself gives clues about the order in which students should present information when writing about their park. First they should describe and explain the features of the park. Then they should write their opinion about how the park will benefit the community. Last they should plan for their drawing of the park. Remind them that each paragraph should include a main topic and details and evidence that support this main topic.

ENGLISH LANGUAGE LEARNERS

If . . . students cannot think of the vocabulary needed to present their ideas about how the park features will be used,

then . . . provide them with sentence frames for them to complete and use to present their ideas. For example, If we build a ___, then the people can ___. This will benefit the community because ___. Review the Vocabulary Activities in Part 3 that were used throughout the unit to recall key vocabulary from the selections that students can use to complete the frames.

STRUGGLING WRITERS

If . . . students struggle to understand the relationship between their drawings and their writing,

then . . . help them recall how authors use text to explain information shown in a drawing, while drawings are used to help viewers understand better what something an author is talking about looks like. Note that when students describe and explain the features of their park, they may choose to write about only the most important characteristics of each feature, while their drawings can illustrate some interesting but less important details that they do not mention in the text.

MONITOR AND SUPPORT

Write

Work with students to create a chart that describes the elements that should be included. Remind them that they should provide facts and details to help a viewer understand the park features illustrated by the plan and specific words and phrases to help a reader understand the benefits of these features. Creating a chart such as the one below can be especially helpful for struggling writers. Invite students to give examples for each row in the chart. This chart may also be used to assess student understanding.

Element	Definition	Example
Explanation	• Written to support a visual • Identifies and describes the parts of the plan • Uses facts and details to explain the qualities and characteristics of these parts • Uses formal language	A large, oval skating rink is located in the center of the park. In the summer, people can roller blade on its smooth concrete top. In the winter, the park will freeze water in the rink so that people can ice skate. At the red booth on the left, people can rent skates all year round.
Statement of Benefits	• Clearly states an opinion • Provides reasons and evidence to support this opinion • Uses linking words to connect the opinion with the reasons • Uses formal language	The park will help people in the community get to know each other better because it gives them a place to work and play together. Grown-ups can meet each other while working in the garden. Kids can make new friends on the playground.

ENGLISH LANGUAGE LEARNERS

If . . . students have trouble coming up with ideas for their drawings,

then . . . help them make a list of the features of the park they want to be certain to include in their drawing. If necessary, help them locate pictures on the Internet to help them know what each feature looks like.

STRUGGLING WRITERS

If . . . students have trouble brainstorming rich adjectives to describe the parts of their park,

then . . . view their illustrated plans with them and prompt their thinking about each feature with questions such as, What shape is this skating rink? What size is the slide on this playground? What colors are the plants grown in this garden? Students can use a web graphic organizer to record the words they brainstorm for each feature.

Look Closely

LOOK AT CONVENTIONS

SENTENCES Review examples of simple and compound sentences that use descriptive adjectives and specific words and phrases. Have students revisit their writing to locate examples of correctly formed simple and compound sentences. Using examples from the texts, show students how short, simple sentences can introduce a new idea, while more descriptive and complicated compound sentences can be used to provide more detailed information. Encourage students to add variety to their writing by rearranging sentences and adding adverbs and adjectives.

PREPOSITIONS Recall that prepositions usually precede a noun to describe where or when it is located in space or time. Have students review their drawings and writing to identify places where prepositional phrases could help to clarify where different park features are located.

CONJUNCTIONS Discuss how conjunctions such as *and* or *or* can connect two clauses, sentences, or words. Review how conjunctions are used as part of a compound subject or verb. Display examples of sentences with conjunctions from the texts for students to use as models when checking their own writing to make sure they have properly used conjunctions.

LOOK AT CRAFT

SENTENCES Have students review each paragraph for a topic sentence that introduces the main idea and a concluding sentence that wraps it up. Remind them that when writing an explanatory text, they should include many supporting details in the other sentences to tell the characteristics of the thing they are explaining.

FORMAL AND INFORMAL LANGUAGE Remind students that writers change the type of language they use, or tone, depending upon their intended audience. Encourage students to look at the tone of their writing to see if it is formal enough. Have them search for places where they might have used slang or informal expressions. Point out examples of formal language from the text as necessary.

ENGLISH LANGUAGE LEARNERS

If . . . students use the wrong conjunctions to join a compound subject,

then . . . review the meaning of different conjunctions to make sure students understand that conjunctions are not interchangeable and that the meaning of a sentence will change depending upon the conjunction used. For example, a writer can use *and* to talk about two people who are doing the same thing (Fred *and* Marcy will make the garden) or *or* to talk about when one or another person will be doing the same thing (Fred *or* Marcy will make the garden), but it does not ever make sense to use *but* to join two subjects.

STRUGGLING WRITERS

If . . . students struggle to revise informal language to make it sound more formal,

then . . . help them visualize their intended audience more clearly. Have them imagine that the principal of their school or the mayor of their town will be reading their work, and tell them to think about how they would explain these same ideas in person to these people. Then tell them to go back through their writing and cross out and replace any words or phrases they would not use when speaking to such an audience.

Name_____

Title_____

Design a Park Writing Checklist

❏ Did I identify the most important features of my park?

❏ Did I describe and explain the qualities and characteristics of these features?

❏ Did I include only the most important details about the park features?

❏ Did I state how this park will benefit the community?

❏ Did I use reasons and evidence to support my opinion regarding how this park will benefit the community?

❏ Did I use *Change Makers* and *City Green* as inspiration?

❏ Did I use adjectives to describe things? Example:

_____

❏ Did I use formal language?

❏ Did I use conjunctions correctly? Example:

_____

❏ Did I use prepositions correctly? Example:

_____

❏ Did I review my work for correct capitalization, punctuation, and spelling?

Unlock the Task: Write About Henry and Chin

Distribute copies of the task found on page 146 of the Teacher's Guide and read it together. Have students suggest important key words or phrases to highlight in the task that will help them understand how to complete this task. Have them highlight the agreed-upon key words and phrases.

> You will write a short story about Henry and Chin from *The Earth Dragon Awakes* that describes an adventure the boys might have during the rebuilding of San Francisco after the earthquake.

Display the following questions, which students should be able to answer in order to demonstrate their understanding of the task. Remind students to review the words and phrases they highlighted to help them answer the questions. Alternatively, provide the questions as a handout. Monitor students to determine who needs more support and who can work independently.

- **What type of writing is this?** (narrative)
- **What will the text of my writing look like?** (a new scene from the story)
- **What text should I reference?** *(The Earth Dragon Awakes)*
- **What details should I give?** (the characters' thoughts, feelings, and actions)
- **What do I need to include?** (a short sequence of events; temporal words such as *first, then, next, finally*; details that describe how the characters feel and what they are thinking; a conclusion)

Have students restate the task in their own words. Check for possible misunderstandings or missing elements.

ENGLISH LANGUAGE LEARNERS

If . . . students have difficulty understanding the concept of rebuilding,

then . . . have students think about the devastation that the earthquake caused. Ask them what they think needed to happen for San Francisco to become a city again. Ask if they are aware of any natural disasters in their native country.

STRUGGLING WRITERS

If . . . students have difficulty understanding how to approach this task,

then . . . have them discuss with you the main event for their narrative. Have them write down one or two events that might happen in the beginning of their narrative, and one or two events that might happen in the middle. Finish by asking them to describe how their narrative might end.

Prepare to Write

DETERMINE FOCUS

Once students clearly understand the writing task, have them review the selection *The Earth Dragon Awakes*. Have them consider what kind of adventure Henry and Chin might have during the rebuilding of San Francisco, and what events they want to include. Some students may benefit from making a list of their ideas. Suggest they put a check mark next to their favorite ideas, and cross out any ideas that they don't wish to pursue.

Have students narrow their list to one particular scene that will be the focus of their narrative. Remind them that this scene should provide plenty of opportunity for writing about each character's thoughts, feelings, and actions. If students have difficulty choosing between two scenes, have them consider which scene includes events that would best fit with what they learned about Henry and Chin from reading the selection. One scene may lend itself to being expanded upon in richer detail.

GATHER IDEAS

Suggest that students use note cards or sticky notes to gather and brainstorm general character and scene details without putting them in any particular order yet. Students can use a three-column chart to organize what each character thinks, feels, and does during this scene. Point out that they should pay attention to the order in which the characters perform the actions and record them in temporal order in their chart, so that the actions will be in the correct sequence when students are ready to write their narratives.

Remind students that the details they include should be the most important and interesting ones. If writers become stalled or unfocused, have them imagine themselves in an adventure like the one they are creating for Henry and Chin. How would they react? What feelings would they have? What types of things might they do?

ACCELERATED WRITERS

If . . . students have easily developed their scene to describe a new adventure for Henry and Chin,

then . . . have students do research to determine what events may have taken place during the actual rebuilding of San Francisco. Have them determine if they would like to incorporate any of the real information into their scene.

Have students talk through their narrative with a partner to help them get their ideas together. Students may benefit from modeling these prewriting conversations or reviewing some questions the writer might ask a listener.

Questions a Writer Might Ask

- What were the main things that happened in this scene?
- What details and descriptions were most interesting?
- What other details might be useful to know about each character's thoughts, feelings, and actions?
- How clearly could you follow the sequence of events?
- What words might help to make the sequence of events clearer?
- What might be missing?
- Was there anything that should be left out?

Encourage students to also formulate questions of their own.

Have students think about the feedback they received when talking through their scene with a partner. Remind them that using this feedback to organize their narrative will save them time and effort when writing and rewriting.

Have students finalize the order of the events that they will narrate in this scene, including what exciting or important moment will start the narrative, and which will provide it with a strong sense of closure at the end. Then have students determine which details they will include as part of their description of each moment. Remind them to include only the details that will best fit the events that make up this scene.

ENGLISH LANGUAGE LEARNERS

If . . . students have difficulty talking through their scene with a partner,

then . . . have them share their prewriting notes, graphic organizers, and drawings with their partner as they walk through the events of their scene together. Have partners ask questions to prompt the conversation, such as, What happens next? How does each character feel about that event? What will the character do in response to that event? Remind partners to be sure to only ask questions, and not tell the events of their partner's scene for their partner.

STRUGGLING WRITERS

If . . . students have difficulty organizing their thoughts when deciding which details to include during each moment of their narrative,

then . . . have students use a story map to list each moment from the beginning to the end of their narrative. Then have them focus on each moment one by one. Tell them to summarize in one sentence the most important thing the reader should know about Harry and Chin's new adventure. Then have them list in the box two or three details that best describe the adventure and the characters' thoughts, feelings, and actions.

Write

Work with students to create a chart that describes the elements of a narrative. Remind them that, like any good narrator, they should include the story elements of character, setting, and plot. Creating a chart such as the one below can be especially helpful for struggling writers. Invite students to give examples for each row in the chart. This chart may also be used to assess student understanding.

Element	Definition	Example
Heading	• Tells time and date • Tells setting, maybe including both place and city	5:12 A.M. Wednesday, April 18, 1906 Chin's apartment in Chinatown
Beginning	• Catches readers' attention • Makes it clear whose point of view is the main one • Includes details to tell what the character feels or is thinking	The first tremble surprises Chin. He has heard many stories from his father about earthquakes back in China. But Chin has never realized just how quickly one can start.
Middle	• Tells about a series of events • Uses words to signal the order of events • Includes descriptions that tell about the main character's actions • Includes details to tell what the main character feels or thinks	Chin's knees hurt because they hit the floor so hard. He can hear his heart beating faster and faster. He has never felt so scared. Then Chin hears his father laugh. He wonders how Ah Sing can be so brave, but it makes him feel a bit better. Maybe he can be as brave as his father.
End	• Includes details to tell what the main character feels or thinks. • Uses words to signal that this event is the last. • Ends with an event that provides a sense of closure	Finally the floor stops moving. Chin blinks and watches dust float through the air. He is almost too surprised to be scared. Did he just live through an earthquake? The apartment is broken all around them. But amazingly, he and Ah Sing seem to be okay.

ENGLISH LANGUAGE LEARNERS

If . . . students struggle to include adequate use of each character's thoughts, feelings, and actions as they write their scene,

then . . . provide them with a three-column chart to list thoughts, feelings, and actions from their writing to give them a visual representation of how much of each they are including in their writing. If students do not have items listed in the column for each character's feelings, guide them to review their writing to locate where they could add words that describe what characters are feeling.

STRUGGLING WRITERS

If . . . students lack the stamina to write the whole narrative at once,

then . . . have students refer back to their story map and work on narrating one event at a time. Then have them go back and focus on checking that they have used strong temporal words to link the events together. Breaking the writing into smaller, more manageable pieces can help them pace their work better.

Look Closely

SENTENCES Remind students that they have worked recently on writing complete sentences that contain both a noun (or pronoun) and a verb. Tell students to review their writing to confirm that all of their sentences are complete. Then, using examples from the texts, show students how a pronoun can be substituted for a noun or a noun can be substituted for a pronoun. Encourage students to add variety to their writing by switching between using sentences with nouns as the subject and pronouns as the subject.

IRREGULAR PLURAL NOUNS Remind students that they recently practiced how to use irregular plural nouns correctly. Have students review their writing to make sure that they have used the correct plural form of any nouns.

REFLEXIVE PRONOUNS Focus attention on the use of reflexive pronouns when the subject of a sentence is acting on itself. Have students review their writing to determine whether there are places where they should use reflexive pronouns and to make sure that any existing reflexive pronouns have been used correctly.

SENTENCES Have students look closely to see that their sentences work together within each paragraph to build a picture of each event. Remind students to make sure no sentences provide extra or confusing information that does not relate to the action at hand. Remind them that, in a narrative, some sentences may contain dialogue that should be set off with quotation marks. Tell students to review their work for details and descriptions that provide information about how each character thinks, feels, and acts.

PAST AND PRESENT VERB TENSES Remind students that they worked a great deal on verb tenses recently, and their writing should reflect what they have learned. Have students think more deeply about the tense in which they have written their narratives. Are they narrating the scene as if it has already happened or as if the character is describing the action while it happens? Have students review their narratives and check that they have been consistent in using the same verb tense throughout.

ENGLISH LANGUAGE LEARNERS

If . . . students have difficulty remembering when to use the different reflexive pronouns,

then . . . help students make a chart that relates the reflexive pronouns with their matching subjects—for example, *I/myself, we/ourselves, he/himself, she/herself, you/yourself/yourselves, they/themselves.* Have students practice using each pair aloud to gain experience with hearing them used together. Provide as many models and opportunities to practice as possible.

STRUGGLING WRITERS

If . . . students have difficulty determining whether the sentences they are writing are complete,

then . . . remind students that a complete sentence must have both a noun (or pronoun) and a verb. Model how to review a sentence to determine whether it is a complete sentence. Ask: Who or what is doing something? What is being done? Then have students work with a partner to review their own writing and ask and answer these questions about each sentence, adding nouns (or pronouns) and verbs as necessary.

Name_____

Title_____

Write About Henry and Chin Writing Checklist

❏ Did I include an attention-grabbing beginning?

❏ Did I use information from *The Earth Dragon Awakes*?

❏ Did I include descriptions of each character's actions?

❏ Did I include concrete details that tell about each character's thoughts and feelings?

❏ Did I include a clear beginning, middle, and ending?

❏ Did I narrate a sequence of events in logical order?

❏ Did I use temporal words when needed to signal the order of events? Example:

_____

❏ Did I use irregular plural nouns correctly? Example:

_____

❏ Did I use the correct verb tense in each sentence and the same verb tense consistently? Example:

_____

❏ Did I include a strong ending that concludes the action and provides the reader with a sense of closure?

❏ Did I review my work for correct capitalization, punctuation, and spelling?

Unlock the Task: Write a Magazine Article

BREAK APART THE TASK

Distribute copies of the task found on page 286 of the Teacher's Guide and read it together. Have students suggest important key words or phrases to highlight in the task that will help them understand how to complete this task. Have them highlight the agreed-upon key words and phrases.

Use information you have learned from *Disaster Alert!* and *Danger! Earthquakes* to write an informative magazine article explaining a natural event. You will introduce your topic, use facts and definitions to develop information, and provide a conclusion.

ANSWER QUESTIONS ABOUT THE TASK

Display the following questions, which students should be able to answer in order to demonstrate their understanding of the task. Remind students to review the words and phrases they highlighted to help them answer the questions. Alternatively, provide the questions as a handout. Monitor students to determine who needs more support and who can work independently.

- **What type of writing is this?** (informative)
- **What will the text of my writing look like?** (a magazine article)
- **What texts should I reference?** *(Disaster Alert!* and *Danger! Earthquakes)*
- **What information should I give?** (how a natural event occurs)
- **What do I need to include?** (introduction; facts and definitions to develop information; conclusion)

RESTATE THE TASK

Have students restate the task in their own words. Check for possible misunderstandings or missing elements.

ENGLISH LANGUAGE LEARNERS

If . . . students have difficulty answering the questions about the task on their own,

then . . . place students in pairs to work through the answers together. Guide students to review the highlighted words and phrases and restate them to their partner in their own words. Then have partners work together to determine how the highlighted text and the bullet points can help them to best answer the questions about the task.

STRUGGLING WRITERS

If . . . students have difficulty understanding why it might be useful to do additional research,

then . . . have students identify the kinds of information they will be collecting from the selections—facts, definitions, and descriptive details that tell about a natural event. Point out that students might want to find additional facts about and descriptions of their specific natural event. Work with students to brainstorm resources that might offer more information about their natural event, such as encyclopedias, science magazines, scientific web sites, and nonfiction books.

MONITOR AND SUPPORT

Prepare to Write

Once students clearly understand the task, have them review the selections *Disaster Alert!* and *Danger! Earthquakes* and any other resources they might use for doing further research. Have students make a list of natural events they might want to report on in their magazine article. Students may benefit from putting sticky notes next to sentences or on pictures that spark ideas for them.

Have students review their list and pick one natural event for the focus of their article. Remind them that there should be plenty of facts and details available to use in their article. If students struggle to choose between two natural events, have them make a quick list of facts and descriptions of each event. One topic may spark more interest than the other.

GATHER IDEAS

Have students put together ideas for their magazine articles using note cards to gather facts and definitions. A cause-and-effect chart can be used to sort the information into details that tell about the natural event and the impact it has on a community and its people. Note that students should keep track of where each bit of information comes from (either one of the two selections or another resource) so that they can cite each fact properly later.

Have students think about the questions a reader may have about this event and its effects on Earth to ensure that they have collected enough information. Have them use a two-column chart to list questions in the first column, and then make sure they have located facts and definitions that will provide the reader with good answers for each question in the other column.

ACCELERATED WRITERS

If . . . students want to add more detail, such as first-hand experience with a natural event, to their writing,

then . . . help students locate student-friendly resources that might allow them to add quotations from those who have experienced their natural event or scientists who have done extensive research on warning signs or safety precautions for their natural event. Remind students to be sure to properly cite their direct quotes in their writing.

TALK IT THROUGH

Have students talk through their magazine article with a partner to help them get their ideas together. Students may benefit from modeling these prewriting conversations or reviewing some questions the writer might ask a listener.

Questions a Writer Might Ask

- What natural event am I describing?
- What are the main ways that this natural event causes change?
- What facts and definitions will be most important?
- Which descriptions could use more adjectives and adverbs to make them more detailed and interesting?
- What might be missing?
- Was there anything that should be left out?

Encourage students to also formulate questions of their own.

GET ORGANIZED

Have students think about the feedback they received when talking through their article with a partner. Remind them that using this feedback to organize their magazine article will save them time and effort when writing and rewriting.

Have students make sure that they are clear about what their main idea is and which facts, descriptions, and supporting details they are including to develop this main idea. Explain that they must begin with a focused introductory paragraph that makes this main idea obvious from the first sentence of their article. Students should then be sure to end with a strong concluding statement that helps the reader understand why this natural event and its effect on Earth are so important to life on Earth.

ENGLISH LANGUAGE LEARNERS

If . . . students have difficulty finding the words to describe what happens during the course of their chosen natural event,

then . . . have them use information from the selection texts (or information from other research) to draw illustrations or diagrams that depict the event and its impact on Earth. Then work with students to find language they can use to write labels and captions to add to their pictures. Students can then expand upon these labels and captions to write their magazine article.

STRUGGLING WRITERS

If . . . students have difficulty providing adequate feedback to their partner,

then . . . have partners repeat the information the writer told them. Hearing the information repeated will allow students to identify whether their partner understood their ideas. If a partner repeats any information in a confusing manner, this will tell the writer that he or she should consider revising that part of the article.

MONITOR AND SUPPORT

Write

Work with students to create a chart that describes the elements of a magazine article. Remind them to answer any questions readers might have about their natural event. Creating a chart such as the one below can be especially helpful for struggling writers. Invite students to give examples for each row in the chart. This chart may also be used to assess student understanding.

Element	Definition	Example
Headline	• Catches attention • Gives a quick introduction of the main idea	Shaken Up! Moved by Earthquakes
Introduction or Lead	• Includes most important information • Answers questions for readers	When an earthquake shakes a place, life changes. The land can crack, buildings and roads can be damaged, and people can be hurt or killed.
Body	• Provides details • Includes facts that develop the main idea and points • Includes definitions of difficult or scientific words • Includes descriptions that help explain the event	Some people live near fault zones, or areas where there is a crack in Earth's crust. These people are in the most danger from earthquakes. Rocks on the sides of the crack push against each other. If the rocks slip and move, Earth shakes. This causes an earthquake.
Conclusion	• Gives readers a short summary • Includes a final statement that draws a conclusion about the event and its effects on Earth	Life is different in a place after an earthquake. People must rebuild homes and roads. They might try to build buildings in new ways to make them stronger if another earthquake shakes them. However, people on Earth may always be in danger from this natural event.

ENGLISH LANGUAGE LEARNERS

If . . . students have difficulty thinking of adjectives and adverbs to make their descriptions more vivid and specific,

then . . . have them locate images in the texts (or research materials) that relate to their topic. Have them point to and tell about different aspects of the images. Ask guiding questions to elicit detailed descriptions related to size, color, or texture. Help students create a list of vivid adjectives and adverbs to use in their writing.

STRUGGLING WRITERS

If . . . students struggle to come up with a strong concluding statement,

then . . . have them restate their main idea in different words. Then tell them to explain to a partner why they think this main idea is important or interesting to know about. Then have them use their work from these two steps as material for crafting a conclusion.

Look Closely

LOOK AT CONVENTIONS

SENTENCES Review examples of sentences that use adjectives and adverbs to provide more precise and descriptive information about a topic. Have students edit their writing to include adjectives that tell additional information about a thing, such as answering the questions *how many, what color,* or *what size.* Then have them edit sentences to include adverbs that tell *how, where, when, why,* or *to what extent* something is done. Encourage students to make their descriptions richer by adding other adjectives and adverbs.

ADVERBS Encourage students to review their writing to find places where they could clarify a description by providing more information about how, where, when, or why an event takes place. For example, including the word *suddenly* in the statement "the land shakes" makes it clearer how quickly an earthquake can start.

CONTRACTIONS Review that contractions combine two words and that an apostrophe should take the place of the missing letter or letters when the two words are put together. Suggest that students check back through their article to check for proper use of contractions.

LOOK AT CRAFT

SENTENCES Remind students that all of their sentences should work together to support the main idea of the paragraph. Have them check to make sure no sentences provide extra or confusing content that does not relate to the main idea of the paragraph (and the entire article). Have students review their work for information that clearly presents the natural event and the connection between it and the planet changes it causes.

ADJECTIVES Remind students to use a variety of adjectives in their writing. Have students review their writing to determine where they could edit their descriptions of things to help the reader picture it better, such as how big or small something is. Point out examples from the texts that show a variety of adjectives.

ENGLISH LANGUAGE LEARNERS

If . . . students have difficulty coming up with a rich range of descriptive adjectives to use,

then . . . have students work with a partner to brainstorm and share synonyms. For example, if one student is overusing *big* to describe the size of an earthquake, a partner might come up with alternate words to use, such as *large, enormous,* or *huge.* Working together, students can provide one another with ideas that individual students might not have come up with on their own.

STRUGGLING WRITERS

If . . . students have difficulty checking that they have used contractions correctly,

then . . . have them expand each contraction back to its individual words and then double-check with a partner that they have removed only the letters that should be deleted and placed the apostrophe in the right place.

MONITOR AND SUPPORT

Name_____

Title_____

Write a Magazine Article Writing Checklist

❑ Did I include an attention-grabbing introduction?

❑ Did I make it clear what natural event I am describing?

❑ Did I use information from *Disaster Alert!* and *Danger! Earthquakes*? Example:

_____

❑ Did I show the relationship between a natural event and the change it causes?

❑ Did I use facts and definitions to develop my main idea?

❑ Did all of my facts and definitions relate to the main idea?

❑ Did I use specific adjectives and adverbs? Example:

_____

❑ Did I include a strong conclusion?

❑ Did I review my work for correct capitalization, punctuation, and spelling?

❑ (Optional) Did I type my article and use the Internet to get information about the natural event and find images or audio clips to include?

Unlock the Task: Write About Lessons

Distribute copies of the task found on page 146 of the Teacher's Guide and read it together. Have students suggest important key words or phrases to highlight in the task that will help them understand how to complete this task. Have them highlight the agreed-upon key words and phrases.

Think about some of the lessons that you can learn from Johnny Appleseed, such as use what you have, share what you have, and respect nature. Choose one of the three lessons and write your opinion about why you think the lesson is still important to follow in today's world. You will introduce the lesson you choose, state an opinion about the lesson, and supply reasons that support your opinion. Use linking words to connect the opinion and reasons, and provide a conclusion.

Display or distribute the questions students should be able to answer to demonstrate their understanding of the task. Students should use what they highlighted to help them answer the questions.

- **What type of writing is this?** (opinion)
- **What will the text of my writing look like?** (an opinion piece)
- **What texts should I reference?** (*John Chapman: Planter and Pioneer* and *Johnny Appleseed*)
- **What information should I give?** (opinion statement about one of the three lessons; reasons and evidence to support my opinion)
- **What do I need to include?** (an introduction to the topic; linking words that connect opinions and reasons; a conclusion)

Have students restate the task in their own words. Check for possible misunderstandings or missing elements.

ENGLISH LANGUAGE LEARNERS

If . . . students are unclear about the meaning of Johnny Appleseed's lessons, use what you have, share what you have, and respect nature,

then . . . discuss the meaning of each lesson in more depth. For example, "use what you have" does not refer to physical belongings, but to the things they do the best, or the things that come naturally to them.

STRUGGLING WRITERS

If . . . students have difficulty understanding how to approach this task,

then . . . have them break the task down into manageable pieces by rereading the task sentence by sentence and making a list of the steps to follow. For example: 1) Review Johnny Appleseed's lessons. 2) Pick one lesson to write about. 3) Decide why this lesson is still important today. 4) Find textual evidence that explains how Johnny lived by this lesson. 5) Explain how I can live by this lesson.

MONITOR AND SUPPORT

Prepare to Write

DETERMINE FOCUS

Once students clearly understand the writing task, have them review the selections *John Chapman: Planter and Pioneer* and *Johnny Appleseed* and the lessons Johnny Appleseed taught as they are summarized in the writing task. Have students decide which lesson they would be most interested in writing about and begin by searching for details from the selections that might help them form and support an opinion about the lessons. Tell students to use sticky notes to mark parts of the texts that relate to the lesson.

Once students have chosen a lesson to focus on, help them begin to develop their opinion statement. Remind them that they must be able to express and support an opinion about the importance of this lesson in today's world and find details in the selections about how Johnny lived by this lesson. If students have difficulty choosing just one of the lessons, tell them to determine how many reasons they are able to come up with to support their opinion about each lesson. Students may find that their opinion about one lesson is easier to support than their opinion about another lesson.

GATHER IDEAS

Have students brainstorm ideas for their opinion pieces. Remind students to use the pages they marked with sticky notes to help them. Give each student a two-column chart and have them label the left-hand column *Then* and the right-hand column *Now*. Some students may also want to write the lesson they have chosen at the top of the page. Tell students to list ideas about how Johnny Appleseed lived by the lesson in the *Then* column and ideas about how people still live by the lesson today in the *Now* column. Once students have recorded their ideas, have them use examples in both columns to state an opinion about why it is important for people today to follow the lesson. If students find that they cannot support their opinion with strong reasons, they may need to return to the selections to look for additional information or modify their opinion.

ACCELERATED WRITERS

If . . . students can easily state their opinion and reasons for their opinion piece,

then . . . challenge them to think of a powerful conclusion that will persuade their readers not only to agree with them, but to take some action to spread the message of the opinion piece. For example, students should inform the reader how they are living by this lesson and encourage the reader to do the same. Students should try writing different conclusions that will compel readers to follow the lesson in their own lives.

Have students talk through their opinion piece with a partner. It may help to model these prewriting conversations or review some questions a writer might ask.

Questions a Writer Might Ask

- What lesson do I think is important to follow in today's world?
- What evidence do I give for how Johnny Appleseed followed this lesson?
- What evidence do I give for how people today can follow this lesson?
- What reasons best support my opinion?
- Does any part of my opinion need more support?
- What linking words could I use to connect my opinion and reasons?
- Was there anything that I should leave out?

Encourage students to also formulate questions of their own.

Tell students to think about the feedback they received when talking through the topic with a partner. Remind them that using this feedback to organize their opinion piece will save them time and effort when writing and rewriting.

Have students decide what their final opinion is and determine which reasons they will use to support this opinion, as well as the order in which they will present these reasons. Remind them to include only strong reasons, particularly the ones identified by their partner as being the most persuasive. Then have students consider what linking words and phrases they can use to connect their opinion with the reasons that support it. Lead a discussion with students about the importance of considering their audience when writing their opinion piece. Decide with students what the proper tone of the writing should be.

ENGLISH LANGUAGE LEARNERS

If . . . students have difficulty choosing the words to express their opinion,

then . . . provide them with sentence frames they can complete. For example: I think that the most important lesson Johnny taught is___. This is an important lesson for people today because___. Johnny lived this lesson by___. I can live this lesson by___.

STRUGGLING WRITERS

If . . . students have difficulty stating their opinion and finding specific reasons that support it,

then . . . prompt them by asking questions. For example: Which of the lessons do you think is the most important? Why do you think that respecting nature is the most important lesson? How did Johnny's actions show his respect for nature? How do you show your respect for nature?

MONITOR AND SUPPORT

Write

Work with students to create a chart that describes the elements of an opinion piece. Remind them that to persuade the reader to agree with their opinion, they must first clearly state their opinion and then provide specific, logical reasons and examples that support this opinion. Creating a chart such as the one below can be especially helpful for struggling writers. Call on students to give examples for each row in the chart. This chart may also be used to assess student understanding.

Element	Definition	Example
Introduction	• Catches the reader's attention • Introduces the main topic • States the opinion clearly	Johnny Chapman changed the world. He taught people to share what they have. This is an important lesson because it allows everyone to have enough to live on.
Reasons and Evidence	• Support the author's opinion • Linking words connect the opinion and reasons	Johnny Chapman shared the things he owned. He collected apple seeds and apple trees. He shared these things when he sold them to settlers and helped the settlers use them to plant orchards. Johnny Chapman also shared the things he knew. He read to settlers, and he told them stories. People can share things they have, like food, and people can share things they know, like skills or technology.
Conclusion	• Gives readers a short summary of the opinion • Restates why the opinion is important • Gives the writing a sense of closure	Following Johnny Chapman's example will make the world better. Like Johnny Chapman, we can help other people by sharing what we have. When people share, everybody wins.

ENGLISH LANGUAGE LEARNERS

If . . . students have difficulty remembering how different linking words are used,

then . . . review common linking words (*because, and, also*) and then discuss situations when each might be used. For example, note that *because* works well in situations when students are writing about a cause-and-effect relationship, while *and* or *also* are good choices to use in situations when students are describing a new supporting reason that is equal in weight or similar to the one they have just presented.

STRUGGLING WRITERS

If . . . students have difficulty writing logical supporting reasons,

then . . . remind students that they should use evidence from the texts or detailed real-life examples to support the statements they are making. Review their writing for places where they make a claim without any support and then have them explain what evidence from real-life or a text makes them believe this is true. If they cannot support the statement, have them return to the texts to gather more evidence or delete the statement from their opinion piece.

Look Closely

SENTENCES Review how to use a compound verb to combine two related simple sentences into one expanded sentence. Write the following sentence pairs: *John sold trees. John traded trees. John liked to read. John liked to tell stories.* Have students explain how each pair of sentences can be combined into one longer sentence using a compound verb. (*John sold and traded trees. John liked to read and tell stories.*) Have students review their writing to locate examples of short, simple sentences. Encourage them to add variety to their writing by finding one or two places where they can use a compound verb to combine two simple sentences.

SINGULAR AND PLURAL POSSESSIVES Remind students that when using singular and plural possessives in their writing, they must place the apostrophe in each word correctly. Call on students to explain when the apostrophe goes before the *s* and when the apostrophe goes after the *s*. Then have students revise their writing to correct any apostrophe errors.

POSSESSIVE PRONOUNS Remind students that possessive pronouns (*my, your, our, his, her, its, their*) act like adjectives that modify nouns. Encourage students to review their writing to make sure that they have used the correct possessive pronouns throughout.

SENTENCES Remind students that adding adjectives to simple sentences makes their reasons and opinions more vivid and descriptive. Write the following sentence: *Johnny walked through the forest*. Have students suggest adjectives to add in order to make this sentence more vivid. (*Johnny walked through the dark, silent forest.*) Have students review their work to add descriptive adjectives.

LINKING WORDS Provide examples from the text that show how linking words connect opinions and reasons. Have students locate places in their writing where they can add linking words and phrases. Encourage them to use variety to make their writing more interesting.

ENGLISH LANGUAGE LEARNERS

If . . . students have difficulty remembering when to use the different possessive pronouns,

then . . . help students make a chart that relates the possessive pronouns with the subject pronouns with which they should be used—for example, *I/my, he/his, she/her, you/yours, we/our, they/their*. Have students practice using each pair aloud to gain experience with hearing them used together. Provide as many models and opportunities to practice as possible.

STRUGGLING WRITERS

If . . . students have difficulty placing the apostrophe correctly in a singular or plural possessive,

then . . . point out that the apostrophe is like a hanger that hooks the *s* onto the end of a word that names a person or thing something belongs to. Remind them that in cases where the possessive noun already ends in -*s*, they only need to add the apostrophe.

Name_____

Title_____

Write About Lessons
Writing Checklist

❏ Did I include an attention-grabbing beginning?

❏ Did I state my opinion clearly?

❏ Did I use information from *John Chapman* and *Johnny Appleseed*?

❏ Did I include reasons and examples that support my opinion?

❏ Did I use linking words and phrases to connect my opinion and reasons? Example:

_____

❏ Did I use singular and plural possessives correctly? Example:

_____

❏ Did I use possessive pronouns correctly? Example:

_____

❏ Did I include a strong conclusion that provides the reader with a sense of closure?

❏ Did I review my work for correct capitalization, punctuation, and spelling?

Unlock the Task: Write About a Journey West

Distribute copies of the task found on page 286 of the Teacher's Guide and read it together. Have students suggest important key words or phrases to highlight in the task that will help them understand how to complete this task. Have them highlight the agreed-upon key words and phrases.

Write a short story about a pioneer child who shows bravery using ideas and information from the texts you read. You will recount a well-elaborated event or short sequence of events. Include details to describe actions, thoughts, and feelings. Use temporal words to signal event order. Provide a conclusion.

ANSWER QUESTIONS ABOUT THE TASK

Display or distribute the questions students should be able to answer to demonstrate their understanding of the task. Students should use what they highlighted to help them answer the questions.

- **What type of writing is this?** (narrative)
- **What will the text of my writing look like?** (a story)
- **What texts should I reference?** *(Pioneers to the West* and *Going West)*
- **What details should I give?** (actions, thoughts, and feelings of my character; information about how a pioneer child showed bravery)
- **What do I need to include?** (a single event or a short sequence of events; details; temporal words; a conclusion)

RESTATE THE TASK

Have students restate the task in their own words. Check for possible misunderstandings or missing elements.

ENGLISH LANGUAGE LEARNERS

If . . . students are unclear about the meaning of the term *bravery,*

then . . . discuss how a person shows bravery by being strong when facing a challenge. If necessary, flip through the texts with students and work together to identify some examples of pioneer children showing bravery.

STRUGGLING WRITERS

If . . . students have difficulty understanding what type of narrative they are to write,

then . . . explain that some narratives are based on real-life people and events while others are completely imaginary. Clarify that students are to write a narrative based on the lives of real-life pioneer children. Although the character they write about will not be real, the events in their stories will be things that could have happened to real pioneer children.

Prepare to Write

Once students clearly understand the writing task, have them review the selections *Pioneers to the West* and *Going West*. Have students make a list of ideas for character traits, actions, and significant events they might want to include in their narratives. Some students may also want to put sticky notes next to sentences or on pictures that spark ideas for them.

Have students review their list and pick one event or series of events that they think could be the focus of their narrative. Remind them that they should describe a difficult situation in which their charcter was able to show bravery and should illustrate why it was so hard for pioneers to move west. They also need to be able to find plenty of facts and details about this situation in the texts that they can use in their narrative. If students have difficulty choosing between two difficult situations, have them consider which poses the greatest challenge for their character to overcome. One situation may make it more vividly clear to a reader why life in the west was hard. If both situations seem equal, ask students which event seems more interesting to write about.

GATHER IDEAS

Have students brainstorm ideas for their narratives. They might use note cards or sticky notes to write details without putting them in any particular order yet. Students can then use a cause-and-effect chart to sort the information into details that tell about the difficult situation and details that describe what the character thinks, feels, and does when responding to the situation. Remind students that they should pay attention to the order in which the character performs the actions so that the actions will be in the correct sequence when students are ready to write their narratives. Suggest that students record character actions in temporal order in their chart or number their events after they have finished recording all of their ideas.

Remind students that in a historical narrative such as this one, some details may be more important to include than others. For example, point out that because the setting and events may be unfamiliar to a reader who lives in modern times, the writer must be sure to include descriptions and explanations that tell what the west was like in the past and what people had to do to survive in this environment.

ACCELERATED WRITERS

If . . . students find it easy to write about one event or a short sequence of events,

then . . . encourage them to focus on creating interest and building suspense. Have them identify what the problem and solution in their story will be and pinpoint the moment when the action will rise to a climax. Then have them consider how they can present the events leading up to the climax in a way that heightens the reader's awareness that something important is going to happen—for example, by including foreshadowing that hints at a coming disaster and adjectives that create a tense atmosphere.

TALK IT THROUGH

Have students talk through their narrative with a partner to help them organize their ideas. It may help to model these prewriting conversations or review some questions a writer might ask.

Questions a Writer Might Ask

- What are the main events that happen during my narrative?
- How does the main character think and feel about these events?
- What does the main character do because of these events?
- What details and descriptions will be most important?
- What other details might be useful for the reader to know, and should be added to my narrative?
- Does the sequence of events make sense?
- Do I have an idea for providing a sense of closure?
- What might be missing?
- Was there anything that I should leave out?

Encourage students to also formulate questions of their own.

GET ORGANIZED

Tell students to think about the feedback they received when talking with a partner. Remind them that using this feedback to organize their narrative will save them time and effort when writing and rewriting.

Have students finalize the order of the events that they will narrate, including which moment will start the narrative and which will provide a strong sense of closure at the end. Then have students decide which details about their character's thoughts, feelings, and actions they will include during their description of each event in their narrative. Remind them to include only the most relevant details.

ENGLISH LANGUAGE LEARNERS

If . . . students have difficulty finding the words to tell what happens during the events of their narrative,

then . . . discuss what they think the hardest part of moving west to a new land was and how their character might be brave during this experience. As students talk, take notes to record any rich vocabulary they use to answer these questions. Then provide students with a list of these words to use when writing their narrative.

STRUGGLING WRITERS

If . . . students have difficulty figuring out what events to include as part of their narrative,

then . . . have them explain what they think the hardest part of moving west was. Then, have them decide if there is an event that comes before this one that the reader needs to know about to understand this hardship. Have students consider events that might occur after this moment that might need to be included to provide the reader with a sense of closure. If necessary, have them record their ideas in a Story Sequence B Graphic Organizer in Part 3.

Write

BREAK IT DOWN

Work with students to create a chart that describes the elements of a narrative. Remind them that, because they are narrating historical events, they should include very clear and detailed information about their character and setting. Creating a chart such as the one below can be especially helpful for struggling writers. Have students give examples for each row in the chart. This chart may also be used to assess student understanding.

Element	Definition	Example
Beginning	• Catches the reader's attention • Introduces the main character • Establishes the setting	Minnie Wheeler shivered so hard that her shawl almost fell off of her shoulders. Rain dripped through the roof of her wagon, but she didn't care. She was already so cold and wet that more rain would not make her any wetter. Everything her family owned was packed into this one covered wagon as they traveled west. And today all of their things were soaked.
Middle	• Uses temporal words to tell about a sequence of events • Includes descriptions that tell about the main character's actions • Includes details that tell what the main character is thinking and how the main character feels	The next morning, Minnie's throat felt like it was on fire. Minnie could not breathe without coughing hard. She was sure she was sick. By afternoon, she felt so bad that she could not stand to be in the rocking wagon any more. Minnie did not want to slow her family down. They needed to reach their new land and start building their farm before winter arrived. But how would they get there soon enough now that Minnie was too sick to travel?
End	• Includes details that tell what the main character feels, does, or thinks • Uses temporal words to show that the story is ending • Ends with an event that provides a sense of closure	Minnie was sad to see her family's wagon roll away from town. She knew she was doing the right thing, though. She would be brave and stay with the people in this town until she was better. In spring, Papa would come back to get her. Then, she would join her family again.

ENGLISH LANGUAGE LEARNERS

If . . . students have difficulty thinking of vocabulary to use to describe the setting and events in their narrative,

then . . . have them flip through *Pioneers to the West* and *Going West* to find images that relate to the setting and events of their narrative. Help them search the text and captions of the selections for words to use.

STRUGGLING WRITERS

If . . . students struggle to come up with an ending that provides a strong sense of closure,

then . . . have them talk with a partner about the hardship they chose to write about, how their character showed bravery during this hardship, and what they think the character learned from this experience. Encourage them to end their narrative by having their main character think back on the events and consider what he or she learned from this experience about life in the west.

MONITOR AND SUPPORT

Look Closely

SENTENCES Review examples of simple, compound, and complex sentences. Point out that students can add variety to their writing by expanding simple sentences into compound sentences that use *and, but,* or *or,* and they can rearrange sentences by adding adjectives, adverbs, and prepositional phrases to make their writing more interesting to read. Have students add variety to their writing by finding one or two places where they can rearrange their sentences or expand simple sentences into compound sentences.

PREPOSITIONAL PHRASES Remind students that prepositional phrases include a preposition and the object of that preposition. Provide examples from the texts and have students locate the prepositional phrase and identify the preposition. Discuss how the prepositional phrases show the relationship between a noun or pronoun and another word in the sentence. Have students check their narratives to make sure that they have formed each prepositional phrase correctly. Have them also check for places where they could clarify a description or a sequence of events by using prepositional phrases to provide more details about when or where something happens.

SENTENCES Remind students that the sentences in their narratives should work together to recount each event that makes up the narrative without including unnecessary information. Have them check to make sure their sentences do not provide extra or confusing details about the events or thoughts and actions of the main character that the reader does not need to know.

LINKING WORDS Call on students to explain how writers use temporal words. Remind them that some temporal words and phrases make more sense when used in the beginning, middle, or end of a narrative. Encourage students to look for temporal words they have used in their narratives and to check for opportunities to use a greater variety of temporal words and phrases to show event order. Point out good examples from the texts as models whenever possible.

ENGLISH LANGUAGE LEARNERS

If . . . students have difficulty adding prepositional phrases to their writing,

then . . . provide students with a list of models they can fill in and use, such as *in [year], in [season], during the [time of day], at [time], over the [place], across the [place],* and so on. Have them work with a partner to double-check that they have used prepositional phrases correctly in their narrative.

STRUGGLING WRITERS

If . . . students use only simple sentences,

then . . . remind them that they can combine related simple sentences into a compound sentence to add variety to their writing. Scan their writing for simple sentences that could go together and model how to join them correctly, using a conjunction and a comma. Remind students to consider which conjunction would make the most sense to use because *and, but,* and *or* are not interchangeable.

Name_____

Title_____

A Journey West Writing Checklist

❏ Did I include an interesting beginning that will grab the reader's attention?

❏ Did I make it clear when and where this narrative takes place?

❏ Did I use details from *Pioneers to the West* and *Going West*?

❏ Did I include descriptions of my main character's actions?

❏ Did I include specific details that tell about the way my character thinks and feels? Example:

_____

❏ Did I include a clear beginning, middle, and end?

❏ Did I arrange the events of my story in an order that makes sense?

❏ Did I use temporal words and phrases to signal the order of events? Example:

_____

❏ Did I use prepositional phrases correctly? Example:

_____

❏ Did I include a strong ending that concludes the action and provides the reader with a sense of closure?

❏ Did I review my work for correct capitalization, punctuation, and spelling?

Unlock the Task: Write a Book Review

Distribute copies of the task found on page 146 of the Teacher's Guide and read it together. Have students suggest important key words or phrases to highlight in the task that will help them understand how to complete this task. Have students highlight the agreed-upon key words and phrases.

> You will write a book review about which of the selections you liked best, *68 Ways to Save the Planet Before Bedtime* or *On Meadowview Street*. Introduce the book you chose, state an opinion about the book, and supply reasons that support your opinion. Use linking words to connect opinion to reasons, and then provide a conclusion.

Display the following questions, which students should be able to answer in order to demonstrate their understanding of the task. Remind students to review the words and phrases they highlighted to help them answer the questions. Alternatively, provide the questions as a handout. Monitor students to determine who needs more support and who can work independently.

- **What type of writing is this?** (opinion)
- **What will the text of my writing look like?** (a book review)
- **What texts should I reference?** *(68 Ways to Save the Planet Before Bedtime* and *On Meadowview Street.)*
- **What information should I give?** (a clearly stated opinion, at least three reasons that support this opinion)
- **What do I need to include?** (the book you choose, an opinion statement, linking words, at least three reasons, a conclusion)

Have students restate the task in their own words. Check for possible misunderstandings or missing elements.

ENGLISH LANGUAGE LEARNERS

If . . . students are unclear about what a book review is,

then . . . explain that the author of a book review presents a clear opinion about why people might want to read the book or how the book might change people's opinions about a topic. Discuss how a review not only summarizes the contents of a book, but also analyzes the contents and passes some sort of judgment on its worth. If available, provide age-appropriate examples of book reviews to students.

STRUGGLING WRITERS

If . . . students have difficulty understanding what they should do during this task,

then . . . help them break the task into pieces by asking questions such as: What should you write? (a book review) What should the book review explain? (whether the book inspires me or might inspire other people)

Prepare to Write

Once students clearly understand the writing task, have them review the selections *68 Ways to Save the Planet Before Bedtime* and *On Meadowview Street*. Have students write down which of the two books their opinion piece will be about and write the main reason for their choice.

If students have difficulty choosing the book they liked best, have them list the things they liked about each book. Have them determine which selection will be the focus of their opinion piece based on their lists.

GATHER IDEAS

Once students have decided on the focus of their opinion piece, tell them to pull together ideas for their book reviews. They might use note cards or sticky notes to gather details that support their opinion. Students might find a two-column chart useful to use. Have them label the left column *What Happened* and the right column *What I Think About It.* Guide them to list events and details in the appropriate columns. Then have students go back and identify which of the details they will include in their opinion piece. Remind them to be sure that they have enough reasons to back up their opinion. Have students begin to think about their conclusion. Suggest they include a statement that tells why other readers should choose the book.

ACCELERATED WRITERS

If . . . students have many more reasons than needed to support their opinion,

then . . . ask them to prioritize their reasons by deciding which ones best support their opinion statement. Remind students to only include those supporting facts and details that will best help readers understand their opinion statement.

TALK IT THROUGH

Have students talk through their book review with a partner to help them get their ideas together. Students may benefit from modeling these prewriting conversations or reviewing some questions the writer might ask a listener.

Questions a Writer Might Ask

- Which book did I choose, and what is the main reason for my opinion?
- What reasons best support my opinion?
- How could I offer more support for my opinion?
- Which linking words could I use to connect my reasons with my opinion?
- How can I make a strong conclusion?
- What might be missing?
- Is there anything I should leave out?

Encourage students to also formulate questions of their own.

GET ORGANIZED

Have students think about the feedback they received when talking through the topic with a partner. Remind them that using this feedback to organize their book review will save them time and effort when writing and rewriting.

Have students go back over the evidence that supports their opinion and decide what bits of information are the most convincing. Then have students consider what linking words and phrases they can use to connect their opinion with the reasons that support it. Remind them to include only pertinent and strong supporting reasons.

ENGLISH LANGUAGE LEARNERS

If . . . students have difficulty finding the words to use to express their opinion of this book,

then . . . have them draw pictures of what they find most inspiring about the book. Then have them talk about their pictures while you record any words or phrases they could use in their review.

STRUGGLING WRITERS

If . . . students lean toward retelling the whole book instead of pulling out a few carefully selected details to use as support,

then . . . remind them that it may be confusing or even boring for their reader to hear their views about every bit of material in the book. Explain that instead they should focus on including only the details that most strongly support their reason for choosing the book they did. Have them review the evidence they collected and decide which points best serve as reasons for their choice.

MONITOR AND SUPPORT

Write

Work with students to create a chart that describes the elements of a book review. Remind them that they must first clearly state their opinion and then provide specific and logical reasons and examples that support this opinion to convince the reader that it is correct. Invite students to give examples for each row in the chart. This chart may also be used to assess student understanding.

Element	Definition	Example
Introduction	• Catches the reader's attention • Introduces the book • States the main opinion clearly	Sometimes people do not try to make changes because they don't think their actions will make a difference. However, reading *68 Ways to Save the Planet Before Bedtime* can inspire children to change the world by taking small steps.
Reasons and Evidence	• Provides reasons that support the author's opinion • Uses linking words to connect reasons to the opinion	We think that making changes to help save our planet is hard, but this book gives us simple things we can do every day. It's easy to turn off lights when you leave a room and recycle some of the trash at home.
Conclusion	• Gives readers a short summary of the opinion • Restates why this opinion is important • Gives the writing a sense of closure	*68 Ways to Save the Planet Before Bedtime* is an important book to read because it will inspire readers to make changes to help the environment. It teaches us that anyone can change the world.

ENGLISH LANGUAGE LEARNERS

If . . . students struggle to find the words to transition clearly between the reasons that support their opinions,

then . . . suggest that they use sequence words such as *first, second,* and *third* to introduce each reason and to signal a new piece of evidence.

STRUGGLING WRITERS

If . . . students are intimidated by the task,

then . . . encourage students to work on one section at a time. Breaking the task into smaller, more manageable pieces can remove some of the anxiety and make the task seem more achievable.

Look Closely

SENTENCES Review the importance of writing complete sentences. Have students review their writing to make sure their sentences begin with an uppercase letter, end with the correct punctuation, and express a complete thought. Work with students to revise and fix any sentences that do not meet these criteria.

SPELLING PATTERNS Review that vowel digraphs are two vowels that join to make one sound, though some of these vowel digraphs have exceptions (such as *bear* and *year*). Note that when using words that are spelled with diphthongs, such as *oi* and *oy*, students must make sure they are using the correct spelling since some diphthongs sound alike. Finish by reviewing how the letter *g* can be used to spell different sounds and can be silent when coupled with an *h.*

PREFIXES AND ROOT WORDS Have students recall what they learned about using prefixes and root words. Have them review their writing to make sure they correctly spelled words with prefixes.

LOOK AT CRAFT

SENTENCES Review how using precise nouns, verbs, adjectives, and adverbs can help students express their meaning more clearly. Add that using words with a more positive or negative meaning can persuade a reader to agree with your opinion. Have students review their work looking for places where they can make their reasons more compelling by choosing to use another word that has a slightly different meaning.

LINKING WORDS Review examples of sentences showing linking words connecting opinions with supporting reasons. Have students look closely at the linking words in their book review and search for opportunities to add or edit linking words and phrases. Remind them to use a variety of different linking words and phrases.

ENGLISH LANGUAGE LEARNERS

If . . . students have difficulty strengthening their writing by coming up with alternate words with different shades of meaning to use,

then . . . pair students and have them work together to brainstorm possibilities. Together, they may have a larger pool of potential vocabulary words from which to draw. Partners could make a chart with words going across from negative to positive, such as *yucky/bad/ okay/good/delicious; stinky/smelly/unscented/fresh/ fragrant.*

STRUGGLING WRITERS

If . . . students struggle to spell words with difficult spelling patterns correctly,

then . . . provide them with a list of sample words that follow each pattern to use for reference. Over time, have them add more examples, as well as exceptions, to the list.

Name_____

Title_____

Write a Book Review
Writing Checklist

❏ Did I clearly indicate whether my opinion piece will be about *68 Ways to Save the Planet Before Bedtime* or *On Meadowview Street?*

❏ Did I clearly state my opinion in the beginning of my writing?

❏ Did I use information from my chosen book?

❏ Did I include at least three reasons that clearly support my opinion?

❏ Did I use linking words and phrases when needed to connect my opinion and reasons?

❏ Did I spell words that follow difficult spelling patterns (such as silent *gh* or vowel digraphs) correctly? Example:

_____

❏ Did I spell prefixes and root words correctly? Example:

_____

❏ Did I include a strong conclusion that provides the reader with a sense of closure?

❏ Did I review my work for correct capitalization, punctuation, and spelling?

Unlock the Task: Agree or Disagree

BREAK APART THE TASK

Distribute copies of the task found on page 286 of the Teacher's Guide and read it together. Have students suggest important key words or phrases to highlight in the task that will help them understand how to complete it. Have students highlight the agreed-upon key words and phrases.

Using *Alfred Nobel: The Man Behind the Peace Prize* or *A Picture Book of Eleanor Roosevelt*, identify an opinion the author includes about Nobel or Roosevelt. State whether you agree or disagree with the opinion. Use text evidence to support your own opinion.

ANSWER QUESTIONS ABOUT THE TASK

Display or distribute the questions students should be able to answer to demonstrate their understanding of the task. Students should use what they highlighted to help them answer the questions.

- **What type of writing is this?** (opinion)
- **What will the text of my writing look like?** (an opinion piece)
- **What texts should I reference?** *(Alfred Nobel: The Man Behind the Peace Prize* or *A Picture Book of Eleanor Roosevelt)*
- **What information should I give?** (a clearly stated opinion, at least three reasons that support this opinion)
- **What do I need to include?** (an introduction; a clear opinion statement; linking words; at least three reasons; a conclusion)

RESTATE THE TASK

Have students restate the task in their own words. Check for possible misunderstandings or missing elements.

ENGLISH LANGUAGE LEARNERS

If . . . students are not familiar with what it means to agree or disagree with an opinion,

then . . . discuss how when you agree with someone, you think that their view on a subject is correct and it is typically the same as your own opinion. On the other hand, when you disagree with someone, you hold a different view on a subject and do not think their opinion is correct. Provide students with some examples of how you might agree or disagree with someone's opinion.

STRUGGLING WRITERS

If . . . students are confused about what opinion they are to include in this opinion piece,

then . . . help them distinguish between the opinion held by the author of the book and their own opinion. Clarify that they are supposed to 1) identify the part of the book they will be writing about and then 2) give their opinion about what the author thinks, explaining whether they think the author's view of the person is right or not.

MONITOR AND SUPPORT

Prepare to Write

DETERMINE FOCUS

Once students clearly understand the writing task, have them review the selections *Alfred Nobel: The Man Behind the Peace Prize* and *A Picture Book of Eleanor Roosevelt*. Have students record interesting points that the authors of each piece make about their subjects, thinking about how these points help the reader understand the authors' opinions about their subjects. Some students may benefit from putting sticky notes next to sentences or on pictures that spark ideas for them.

Then have students narrow their topic, first by picking one person about whom to write and then by picking one particular point the author makes about this person. Note that each author expresses several opinions about the respective person, so students must decide which opinion they will judge. If students have difficulty choosing between the two selections, tell them to consider which person they find more interesting. If students have difficulty selecting one opinion to write about, remind them that they will need to be able to provide several reasons to support why they agree or disagree with the author's opinion.

GATHER IDEAS

Have students put together ideas for their opinion piece. They might use note cards or a graphic organizer to gather details about the author's opinion of the person. Students can write the author's opinion in the center oval of a Word Web and then record reasons the author includes to support this opinion in the surrounding ovals. Once students have collected information, have them decide whether they agree with each of the author's reasons they listed and why. Once students have evaluated each reason, have them decide what their overall opinion of the text is, and what they could say to support their opinion.

Have students talk through their opinion piece with a partner to help them get their ideas together. Students may benefit from modeling these prewriting conversations or reviewing some questions the writer might ask a listener.

Questions a Writer Might Ask

- What is the author's opinion of this person?
- What reasons does the author offer to support this opinion?
- What is my opinion about the author's viewpoints?
- What reasons best support my opinion?
- In what ways does my opinion need more support?
- Where could I add linking words to connect my reasons with my opinion?
- How can I make a strong concluding statement?
- What might be missing?
- Is there anything I should leave out?

Encourage students to also formulate questions of their own.

GET ORGANIZED

Tell students to think about the feedback they received when talking through their opinion piece with a partner. Remind them that using this feedback to organize their opinion piece will save them time and effort when writing and rewriting.

Have students decide what their final opinion is and determine which reasons they will use to support this opinion, as well as the order in which they will present these reasons. Then have students consider what linking words and phrases they can use to connect their opinion with the reasons that support it. Remind them to include only pertinent and strong supporting reasons, particularly the ones their partner identified as being the most persuasive.

ENGLISH LANGUAGE LEARNERS

If . . . students have difficulty finding the words to tell why they agree or disagree with the author's opinion,

then . . . have them flip to the part of the selection where the author expresses this opinion. Have them use the pictures and the words from the text in this part to summarize the author's opinion. Guide them to use their own words to talk aloud about what they think of this opinion and use what they say in their drafts.

STRUGGLING WRITERS

If . . . students have difficulty figuring out what information they should include in their writing to present the author's opinion,

then . . . point out that each book is full of many details and descriptions of things that happened to the person. However, students should only include information that directly relates to the author's opinion. Have students first state the author's opinion as concisely as possible and then review the information they are planning to include to make sure it all relates to this opinion.

Write

Work with students to create a chart that describes the elements of an opinion piece. Remind them that they must first clearly state their opinion and then provide specific and logical reasons and examples that support this opinion to convince the reader that this opinion is correct. Invite students to give examples for each row in the chart. This chart may also be used to assess student understanding.

Element	Definition	Example
Introduction	• Catches the reader's attention • Introduces the main topic • States an opinion clearly	In *Alfred Nobel: The Man Behind the Peace Prize,* Kathy-Jo Wargin argues that Alfred was a man who loved peace. I think that she is right because Alfred invented dynamite and set up the Nobel prizes for good reasons.
Reasons and Evidence	• Provides reasons that support the writer's opinion • Uses linking words to connect reasons to the opinion	The author says that Alfred hoped his inventions would prevent war. She tells the reader that Alfred thought that if people were afraid of what dynamite could do, maybe they would settle their problems peacefully. I agree that this shows Alfred loved peace. Not only did he want people to settle their problems peacefully, but he also was sad when people used his inventions to hurt each other.
Conclusion	• Gives readers a short summary of the opinion • Restates why this opinion is important • Ends with a concluding statement that gives the writing a sense of closure	Kathy-Jo Wargin picked a good title for her book about Alfred. I agree that he should be remembered as the man behind the Peace Prize, because he did love peace. He never meant for his inventions to hurt people, and he did everything he could to get the people of the world to act peacefully.

ENGLISH LANGUAGE LEARNERS

If . . . students struggle to use appropriate linking words in their writing,

then . . . review possibilities for linking words they could use—such as *not only/but also, so that,* and *because*—and have students work with a partner to review their writing and identify places where they have used the same linking word or words too many times in a row. Then have partners offer each other suggestions for alternative linking words to use to break up the repetition.

STRUGGLING WRITERS

If . . . students do not provide enough reasons to support their opinions,

then . . . provide them with a list of questions they can use to double-check that they have included reasons to support each part of their opinions. For example: *What is the author's opinion? What is one reason why the author holds this opinion? What is one reason why you agree/disagree with this reason? What is another reason you agree/disagree with this reason? What is a second reason why the author holds this opinion? What are two reasons why you agree/disagree with this reason?*

Look Closely

SENTENCES Clarify that each paragraph should include a strong topic sentence that tells the main idea of the paragraph, as well as several supporting sentences that tell more about this topic. Use examples from the texts to give students practice with identifying the topic sentence of a paragraph. Have students use these examples as models for revising their written paragraphs as necessary, creating clear topic sentences and deleting or moving any sentences that do not relate to this main topic.

ROOT WORDS AND PREFIXES Review examples of root words and prefixes. Then have students review their writing to confirm that they have used prefixes correctly and have not used the wrong form of words that contain root words.

DICTIONARIES Focus attention on how to use dictionaries to check the definition of words. Remind students to look up words in a dictionary before using them in their writing to confirm the word means what they think it does. Have students check back through their writing to confirm that they have used the words they intended to use.

SENTENCES Remind students that they can use connecting words within their sentences to help readers better understand their topic. Review how connecting words like *such as* and *for example* can help a reader use context clues to figure out the meaning of unfamiliar words. Have students check their writing for places where they can add or edit connecting words so that their writing and reasons are as clear as possible.

LINKING WORDS Have students recall how writers use linking words such as *because, so that,* and *as a result,* to connect opinions with the reasons that support them. Have students check that they have used a variety of linking words in their opinion pieces and search for opportunities to use additional linking words and phrases.

ENGLISH LANGUAGE LEARNERS

If . . . students have difficulty thinking of connecting words to use in their writing,

then . . . arrange students in groups of three or four. Have group members read each other's writing, identify places where words could be revised to explain a topic better, and discuss which new words might best work in these places.

STRUGGLING WRITERS

If . . . students struggle to develop topic sentences,

then . . . provide them with the Main Idea and Details Graphic Organizer in Part 3 to record the information they plan to include in each paragraph. Have them write their facts, supporting reasons, and descriptive details in the *Details* boxes. Then have them combine this information, using a key word from each *Detail* box, to write their topic sentence in the *Main Idea* box.

Name_____

Title_____

Agree or Disagree Writing Checklist

❏ Did I include an attention-grabbing beginning?

❏ Did I fully introduce the topic, including the author's opinion?

❏ Did I state clearly in the beginning what my opinion is?

❏ Did I use information from *Alfred Nobel: The Man Behind the Peace Prize* or *A Picture Book of Eleanor Roosevelt?* Example:

_____

❏ Did I include at least three reasons that clearly support my opinion?

❏ Did I use linking words and phrases when needed to connect my opinion and reasons? Example:

_____

❏ Did I use root words and prefixes correctly? Example:

_____

❏ Did I include a strong concluding statement that provides the reader with a sense of closure?

❏ Did I review my work for correct capitalization, punctuation, and spelling?

❏ (optional) Did I include images or videos from the Internet of my chosen subject to support my opinion?

Scaffolded Lessons for the Writing Types

Unlock Opinion Writing

INTRODUCE

Show students an example of an opinion text from a student newspaper editorial, from a magazine article, or from a text that you have read in class. Explain to students that this is an example of an opinion piece and that an opinion is a belief or something that a person thinks is true. In an opinion piece, a writer is telling his or her view about something. Engage students in a discussion about opinions. Ask them if they have opinions about different things, such as what the school cafeteria should serve for lunch or how much time they should have for recess. Invite students to share their opinions, and then point out that not everyone shares the same opinion.

Explain to students that when they read opinion pieces, they may or may not agree with what the writer has to say. Some opinion writing is based on the writer's feelings or what the writer has heard or been told, while other opinion writing is supported with facts. Tell students that, either way, a writer should use reasons to support his or her opinion.

UNDERSTAND TASK AND TONE

Tell students that in opinion writing they are often given a topic to write about, but that they can choose what their opinion about the topic is. Remind students that before they begin writing, they must carefully read the assignment and understand all of its parts. Explain that most school assignments will be read by you, their teacher, so they should use a formal tone.

REFOCUS ON THE WRITING TYPE

Throughout the year as students read or are asked to write opinion texts, remind them of the key features of this text type. Opinion writing

- states an opinion about the topic.
- gives reasons that support the opinion.
- connects the opinion and the reasons.
- includes a concluding statement.

Introduce a Topic

What Students Should KNOW	What Students Will DO
• Distinguish between facts and opinions. • Identify topics for which opinions can be given. • Write a sentence that introduces a topic and states an opinion.	• Introduce the topic or book they are writing about. • State an opinion.

MODEL AND PRACTICE

Guide students in choosing a topic for an opinion piece. Begin by talking about topics that interest students or topics that students feel strongly about. Read aloud several fact or opinion statements to see if students can distinguish between facts and opinions. As you read, invite students to raise their hand when they hear an opinion and snap their fingers when they hear a fact. Review the topic of the text and how the writer introduced it. Did the writer state his or her opinion to introduce the topic, or did the writer introduce the topic by stating a fact? Tell students that these are both effective ways to introduce a topic when writing an opinion piece.

MODEL Which of these topics would work best for opinion writing—how to blow a bubble or what type of pizza tastes better? If I write about how to blow a bubble, I need to tell the reader how to do something. That doesn't sound like an opinion. The topic about pizza would be good for opinion writing, because I have a strong opinion about the topic. To introduce the topic I might write, "Cheese pizza and pepperoni pizza are both popular, but I think cheese pizza tastes better." I stated and introduced the topic and stated my opinion.

PRACTICE Work together to brainstorm a list of possible topics for an opinion piece. Then suggest some topics that would not work well for an opinion piece, and see whether students can explain the difference. Then have students vote to choose a topic that works well.

DEEPER PRACTICE Using the information from the group practice, instruct students to work with a partner to write a complete sentence that introduces the topic and states an opinion about the topic.

ENGLISH LANGUAGE LEARNERS

If . . . students confuse the difference between fact and opinion,

then . . . give them practice with familiar topics, such as sandwiches. Model a fact and an opinion about the topic. Say: A sandwich has bread. Cheese sandwiches are the best. Make sure students understand which statement is a fact and which is an opinion and why. Have students work in pairs to provide examples of facts and opinions about sandwiches.

STRUGGLING WRITERS

If . . . students write a sentence that states an opinion but doesn't introduce the topic,

then . . . work through some sample sentences together to help them see the difference between stating an opinion and introducing a topic. Remind students that the sentence can include a fact but should also clearly introduce the topic to the reader. Point out that simply stating an opinion, such as "I like cheese pizza," does not introduce the topic clearly, but, rather, just states the writer's opinion.

MONITOR AND SUPPORT

Provide Reasons

What Students Should KNOW	What Students Will DO
• Write a sentence that gives at least one reason for an opinion. • Identify words that can link opinions and reasons.	• Supply reasons that support the opinion. • Use linking words (*because, and, also*) to connect opinions and reasons.

MODEL AND PRACTICE

Tell students that good opinion pieces include reasons to support the writer's opinion. Point out that students should have at least one reason for an opinion statement. Ask students what they would think if you said you like apples just because you like them. Help students understand the value of reasons to support opinions. As you provide reasons that support an opinion for liking apples, ask students to also listen for linking words, such as *and, also,* and *because,* that connect the reasons to your opinion.

MODEL If I am writing about why I like cheese pizza better than pepperoni pizza, I need to look for reasons to support this opinion. I might write that I like cheese because pepperoni is sometimes too spicy for me. This can be a reason to support my opinion statement. I could also try to find facts that support this reason. I could do research. I could learn if cheese pizza is more or less expensive or has more or fewer calories.

PRACTICE Have students work with a partner to identify linking words in opinion pieces. Ask students to list the linking words they find. Then instruct them to tell which reason and opinion each linking word connects.

DEEPER PRACTICE Ask students to work in groups to brainstorm additional reasons for the topic of liking cheese pizza better than pepperoni pizza. Have students work together to write a complete sentence that includes the reason. Challenge them to include a linking word.

ENGLISH LANGUAGE LEARNERS

If . . . students have trouble understanding what linking words are,

then . . . write linking words on note cards. Write an opinion on a piece of paper and a reason on another piece of paper. Then have two students stand, one holding the opinion and one holding the reason, and link arms to hold up the linking words. Work with students to determine which linking word best connects the opinion and reason. Try several more examples.

STRUGGLING WRITERS

If . . . students have difficulty thinking of reasons to support an opinion,

then . . . have them use a word web to help organize ideas. Ask them to write the topic and/or introductory sentence in the center circle and then brainstorm ideas in the outer circles. Then provide model reason sentence frames, such as "[insert introductory sentence] [insert topic] because [reason 1] and [reason 2].

Write a Conclusion

What Students Should KNOW	What Students Will DO
• Identify conclusions in opinion texts students have read. • Write a sentence or sentences that conclude the opinion piece.	• Provide a concluding statement or section.

MODEL AND PRACTICE

Explain to students why opinion writing should have a strong concluding statement or section. The conclusion should wrap up or restate the writer's opinion about the topic and come to a close. It should not introduce new ideas that have not yet been introduced. Tell students that an opinion piece can end with a strong statement that gives the reader something to think about and that is related to the topic, the opinion that was expressed, or both.

MODEL I want to wrap up my opinion piece about cheese pizza. I will restate my opinion once more and talk about the reasons I used. Should I go on to talk about sausage pizza? No, that would not be connected to the topic or my opinion. I want to leave the reader with something to think about that connects to my topic. I can write, "The next time you get to pick a kind of pizza, think about voting with your stomach for my favorite, cheese pizza." This concluding sentence wraps up my writing and leaves the reader with something to think about.

PRACTICE Work with students to list the elements that a strong conclusion for an opinion piece would need. Write the list on the board or a chart and create several strong conclusions together. Write the conclusion and check that each element is included.

DEEPER PRACTICE Ask each student to write two or more sentences that wrap up the opinion piece about cheese pizza. Point out that one concluding sentence has already been provided for them as a model.

ENGLISH LANGUAGE LEARNERS

If . . . students have trouble wrapping up an opinion piece,

then . . . provide a model conclusion. Replace key words one at a time that relate to the topic. Model reading the sentences with each change and have students read after you.

STRUGGLING WRITERS

If . . . students write conclusions that are not connected to the opinion or to reasons with linking words,

then . . . remind students that they can use linking words or phrases to help them. Have them work with a partner to make a list of linking words, and then try each one in their conclusion to determine which fits best.

Support for Extended Writing

Refer to this process when students are writing a longer passage that requires development and organization to produce an opinion text. Remind students of the importance of revising and editing their work to make it stronger.

UNDERSTAND THE TASK Tell students to review their writing prompt or writing assignment carefully to be sure they understand what is being asked and that they answer all parts of it. Consider having them answer these questions: What is the topic? What is my opinion about the topic? Do I need to reference or cite another text? What reasons will I use to support my opinion? How many parts are there in this writing assignment?

BRAINSTORM Provide students with assistance as they brainstorm ideas for their topic. Point out that sometimes having a strong opinion can help lead them to a topic choice. Then ask them to consider how they will introduce their topic once they have selected it.

PROVIDE REASONS Have students focus on the part of the writing in which they list reasons for their opinion. Work with students to locate print and/or digital resources that may be helpful to them to gather facts for their reasons. Model for them how to use facts as supporting reasons.

ORGANIZE INFORMATION Have students focus on the way they will organize their writing, especially how they will list the reasons to support their opinion. Point out that students need to decide how many reasons they will use to support their opinion and what linking words work best to connect them. Remind students to think about how they will provide closure for their opinion piece before they begin to write. You might provide a framework that includes a box for the introduction and opinion statement, a larger box for the reasons, and a box for the conclusion. A visual model such as this may help students remember to include all of the parts.

FOCUS ON LINKING WORDS Have students review their own writing and look for opportunities to add linking words. A peer reviewer might be able to suggest some possible locations that would benefit from the additional support of linking words.

WRITE

Provide students with encouraging tips to guide them through their writing process. Some tips might include:

- Remind students that their draft should focus on making their opinion and reasons clear to the reader, and they do not need to worry about every detail in grammar, spelling, or punctuation at this point.
- Explain to students that if they get stuck, they can use any graphic organizers or checklists to help guide them through the writing process.
- Tell students to give their own opinion about the topic and not to worry about what other people think of their opinion.
- Remind students to state their opinion in both their introduction and conclusion.
- Encourage students to check that their opinion is supported by reasons and facts and that all are connected by linking words.
- When students are finished, have them double check that they have answered all parts of the writing prompt or assignment.

REVISE AND EDIT

Guide students through the revising and editing process. Work with them to develop writing and reviewing checklists to help them look for details that they might address in their revision. You may choose to reproduce the checklists on the following pages and work with students to add task-specific items to the lists. After revising their work, have students review one another's work to further strengthen their writing.

PUBLISH

Provide students with support in presenting their final version. You may want to create a show called "Opinions 'R Us" to provide an opportunity for students to share their opinion pieces with the class. Consider recording their "show" with audio or video, and then play it back for students to listen to or watch.

ACCELERATED WRITERS

If . . . students are comfortable stating and writing their opinions,

then . . . encourage them to write an opinion piece that takes the opposite opinion from their own. Remind them that this opposite opinion should also be supported with reasons.

Writer's Checklist

Name_____

Title _____

❏ Did I include a strong introduction?

❏ Did I give reasons to support my opinion?

❏ Did I use facts to support my reasons?

❏ Did I explain my opinion clearly so that the reader understands it?

❏ Did I use linking words to connect my opinion and reasons?

❏ Did I restate my opinion and reason in the concluding statement or section?

❏ Did I address all parts of the prompt or writing assignment?

❏ Did I review my work for correct capitalization, punctuation, and spelling?

❏ _____

❏ _____

Peer Review Checklist

Name_____

Writer's Name_____

Title _____

❏ Does the writer give a reason or reasons
to support his or her opinion?

❏ Does the writing use facts to support reasons?

❏ Is the writing clearly organized?

❏ Does the writing include linking words to connect
the stated opinion and reasons?

❏ Does the concluding statement restate the
writer's opinion and reason?

❏ Does the writing have linking words or phrases
to connect or clarify ideas?

❏ Are all parts of the prompt or assignment
addressed clearly in the writing?

❏ _____

❏ _____

❏ _____

Unlock Informative/ Explanatory Writing

Show examples of informative/explanatory texts that are familiar to students. You may choose texts from your classroom library or one that you have recently read, such as a biography. Explain to students that the text is an example of informative/ explanatory writing. Tell students that the writer researched facts about the topic of the text to give the reader information about it. Allow students to look through the text and decide what the topic of the text is.

Explain to students that the purpose of informative/explanatory writing is to explain a topic and to share ideas and information clearly. Point out that the words *informative* and *explanatory* include the words *inform* and *explain.* Provide a few examples of this type of writing, and have students brainstorm with you to create a comprehensive list. You may add to the list throughout the year. Examples may include but are not limited to:

- newspaper articles
- recipes
- nature guides
- biographies
- magazine articles
- how-to books
- travel brochures
- textbooks

Have volunteers talk about the tone, or voice, of informative/explanatory writing they have come across, and discuss what makes it different from other forms that tell a story or give an opinion. Guide students to understand that the tone of a particular kind of writing depends on its purpose and audience. Many informative/ explanatory texts have a formal tone, which is the tone students will need to use for most of their nonfiction writing.

UNDERSTAND PURPOSE

Explain to students that they will sometimes be asked to write informative/ explanatory texts as part of their assignments or assessments. Tell students that they are often given a topic to write about, which is sometimes called a writing prompt. Explain that before they begin writing, they must carefully read the assignment and understand all of its parts. They should also make sure they understand the purpose of their writing and who their audience is.

Introduce a Topic

What Students Should KNOW	What Students Will DO
• Identify how topics are introduced in texts students read. • Understand the goal of an introduction for informative/explanatory writing. • Identify and use introductory words and phrases. • Write an introductory sentence.	• Introduce a topic.

MODEL AND PRACTICE

Discuss the importance of an introduction when writing informative/explanatory texts.

MODEL Introductions are important because they help get the readers' attention. They tell the audience what the text will be about. My assignment is to write about an admirable woman. I think about how best to introduce my topic. First, I thought of several admirable women in history and selected Sacagawea. I found several books about her in the library. My introductory sentence lets the reader know that Sacagawea helped Lewis and Clark explore the West. This is a clear and simple way to introduce my topic.

PRACTICE Ask each student to write an introductory sentence about a topic. Have students exchange introductory sentences with partners. Ask partners to tell what they think the rest of the text will be about, based only on reading the one sentence. Encourage them to identify the words that were most helpful.

DEEPER PRACTICE Have students work with a partner to find three introductory sentences in texts in the classroom. Have students copy the sentences and then ask another pair to tell which sentence came from which piece of text.

ENGLISH LANGUAGE LEARNERS

If . . . students have trouble determining what to include in an introductory sentence or sentences,

then . . . have them draw pictures showing what they want to share about a topic. Ask students to decide what is most important about each topic. Help each student form a complete sentence about the topic and say the sentence together. Once comfortable saying the sentence, ask each student to write the sentence and read it to a partner.

STRUGGLING WRITERS

If . . . students have difficulty staying focused when deciding how to introduce a topic,

then . . . have them write the name of the topic on the top of a piece of paper or a blank note card. Ask students to write one or two words that are most important for a reader to know about their topic. Suggest that students build the introduction based on those few words.

MONITOR AND SUPPORT

Use Facts and Definitions

What Students Should KNOW	What Students Will DO
• Identify facts in texts students have read. • Gather information related to the topic. • State the points students want to develop related to the topic.	• Use facts to develop points.
• Identify important words to define that help develop points related to the topic. • Know how to write a definition.	• Use definitions to develop points.

MODEL AND PRACTICE

Provide students with examples of facts from informative/explanatory texts. Explain that unlike opinion statements, facts are statements that can be proven. Discuss how providing definitions for difficult or unfamiliar words in a fact can help make the topic clearer.

MODEL I'm going to write about Sacagawea. I want to tell who she was and what she did. I will find facts about her travels. I'd better define the words *expedition* and *Shoshone*. I know that they may be unfamiliar to my readers. I'll use a dictionary to find the definitions of these words, but I'll write the definitions in my own words.

PRACTICE Invite students to identify examples of facts in informative/explanatory texts that they think make a topic clearer and more interesting. Have students locate vocabulary, content, or academic words that are defined. Ask them to work with a partner to identify the word, read the sentence that provides the definition, and identify the fact that it supports.

DEEPER PRACTICE Have students brainstorm a list of additional facts that could be added to help to develop points, or ask questions about the topic that could be answered using facts. Ask students to identify where they would insert definitions in the text and to explain their choices.

ENGLISH LANGUAGE LEARNERS

If . . . students have trouble identifying which facts help develop the same point,

then . . . ask students to use colored highlighters or crayons to color-code related information. Ask students to explain how the same color items are connected.

STRUGGLING WRITERS

If . . . students have trouble identifying vocabulary, content, or academic words that are defined or need definitions,

then . . . ask students to use text elements to help them locate these words. Explain that such words are often in dark letters or highlighted in a text so that the reader can locate them easily. Then ask students to read the sentence before and after the sentence in which the word is defined. Point out that often a vocabulary word is introduced in a fact before it is defined.

Provide a Conclusion

What Students Should KNOW	What Students Will DO
• Identify the concluding statements or section in texts students have read. • Understand the goal of a concluding statement or section for informative/explanatory writing. • Identify and use concluding words and phrases.	• Provide a concluding statement or section.

MODEL AND PRACTICE

Explain that informative/explanatory writing should have a clear conclusion that provides an end to, or a wrap-up of, the text. The conclusion often restates or repeats the topic and the main points that the writer made. Tell students that some conclusions end with a question or a statement that gives the reader something to think about.

MODEL I'm getting ready to end my informative text about Sacagawea. I must think about what I told the reader in my introduction. I want to restate the topic and the main points, but I also want to end the text in a way that will keep the reader thinking about Sacagawea. Maybe I can write, "As you can see, Sacagawea was a Native American woman who helped lead American explorers. What made her an American hero?" The last sentence does not introduce new information to the reader, but it asks the reader to think about how the actions of Sacagawea made her an American hero.

PRACTICE Provide students with a few examples of informative/explanatory texts. Ask small groups to locate and read aloud each conclusion. Have them identify how the concluding statement restated the topic and the main points from the introduction. Ask if the concluding statement left the reader with a question or something to think about.

DEEPER PRACTICE Ask students to vote in their group to choose one of the concluding statements. Then have them write a question or statement to make the reader think more about the topic. Encourage students to rewrite the concluding sentence with this additional text.

ENGLISH LANGUAGE LEARNERS

If . . . students have trouble writing a concluding statement,

then . . . ask them to reread their introductory sentence. Ask students to suppose they are telling a younger child about this topic. What would they want that child to remember? Encourage students to restate that important information in the conclusion.

STRUGGLING WRITERS

If . . . students have trouble identifying the concluding statement,

then . . . ask them to look at the first and last paragraphs of the text. Have them underline important words and phrases about the topic in both paragraphs. Then ask them to look for those words and phrases in both paragraphs that are alike.

Support for Extended Writing

Refer to this process when students are writing a passage that requires development and strengthening to produce an informative/explanatory text.

UNDERSTAND THE TASK Tell students to review their writing prompt or writing assignment carefully to be sure they understand what is being asked. Have them answer these questions: What am I asked to write about? How can I restate what I need to write about in my own words? Do I know where to find the information to answer the question or prompt?

RESEARCH Provide students with guidance and support to focus on their writing topic. You might group together students with similar topics. Organize a trip to the school library or media center to gather information or to conduct online research. Review examples of Web sites that are appropriate to use to gather information.

GATHER INFORMATION Demonstrate how to gather several books or other reference sources on the same topic. Model how to record information from the sources without writing it down word for word. Have students work with a partner or small group to gather sources and record some of the information.

ORGANIZE INFORMATION Model organizing facts and information to support the points in your writing. Help students align the facts and definitions with the key points they want to include. Remind students of the three main parts of their writing: the introduction, the points supported with facts and definitions, and the conclusion.

FOCUS ON DEFINITIONS Provide students with examples of sentences that include definitions. Review together the signals for a definition. Help students see that words like *meaning* and *which means*, or a comma followed by a short, defining phrase can all be helpful.

Provide students with encouraging tips to guide them through the writing process. Some tips might include:

- Remind students that they are beginning with a draft, and they should concentrate on focusing their topic, using the best facts and definitions that develop their topic.

- Explain to students that they must use their own words when writing about what they learned from other sources.

- If students have difficulty beginning to write their first draft, encourage them to write one sentence for each fact. Then ask them to number each sentence to determine in what order they should arrange the sentences so that the topic is clear. Encourage them to read aloud each sentence to help them with this task.

- Remind students to concentrate on writing an effective introductory sentence and concluding statement.

REVISE AND EDIT

Guide students through the revising and editing process. Work with students to develop writing and reviewing checklists to help them look for details that they might address in their revision. After revising their work, have students exchange papers with a partner and review each other's work to further strengthen their writing.

PUBLISH

Provide students with support in presenting their final version. You may want to arrange classroom time for students to read their texts aloud. Provide a space for students to display the final texts. You might provide them with time to enter their final drafts into a computer software program or to present it on a classroom or school Web site.

ACCELERATED WRITERS

If . . . students have difficulty finding anything in their own work to revise,

then . . . encourage students to go sentence by sentence to stretch and strengthen each sentence. Model making these changes in your own writing, and explain that making changes is what good writers do. Some students may see it as a sign of having made a mistake.

Writer's Checklist

Name_____

Title _____

❑ Did I introduce my topic?

❑ Did I use facts to develop points about my topic?

❑ Did I state the facts clearly?

❑ Did I include definitions for words that readers may not know?

❑ Did the definitions help to develop my points?

❑ Did I add a concluding statement or section?

❑ Did I review my work for correct capitalization, punctuation, and spelling?

❑ _____

❑ _____

❑ _____

❑ _____

❑ _____

Peer Review Checklist

Name_____

Writer's Name_____

Title_____

- ❏ Does the introduction tell the reader about the topic?

- ❏ Do the facts help to support the points?

- ❏ Are the facts stated clearly?

- ❏ Does the writing have definitions of content words?

- ❏ Do the definitions help to develop points?

- ❏ Does the writing have a strong concluding statement or section?

- ❏ _____

- ❏ _____

- ❏ _____

- ❏ _____

- ❏ _____

Unlock Narrative Writing

Ask students if they have ever told or written a real or make-believe story that is based on something that happened to them or someone they know. Point out that when they tell a story, they are the storyteller or the narrator. Explain to them that a story is also called a narrative. Show students an example of a narrative text that they have read in the classroom. Tell students that the writer wrote a story, which is different from an opinion piece or a text that explains or teaches by giving information. Show examples of the other two kinds of texts that students have read so that they can see how narrative writing is different. Then make a list on the board of questions you can answer when reading narrative writing, using *who, what, where, when, why,* and *how.* Then use a familiar narrative text to go through with students to find the answers to the following questions: What is the story about? Where and when does the story take place? Who is in the story? Why do some things happen in the story? How does the story end?

UNDERSTAND TASK AND TONE

Remind students that before they begin writing a narrative, they must read the assignment carefully and understand all of its parts. Tell students that they may be given a question or a writing prompt as an assignment for narrative writing. For example, the writing prompt may be, "Tell about something that you did during the summer break" or "What did you do during the summer break?" Point out to students that even though the topic of their narrative text may be casual or fun, they need to write in complete sentences.

REFOCUS ON THE WRITING TYPE

Throughout the year as students read or are asked to write narrative texts, remind them of the key features of this text type. Narrative writing

- tells about a real or make-believe experience or event.
- gives descriptive details about events and characters.
- tells about events in sequence.
- provides an ending that wraps up the story.

Sequence Events

What Students Should KNOW	What Students Will DO
• Retell events in the correct sequence.	• Recount a well-elaborated event or short sequence of events.
• Identify words that show sequence in texts students read. • Determine possible temporal words to use in narrative text.	• Use temporal words to signal event order.

MODEL AND PRACTICE

Narrative writing often tells about an event or experience in the order events happened. Help students identify the events or experiences in a familiar story. Explain that using sequence words helps the narrator retell an event or experience in the order in which it happened, which makes it easier and clearer for the reader to follow. Display for students a list of sequence words, such as *first, next, last, before, after,* and *finally.*

MODEL I will write a narrative about the time I learned how to ride a bike. I will think about the things that I had to learn and remember in order to ride a bike. Then I will write those things in a list. (Write the items in random, rather than sequential, order.) Please help me move around the things on my list so that they are in the correct order. Then I will number my list to help me keep track of the order.

PRACTICE Provide small groups with an example of something they have most likely learned or experienced. Encourage students to write the events on strips of paper. Then have them stand up and walk through each part of that event, using their strips of paper as a guide. If they realize that they have something out of order, ask them to rearrange the strips of paper. Talk about words that could help show sequence.

DEEPER PRACTICE Work with small groups to go through a familiar narrative text and identify places where they could add temporal words to help the reader follow the story. On the board, show the text and highlight or underline sequence words that are already present in the text. Work together to add sequence words. Check students' understanding by adding a sequence word in a place where it doesn't fit or make sense to see if students can catch your "mistake."

ENGLISH LANGUAGE LEARNERS

If . . . students have difficulty using temporal words,

then . . . draw simple drawings on three cards, such as a seed, a seed with small roots and a stem, and a stem with a flower. Write temporal words *first, next,* and *last* on cards. Ask students to arrange the picture cards in the correct order then place the word cards next to the pictures where they would be used to retell the sequence.

STRUGGLING WRITERS

If . . . students cannot think of what might happen next in a story,

then . . . have them fold a paper in three sections and draw what happened first in the first section. Talk about what changed or happened next, and have students draw that picture. Have students complete the three pictures and then tell the story.

Include Details

What Students Should KNOW	What Students Will DO
• Identify details that describe actions, thoughts, and feelings in texts students read. • Expand sentences to include descriptive details.	• Include details to describe actions, thoughts, and feelings.

MODEL AND PRACTICE

Explain to students that they can develop their story, or narrative, in different ways to make it interesting. One way is to use details that describe, or tell about, events that happen in the story or how the writer thought or felt about the event. Tell students that readers can relate to a story better when they can paint a picture in their heads of what was going on. Select a few narrative texts that students have read, and help them identify details that describe actions, thoughts, and feelings.

MODEL In my story about riding a bike for the first time, I try to write about what I did, thought, and felt. Since descriptions tell more about what happened, what I was thinking about, or what I was feeling, I might write, "I was scared that I might fall off my bike. I didn't want my dad to let go." I want to expand my sentences using descriptive details. That way I can tell more about what I did, thought, or felt so that my readers can imagine that they were actually there. I can use a three-column chart to help me organize details about my actions, thoughts, and feelings. I'll write, "I was scared that I might fall off my bike" in the column labeled *Feelings.* Then I can think about why I was scared. I can add more details to tell about that feeling.

PRACTICE Provide a three-column chart and label the columns *Actions, Thoughts,* and *Feelings.* Ask students to work with a partner to choose a common experience to retell and then write sentences with details in each column.

DEEPER PRACTICE Have students use their charts to help them practice expanding sentences to include descriptive details. Ask them to choose one detail from each column of their chart. Instruct them to decide with their partner which description they will add to each detail to make a longer and more interesting sentence.

ENGLISH LANGUAGE LEARNERS

If . . . students have trouble adding descriptive details in narrative text,

then . . . have students look at a picture and tell a short story about what they see. Write one sentence from the story they tell on a sentence strip. Write it again on another strip and cut it apart into individual words. Model adding some descriptive details on word cards to expand the sentence. Have students read both sentences. Encourage students to try this with another sentence.

STRUGGLING WRITERS

If . . . students' narratives include only events,

then . . . have them use colored highlighters to underline sentences that describe events in one color, thoughts in another, and feelings in a third color. Have students review their story to see what might be lacking. Help students add sentences to create a more "colorful" story.

Provide Some Sense of Closure

What Students Should KNOW	What Students Will DO
• Identify examples of closure in texts students read. • Write a concluding sentence.	• Provide some sense of closure.

Tell students that a concluding sentence can tell the last event that happened and alert the reader that the story has ended. Students may have seen stories that end with the characters living happily ever after or returning home to a family after being lost. Review together some examples of narrative texts that you have read. Discuss how they are alike and different, as well as what elements make a strong concluding sentence.

MODEL When I come to the end of my story, I need to think about how to close, or end, it. I may use one or a few sentences, depending on my topic. In my story about learning how to ride a bike, I might say something about my thoughts, actions, or feelings. Just writing "The End" doesn't seem like enough. I might write, "At last, the hard work worked. My dad let go of me, and I rode down the sidewalk by myself. I was a very happy biker."

PRACTICE Work together to create several other endings for the story you modeled. Encourage pairs of students to work together to suggest sentences that might be used. Share the ideas from the pairs and review what the closing sentences have in common.

DEEPER PRACTICE Provide students with different examples of narrative texts that they have read. Ask them to identify the concluding sentences. Then have them write a different concluding sentence that makes sense with the story.

ENGLISH LANGUAGE LEARNERS

If . . . students have trouble writing an ending,

then . . . ask them to act out or draw a picture that shows how the story ends. Have students put the ending into words. Model rephrasing those words as needed into a complete sentence that could serve as a closing sentence. Ask students to repeat the sentence. If students are satisfied with the ending, write the sentence and ask them to read the new closing sentence.

STRUGGLING WRITERS

If . . . students end stories abruptly,

then . . . model ending a story abruptly. Example: "The car was headed for the kitten in the street. The end." Remind students that the ending for the story should make readers feel like they know what happened and that everything is all right now. Ask students to say what happened to the main character at the end of the story. Encourage students to write a sentence that tells how the character felt about what happened at the end.

Support for Extended Writing

Refer to this process when students are writing a longer passage that requires development, organization, revising, and editing to produce a narrative text.

UNDERSTAND THE TASK Tell students to reread their writing prompt or assignment carefully to be sure they understand the task and what is being asked. Have them answer these questions: What am I asked to write about? Am I being asked to cite or reference another text? How many parts are there to this writing assignment? In what order should I write about this topic?

BRAINSTORM Provide students with guidance and support as they determine a topic for their narrative. Explain that they can use a graphic organizer to jot down ideas for their topic. Remind students to keep in mind that the first idea they think of might not always be the best to use. Encourage them to share their ideas for a topic with a partner. Then work with students to help them choose what they think is the strongest idea that will enable them to answer all parts of the writing prompt.

TAKE NOTES Model for students how to write ideas for their topic. Point out that these can be a word or a few words, but they should focus on the big ideas about their topic. Have them write down *who, what, when, where, why,* and *how,* and then help guide them to provide the information for each question word.

ORGANIZE INFORMATION Use a story map graphic organizer. Explain that the organizer has a box for each part of their story: the beginning, middle, and end. Show students how to use the boxes to record the parts of the story so that they can refer to it as they write. Explain that putting the parts of the story in the correct sequence is important to make their writing clear. Point out that the reader will be able to better follow the story if students keep focused on what happened first, next, and last.

WRITE

Provide students with encouraging tips to guide them through their writing process. Some tips might include:

- Remind students that they are writing a first draft and that they need to be focused on the overall structure of the story. They do not need to make sure that everything is perfect at this point in the writing process.

- Explain to students that they will be able to write a clearer and more organized story if they think through the story and write down their ideas ahead of time.

- If students have difficulty starting to write, encourage them to look at their notes and think of or say one sentence aloud before writing it. Then ask them to think about where that sentence should go in the story (beginning, middle, or end). Encourage them to work on one idea at a time and to find a place for that idea in the overall narrative before moving onto the next idea.

- Remind students to write a clear and focused introduction and conclusion.

- When students are finished, have them double check that they have answered all parts of the writing prompt or assignment.

REVISE AND EDIT

Guide students through the revising and editing process. Work with them to develop writing and reviewing checklists to help them look for details that they might address in their revision. After revising their work, have students review one another's work to further strengthen their writing.

PUBLISH

Set aside classroom time for students to read their texts aloud. Consider having students draw an illustration for their story and post their completed work on a story wall in the classroom. You may choose to create a story blog on your school or classroom website for students' completed work.

ACCELERATED WRITERS

If . . . students have difficulty telling their peers about revisions they could make to their stories,

then . . . encourage students to first write down or point out two things that they liked about the narrative. Then ask them to show the writer the parts in the narrative that could use some revision.

MONITOR AND SUPPORT

Writer's Checklist

Name_____

Title _____

❏ Did I write an introduction?

❏ Did I put the events in the correct order or sequence?

❏ Did I use descriptive details to tell about actions, thoughts, and feelings?

❏ Did I use sequence words to show how events in the story happened?

❏ Did I provide a strong conclusion?

❏ Did I address all parts of the prompt or writing assignment?

❏ Did I cite or reference any other text I was asked to include?

❏ Did I review my work for correct capitalization, punctuation, and spelling?

❏ _____

❏ _____

Peer Review Checklist

Name_____

Writer's Name_____

Title _____

- ❏ Does the introduction describe what the writing will be about?

- ❏ Is the writing clear, and does it make sense?

- ❏ Is it easy to follow what happens in the story?

- ❏ Did the writing include sequence words to make it easier to follow what happens in the story?

- ❏ Does the writing include descriptive details about actions, thoughts, and feelings?

- ❏ Does the writing have a strong conclusion?

- ❏ Are all parts of the prompt or assignment addressed clearly in the writing?

- ❏ _____

- ❏ _____

- ❏ _____

PART 3

Routines and Activities

Part 3 Routines and Activities

Listening and Speaking Routines

Language Routines and Activities:
Vocabulary and Conventions

Noun Activities

Pronoun Activities

Verb Activities

Adjective Activities

Adverb Activities

Sentence Activities

Punctuation Activities

Word Study Activities

Vocabulary Activities and Games

Quick Write and Share

PURPOSE

Use this routine to activate and build on students' prior knowledge before reading a selection.

PROCEDURE

1. Before reading a selection, pose a question to activate students' prior knowledge about a topic they will read about. Give students a few minutes to jot down their ideas. Because this is a quick write, tell students that they do not need to worry about grammar or spelling. They can also use pictures.

2. Review class rules for discussion. Remind students of the proper methods for sharing ideas, such as who goes first, what to do while someone else is speaking, and when it is okay to take your turn.

3. As a class, or in small groups or pairs, ask students to share their ideas with others in their group. Again, remind students that each person should speak without interruption so that everyone has a chance to share. During this discussion, assess students' prior knowledge and clarify any questions.

TEACHING TIPS

- When creating questions for step one, make sure they are text specific and that answering them will help students unlock ideas in the text. For example, before starting a book on animals, ask questions such as, *How can hares tell it is wintertime? How do they survive in winter?* These questions are appropriate because they are specific to the text and ask students to recall information that will help them when reading. An inappropriate question would be *Do you like hares?* because it is not text specific, and responding to the question will not help students unlock ideas in the text.

- Additionally, it may benefit students to read aloud a short paragraph or excerpt relating to a key idea or topic in the text. This will help students gain confidence going into the text, because it will ensure that everyone will have some foundational understanding of the text.

EXTEND

Have one student from each group or pair share ideas from their discussion with the class. Use student responses to create a class list or web of prior knowledge, and display the list/web permanently in the classroom. This will act as a continual reminder to students of what they already know. As students acquire new knowledge, the information can be added to the list/web so they can see how their understanding is growing.

Two-Column Chart

PURPOSE

Use this routine with the Two-Column Chart Graphic Organizer. This is a multipurpose graphic organizer that is helpful when exploring and comparing ideas, story elements, or vocabulary words. Students can chart ideas within and across texts, such as how two texts address similar themes or topics, or between prior knowledge and new ideas. Students might also analyze and compare the structure of two texts.

PROCEDURE

1. Model using the chart. Display the chart and write two topics being studied on the chart, one topic per column, such as Cow and Bull.
2. Read the text.
3. Elicit responses from students based on the topics chosen. Model how to list ideas or examples in the correct columns. For example, under Cow write: *gives birth and stays with her baby.* Under Bull write: *leaves mom as a young calf.* Students' responses should refer directly to the text.

TEACHING TIPS

- Students can write in the chart, but they can also draw and list or label.
- Students can use the chart to compare similar topics across texts, such as the behaviors of different animals.
- Use the chart to organize ideas gathered in a class brainstorming session.
- Use the chart to explore two vocabulary words. Write the words at the tops of the columns. Then under each word, students can sketch the word, write a definition, or write a sentence using the word.

EXTEND

Students can work with partners, each partner completing one half of the chart. Then pairs can share their work with the rest of the class.

Two-Column Chart

Three-Column Chart

PURPOSE

Use this routine with the Three-Column Chart Graphic Organizer. This is a multipurpose graphic organizer that works well for exploring and organizing ideas for three concepts, words, or topics. It works well with many selections and can aid students in exploring or classifying ideas, story elements, genres, or vocabulary features. It can also help students recognize comparisons and contrasts, or chart ideas within and across texts.

PROCEDURE

1. Display the chart. Choose three headings and write them on the chart, such as three different vocabulary words or characters.

2. Ask students for details or examples for each heading and record them in the appropriate column on the chart. Details or examples should directly reference the text.

3. Point out that this chart helps students organize information or identify comparisons among ideas or topics in the text or across texts.

TEACHING TIPS

- Once you have modeled how to use the chart, students can complete the chart independently or in pairs or small groups.

- Students can draw in the charts as well as list ideas.

- Students can use the chart to explore story characteristics or characteristics of genre.

- Students can use the chart to organize ideas they generate during brainstorming.

- Show students how they can use the chart to record similarities or differences across texts.

EXTEND

- Students can use the chart to record ideas that follow the format of before, during, and after.

- Students can compare and contrast story characteristics or elements across selections. For example, ask them to record details of three different characters. Have them chart personality traits or reactions to conflicts or situations.

- After completing the class activity, have students use the chart in pairs or individually with other selections.

Three-Column Chart

Story Map A

PURPOSE

Use this routine with the Story Map A Graphic Organizer. This organizer works well with any selection with a clear sequence of events. This graphic organizer can aid students in recording the sequence of events in a selection.

PROCEDURE

1. Display the graphic organizer. Write the title of the selection at the top of the graphic organizer.

2. Start reading. Pause to ask: What happens first? Record what happens first on the organizer in the Beginning box.

3. Focus on events in the middle of the story, pausing for students to identify them. Record them on the graphic organizer in the Middle box.

4. As you finish the selection, record important events from the end of the selection.

TEACHING TIPS

- Make a list of words that tell time order, such as *after, later, first,* and *next.* Provide sentence frames to help students use the time-order words.

- Encourage students to use story maps to retell the events to partners.

EXTEND

- After completing this activity with the class, have students use the graphic organizer in pairs or teacher-led small groups with other selections. Have students draw pictures of events in the organizer. They can label or dictate words for the pictures.

- Have students work in small groups to discuss how they might change the end of a story. Describe what must change in the middle section in order for the ending to be different in their versions. Have one student from each group present their ideas to the rest of the class.

Story Map A

Title _____

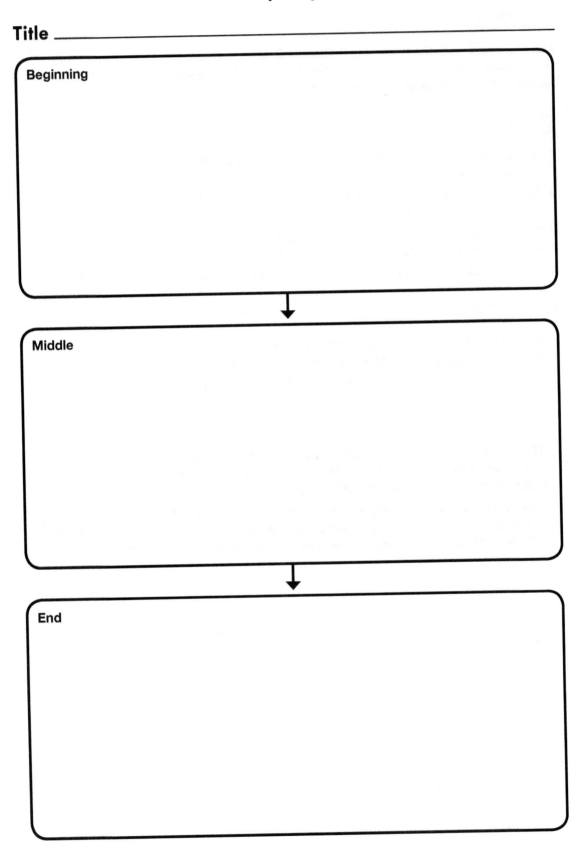

Beginning

Middle

End

Story Map B

PURPOSE

Use this routine with the Story Map B Graphic Organizer. This graphic organizer works well with any text that has a clear sequence of events. This organizer can help students identify different story elements.

PROCEDURE

1. Display the graphic organizer. Write the title of the selection on the organizer.

2. Read the selection. Pause to think aloud and record information about the characters on the graphic organizer.

3. As you read, pause to ask: Where does the story take place? When does the story take place? Record those details in the Setting section.

4. As you read, pause to record information about the sequence of events.

TEACHING TIPS

- Model talking about characters and setting: ___ is a person/animal in this story. This story takes place ___. (in the future, in the past, today)

- Have students draw pictures of events in the graphic organizer. They can label or dictate words for the pictures to describe those events.

- Students may not need all the lines, or they may need more. Help them modify the organizer depending on the story.

EXTEND

- After completing this activity with the class, have students use the graphic organizer in pairs or teacher-led small groups with other texts.

- Help students think of words to describe characters or events. Make a list and have students add to it.

- Help students look for clue words for sequence. Make a list of clue words to display for students' reference. For example, words and phrases such as *first, in the beginning, next, then, later,* or *finally* signal time and its progression. Students may get a sense of where they are in the story when they read these clue words. This will help them to trace the sequence of events in a text. Ask students to identify other clue words that help them trace sequence.

- Help students map characters and settings by analyzing descriptions. Sensory details shape the reader's image of who the characters are and where the story takes place. First have students name the five senses: sight, hearing, taste, touch, smell. Then have students find examples of each in the text.

Story Map B

Title

_____

Characters

Who is in the story?

_____

Setting

Where does the story happen?

_____

When does the story happen?

_____

Events

What happens in the story?

_____

_____

_____

_____

_____

_____

Venn Diagram

PURPOSE

Use this routine with the Venn Diagram Graphic Organizer. This graphic organizer works well in any situation that lends itself to comparing and contrasting. Students can use this graphic organizer to record similarities and differences between places, ideas, characters, or other elements of fiction or nonfiction.

PROCEDURE

1. Start by comparing and contrasting something simple, such as cats and dogs. Write or draw the subjects you are comparing at the top of each circle of the diagram.

2. Point to where the circles overlap. Let students know that in this section, you'll write similarities between the two, or how the two things are alike. Ask how the two subjects are alike, and record students' responses. For example, you might write: *both have fur*.

3. Point to an individual circle and let students know that, in this section, you'll write details that describe only what is labeled at the top of the circle. Ask students to share details as you record them. Then ask how the two subjects are different and record students' responses.

TEACHING TIPS

- It might help students if you ask questions that lead to details to write in the diagram. For example, when discussing the characters in two different stories, ask: What do these characters have in common? How are they different?

- Help students by providing sentence frames, such as: These two things are alike because___. These two things are different because___. Help students identify words and phrases in the text that describe the the two things being compared.

- List words that signal comparing and contrasting, such as *alike*, *different*, or *but*. Instruct students to identify those words in the text as they read.

EXTEND

Students can use the Venn diagram to compare ideas in informational texts, such as two people or two events.

Venn Diagram

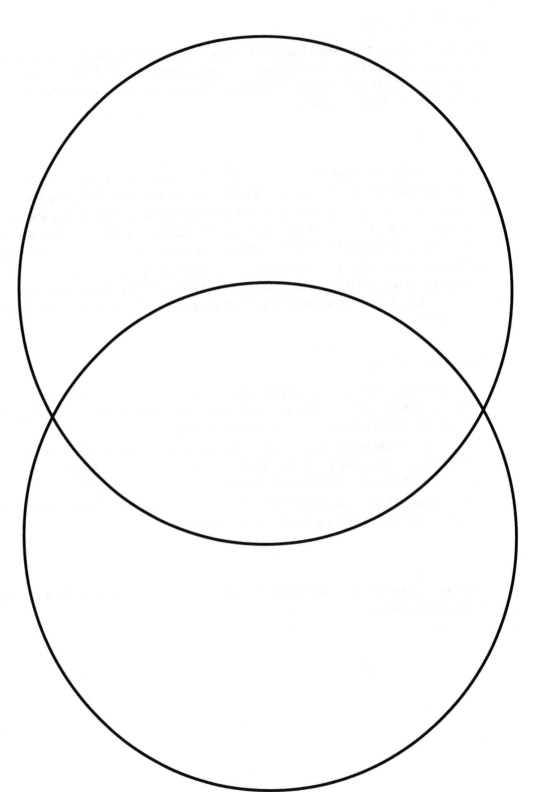

Web

PURPOSE

Use this routine with the Web Graphic Organizer. This graphic organizer has multiple uses and is appropriate for all levels of learners. It will aid students in exploring their prior knowledge as they brainstorm related ideas, recognize concept relationships, and organize information. Students can highlight a central concept and connect it to related words, ideas, or details.

PROCEDURE

1. After students have read the text, display the graphic organizer. Write or draw a central idea or topic in the middle of the web. This can be a character name, a setting, or an idea from the text, for example, *calves*.
2. Ask students for ideas that are related to the central idea. Record those ideas in the circles attached to the middle circle, for example, *Cows protect calves. They are born one at a time. Calves drink milk.*
3. Point out that the lines show connections. Explain to students how the information in each outer circle connects to the main topic, calves.

TEACHING TIPS

- Once you have modeled how to use the web, have students complete the web independently, in pairs, or in small groups.
- Encourage students to explain how the ideas in the outer circles of the web are related to the central idea. Provide sentence frames to help students talk about the web: The important idea is ___. Some ideas related to this are ___.
- Use this web to organize information, explore main ideas and details, identify character names and their traits, or record vocabulary words and their synonyms.
- Encourage students to use pictures or have them dictate the words to fill in the web.
- After students create a web, have them write a sentence or short paragraph telling how the concepts are connected. Ask them to explain why they are making these connections by using examples from the text to support their ideas.

EXTEND

- Students can use the web to record ideas about a topic in content-area reading, such as things plants need to grow.
- Have students use the web to record background knowledge about a topic. Use the webs to assess gaps in understanding as you plan instruction.

Web

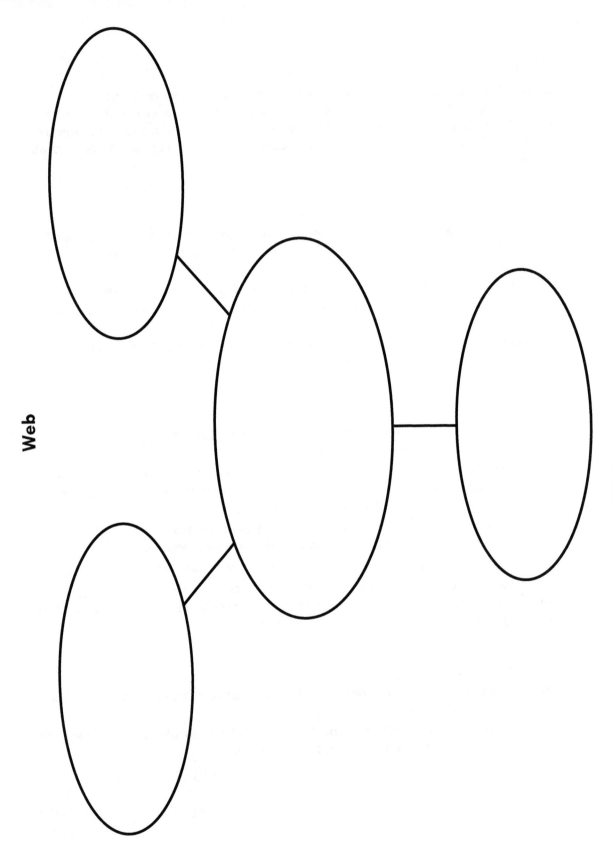

Time Line

PURPOSE

Use this routine along with the Time Line Graphic Organizer to organize events from fiction or nonfiction texts in sequential order along a continuum.

PROCEDURE

1. After reading a selection, ask students what happened first. Record the first event on the time line.

2. Continue asking students to name events in order, placing them on the continuum. Point out that they will use this time line the same way they read, from left to right.

3. It may be helpful to list all of the events first, and then place them in order on the time line to ensure that the important events are included.

4. If there are specific dates or references to a specific time (Tuesday, July), record those under the event.

TEACHING TIPS

- Remind students to look for clues in the text that signify the order in which things happen. They might find dates or clue words, such as *first*, *next*, *then*, and *last*.

- If students need extra support, write events from the text on sentence strips. Have students work in pairs or small groups to place the strips in order, and then write the events on the time line.

EXTEND

- When students are reading fiction selections, have them use their time lines to retell the stories. They can use this graphic organizer with other selections as a group or in small teacher-led groups.

- Have students create a time line of special events for the school year to display in the classroom. In addition to Columbus Day and Thanksgiving, for example, you may add events such as Report Card Day, School Olympics, or Exam Week to the time line. Record the dates under each event.

Time Line

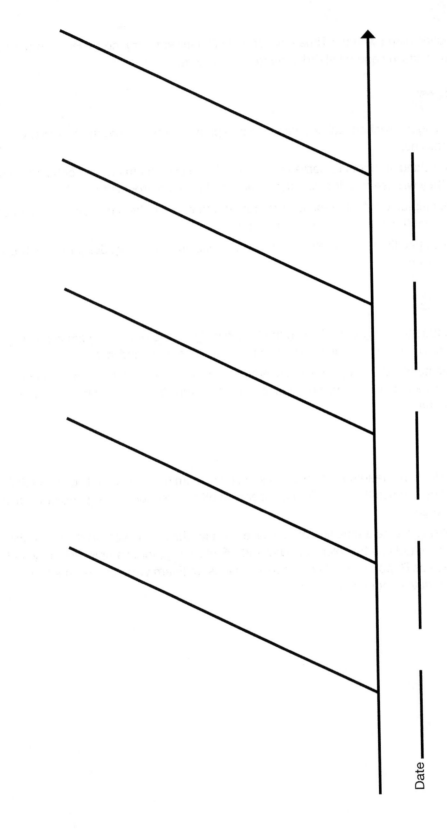

Date

Sequence of Events

Use this routine with the Sequence of Events Graphic Organizer. This graphic organizer works well with any fictional selection that has a clear series of events. It can help students understand how the characters, setting, and events in a story all fit together.

1. Display the graphic organizer. Write the title of the selection or chapter on the on the Title section.
2. Read the selection together. Ask students where and when the story takes place. Record those details in the Setting section.
3. As you read, use a think aloud to model how to record information about the characters. For example: I noticed that Vern says Chris is his best friend. But we haven't met Chris yet. I wonder who he or she is. I will write Chris's name in the left column under Characters. As I read, I will look for information about Chris and other characters we read about.
4. Then pause occasionally to record information about the events that happen in the boxes under the Character and Setting sections.

* Provide sentence frames for talking about characters and setting. For example: ___ is a person/animal in this story. This story takes place in ___.
* Help students look for clue words in the story that signal the order of events. Make a list of clue words to display for students' reference, such as *first, next, then, finally.*
* Modify the graphic organizer as needed to include more or fewer boxes.
* Allow students to draw the events in the events boxes and dictate a phrase or sentence.

* After completing this activity as a class exercise, have students use the graphic organizer in pairs, small groups, or independently with other texts.
* Help students think of words that describe the characters or setting. Make a list and have students add to it as they read. Have students identify sensory details in the text; guide them by first naming the five senses. Then ask them to find examples in the text that use these senses to describe characters, objects, or locations.
* After completing the graphic organizer, have students retell the story to a partner, a small group, or the class, using their graphic organizer.

Sequence of Events

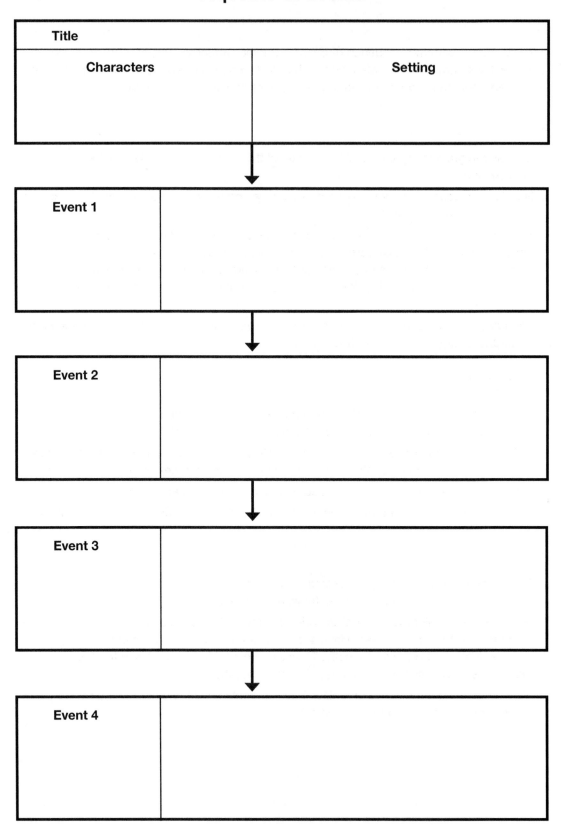

Title	
Characters	**Setting**

Event 1

Event 2

Event 3

Event 4

KWL Chart

PURPOSE

Use this routine with the KWL Chart Graphic Organizer. Students can build prior knowledge about a text, ask questions to set purposes for reading, and record what they learn as they read. This graphic organizer works well with expository texts.

PROCEDURE

1. Display the graphic organizer.
2. Identify a topic to model using the graphic organizer (for example, Dogs). Write the word *Know* on the board. Underline the *K*. Tell students that the *K* stands for What Do I Know? Ask students what they know about dogs and record their responses on the graphic organizer.
3. Write *Want* on the board and underline the *W*. Tell students that the *W* stands for What Do I Want to Learn? Ask students what they want to know about dogs. Model recording on the graphic organizer their responses in the form of questions. (*Is it hard to train a dog? Do some dogs make better pets than other dogs?*)
4. Write *Learn* on the board. Underline the *L*. Tell students that the *L* stands for What Did I Learn? As you read, ask students what they are learning. They should try to answer the questions they wrote in the *W* column.

TEACHING TIPS

- After modeling, students can complete the graphic organizer in pairs or small groups. You might brainstorm ideas as a class for the *K* column, and have students work together to write questions for the *W* column.
- Model how to write a question with a capital letter and a question mark.
- Modify the graphic organizer if necessary by changing the headings into sentence frames: I know ___. I want to know ___. I learned ___.

EXTEND

- Use the graphic organizer as you learn about different topics in content areas, such as social studies and science, and post them around the room. Students can add to the *L* columns of the graphic organizers as they learn more.
- Have students work in pairs to read an article at their reading level or to listen to an article you read aloud. They can use the graphic organizer to organize their thinking.
- Have students revisit their graphic organizers after reading the selected text and review what they recorded under What Do I Want to Learn? Identify any topics that students still have questions about and were not answered by reading the text. Discuss the ways students can find answers to their questions.

KWL Chart

Topic _____

What Do I **K** now?	What Do I **W** ant to Learn?	What Did I **L** earn?

Main Idea and Details

PURPOSE

Use this routine with the Main Idea and Details Graphic Organizer. With this graphic organizer, students can recognize a main idea and distinguish between the main idea and the supporting details. This graphic organizer works especially well with nonfiction selections that are organized around main ideas and details.

PROCEDURE

1. Display the graphic organizer.

2. Read a selection. Record the main idea in the top box. (For example, *Earthquakes cause a lot of damage.*) Define *main idea* as "the most important idea."

3. Model by recording details that support, or tell more about, the main idea, such as *knock down buildings, wreck highways, destroy cities and towns,* and *injure people.* Have students supply additional supporting details as you record them.

4. Once you have modeled how to use the graphic organizer, have students complete the organizer independently, in pairs, or in small groups.

TEACHING TIPS

- Supply a sentence frame about main ideas: The most important idea is ___. Supply a sentence frame about supporting details: One detail about this idea is ___. You may also prompt students by asking them first to suggest a statement that tells what the text is about. Then ask them to identify information that supports the main idea.

- Display part of a selection and model highlighting important ideas. You may want to highlight the main idea in one color and highlight details in another color. Ask: What is this text mostly about? This is the main idea. Which sentences tell you more information about this main idea? These are the supporting details. Record the important ideas in the graphic organizer.

- Extend or add additional boxes to the graphic organizer, if necessary, to include more supporting details.

EXTEND

- Have students use the graphic organizer to record ideas for writing pieces of their own. Make sure they record one main idea and the details that tell more about it. Then have them write a paragraph using the information they have recorded in the graphic organizer.

- Have students use the graphic organizer in pairs or small groups to record important ideas from content-area reading, such as in social studies or science.

Main Idea and Details

Main Idea

Details

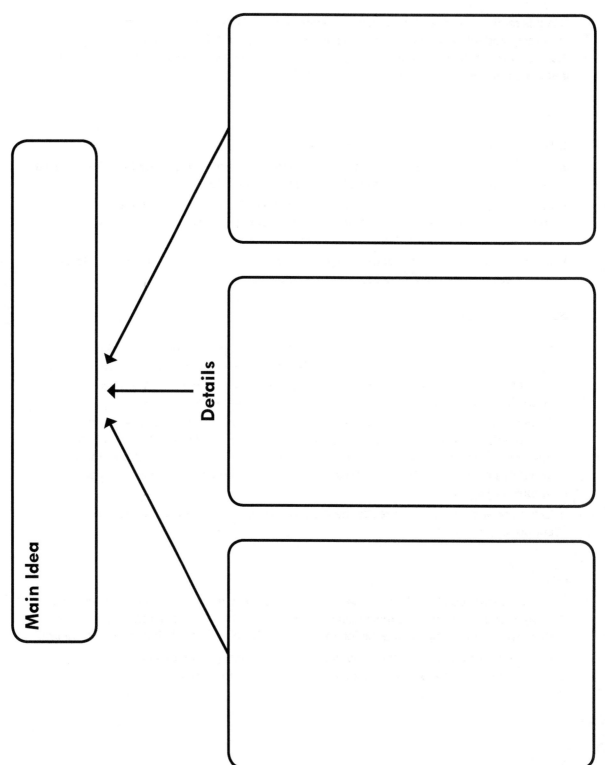

Story Predictions Chart

PURPOSE

Use this routine with the Story Predictions Chart Graphic Organizer. Students will preview the text's title and illustrations and then predict what might happen in the text. This graphic organizer works well with any text in which the title and/or pictures suggest clues about the events in a story. Consider using it for content-area texts as well.

PROCEDURE

1. Display the graphic organizer.

2. Preview the text with students. Read the title and lead a picture walk. Ask students: What do you think this story will be about? Remind them to use what they know about the topic as well as what they see during the picture walk. Record their predictions in the graphic organizer under What might happen? Students may draw their predictions if they wish.

3. Ask students what helped them guess what might happen. Ask: Have you read a story like this before? What evidence from the pictures helped you make a guess about what would happen next? Record their clues in the graphic organizer under What clues do I have?

4. After reading, look back at the predictions. Ask: What actually happened in the story? Write what actually happened under What did happen? Ask students if their predictions were different from what happened. Ask: What happened in the story that is different from your prediction? How is making a prediction helpful?

TEACHING TIPS

- Focus on clues in illustrations. What details in the illustrations help students make predictions?

- Model sentence frames for predicting: I think ___ will happen. I think this will happen because ___.

- Reassure students that even if their predictions turn out differently, making predictions is a useful skill because it helps them understand the story at a deeper level.

EXTEND

- After completing this activity as a class exercise, have students use the graphic organizer in pairs, small groups, or independently with other selections.

- Use the graphic organizer with content-area texts. Focus on the content, giving students a sentence frame to use: I think I will learn about ___ because ___. Ask students to explain how they make their predictions and connect their explanations to the text.

Story Predictions Chart

Title _____

What might happen?	What clues do I have?	What did happen?

Story Comparison

PURPOSE

Use this routine with the Story Comparison Graphic Organizer. Students can use this graphic organizer to record how two texts are similar and different. This graphic organizer works well with texts that have something in common. It is a useful tool for comparing texts by the same author, about the same topic, or in the same genre.

PROCEDURE

1. Display the graphic organizer.
2. Choose two stories to compare. Write their titles on the graphic organizer.
3. Ask questions to elicit characters, settings, and plot events. Use information from the texts and illustrations/photographs that will help students identify details about characters, settings, and events.
4. Record details on the graphic organizer.

TEACHING TIPS

- After you model how to use the graphic organizer, students can work on their own graphic organizer with partners or in small groups.
- Provide sentence frames for comparison and model how to use them, such as: The characters in the first story are ___, but the characters in the second story are ___. Ask students to describe how the characters respond to major obstacles and challenges.
- Invite students to use the graphic organizer to retell stories and then to determine the themes, or central messages. Have students cite details from the texts to support their ideas.

EXTEND

- Students can use the graphic organizer to compare a story and a nonfiction text about the same topic. Ask: What are some details that one text offers and the other doesn't?
- Have students use one half of the graphic organizer to plan the writing of their own story. Ask volunteers to share their work with the rest of the class.

Story Comparison

Title A _____

_____

Title B _____

_____

Characters

Who is in the story?

Characters

Who is in the story?

Setting

Where and **when** does it happen?

Setting

Where and **when** does it happen?

Events

What happens in the story?

Events

What happens in the story?

Ask and Answer Questions

PURPOSE

Use this routine to build on students' use of asking and answering questions to better understand a text.

PROCEDURE

1. Use the text that the class is currently reading. As a warm-up activity, review *how* and *wh-* questions. For example: Where does the princess live with the frogs? How do spiders spin a web? What is a fairy tale? Where do giraffes live? Why does it rain? Have students take turns asking questions orally. (If students want to answer questions, give them the chance to do so.)

2. Choose a short passage, paragraph, or chapter from the text the class is currently reading. Read the text aloud as students follow along.

3. Model specific examples of questions relating to the text, such as *How do seeds travel? What do seeds need to grow?* Invite students to think of their own questions to ask about the text.

4. Hand out copies of the worksheet on the following page and direct students to the text. Explain that students should refer directly to the text to ask and answer questions about it.

TEACHING TIP

Encourage students to ask themselves questions as they read on their own. For fiction, students might ask: *Who is the main character? Why did the main character run away? What is happening in the story now?* For informational text, students might ask: *What interesting facts did I learn so far? What else do I want to learn?* Answering these questions will help students understand and remember what they read.

EXTEND

- After completing Step B on the worksheet, ask students to share their most challenging questions with the class and have other students try to answer them. This will allow students to both understand the text more fully and share what they already know.

- Have students revisit their questions and discuss ideas for further reading and research.

Ask and Answer Questions

A. Read the text. Write two questions you have about the text. The questions may be about details or about the big idea.

1. Question:_____

_____

_____

_____

2. Question:_____

_____

_____

_____

B. Trade papers with a classmate. Read your classmate's questions from Step A. Write your answers to the questions.

1. Response: _____

_____

_____

_____

2. Response: _____

_____

_____

_____

Problem and Solution

PURPOSE

Use this routine with the Problem and Solution Graphic Organizer. This graphic organizer works well with any selection with clear problems and solutions. The organizer can aid students in identifying problems and solutions presented in fiction or nonfiction.

PROCEDURE

1. Talk with students about what a problem is. Elicit from students that a problem is something that needs to be solved. Give an example of a problem from a selection.

2. Record the problem in the Problem section of the graphic organizer.

3. Ask students what happens in the selection to fix the problem. Tell students that fixing a problem is the same as solving a problem.

4. Record students' responses in the Solution section. Student responses should reference the text directly.

TEACHING TIPS

- Once students understand how to use the graphic organizer, focus on a different problem and solution from the selection. There may be different solutions to one problem. Guide students as they identify additional examples.

- Provide sentence frames to help students discuss problems and solutions: One problem in the text is ___. One way to solve it is ___.

- Students can draw problems in the graphic organizer and then label them with words or phrases.

EXTEND

- Have students work individually or in pairs to find more problems in the text. Then use the graphic organizer to list them along with the solutions.

- Discuss a problem in the school, classroom, or community. Collect written examples and place them in the Problems box, and have students work in pairs or small groups to brainstorm solutions.

Problem and Solution

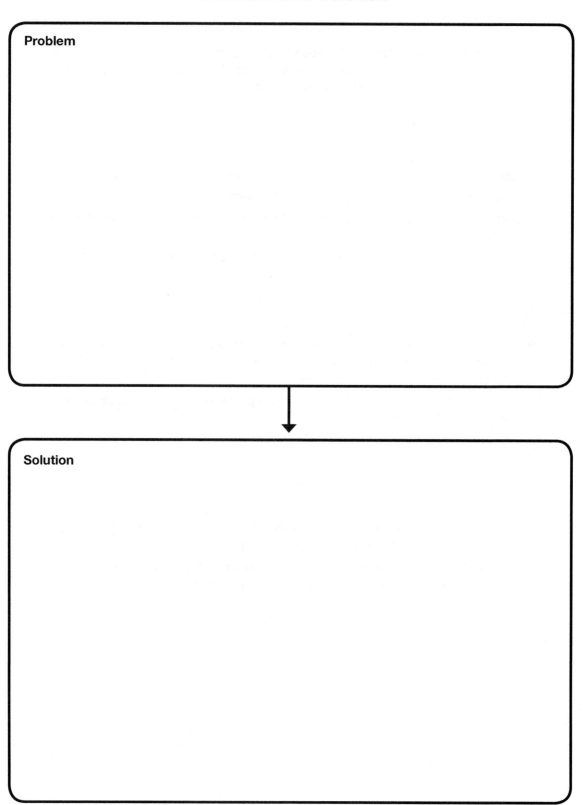

Problem

Solution

Cause and Effect

PURPOSE

Use this routine with the Cause and Effect Graphic Organizer. This graphic organizer works well with any selection that has clear cause-and-effect relationships. It can help students identify cause-and-effect relationships in either fiction or nonfiction.

PROCEDURE

1. Discuss the meaning of the word *effect* with students. Explain that something that happens is an effect. Record or draw an effect on the graphic organizer. (I got out my umbrella.)

2. Then ask students: Why did that happen? Explain to students that the reason something happens is a cause. Record or draw the cause on the graphic organizer. (It started to rain.)

3. Tell students: Cause comes first. It is why something happens. Effect comes next. It happens after the cause. Restate the cause and effect: It started to rain, so I got out my umbrella.

TEACHING TIPS

- Remind students to ask themselves questions, such as *What happened next?* and *Why did the character do or say this?* to identify effects and causes. It is usually easier to identify the effects first, before the causes. Use sentence frames to guide students: ___ happened because ___.

- List clue words that signal causes and effects, such as *because* and *so*. Look over the clue words with students, but remind them that not all causes and effects in selections have clue words. Help them identify causes and effects in the selections when no clue words are used.

EXTEND

- Students can draw, write, or dictate causes and effects from the selections they are currently reading. They could record, for example, causes of thunderstorms or of events in history.

- If students need extra assistance, fill in either causes or effects before distributing the graphic organizer.

ROUTINE

Cause and Effect

Cause

Why did it happen?

Effect

What happened?

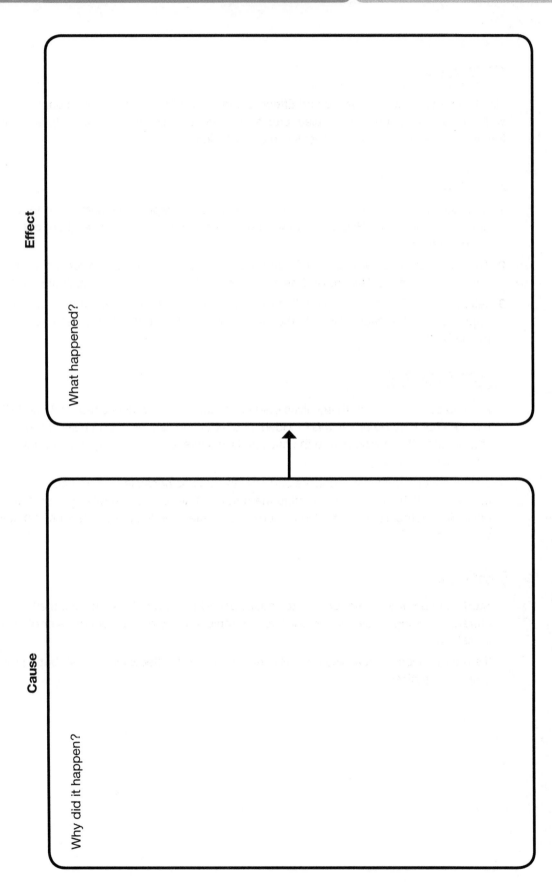

Steps in a Process

PURPOSE

Use this routine with the Steps in a Process Graphic Organizer. This graphic organizer aids students in breaking down a process into simple steps or directions. This graphic organizer works well with any procedure that has relatively few steps. If students need more or fewer steps, help them redesign the graphic organizer.

PROCEDURE

1. Display the graphic organizer. Write a title on the Process line, such as Making a Peanut Butter Sandwich.
2. Say: First, let's think about what we will need, such as a plate, knife, and bread. Do we need anything else? If we have all that we need, what do we do first? Record the first step in the graphic organizer.
3. Write the remaining steps in the graphic organizer in order as students supply them.

TEACHING TIPS

- Once students can contribute to the graphic organizer, have them work in pairs or small groups to write the steps of a simple process. You may provide prompts for activities that students will already know how to do, such as tying shoelaces or making lemonade. Or, students may come up with their own ideas. Provide feedback and guidance as needed to ensure that ideas are simple enough to include a few steps.
- Ask students to review their processes, checking each step and deciding whether it is clear or needs to be broken down further. Ask: Is this process easy to follow? Which step might become two or three smaller steps?
- Encourage students to look in the text for clue words to sequence, such as *first, next,* and *later,* to help them sequence the steps.

EXTEND

- Students may draw the steps in the graphic organizer and label them with words or phrases.
- Have students use the graphic organizer to show steps in a recipe, steps for doing a science project, steps for playing a game, or steps in another content area. Have students test each other's processes and provide feedback.

Steps in a Process

Process _____

Step 1

Step 2

Step 3

Narrative Writing

PURPOSE

Use this routine along with the Narrative Writing Graphic Organizer to help students plan and write a narrative story or to add narrative details to a description of a place or an event. (See also the Unlock Narrative Writing lesson in Part 2 of this handbook.)

PROCEDURE

1. Begin by asking students: What is narrative writing? Explain: It is a story told by a narrator.

2. Show examples of narrative writing they've read recently. Say: Narrative writing may be fiction (made up), such as a short story, or nonfiction (true), such as a biography.

3. Explain that a narrative story has a beginning, middle, and end. Say: Stories should tell what happens first, then what happens next, and finally, come to an end.

4. To demonstrate how to write a narrative paragraph, use a sentence frame as a story starter. For example: It was a warm and sunny day, so we ____.

5. Write the sentence frame on the board and read it aloud. Brainstorm ideas for what should happen first in the narrative. Write the ideas on the board.

6. Work with students to choose the best ideas. Use these to write a few sentences for the beginning of the narrative. Display the graphic organizer and model how to fill it in.

7. Repeat the process with the middle part of the narrative. Ask: What happens next in our story? Guide students in making sure that what happens is a logical progression from the start of the story.

8. Then discuss with students how the narrative might end, and create an ending or conclusion together. The end should follow logically from the sequence of events.

9. Now ask students to write their own narrative using the graphic organizer. Provide them with several sentence frames to start. Challenge students by having them set the scene by providing a description of where the story takes place or define character by describing the main character of the narrative. Ask students questions, such as *What is the weather like? Is your character a boy or girl? Does your story happen at home or in school? What other qualities does your character have?*

10. Invite volunteers to read their narrative aloud to a partner or small group.

TEACHING TIPS

- Make sure students understand the story starters. Supply an alternative sentence frame if needed.

- Have students draw their narrative first to help them visualize the characters or sequence of events.

- Remind students to go through the self-monitoring questions in Step C on the graphic organizer.

EXTEND

- Have students publish their narratives in a blog or class or school Web site.

- Have them illustrate their work and post it in the classroom.

- Ensure that students' work follows correct conventions and proper capitalization and spelling.

Narrative Writing

A. Read the story starters. Choose one and brainstorm ideas for your narrative. Write down these ideas on a separate sheet of paper.

B. Use your ideas to write sentences in the graphic organizer. Read the information in the left column and write your ideas in the right column.

The **beginning** of the narrative tells what happens first.	
The **middle** of the narrative tells what happens next.	
The **end** of the narrative tells what happens last.	

C. Read your narrative piece. Ask yourself:
- Does the beginning tell what happens first?
- Does the middle tell what happens next?
- Does the end tell what happens last and provide a conclusion?

D. Read aloud your narrative to a partner, small group, or the class.

Informative/Explanatory Writing

PURPOSE

Use this routine along with the Informative/Explanatory Writing Graphic Organizer to help students plan and write an informative/explanatory piece of writing. (See also the Unlock Informative/Explanatory Writing lesson in Part 2 of this handbook.)

PROCEDURE

1. Ask students: What is informative/explanatory writing? Say: Its purpose is to explain a topic and give readers information specific to the topic.

2. Show examples of informative/explanatory writing that students have read recently. Say: Informative/explanatory writing is nonfiction. It is factual and not made up. Newspaper articles, magazine articles, and textbooks are examples of informative/explanatory writing.

3. Display the graphic organizer. Say: The first step in planning and writing an informative/explanatory piece is to decide on and name the topic. This will be part of your introduction. The next step is to do research and supply facts about the topic. Then you'll need to develop your topic and put your facts on paper. These details can include definitions or examples that tell more about the points you are trying to make. And finally, you'll need to provide a concluding statement.

4. Model how to complete the graphic organizer. Give students a sample topic to begin, such as what animals need to grow. Have students choose an animal to write about. Ask them to think of sources they might use to gather more information about their chosen animal.

5. Then have students write an informative/explanatory paragraph, using the ideas and facts they have collected in their graphic organizers.

TEACHING TIP

Have students refer to the checklist on the graphic organizer as they write.

EXTEND

- Have students add illustrations, photographs, and/or diagrams that support their writing.
- Have students share their writing with the class. Then display student writing in the classroom.

Informative/Explanatory Writing

Name the Topic: _____

Facts About Topic

Conclusion

Use this checklist to remind yourself to

☐ name the topic.

☐ supply some facts about the topic.

☐ provide some closure.

Opinion Writing

PURPOSE

Use this routine with the Opinion Writing Graphic Organizer to help students plan and write an opinion piece. (See also the Unlock Opinion Writing lesson in Part 2 of this handbook.)

PROCEDURE

1. Explain that an opinion is how someone feels or what he or she believes about something. Say: An opinion cannot be proven true or false because it is not a fact. A fact can be proven to be true. Select two topics about which students can formulate an opinion. For example: Should students have homework every night? or Should students go to school during the summer? Use one topic to model instruction and the other for independent writing.

2. Explain that opinion writing involves the following steps:

   a. Students will first introduce the topic that they are writing about. This includes stating their opinion about the topic. They may answer the prompt or think of a topic they have an opinion on.

   b. Next, students will provide a reason or reasons for their opinion. Remind them that they should explain why they feel/believe as they do in two or three sentences.

   c. Finally, students will provide a sense of closure or a concluding statement.

3. Display the graphic organizer and model filling it in. Begin by filling in information about the topic, and then write the statement of opinion.

4. Next, fill in at least one reason for the opinion. Remind students to keep in mind the reason for their opinion as they write.

5. Finally, model writing an opinion piece using the information in the graphic organizer.

TEACHING TIPS

- Provide students with sentence frames to help them state an opinion: I think ____. I believe ____.
- Have students work in pairs to describe their topic and to determine possible reasons.
- Have students use linking words and phrases (because, therefore, since, for example) to connect their reasons to their opinions.

EXTEND

- Have students with opposite views on one topic present their opinions in a debate format.
- Have pairs exchange papers and review their partner's writing against the checklist in the graphic organizer to make sure they are meeting checklist criteria.

Opinion Writing

Topic: _____

Information About Topic

Opinion Statement: _____

Reason For Opinion

Use this checklist to remind yourself to

☐ introduce the topic and your opinion.

☐ give a reason or reasons to support your opinion.

☐ provide closure or a concluding statement.

Writing Directions

PURPOSE

Use this routine to help students learn how to give directions in sequential order.

PROCEDURE

1. Explain that when giving directions for a task, it is important that the steps are both clear and in the right order.

2. Provide a simple scenario for students, such as getting from the classroom to the lunchroom. Have students provide steps as you write them on the board. Remind them to use sequence (order) words, such as *first, next, then,* and *last.*

3. Guide students to use clear directions. Ask: How can we make that direction easier to understand? Can we break that up into more than one step? Are those steps in the right order? Can you describe that step with more details?

4. Read the directions back. Can students use the directions to find the lunchroom? Display the worksheet on the following page and, with students, assess a rating of their directions using the rubric.

5. Pair students and have partners take turns giving directions orally for a simple task, such as sharpening a pencil, making a sandwich, or drawing a triangle. The student performing the action must do exactly as the partner directs, and the student giving the directions must use sequence (order) words. After completing the task, have the students following the directions offer feedback to their partners based on the rubric.

TEACHING TIPS

- On index cards, draw pictures for a simple process. Put one step on each card. Give the cards to groups of students and have them work together to place the cards in order. After they have figured out the order, students can say or write the directions using the sentence starters from the worksheet.

- Give an example of directions that are out of order or missing steps. Guide students to test the directions to show how they do not make sense when they are out of order or unclear.

EXTEND

- Provide out-of-order directions without order words. Have students place the directions in order and rewrite the directions, inserting sequence words to add organization.

- Have students write directions for common classroom procedures. Compile the directions to create a Classroom Procedures Guide to help guests or new students.

Writing Directions

Write order words in the box. Look at the examples.

> **Sequence Words**
>
> **first**   **next**
> **second**   **last**

Use the sentence starters to give directions.

First, you should . . .
Second, . . .
Next, . . .
After that, . . .
Finally, . . .

Ask a friend to follow your directions. Can your friend follow them? How can you make them better?

Circle a picture for each sentence. **Tell** how you give directions.

I can give directions with
more than one or two steps.

I use order words
(first, second, next, last).

My directions are clear.
People can follow them.

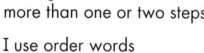

Monitor Understanding: Listening Skills Log

PURPOSE

Use this routine with the Listening Skills Log to help students monitor their understanding and learn how to take helpful class notes.

PROCEDURE

1. Explain the purpose of the Listening Skills Log to students. Begin with a question, such as *Why is it important to listen?*

2. Distribute the Listening Skills Log and use a media or audio selection to model filling it out. Explain to students that good listeners jot down important words that a speaker says, not every detail. They listen for main ideas. Review the difference between a main idea and a detail.

3. Display the log you created in Step 2 as a model. Have students view the log while listening to the same media or audio selection. Afterwards, discuss why you chose to write down what you did, and allow students to ask questions.

4. Read a text aloud, or present information using a form of media. When using media, preview the selection so you can pause after main ideas. This will allow students to practice listening for and writing down main ideas or important words.

5. Have students compare their log entries in small groups prior to discussing them with the class. Encourage students to ask about any words they did not understand.

TEACHING TIPS

- Speak at a normal rate and enunciate clearly. Pause at appropriate places to allow students time to process the information and ask clarifying questions. Ask questions, such as *Does it make sense? What have you learned?*

- If students have difficulty with a passage, pause to explain new words and concepts. As students become more proficient listeners, gradually increase the length and difficulty of the passages.

- Reread or replay the same text or media so students have multiple chances to catch main ideas.

- Allow students to reread the selection to compare their Listening Skills Log to what was in the text. As they reread the selection, students can code the text with sticky notes to indicate *I understand. I need help. I figured it out.*

EXTEND

- Have students write a sentence or two from their notes.

- After listening to a selection or media and filling out the organizer, have partners use classroom resources to find answers to their own questions, define unknown words, and clarify any misunderstandings. Pairs can present their findings to the class, and explain how they came to their answers.

Listening Skills Log

Main Idea	
Important Words	
My Questions	
New Words	

Tell a Story

Use this routine to help students organize their ideas for telling a story, and later rating themselves on their story telling. This is a good tool for telling stories or for giving speeches.

1. Display the worksheet on the following page. Choose a familiar story to model telling, and write the title on the worksheet.

2. Ask students for ideas about how you should tell the story. Then model writing or drawing the ideas on the worksheet.

3. Tell the first part of the story two times. As you tell it the first time, mumble and don't make much eye contact. Ask: Could you hear what I was saying? Did my story make sense? How could I do better? Model rating yourself, using the rubric on the worksheet.

4. Then tell the story again using the feedback. Call attention to making eye contact and speaking loudly enough so everyone can hear. Say: When I am telling a story to a group, the voice I use is different from the voice I use when talking to a friend. I speak clearly and loudly enough so everyone in the group can hear. I look at the group when I speak. I tell the events of the story in order.

5. Review the rubric on the worksheet and have students again provide a rating to demonstrate their understanding of your improved story telling.

- After you have modeled telling a story, have partners take turns telling simple stories they are familiar with. Partners can offer feedback. Can they hear their partner? Did the story make sense? Explain that their comments should be helpful and respectful and should also include at least one positive comment. They can refer to the rubric to structure their feedback.

- Give students a chance to plan what they will say. They can also write their ideas on the worksheet. Talk to them about the sequence of events in the story so they can think about how they will tell it.

- Review sequencing words, such as *first, next, then,* and *last,* to aid students in telling their story in order.

- Have each student tell their story to a larger group. Ask listeners to use the rubric on the worksheet to provide constructive feedback.

- Have students work on elaborating. Lead them by explaining that stories are more interesting if they use describing words that tell how something looked, felt, smelled, or sounded.

- Guide students in adding dialogue to their stories. Model how to use words to introduce dialogue, such as *and then the wolf said . . . .* Help them to use different voices that show the personalities of the different characters from the story.

Tell a Story

Use the planner to organize ideas for telling a story.

Write the title of the story.

Draw how you will introduce your speech.

Use your drawings to tell the story.

Title:

_____

Rate your story telling.

People could hear me.

People could understand my words.

I told the ideas in order.

My story made sense.

Tell What You Think

PURPOSE

Use this routine to help students form and organize opinions.

PROCEDURE

1. Explain the meaning of an opinion to students. Say: We tell our opinions to show what we think or believe. We cannot prove whether an opinion is true or false. People have many different ideas or feelings. We can listen to other people's opinions and respect them, even if we don't agree.

2. Display the worksheet on the following page. Model stating an opinion using a word or phrase from the box, for example: I do not like Brussels sprouts. I am saying what I think or believe, but others may not agree. This is an opinion.

3. Have students work with partners to state opinions about sports, food, television shows, or books. Have them use the words and phrases in the box on the worksheet. Point out that the sentence frames will help them express opinions correctly.

TEACHING TIPS

- Have students write statements of opinion and then say them aloud with partners.
- Write sentence frames on index cards and distribute them to students. Have them work in pairs to state opinions using the frames.
- Have students use phrases, such as I like or I do not like, rather than single words.
- Remind students that opinions are neither wrong nor right, but are statements of how someone thinks or feels. Ask students to be respectful and listen to others' opinions.

EXTEND

- Have students state an opinion to a partner and then support it with reasons.
- Have students add other opinion words or phrases to the box and write additional sentence frames. They can use the frames to state opinions.

Tell What You Think

> **Opinion Words**
>
> | I think | I believe | my opinion is | I agree |
> |---------|-----------|---------------|---------|
> | I disagree | I like | I do not like | |
> | best | worst | good | bad |

Complete opinions using these sentence frames:

I like _____

_____.

I think _____

_____.

I believe _____

_____.

I do not like _____

_____.

My opinion is _____

_____.

Challenge! Add more details to your sentence.

I like _____

because _____.

My friend's opinion is _____

because _____.

Have a Discussion

PURPOSE

Use this routine to help students learn to participate in collaborative discussions.

PROCEDURE

1. Ask: When do we have discussions? I talk with my family at the dinner table. I discuss ideas with other teachers at school. In a discussion, we speak and we listen. We respect other people's ideas, and we ask questions when we are unsure of what the speaker means.

2. Introduce an easy discussion topic, such as a recently read selection. Model the discussion behaviors from the rubric on the worksheet on the following page. For example, say: I laughed really hard when I read this story because the characters were so funny. What did you think? Then continue the discussion by building upon each student's response to your question.

3. As you model having a collaborative discussion, pause to think aloud. Say: Ethan took his turn in the conversation and then I responded, so Ethan knows that I understood him. He also knows I was listening. We took turns speaking. It is important to take turns being a good listener and a good speaker.

4. Point out that it is also important that the listener understands the speaker. Say: When we are having a discussion about a topic or a selection, it is important that everyone understands one another. Ask: What can you do if you are the listener and you do not understand what someone has said? (Ask questions.)

5. Explain the rules of discussions with one or more people.
- Listen carefully.
- Speak one at a time.
- When it is your turn to speak, talk about the discussion topic.
- Ask questions when you don't understand.
- Wait your turn.

6. Have students use the worksheet on the following page to rate themselves when they have a discussion with classmates.

TEACHING TIPS

- As students discuss, monitor and encourage the positive behaviors you observe. Share these positive behaviors with the class, and have students identify other positive behaviors they know.
- Stress the importance of active listening and the behaviors that go with it. Model examples of nonverbal communication skills that an active listener uses, such as nodding and making eye contact.

EXTEND

Have a pair of volunteers model a discussion (based on a topic you provide, or one they decide on) while the rest of the class listens. Have the listeners rate the discussion using the worksheet. Ask them to point out areas that the volunteers did well or could improve upon.

Have a Discussion

Rate what you do during discussions with your classmates.

I share ideas.

I answer questions.

I listen to other people.

I look at people when I talk.

I repeat back what other people say.

I am friendly to classmates.

What do you want to talk about?

Make a list.

Pick something to talk about!

_____

_____

_____

_____

_____

Ask Questions

PURPOSE

Use this routine to help students form questions to ask you or their classmates.

PROCEDURE

1. Explain to students: If I don't understand something, I need to ask the person speaking to repeat what he or she said. Then I can understand it. That is called clarifying. I ask questions to be sure I understand. I also ask questions when I am reading. I ask questions before I read, while I read, and after I read. That helps me understand what I am reading.

2. Share the worksheet on the following page with students, and talk about situations in which students would use each of the clarifying questions. Ask: Which question would you ask if you solved part of a problem but are unsure of how to get to the correct solution? (*What should I do next?*)

3. Point out the sentence frames on the worksheet. Have students use the sentence frames to ask questions about a selection you have recently read.

TEACHING TIPS

- Work with a student to role-play a situation in which you would ask a clarifying question. Have the student give you simple directions for doing something. As the student speaks, find an opportunity to ask a question, such as *What does that mean? Can you repeat that, please? How do you do that?*

- Provide multiple opportunities to practice using sentence frames to ask and answer questions.

EXTEND

- Have students use question words (*how, when, where, why, who, what*) to ask and answer questions about a text.

- Present situations for students to discuss in small groups. Have them identify questions they would ask the teacher, their parents, or other students in a group to clarify their understanding.

Ask Questions

Look at the examples of questions.

Use them when speaking with classmates and your teachers.

Read clues in the word box for help.

right	wrong	again	slower	louder	help
what	where	when	how	first	next

"Is this right?"

"Can you please help me?"

"What should I do next?"

Use these sentence frames to ask questions. **Use** the sentence frames to answer questions, too.

Who is _____? That person is _____.

What is _____? That is _____.

When did _____ happen? It happened _____.

Where is _____? The _____ is _____.

Why did _____ happen? It happened because _____.

Retell or Summarize

PURPOSE

Use this routine with the Retell or Summarize Graphic Organizer.

PROCEDURE

1. Model thinking aloud an example of summarizing: I saw a movie yesterday. When my friends asked me about it, I did not tell every detail from the beginning to the end. Instead, I told the most important details. This is called summarizing. When I summarize, I know to sort out the most important details of things that I have seen, read, and heard. A summary includes only important details. Retelling is different. When you retell something, you listen to or read the message, and then you say it in your own words to show you understand it.

2. Ask students to listen carefully as you read a short passage aloud. After you read, ask students to contribute to a summary of the passage. Say: A summary should answer the question, *What was it about?*

3. Help frame students' thinking as you list their ideas to create a summary. Help students distinguish between the need-to-know details and the nice-to-know details by looking at big ideas. Have pairs of students read the complete summary together.

4. Reread the passage. Have pairs decide if the summary lists the most important details. Ask: What should be added or changed? Discuss and clarify answers. Repeat this process with another story to focus on retelling. Remind students that in both summarizing and retelling, they must use their own words.

5. Have students use the graphic organizer to list details from a written or spoken passage. In the box at the bottom, students can write their summaries. Encourage them to keep their summaries short and to the point. Have them read their summaries aloud to a partner.

TEACHING TIPS

- Use questions, such as *What happened? Who was involved? How did the story end?* to help students summarize.

- Have students orally summarize a simple spoken message or a simple text, such as a comic strip. They can work in pairs to practice and then share oral summaries.

- Students can use the sentence starters at the bottom of the graphic organizer to guide their writing.

EXTEND

- Provide a simple text and a sample summary or retelling that is missing some information. Have students read and discuss in pairs to determine what details are missing.

- Provide a sample summary or retelling that includes too much information. Have students determine which details do not need to be included.

- Have pairs of students create directions for summarizing or retelling. Have them share their directions and sample summaries with the class.

Retell or Summarize

Use the graphic organizer to list important details.

Write a summary in the box.

Say the summary aloud.

Use the summary starters if you need to.

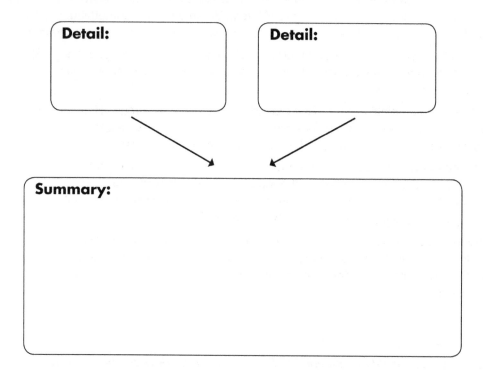

Detail:

Detail:

Summary:

Summary language:

In summary, . . .

The most important ideas are . . .

What we need to remember is . . .

Nondecodable Words

PURPOSE

Use the Nondecodable Words Routine to help students learn words that do not sound like they are spelled by recognizing familiar letters and remembering them.

PROCEDURE

1. Explain to students that some English words do not sound like their spellings. Say: We learn how to say these words by remembering the letters. We will say and spell the words together.

2. Display the word on the board. Point to the word as you read it aloud. Identify the letters in the word, and indicate the number of letters in the word. For example: This is the word *do*. It has two letters. The letters are *d* and *o*.

3. Have students repeat the word, the letters of the word, and the number of letters in the word with you. Then, have the students do this on their own.

4. Remind students to watch how you move your mouth. Point out any letters that do not follow the standard rules.

5. Have students use the nondecodable word in a sentence to demonstrate usage of the word.

TEACHING TIPS

- Provide an example sentence that relates to students' experiences and uses the word in the same context as the text.

- Provide pictures, examples, or visual clues to help students understand the word's proper usage.

- If students pronounce the word incorrectly, model each sound in the word. For example: This is the letter *d*. It makes the sound /d/. The letter *o* in this word does not make its usual sound. It makes the /ü/ sound. Let's try the word again: *do*.

EXTEND

- Have students find a rhyming word for the nondecodable word to help them remember the proper pronunciation.

- Find short poems to have students recite aloud. Ask them to identify examples of nondecodable words.

Preview and Review Vocabulary

Use this routine to assess what students know about words they will encounter in a reading selection. This activity also is a way to review the vocabulary from previous selections so that students internalize the words.

PROCEDURE

1. Select 8–10 words for vocabulary study. Use words from the vocabulary list in the Teacher's Guide and select the remaining words based on the needs of your students. Include on the list 2–3 words from a previous selection.

2. Display the words and read each one aloud to students. Have students record words in a vocabulary notebook for later reference. Then have students read each word with you.

3. Ask them first to decide which words they think will be in the selection before joining a partner for the following step.

4. Have students explain to a partner why they chose each word and why they didn't choose others. Afterward, pairs can explain their choices to the class. Explaining why is a very important step, because students will use their background knowledge of the word to predict the content of the selection. These explanations also demonstrate what students know about a word. It helps to provide more background to students who may not be familiar with the words.

OPTIONS FOR VARYING THIS ROUTINE Replace Steps 3–4 with one of the following:

- Select words they want to know more about.
- Select words they don't know or understand.

EXTEND

- Have students create a word web relating the vocabulary terms to other words they know. These can be words with similar affixes, sounds, or meanings.

- When reading a fiction selection, choose 10 words from the text that exemplify the story's characters, setting, and problem. Have students sort the words into three categories: Characters, Setting, Problem. Then, work together as a class to create a 1–3 sentence prediction about the story. Make sure the prediction includes many of the vocabulary words. The purpose is to have students use new words to practice making predictions, so it is okay if the predictions are "wrong."

- After reading, have students review the words they still do not know. Reread the words in the context of the selection and provide a student-friendly definition. Have students write another sentence using the word.

Act Out or Draw Meaning

PURPOSE

Use this routine with the Act Out or Draw Meaning Graphic Organizer to help students learn and remember new vocabulary. Explain that one way to learn and remember new words is to draw or act out new words.

PROCEDURE

1. Provide a model from something that students have recently read: I just read a new word: *cross*. It can mean "to get from one side to another" or "to draw a line or an x" or "an object formed by two short lines or pieces." I drew a picture of something being crossed out. (Display the picture.) I can also act out the meaning by moving from this side of the room to the other side, or I can make an *x* with my arms.

2. Divide the class into small groups. Introduce words from the selection. Choose "picturable" words and give each group a word.

3. Have students work together to create a picture and/or demonstrate the meanings of the words. Say: Talk about what this word means. Then explain by drawing a picture of it or showing us what it means.

4. Have volunteers explain their drawings to the class. Clear up any misconceptions.

5. Ask: How did drawing the word or acting it out help you remember what it means?

TEACHING TIPS

- Drawing a word aids understanding because it requires students to express ideas in a different format. If students doubt their artistic ability, reassure them that they will not be evaluated based on how their drawings look, but rather on their ability to explain how their drawings help them understand new words.

- Consider modifying the graphic organizer to include a place to record synonyms as well as dictionary definitions.

EXTEND

- Play a guessing game with students. Distribute words on index cards that students have learned in class. Students can take turns drawing pictures or acting out word meanings for the class to guess.

- Use the graphic organizer for students to create dictionaries of word meanings. Distribute copies of the drawing frames when students learn new words. Have students keep and add to their own personal dictionaries.

- Challenge students by having volunteers act out words and their antonyms. Provide a list of words. After demonstrating the meaning, have students name their antonyms and act those out too.

Act Out or Draw Meaning

Word: _____

Drawing

This word means _____

Word: _____

Drawing

This word means _____

Analyze Cognates

PURPOSE

Identifying cognates in texts is a useful strategy for expanding vocabulary, helping students understand more words in English, validating the home language, and making clear connections between the home language and the target language, English. Use this routine with the Personal Cognate Chart to help students whose home language has many cognates of English words, such as Spanish, Portuguese, French, and Italian.

PROCEDURE

1. Ask students if they know how to say the word for *animal* in another language. Create a chart of the languages and words as students provide them. For example, English: *animal*; Spanish: *animal*; Italian: *animale*. Point out that some of the words are a lot like *animal* in English.

2. Explain that when words look or sound similar and have a similar meaning in different languages, they are called *cognates*. Use pictures to help students connect to the English word. Say: When you see an English word that you do not know, think about whether the word looks or sounds like a word in another language that you have heard before. If it does, use the clues in the surrounding words and in the pictures to decide if it has the same meaning as the word you know in the other language.

3. Display and distribute the Personal Cognate Chart. Using the current selection, preview the selection with students to practice looking for cognates when reading. Use the list of cognates provided for each unit's module as a guide.

4. Have students select a word that they believe is a cognate. Write or draw the word in the English Word column of the chart. Have students write the name of their other language on the line at the top of the second column, and write the word they believe is a cognate in the proper box in that same column.

5. Have students read the sentence containing the word and look at the picture on the page to determine the meaning of the word. Then ask: Does this word look like a word you know from another language? Does it seem to have the same meaning as that word you know from another language? If you can say *yes* to both questions, the words are cognates. If students have answered *yes* to both questions, have them write *yes* in the third column. Ask students to circle the differing letters in the cognates if they are not spelled the same. If students were not able to answer *yes* to both questions, have them write *no* in the third column.

- Point out that cognates in different languages usually share the same base. For example, the Spanish, French, and Italian cognates for the word *family* all share the base *fam*.

- Point out that sometimes words in different languages are "false friends"—they look almost the same, but they don't mean the same thing. For example, the English word *trap* looks like the Spanish word *trapo*, but *trap* is really *trampa* in Spanish, and *trapo* is the Spanish word for *rag*. Ask students if they know other examples of "false friends."

- Have students draw pictures in the English Word column of their Personal Cognate Chart to help them better understand the meanings of the words.

EXTEND

- Share the French and Italian cognates for words, such as *family*, and point out the similarities across various languages. Follow the same routine with the word in each language.

English	Spanish	French	Italian
family	familia	famille	famiglia

- Encourage students to suggest other cognates they know in English and another language. Remind them that cognates can help them understand more words in English.

- Prepare word strips of English words and their cognates. Have students in small groups sort through the words and match cognates with English words. Then have them discuss what the words mean. Allow volunteers to share their work with the class, making sure that they explain how they arrived at their pairings and definitions.

Personal Cognate Chart

English Word	_____ (name of language)	Are they cognates? (yes/no)

Analyze Idioms and Expressions

PURPOSE

Idioms are phrases that have a figurative meaning, such as *hit the road*. An expression is a group of words used as a unit, such as *wise guy*.

Because the meanings of idioms and expressions are not literal, students may need extra support to understand them. Students who speak other languages at home might have added difficulty, since there may not be a similar idiom in their own language they can relate it to. The best approach to teaching idioms and expressions is to discuss them in the context of a classroom text or in conversation. By exposing students to idioms and expressions, they will be better able to recognize and understand them when reading or listening to conversations and media.

PROCEDURE

1. Explain that idioms are phrases that communicate an idea or feeling that cannot be understood based on the meaning of each word in the phrase. Say: When I use an idiom, I don't exactly mean what the words say. For example, what do I mean when I say that Carl talked too much and he spilled the beans about the surprise party? Did he literally spill some beans? No, I mean to say that Carl told the secret about the surprise party.

2. Ask students for other examples of idioms and expressions or supply examples, such as *jumping down my throat, feeling under the weather, bite the dust*.

3. Write them on the board and discuss what they might mean based on the context in which they were heard or read. Talk about why someone might be confused by a particular idiom. For example, *to sleep on it* can be confusing because students might visualize someone sleeping on top of something.

4. Point out idioms and expressions in selections that students are reading or that you read aloud to them. Ask them to figure out the meanings. Clarify any misunderstandings and provide corrective feedback.

TEACHING TIP

If students are having trouble distinguishing the literal from the figurative meaning of idioms, use pictures that illustrate both meanings. For example, to explain *raining cats and dogs,* show a picture of a person under an umbrella shielding himself from many cats and dogs falling from a cloudy gray sky. Show a variation of the same picture that has sheets of rain falling instead of cats and dogs.

EXTEND

- Have students draw the literal meaning of an idiom or expression and describe the figurative meaning. Compile a class book or poster of idioms and expressions to display in the classroom.

- Have pairs work together to write sentences using idioms and then explanations of what they mean. Ask volunteers to share their work with the class.

Analyze Multiple-Meaning Words

PURPOSE

Use this routine to help students determine or clarify the meaning of words and phrases that have more than one meaning.

PROCEDURE

1. Explain that some words have more than one meaning. Say: Words like *bat* have multiple meanings. *Bat* can mean "a type of animal that flies during the night." *Bat* can also mean "a wooden club used in games like baseball." When you come across a word in a text that has more than one meaning, how can you figure out which meaning is being used?

2. Present different strategies that students can use to determine or clarify the meaning of a word that has more than one meaning:

   a. Tell students that they can often use the context of the sentence to figure out what a word or phrase means. Using the context means looking at the other words in the sentence for clues. Say: If I told you that I saw a bat flying in a cave at the zoo, you would know that I am talking about a type of animal.

   b. If the text does not provide enough context to help students figure out the meaning of a word, tell them they can also use prefixes and suffixes that they do know to figure out the meaning of a word. For example, the prefix *un-* means "not" and the suffix *-able* means "able to."

   c. Another strategy is to use base words with which students are familiar. For example: For words like *pop, pops, popped,* and *popping,* students may be familiar with the definitions of *to pop up,* meaning "to jump out," or *to pop,* meaning "to explode."

TEACHING TIPS

- To avoid too many interruptions while reading, have students use sticky notes to flag unknown words, especially those with multiple meanings, while they read.

- Have students draw pictures that illustrate the distinction between the different meanings of multiple-meaning words, such as *bat.*

- Explain to students that they can clarify the meaning of a word by identifying its part of speech. For example, in *Button up—it's cold,* the word *button* is used as a verb. In *I have a loose button on my coat,* the word *button* is used as a noun.

EXTEND

Draw a two-column graphic organizer. Title the columns Word and Meanings. Have students brainstorm additional multiple-meaning words and fill in the columns accordingly.

Common Nouns

INTRODUCE Point to objects in the room, and have students name them. Tell students: We have names for the things around us. A noun is a word that names something or somebody.

TEACH/MODEL After students read the selection, explain that a noun names a person, a place, an animal, or a thing. Have students place the following four words into a chart, like the one below: *boy, school, bird, desk.* Then, provide a list of words from the selection for students to place in the correct column.

Person	Place	Animal	Thing
boy	school	bird	desk

PRACTICE Pairs may look through a selection and say the nouns for people or things in the pictures. Then, have them place the words in the correct column of the chart.

ASSESS Check students' understanding by reviewing the charts that each pair completes.

ENGLISH LANGUAGE LEARNERS

Students' home languages also have words for people, places, animals, and things. To help them learn English nouns, bring items—apples, hats, dolls, stuffed toys, dishes, and so forth—for vocabulary building.

Proper Nouns

INTRODUCE Have students practice writing their names. Point out that each student's name begins with a capital letter. Tell students: Each of us has our own special name. A proper noun is the special name of a person, place, animal, or thing.

TEACH/MODEL Explain that a proper noun names a special person, place, animal, or thing. A proper noun begins with a capital letter. Have students place the following words into the chart in the correct column: *Fluffy, London Bridge, Mexico, Alex.* Then, provide a list of words from the selection for students to place in the chart.

Special Person	Special Place	Special Animal	Special Thing
Alex	Mexico	Fluffy	London Bridge

PRACTICE Pairs may look through the text and point out the names of special people, places, animals, or things in the pictures. Have them place the words in the correct column.

ASSESS Check students' understanding by reviewing the charts that each pair completes.

ENGLISH LANGUAGE LEARNERS

- Students whose home language is nonalphabetic, such as Chinese, Korean, and Japanese, may need extra practice writing names with letters.
- In some Asian languages, family names appear first in persons' names. Point out that, in English, the family name follows the person's first name.

Singular and Plural Nouns

INTRODUCE Point to one book and say: a book. Point to two books and say: books. Repeat with a *girl* and *girls*. Have students name other singular and plural nouns as you point to them. Say: Some nouns name one thing. They are called singular nouns. Some nouns name more than one thing. They are called plural nouns.

TEACH/MODEL Discuss with students that adding -s to most nouns forms the plural. *Plural* means "more than one." Write the words noted above on a chart like the one below. Have students select objects around the room and record them under One or More Than One.

One	More Than One
girl	girls
school	schools
dog	dogs

PRACTICE Provide a list of singular and plural nouns from the current reading selection. Provide a chart like the one above, and have students work independently or in pairs to place the words from the list in the correct column.

ASSESS Review pairs' charts to check that they have the words in the correct columns.

ENGLISH LANGUAGE LEARNERS

In some languages, including Chinese, Hmong, and Vietnamese, nouns do not have plural forms. Instead, the plural is indicated with an adjective.

Plural Nouns That Add -*s* and -*es*

INTRODUCE Point to two chairs and say: chairs. Repeat with boxes or other items represented by a plural noun ending in -*es*. Tell students: We usually add -*s* to form a plural. But if the noun ends in -*ch, -sh, -ss,* or -*x,* we add -*es.*

TEACH/MODEL Explain to students that most nouns add -*s,* such as *books* and *girls.* However, some nouns add -*es: boxes, brushes, classes.* Put these words into a chart like the one below, and help students identify and categorize other plural nouns with -*s* or -*es* endings.

PRACTICE Provide a list of singular words from the text that includes both types of nouns. Using the chart below, have students organize the words into the correct column.

Add -*s*	Add -*es*
chairs	boxes

ASSESS Have students say or write a noun from the reading that adds -*es*. Have students use the word in a sentence.

ENGLISH LANGUAGE LEARNERS

Spanish-speaking students who have begun to read may be familiar with using -*s* and -*es* endings for plural nouns, as in the Spanish words for *plants* and *flowers: plantas* and *flores.*

Plural Nouns That Change Spelling

INTRODUCE Say: *The children brush their teeth. The women tap their feet.* **Tell students:** Most nouns add *-s* or *-es* to form the plural, but some change spelling to form the plural, like *children, teeth, women,* and *feet.*

TEACH/MODEL Present the concept and provide examples:

* Most nouns add *-s* or *-es* to form the plural: *books, girls, boxes, brushes.*
* Some nouns change spelling to form the plural. These are called irregular plural nouns.

Irregular Plural Nouns			
child/children	foot/feet	life/lives	man/men
mouse/mice	tooth/teeth	wolf/wolves	woman/women

PRACTICE Use each of the singular nouns listed above in a sentence. For example, say: *The child hurt his foot.* Have students repeat each sentence. Then have them replace each singular noun with its plural form and say the new sentence aloud.

ENGLISH LANGUAGE LEARNERS

English learners may add *-s* to irregular nouns as they speak or write: *gooses, childrens, wolfs, clothings.* Have students practice with nouns that have different plural forms.

Possessive Nouns

INTRODUCE Give a book to each of three students. Stand near one student and say: *This is [student's name]'s book.* Repeat with the other two students. Then have all three students show their books. Say: *These are the students' books.* Write the four singular nouns (the name of each student and the word *students*) on the board. Explain: *To show that a person, place, or thing has or owns something, add an apostrophe and the letter -s. Add only an apostrophe when the noun is plural and ends with -s.* Punctuate the nouns on the board.

TEACH/MODEL Present the concept and provide examples:

* To form a possessive noun, add an apostrophe (') and *-s* when the noun is singular.
* Just add an apostrophe when the noun is plural and ends in *-s.*

Singular Nouns	Possessive	Plural Nouns	Possessive
friend	friend's name	boys	boys' caps
girl	girl's book	cats	cats' bowls
school	school's library	puppies	puppies' toys

PRACTICE Write the following sentences on the board, and have students identify the correct possessive noun in each sentence: *The* (cats, cats') *toys are on the floor.* (Pauls', Paul's) *bowl is dirty. The two* (frogs', frog's) *legs are green. This is* (Susan's, Susans') *pencil.*

ENGLISH LANGUAGE LEARNERS

In many languages, speakers show possession in phrases rather than noun endings. Show students how to change phrases, such as *the tail.*

Titles and Abbreviations

INTRODUCE Write and read aloud names of people, including titles like *Mr., Mrs.,* and *Dr.* Underline the titles and explain that they are abbreviations, or shortened forms of words.

TEACH/MODEL Present the concept and provide examples:

- Proper names may begin with a title, such as *Mrs., Mr., Ms.,* or *Dr.*
- A title begins with a capital letter. If a title is an abbreviation, it ends with a period.

Abbreviated Title	Example
Mr. (mister)	Mr. Garza
Ms. (miz)	Ms. Prince
Mrs. (missus)	Mrs. Dexter
Dr. (doctor)	Dr. Marco

PRACTICE Have pairs review a recent selection for examples of titles and abbreviations. Have them create a chart like the one above. Remind students that some titles, such as *Senator, President,* and *Professor,* are not abbreviated. Have them add to the chart as they read.

ENGLISH LANGUAGE LEARNERS

- Explain that, in English, the title *Doctor* is used for both men and women.
- In some countries, the word *teacher* is used as a title. Point out that in the U.S., teachers are addressed with a title, such as *Mr., Ms., Mrs.,* or *Miss*.

Days, Months, and Holidays

INTRODUCE Write today's date and point out the capital letters.

TEACH/MODEL Present the concept and provide several examples:

- Days of the week, months of the year, and holidays begin with capital letters.

Days of the Week	Months of the Year		Holidays (Examples)
Sunday	January	July	New Year's Day
Monday	February	August	Valentine's Day
Tuesday	March	September	Thanksgiving
Wednesday	April	October	
Thursday	May	November	
Friday	June	December	
Saturday			

PRACTICE Ask these questions, and have students write their answers: What is your favorite holiday? What day is today? In which month were you born? Check for correct capitalization.

ENGLISH LANGUAGE LEARNERS

In languages including Spanish, French, Polish, and Vietnamese, the names of days and months are not usually capitalized.

Subject Pronouns: *I, You, He, She, It*

INTRODUCE Point to yourself and say: I am a teacher. Point to the students and say: You are students. Point to a boy and say: He is a student. Point to a girl and say: She is a student. Indicate everyone in the room and say: We are at school. Explain to students that pronouns such as *I, you, he, she, we,* and *they* are used in place of nouns or noun phrases, such as people's names. These pronouns are used as the subject of a sentence. We do not say, "Me am a teacher" or "Him is a student."

TEACH/MODEL Present the concept and provide examples from the current reading selection:

- A subject pronoun is used as the subject of a sentence. The singular pronouns are *I, you, he, she,* and *it.*

PRACTICE Say these sentences, or choose examples from the text, and have students rephrase them using subject pronouns: Ana sits in the third row. Max sits here. Ana and Max are cousins. The sandwich is the teacher's lunch.

ENGLISH LANGUAGE LEARNERS

In languages such as Spanish, Chinese, Vietnamese, Korean, and Hmong, some subject pronouns can be omitted from sentences because the context indicates the subject. If students say sentences such as "Is good" (for "It is good") and "Am tired" (for "I am tired"), provide practice using subject pronouns.

Plural Subject Pronouns: *We, You, They*

INTRODUCE Hand out markers or crayons of different colors to pairs of students, giving each pair one color. Indicate everyone and say: We all have markers. Point to and look at a pair of students near you, and say, for example: You have a blue marker. Point to another pair and say: They have a red marker. Explain: The words we, you, and they are pronouns. They tell about more than one.

TEACH/MODEL Present the concept and provide examples:

- *We, you,* and *they* tell about more than one.

PRACTICE Write sentences such as these on strips: *Reina, Tran, and Cali play with cars. The dog and cat run fast. Peter and you will sit.* Cut them into subject and predicate. Create strips with *We, You,* and *They.* Have students replace the noun strips with pronoun strips. Help them read the new sentences.

ENGLISH LANGUAGE LEARNERS

Many languages have different words to indicate *you* singular and *you* plural. Reassure students that in English *you* can refer to one person or more than one person.

Object Pronouns: *Me, You, Him, Her, It*

INTRODUCE Display and read aloud these sentences: Give the book to me. She called you. That book belongs to her. I saw him yesterday. Explain that pronouns such as *me, you, him,* and *her* are used after action verbs or after words such as *for, at, with, to.* They are used in the action parts of sentences. We do not say "Give the book to I" or "You saw he yesterday."

TEACH/MODEL Present the concept and provide examples:

- Different pronouns are used in the action parts of sentences, after an action verb or preposition.
- *You* is used in either part of a sentence.

PRACTICE Pose open-ended sentences, cueing object-pronoun endings by gesturing to different people in the room: I will help... [gesture toward a girl]. Students should finish the sentence: *her.*

ENGLISH LANGUAGE LEARNERS

Spanish, Chinese, and Vietnamese speakers and other English learners may use subject pronouns as objects (*We like she; I saw they*) until they have enough practice in English to recognize and use pronoun forms well.

Plural Object Pronouns: *Us, You, Them*

INTRODUCE Display and read these sentences aloud: Li and Pam sang for us. We heard them. I will sing you a song. Explain that the pronouns *us, them,* and *you* tell about more than one. They are used after action verbs, or after words such as *for, at, with, to.*

TEACH/MODEL Present the concept and provide examples from the current reading selection:

- The pronouns *us, them,* and *you* are used in the action parts of sentences, after an action verb or preposition. For example:

   Mari and I will have a race. Will you watch <u>us</u>?

   The chairs are in the way. Please move <u>them</u>.

   We will race <u>you</u> and Ben. We will run with <u>you</u>.

PRACTICE Display the words *us, them,* and *you.* Have students call out pronouns to finish these rhymes: I bring these flowers for Gina and Clem. These pretty flowers are just for ___. My friends and I ride on the bus. Come along, and ride with ___. My very best friends are you and Sue. I'm glad that I am friends with ___!

Then provide example sentences from the text and have students complete the sentence frames.

ENGLISH LANGUAGE LEARNERS

Some languages distinguish the gender of *them* with two different words. Reassure students that in English, *them* is used for males, females, and things. Also, remind students that *them* does not need –s.

Action Verbs

INTRODUCE Perform these actions as you narrate, and have students repeat your words and actions: I clap. I walk. I sit. Which words tell what I do? (*clap, walk, sit*) A word that tells what we do is called a verb.

TEACH/MODEL Present the concept and provide examples:

- An action verb tells what we do.
  I <u>play</u>. You <u>sing</u>. They <u>jump</u>. The dogs <u>bark</u>.

PRACTICE Ask students to continue thinking of action words, such as *sit, hop, skip, sing, laugh*. Have volunteers share their action words with you and create a list on the board. Then have the students come to the front of the classroom. Call out appropriate words from the list and ask students to act them out.

ENGLISH LANGUAGE LEARNERS

English verb endings are simpler than verb endings in languages such as Spanish and Polish, which use different endings for person and number of subjects. Provide examples of English verbs with no added endings, such as *We eat* and *They can run*.

Verbs for Now: Add -*s*

INTRODUCE Gesture as you narrate: She sits here. He sits here. She sees me. He sees me. The word *sits* is a verb. The word *sees* is a verb. A verb can tell what one person, animal, or thing does now. Many verbs that tell what is happening now end with -*s*: *sits, sees*.

TEACH/MODEL Present the concept and provide examples:

- Verbs in present tense tell what happens now.
  She <u>sees</u> me. He <u>sits</u>. The girl <u>runs</u>. The ball <u>rolls</u>.

PRACTICE Read aloud to students a few pages from a short story written in the present tense. Ask them to clap whenever they hear a verb ending with -*s*. Speak slowly and enunciate carefully to help them catch the -*s* verbs.

ENGLISH LANGUAGE LEARNERS

Students who speak highly inflected languages, such as Russian and Spanish, may need practice adding -*s* to verbs in present tense with third-person singular subjects. Help students see the difference between -*s* on plural nouns and -*s* on verbs: *He bakes a pie; She runs*.

Verbs for Now: Add -*s*, -*es*

INTRODUCE Say these sentences as you act them out: The teacher touches the board. The teacher washes her hands. She passes the papers to us. **Ask:** Which words tell what the teacher is doing? (*touches, washes, passes*) Display the verbs and explain: You know that we add -*s* to a verb to tell what a person, animal, or thing does. But sometimes we add -*es* to a verb. Some verbs are easier to say that way. Demonstrate to students by adding only /s/ to *pass* or *wash*. Then have them add -*es* so they can hear the extra syllable: *passes, washes*.

TEACH/MODEL Present the concept and provide examples:

- Add -*s* to a verb to tell what a person, animal, or thing does.
- Add -*es* if the verb ends in -*ch, -sh, -x,* or -*ss.*

Add -*s*	jumps, plays, paints, runs, walks, eats
Add -*es*	teaches, washes, kisses, brushes, fixes

PRACTICE Write these sentences on the board and have students identify the correct verb in each sentence: *Mom* (fix, fixes) *Lisa's doll. Lisa* (huges, hugs) *Mom. Lisa* (kiss, kisses) *Mom.* Next, have students say a sentence using the word *washes.*

ENGLISH LANGUAGE LEARNERS

Help students recognize that -*s* and -*es* verb endings, although they are spelled differently, are similar. Provide examples in context rather than in word lists: *Ana rides a bike; Tom talks quietly; Mia brushes her hair; Dad fixes a lamp.*

Verbs for Now: Do Not Add -*s*

INTRODUCE Say these sentences, gesturing as you speak: The children play. Two boys jump rope. Three girls run. **Ask:** Which words tell you what they do? (*play, jump, run*) Write the verbs on the board. **Explain:** You know that we add -*s* to a verb to tell what one person, animal, or thing does. To tell what two or more people, animals, or things do, we do not add -*s* to the verb. Also, after the word *I* or the word *you*, we do not add -*s* to the verb: I walk home. You ride the bus.

TEACH/MODEL Present the concept and provide examples:

- Do not add -*s* to a verb that tells what two or more people, animals, or things do. The men <u>plant</u> trees. The birds <u>sing</u>.
- Do not add -*s* to a verb that tells what I do or what you do. You <u>play</u> a game.

PRACTICE Write the following sentences on the board, and have students write on a piece of paper the correct verb to use in each sentence: *Tim and I* (ride, rides) *our bikes. Mom and Dad* (run, runs) *on the path. Tim* (sings, sing) *a silly song. I* (smile, smiles) *at the song.* Then have students write or say a sentence about Mom and Dad, using the verb *sing.*

ENGLISH LANGUAGE LEARNERS

Guide students of various language backgrounds so they do not add -*s* to both the subjects and verbs, as in *The girls walks.* Help them practice saying and/or writing examples such as *The girls walk; The boys smile;* and *We sing.*

Verbs for the Past: -ed with the Sound of /t/ and /d/

INTRODUCE Say these sentences and display the verbs: Yesterday I walked to the park. I played with my dog. He barked at a cat. I pulled at his leash. **Explain:** I did these things yesterday, in the past. Many verbs that tell about the past end with -ed. Sometimes the -ed sounds like /t/, as in walked and barked. Sometimes the -ed sounds like /d/, as in played and pulled.

TEACH/MODEL Present the concept and provide examples:

- Verbs in past tense tell what already happened.
- Many verbs in past tense end with -ed.

Sound of /t/	I <u>asked</u> her to play. We <u>jumped</u> rope. I <u>helped</u> her, and she <u>thanked</u> me.
Sound of /d/	I <u>opened</u> the door and <u>called</u> your name. You <u>cleaned</u> your room.

PRACTICE Read aloud to students a few pages from a short story written in the past tense. Ask them to clap whenever they hear a verb ending with -ed. Speak slowly and enunciate carefully to help them catch the -ed verbs. Help students identify between the /t/ and /d/ sounds at the end of the verbs.

ENGLISH LANGUAGE LEARNERS

In Chinese, Hmong, and Vietnamese, verbs do not change to show the tense. Instead, adverbs or expressions of time indicate when an action has taken place. Help students use past-tense verbs in conversations.

Verbs for the Past: -ed with the Sound of /əd/

INTRODUCE Say, gesturing: Yesterday, I visited my friend. We planted some flowers. I counted four flowers. **Display the verbs and explain:** I did these things in the past: visited, planted, counted. These verbs end with the letters -ed. For these verbs, the -ed sounds like /əd/. Listen: visited, planted, counted.

TEACH/MODEL Present the concept and provide examples:

- Many verbs in past tense end with -ed that sounds like /əd/.

Sound of /əd/	I <u>wanted</u> my water to be cold. I <u>needed</u> some ice. I <u>waited</u> one hour. I <u>lifted</u> my glass. The ice had <u>melted</u>, so I <u>added</u> more ice.

PRACTICE Have students pair up. Ask them to skim through a few pages of their textbooks, looking for past-tense verbs that end with -ed that sounds like /əd/. Tell them to say the verbs aloud to determine if they end with the /əd/ sound. Have partners keep a list of the verbs they find that end with the /əd/ sound. Review the lists as a class.

Verbs for the Future

INTRODUCE Say: What will I do after school today? I will go home. I will eat an orange. Explain: Verbs can tell about action in the future. Write one of the statements. Point to the word *will*. Say: To talk about the future, put the word *will* before the verb.

TEACH/MODEL Present the concept and provide examples:

* Verbs in future tense tell what will happen.

  EXAMPLES: I will visit Ethan.   We will see a movie.   Mom will drive me home.

PRACTICE Write the following words and sentence frames on the board: *will swim, will teach, will grow*; Mama Duck ___ her babies to swim. Soon, the baby ducks ___ big. They all ___ in the pond. Have students fill in the blanks with the appropriate words from the board. Next, have students write or say a sentence about what they think will happen when the baby ducks are grown.

Verbs: *Am, Is, Are, Was,* and *Were*

INTRODUCE Say: I am your teacher. Jacob is a good student. Amara and Chung are friends. Explain: In these sentences, the verbs *am, is,* and *are* do not tell what someone does. They tell what someone is. *Am, is,* and *are* tell about now. Listen to these sentences: Yesterday was Tuesday. Two children were sick on Tuesday. *Was* and *were* tell about the past.

TEACH/MODEL Present the concept and provide examples:

* Use *is* and *was* to tell about one person, place, animal, or thing.
* Use *are* and *were* to tell about more than one.
* Use *am* and *was* with *I*. Use *are* and *were* with *you*.

	Verbs: am, is, are, was, were
Now	I am happy. You are happy. Celine is happy. The cat is happy. Celine and I are happy.
Past	Yesterday my lunch was good. My friends were hungry last night.

PRACTICE Write the following sentences on the board, and have students complete each sentence using the correct verb: *Yesterday, I* (are, was) *sick. Today I* (am, are) *still sick. Last week, my sisters* (was, were) *both sick. Mom* (is, are) *very nice to me. She and I* (are, is) *talking.* Review students' responses. Then have students write or say a sentence about someone being sick, using the verb *is*.

ENGLISH LANGUAGE LEARNERS

In Chinese, Hmong, and Haitian Creole, *to be* is not required in some sentences. If students say "I happy," practice with sentences such as *I am happy.* Tell Spanish speakers that English speakers say "We are hungry" rather than "We have hunger."

Verbs for the Present and for the Past

INTRODUCE Write and say the following expressions: She walks. He talks. Point out that these verbs tell us what happens now, or in the present. Write and say: She walked. He talked. Explain that these verbs tell what happened in the past.

TEACH/MODEL Present the concept and provide examples:

* Some verbs that tell about the past end in -ed.

* Expressions of time, such as *last month, yesterday,* or *last year,* can also help students recognize actions in the past.

Verbs in the Present	helps, plays, paints, walks, fixes, picks
Verbs in the Past	helped, played, painted, walked, fixed, picked

PRACTICE Write these verb stems on the board: *jump, borrow, dance, learn, pick, want.* Have pairs take turns using each verb in a series of sentences set in the present. Then have them reuse each verb in a series of sentences set in the past.

ENGLISH LANGUAGE LEARNERS

In Spanish, French, and Portuguese, verb endings indicate the tense of the verb. In Chinese, Hmong, and Vietnamese, verbs do not change to show the tense. Adverbs or expressions of time indicate when an action takes place.

Verbs for the Past, Present, and Future

INTRODUCE Write and say the following sentences: Mary walked to school. (past) She walks every day. (present) She will walk home later. (future) Identify the action that took place in the past, the action that is happening in the present, and the action that will happen in the future.

TEACH/MODEL Present the concept and provide examples from a reading selection:

* Some verbs tell about the past. They may end in -ed.

* Some verbs tell about the present. They may end in -s or have no ending.

* Verbs in the future tense tell what will happen in the future. We use the helping verb *will* to form the future tense.

Verbs in the Past	waited, called, learned
Verbs in the Present	waits, wait, calls, call, learns, learn
Verbs in the Future	will wait, will call, will learn

PRACTICE Write these signal words: *yesterday, now, tomorrow*. Have partners say and write sentences containing each signal word.

ENGLISH LANGUAGE LEARNERS

In Spanish, the verb can appear before the subject. In Korean, the verb appears at the end of the sentence. Provide extra practice with word order in sentences.

Contractions

INTRODUCE Say these sentences: I am your teacher. I'm your teacher. I said the same thing twice. In the second sentence, I made a contraction from *I am*. We can make a contraction with a pronoun, such as *I, you, he, she,* or *they*. Combine it with a verb, such as *am, will, are,* or *is*.

TEACH/MODEL Present the concept and provide examples:

- Make a contraction with a pronoun plus *am, will, are,* or *is.*

If <u>you are</u> going, <u>I am</u> going too.	If <u>you're</u> going, I'm going too.
<u>She is</u> my sister.	<u>She's</u> my sister.
<u>You are</u> my friend.	<u>You're</u> my friend.
<u>I will</u> go now.	<u>I'll</u> go now.

PRACTICE Provide students with examples of contractions from the text. Have students write the sentences with and without contractions.

ENGLISH LANGUAGE LEARNERS

Students may hear *I'm* and *it's* repeatedly but may not recognize them as contractions. Have students make these word cards: *I, am, I'm, it, is, it's*. Have them match the contraction to its two words.

Contractions with *Not*

INTRODUCE Say and display these sentences: I do not know. I don't know. **Say:** These two sentences mean the same thing. The word *don't* is the words *do* and *not* combined. It is called a contraction. We can make a contraction by putting a verb together with the word *not*. An apostrophe takes the place of the *o* in *not*.

TEACH/MODEL Present the concept and provide examples from the current reading selection:

- A contraction is a short way to put two words together.
- An apostrophe takes the place of the missing letter or letters.

They <u>do not</u> see me.	They <u>don't</u> see me.
You <u>are not</u> walking.	You <u>aren't</u> walking.
I <u>did not</u> get a pen.	I <u>didn't</u> get a pen.
That <u>is not</u> my dog.	That <u>isn't</u> my dog.

PRACTICE Display *don't, isn't, didn't,* and *aren't*. Have students reword these sentences using the contractions: *Cats do not bark. That is not true. I did not know. My dogs are not big.* Students can say or write the reworded sentences.

ENGLISH LANGUAGE LEARNERS

- Spanish-speaking students will know these contractions: *al = a + el; del = de + el*. Explain how the apostrophe is used in English contractions.
- In Spanish, Haitian Creole, and other languages, double negatives are correct (comparable to *I did not do nothing*). Explain how *–n't* is used in English.

Colors

INTRODUCE Display a box of crayons. Pull out a crayon as you point out items in that color: This is a red crayon. What else in this room is red? Ah, here is a red book. Repeat with other colors. Explain: The words *red, yellow, blue, green, orange, brown, purple,* and *black* tell more about things. They are adjectives. Adjectives describe a person, place, or thing. Some adjectives are the names of colors.

TEACH/MODEL Present the concept and provide examples:

- Some adjectives name colors.

  <u>yellow</u> house, <u>red</u> apple, <u>blue</u> car, <u>green</u> grass, <u>orange</u> crayon, <u>brown</u> shoe, <u>purple</u> ball, <u>black</u> cat

PRACTICE Write the following sentences on the board, and ask students to identify in each sentence the adjective that names a color: *Give me some white paper, please. I will use a red crayon to draw an apple. I will use a green crayon to draw leaves on a tree. Would you like to draw a pink flower?* Then display a colorful picture for students and have them describe it, using color adjectives.

ENGLISH LANGUAGE LEARNERS

Speakers of Polish and other languages may express choices among objects using adjectives without nouns, as in *I want the blue.* Help students add the noun that adjectives reference.

Shapes

INTRODUCE Point out items in the room as you draw their shapes in the air with your finger: Here is a round rug (or clock). What else is round? Here is a square block. What else is square? Explain: The words *round* and *square* are adjectives. Some adjectives name shapes.

TEACH/MODEL Present the concept and provide examples:

- Some adjectives name shapes.

  <u>round</u> circle, <u>round</u> dot; <u>square</u> window, <u>square</u> paper; <u>oval</u> egg

PRACTICE Hand each student a cutout of a shape. Show them a series of images, such as an orange, a painting in a square frame, or an oval plate. Have students hold up their hand if their shape matches the shape of the object in the image. Then ask students to describe the object, using the appropriate shape word. For example: The orange is round. The painting is square. The plate is oval.

ENGLISH LANGUAGE LEARNERS

Help students understand that the word *square* can be used both as an adjective and as a shape name (noun). The word *round* is an adjective, but the shape name is *circle.*

Size

INTRODUCE Display pictures of animals and describe their various sizes: Here is a small mouse. Here is a big whale. A giraffe has a long neck. A turtle has short legs. **Explain:** Some adjectives describe size. *Big, small, long,* and *short* are just a few of the adjectives that describe the size of a person, place, animal, or thing.

TEACH/MODEL Present the concept and provide examples:

- Some adjectives describe size.

  <u>big</u> man, <u>small</u> dog, <u>long</u> line, <u>short</u> tree

PRACTICE Display a picture that shows people, animals, or things that are different sizes. Have students use adjectives that describe size to write sentences or phrases about what they see in the picture. Then ask volunteers to share their sentences or phrases.

ENGLISH LANGUAGE LEARNERS

In Spanish and Vietnamese, adjectives may follow nouns, as in the name *Río Grande* ("big river"). Help students write adjectives before nouns in English.

What Kind

INTRODUCE Point out items in the room as you describe them: This is an old table. What kind of table is this? (old) This is a new book. What kind of book is this? (new) Continue with other items around the room. **Explain:** The words *old* and *new* are just a few adjectives that tell what kind.

TEACH/MODEL Present the concept and provide examples:

- Some adjectives tell what kind.

  <u>dark</u> socks, <u>cold</u> milk, <u>loud</u> noise, <u>wet</u> shoes, <u>happy</u> children

PRACTICE Display a picture of a family or group of people. Have students write sentences that describe the people in the picture, using adjectives that tell what kind. Then ask volunteers to share their sentences.

ENGLISH LANGUAGE LEARNERS

Spanish adjective endings match the gender and number of the nouns they modify. Help students understand that English adjectives do not have gender or plural endings. The word *new* stays the same in a *new toy, new toys,* a *new lady,* and *new ladies.* Help students practice with various adjectives and nouns.

How Many

INTRODUCE Present two groups of students, one with two boys and one with three girls. Say: Here are two boys. Here are three girls. There are five children. **Explain:** *Two, three,* and *five* are number words. They can tell how many people, places, animals, or things.

TEACH/MODEL Present the concept and provide examples:

* Some adjectives tell how many.

  <u>three</u> monkeys, <u>four</u> schools, <u>one</u> child, <u>two</u> feet, <u>five</u> fingers

PRACTICE Display a picture of a child's bedroom or another room. Have students write sentences or phrases to describe the room, focusing on how many people, animals, or things are in the room. Then ask volunteers to share their sentences or phrases.

ENGLISH LANGUAGE LEARNERS

Some English number words have cognates in other languages: The Spanish word for *three* is *tres;* the Russian word for *three* sounds similar to *tree;* and the Haitian Creole word for *six* is *sis* (pronounced like *cease*).

That Compare

INTRODUCE Draw two long lines of different lengths on the board. Point to the shorter line and say: This line is long. Point to the longer line and say: This line is longer. Write *long* and *longer.* Say: You know that *long* is an adjective for size. *Longer* compares the two lines. Most adjectives that we can use to compare end with *-er: longer, shorter, happier.* Draw another, longer line. Say: This line is the longest. Write *longest* on the board. Say: *Longest* compares all three lines.

TEACH/MODEL Present the concept and provide examples:

* Add *-er* to most adjectives when you compare two persons, places, animals, or things.
* Add *-est* to most adjectives when you compare three or more persons, places, animals, or things.

  A dog is <u>smaller</u> than a cow.

  If you see a cow, a dog, and a frog, the frog is the <u>smallest</u> of the three.

PRACTICE Have pairs of students find pairs or sets of objects in the classroom to compare. For example, one eraser might be smaller than another, while one book might be the heaviest of three. Have students write sentences comparing their objects. Then have each pair share their sentences with the class.

ENGLISH LANGUAGE LEARNERS

Many languages do not use comparative endings. Students may need extra practice with *-er* and *-est* endings. In Spanish, Korean, and Hmong, comparisons are made with phrases, similar to *more sad.* If students use *more happy* or *most old,* help them learn *happier, happiest, older,* and *oldest.*

Tell *When* and *Where*

INTRODUCE Say these sentences: Yesterday we came to school. **Ask:** <u>When</u> did we come to school? (yesterday) Continue: We played outside. **Ask:** <u>Where</u> did we play? (outside) The word *yesterday* tells more about the verb *came. Outside* tells more about the verb *played.* Words like *yesterday* and *outside* are called adverbs. Adverbs tell more about verbs.

TEACH/MODEL Present the concept and provide examples:

- An adverb tells more about a verb.

- An adverb can tell when and where something happens.

When	I'm leaving <u>now</u>. I'll see you <u>soon</u>.
Where	I sleep <u>here</u>. I walk <u>outside</u>.

PRACTICE Hand each student two flashcards: one labeled "when" and the other labeled "where." Tell students to hold up their "when" flashcards when they hear an adverb describing when something happens and to hold up their "where" flashcards when they hear an adverb describing where something happens. Say these sentences: He plays inside when it's raining. She'll arrive soon. I've never been there. I did my homework yesterday. I want to play later. I want to play inside.

ENGLISH LANGUAGE LEARNERS

If students place adverbs in unusual positions, as in *We today sang a song,* help them understand correct placement of adverbs in English sentences with more varied examples.

Tell *How*

INTRODUCE Say and act out this chant: Slowly I turn. Loudly I clap! Quietly I walk. Quickly I tap! **Explain:** *Slowly, loudly, quietly,* and *quickly* are adverbs. They tell how something happens.

TEACH/MODEL Present the concept and provide examples:

- An adverb can tell how something happens.

- Many adverbs that tell how end in *-ly,* such as *happily* and *sadly.*

I'm walking <u>quickly</u>. She laughed <u>softly</u>.

PRACTICE Write these adverbs on the board: *slowly, quickly, loudly, sleepily, quietly, sneakily.* Have a volunteer choose one. Give a command, such as Walk to the door. The volunteer must walk in the manner of the adverb, and the other students must guess the adverb he or she chose. The student who guesses the adverb takes the next turn.

ENGLISH LANGUAGE LEARNERS

Many languages do not strongly distinguish adjectives from adverbs. Students may use adjectives as adverbs. For example, students may say *run slow* and *talk glad.* Help students recognize adverbs with *-ly* (*slowly, gladly*), but point out that not all *-ly* words are adverbs. For example, *friendly* is an adjective.

Meaningful Word Groups: Phrases

INTRODUCE Say and write these words on the board: *dog, little, the.* Ask: What do these words mean? Let's look at them one at a time. The first word names a kind of animal. The second word tells a size. The word *the* by itself doesn't tell me anything. These words are like pieces of a puzzle. They don't mean very much when they are put together this way. Look what happens when I arrange the words differently: *the little dog.* These words really mean something when they are put together this way. They help me think of a little dog.

TEACH/MODEL Present the concept and provide examples:

- Meaningful word groups make sense when we say or read them together.

Meaningful	a red cat	sat on a mat
Not Meaningful	cat red a	on sat mat a

PRACTICE Write phrases such as these on strips of paper: *the yellow cat; my red car; runs fast.* Cut each phrase apart and mix them up. Read each piece randomly. Have students help you put the pieces together so they form meaningful word groups.

ENGLISH LANGUAGE LEARNERS

Meaningful word groups in English may not always be self-evident to students whose home languages may use different patterns of word order. Restate students' sentences to help familiarize them with correct word order in English.

Meaningful Word Groups: Sentences

INTRODUCE Write these words on large cards: *dog, away, ran, the.* Say them, and post them on the board. Ask: Do these words tell us anything? Can we arrange these words so that they do tell us something? Rearrange the words: *the dog ran away.* Now these words tell us something. They tell us that the dog ran away. We put these words together so they would tell us something. We made a sentence. Write the sentence on the board. When you write a sentence, it starts with a capital letter. It ends with a period. A sentence is made up of a subject, or noun, and a verb.

TEACH/MODEL Present the concept and provide examples:

- A meaningful word group that tells us something, and includes a subject and a verb, is called a sentence.

Meaningful	A fat cat can run.
Not Meaningful	cat run can A fat

PRACTICE Write these words on cards, and post them on the board: *had, the, dog, bone, big, a.* Ask: Do these words make sense together? Do you think they might make sense if we changed their order? Invite students to come up to the board to put the words into a more logical order. The words should be ordered in one of two ways: *the big dog had a bone* or *the dog had a big bone.*

Word Order

INTRODUCE Display these sentences and read them aloud, gesturing: The bird flies. Flies the bird. **Ask:** What is the naming part of the first sentence? (The bird) The second sentence does not sound right. The words are not in the right order to make a sentence. In an English sentence, the naming part usually comes first. The action part usually comes after the naming part.

TEACH/MODEL Present the concept and provide examples:

- Sentences need to have words in the right order.

- In a statement, the naming part usually comes first. The action part usually comes next.

In the Right Order	The dog barks.
Not in the Right Order	Barks the dog.

PRACTICE Help pairs of students make cards or strips of paper with parts of sentences: *My friend / rides a bike. / Rides a bike / my friend. / Plays / the dog. / The dog / plays. / The bird / sings. / Sings / the bird.* Have pairs say the parts and build sentences in correct word order.

ENGLISH LANGUAGE LEARNERS

Help students see that word order strongly affects meaning in English. *The puppy barked at Kay* has a different meaning from *Kay barked at the puppy.* Have students practice changing the word order in sentences to express different meanings.

Complete Sentences

INTRODUCE Display and read aloud these groups of words: Tom went to the library. To the library. **Say:** The first group of words is a sentence. What is the naming part? (Tom) What is the action part? (went to the library) The second group of words, *to the library,* is not a complete sentence. There is no naming part or action part. A complete sentence needs a naming part and an action part.

TEACH/MODEL Present the concept and provide examples:

- A complete sentence needs a naming part and an action part.

Complete	Amelia eats lunch.
Incomplete	Her lunch in a bag.

PRACTICE Read these groups of words, and have students raise their hands each time they hear a complete sentence: *My brother. We walk to school. We ride the bus. In the car. At the park. I eat apples. Mike. After school.* Invite students to say their own complete sentences.

Types of Sentences: Telling Sentences

INTRODUCE Display and read aloud these sentences: We jump rope. My brother plays with toy cars. **Say:** Let's look at these sentences. Each one starts with a capital letter and ends with a period. Each one tells something, so it is a telling sentence. A telling sentence is called a statement. It states, or tells, something.

TEACH/MODEL Present the concept and provide examples from the current reading selection:

- A sentence that tells something is called a statement, or a telling sentence.
- It begins with a capital letter and ends with a period.

EXAMPLES: The cat is black. My mom likes cats. We have two cats.

PRACTICE Make sets of cards using examples from the text: *The cat / sees / the bird. / The bird / sees / the cat.* Mix the cards, and have students form statements. Remind them to put the capital letter at the beginning and the period at the end.

ENGLISH LANGUAGE LEARNERS

Students who read in Spanish may recognize that a sentence begins with a capital letter and ends with a period. The Spanish word for "capital letter" is *mayuscula,* and the period is called *punto,* which can mean "point," "dot," or "period."

Types of Sentences: Questions

INTRODUCE **Say:** Listen to these sentences: What is your name? Where do you live? How old are you? Do you have any cats? **Ask:** How are these sentences different from statements? (They each ask something.) Write two of the sentences on the board. **Ask:** How else are they different? (Each one ends with a question mark.) A sentence that asks something is called a question.

TEACH/MODEL Present the concept and provide examples from the reading selection:

- A sentence that asks something is called a question.
- It starts with a capital letter and ends with a question mark.

EXAMPLES: How are you? What is your teacher's name? Where is your school?

PRACTICE Have students ask each other questions about what they did yesterday. For example: *What did you eat for lunch? Who played games with you?* Then, have students find examples of questions from the text. Remind students that the questions will end with a question mark.

ENGLISH LANGUAGE LEARNERS

Help students understand that questions in English often begin with words such as *who, what, when, where, how, do,* and *did.* Speakers of Asian languages often form questions by adding words to statements, comparable to *The water is cold, no?* Provide extra practice with English questions.

Types of Sentences: Exclamations

INTRODUCE Write and say in an excited voice: I am very happy! Have students repeat, and then ask: What feeling does that sentence tell about? (excitement, happiness) Whenever you say something with strong feeling, you are saying an exclamation. A written exclamation begins with a capital letter and ends with an exclamation mark.

TEACH/MODEL Present the concept and provide examples from the current reading selection:

- An exclamation is a sentence that shows strong feeling.
- It begins with a capital letter and ends with an exclamation mark.

EXAMPLES: This is fun! This swing goes high! I can touch the sky!

PRACTICE Say these sentences, and have students repeat them as exclamations: That dog is big. He is barking. I can't hear you. Have students find and read examples of exclamations in the text. Remind students that the exclamations will end with an exclamation mark.

ENGLISH LANGUAGE LEARNERS

The exclamation mark at the end of an exclamation is the same in English and Spanish. Tell Spanish-speaking students that, in English, there is no exclamation mark at the beginning of the sentence.

Types of Sentences: Commands

INTRODUCE Give students various commands, such as these: Please stand up. Walk to the front of the class. Say hello. Sit down. **Ask:** How are these sentences the same? In each one, I am telling you to do something. A sentence that tells someone to do something is called a command. It begins with a capital letter and ends with a period.

TEACH/MODEL Present the concept and provide examples from the current selection:

- A command is a sentence that tells someone to do something.
- It begins with a capital letter and ends with a period.

EXAMPLES: Come to my house. Play with me. Draw a picture.

PRACTICE Share this poem. Have students mime the actions mentioned in the commands. *1, 2, tie your shoe / 3, 4, touch the floor / 5, 6, pick up sticks / 7, 8, close the gate / 9, 10, twist and bend.* Brainstorm other rhyming commands. Have students find examples of commands in the text. They can write them or read them aloud.

ENGLISH LANGUAGE LEARNERS

Help students recognize that, in English, a command usually does not state the person (you) who is commanded to do something. English commands also may not state that the action should be done now. *Please take this to the office* means "(You) please take this to the office (now)."

Compound Sentences and Commas

INTRODUCE Display and read these sentences: I went to Mimi's house. We ate lunch. Explain: These two sentences have ideas that go together. We can join them to make a longer sentence: I went to Mimi's house, and we ate lunch. **Demonstrate as you talk:** Take out the period in the first sentence; put in a comma instead; and add the word *and.* Add the second sentence, starting with a lowercase letter. To join sentences that have opposite ideas, use the word *but:* I went to the library, but it was closed.

TEACH/MODEL Present the concept and provide examples:

- A compound sentence has two sentences joined by a comma and the word *and* or *but*.

Simple Sentences	• I am 8 years old. I am in the second grade.
	• Joe likes bikes. He does not have one yet.
Compound Sentences	• I am 8 years old, and I am in the second grade.
	• Joe likes bikes, but he does not have one yet.

PRACTICE Provide compound sentence examples from the current selection. Write sentence pairs on sentence strips: *Juanita likes cats. She doesn't like dogs. / Ana loves animals. She has many pets*. On each of four cards, write *and, but,* and two commas. Distribute cards and sentence strips, and have students join the sentences with a comma plus *and* or *but*. Have students read the compound sentence aloud, pausing at each comma.

ENGLISH LANGUAGE LEARNERS

Students may have difficulty seeing the clauses in a compound sentence. Point out the conjunction (and, but) in the examples. Have students also practice finding the subject and verb within independent clauses.

Commas

INTRODUCE Display these examples: July 4, 1776; Thursday, July 4; Chicago, IL 60626; I like blue, red, and yellow. Explain: Commas tell us where to pause, or slow down. We use commas in many ways. We use commas in dates. We use commas in addresses. We use commas to separate three or more things in a list.

TEACH/MODEL Present the concept and provide examples:

- Use commas in dates: February 14, 1963

- Use commas in addresses: Salinas, CA 93908

- Use commas to separate three or more things: Ben, Alma, and Cindy went home.

PRACTICE Write the following sentences on the board, omitting commas: *We took a trip on May 14 2005. We went to Santa Barbara California. We saw Rosa Gus Maria and Eva. We came home on Sunday May 22.* Invite volunteers to come up to the board and insert commas where needed. Then have students write sentences about themselves using these models: *I was born on February 7, 2001. I was born in Houston, Texas.*

ENGLISH LANGUAGE LEARNERS

Students may be familiar with dates in which the day number comes first, as in *4 July 1776.* Show how the comma helps separate the day number from the year number in dates, as written in the United States.

Quotation Marks

INTRODUCE Explain to students that quotation marks are used in a dialogue to set apart the exact words a character or person speaks. Quotation marks are always used in pairs. Display and read examples: My brother said, "I am tired." "You should go to bed," I said. Point out that clue words, such as *I said,* help readers determine who said the words.

TEACH/MODEL Present the concept and provide examples:

- Quotation marks show the beginning and the end of words a person says.

- The speaker's name and words such as *asked* and *said* are not inside the quotation marks. "What is your favorite sport?" asked Lora. I said, "Soccer is my favorite sport."

PRACTICE Display correct and incorrect examples of quotation marks in a sentence: *"She goes to school"* (incorrect) and *She said, "Go to school."* (correct). Offer several examples and ask students to identify correct and incorrect usage.

ENGLISH LANGUAGE LEARNERS

The punctuation for quotations varies across languages. For example, in Spanish, double quotation marks ("") or angled quotation marks (<< >>) may be used. Help students correctly use and write quotation marks in English sentences.

Plurals

INTRODUCE Ask students to point to the clock in your room. Say: Good! We only have one clock in our room. Write the word *clock* on the board. Then ask students to point to a desk. Say: Yes! There are many desks in our room. Write the word *desks* on the board. Then review the two words, pointing at them and saying: Clock, desks. We have one clock. We have many desks. What is at the end of this word (point to *desks*) that tells you it means more than one? Yes, it is the letter *s*. (Underline the *s*.)

TEACH/MODEL Present the different ways to form plurals. Create a simple chart on the board with these headings and examples.

Most Words: Add *-s*	Words That End in *s*, *sh*, *ch*, *x*, or *z*: Add *-es*	Words That End in *y*: Change the *y* to *i*, then add *-es*
book/books pencil/pencils marker/markers	fox/foxes class/classes wish/wishes	bunny/bunnies city/cities story/stories

Point to the chart and talk about each column. Say: Most of the time, we just add an *-s*, as in *book/books*. Sometimes, though, we have to look for certain letters at the end of a word. Say the letters with me. (Point to *s, sh, ch, x,* and *z* in the heading of the second column.) When we see these letters, we add *-es*. This word, *fox,* ends with *x*. So, we add *-es*. We also have to look for a *y* at the end of a word. When we see that, we make a change. We change the *y* to an *i*, then add *-es*. See, *bunny* becomes *bunnies*.

PRACTICE Write these words on sticky notes: *fox, puppy, brush, cap, sky, pin, bunch, girl, dress, slide, baby, box, fly, can*. Have students place the words in the correct column of the chart on the board. Challenge them to write or spell aloud the plural forms.

ENGLISH LANGUAGE LEARNERS

Inflected endings may be challenging for English learners. For example, in Chinese, Hmong, and Korean, nouns do not have a plural form. Students may need practice adding *-s* and *-es* to show plural nouns. In languages such as Polish and Spanish, adjectives, as well as verbs and nouns, have inflected endings. Provide students with extra practice adding inflected endings to nouns and verbs.

Possessives

INTRODUCE Call one boy and one girl to stand next to you. Hand the boy a pen. Say: This is the boy's pen. Write *boy's* on the board. Hand the girl a pen, saying: This is the girl's pen. Write *girl's* on the board. Then divide the class into boys and girls and have them stand on different sides of the room. Motion to the boys' side of the room and say: This is the boys' side of the room. Motion to the girls' side and say: This is the girls' side of the room. Write *boys'* and *girls'* on the board, under *boy's* and *girl's*. Circle all of the apostrophes in the words and say: Today we will learn what these mean. Ask students to return to their seats.

TEACH/MODEL You will be teaching students about singular and plural possessives. Use a simple T-chart on the board:

One Has or Owns It: *'s*	More Than One Has or Owns It: *s'*
boy's girl's	boys' girls'

Refer to the apostrophes you have circled in the words on the board. Say: These are called apostrophes. They can tell you that someone has or owns something. When I gave the pen to [boy student's name], it was his pen. It was the boy's pen. He is only one boy, so I added *'s* to the word *boy*. (Point to the word *boy's*.) Boys, when you were standing over there, that part of the room was yours. It was the boys' side. You are many boys, so I just added an apostrophe to the word *boys*. (Point to the word *boys'*.) Show students the chart and write the words in the correct columns. Repeat these steps for *girl's/girls'*. Ask students to suggest additional examples.

PRACTICE Write the following sentences on the board, and have students identify the correct possessive noun in each sentence: *That* (elephants', elephant's) *ears are huge! In the forest, all the* (trees', tree's) *leaves are green. The teacher looked at all the* (students', student's) *work. I like that* (girls', girl's) *shirt. All the* (boys', boy's) *uniforms got dirty. My* (brother's, brothers') *birthday is next week. The* (puppies', puppy's) *tails were wagging.*

Verb Endings: -*s*, -*ed*, -*ing*

INTRODUCE Write the word *ask* on the board. Say: I like it when you ask me questions. It means you want to learn. Remember yesterday when [name of student] asked me about [topic]? Write the word *asked* above *ask* on the board. Say: This class asks lots of good questions. Write *asks* beside *ask.* I'm surprised that you are not asking me about why I'm writing these words on the board. Write *asking* beside *asks*.

TEACH/MODEL Draw a simple table around the words you have written on the board, adding headings as shown below.

Past	asked		
Now	ask	asks	is/are asking

Point to *ask* and say: We change this word by adding endings to it. Underline the -*ed* in *asked*. This ending says the action already happened. Underline the -*s* in *asks*. This ending says someone is doing the action now. Underline the -*ing* in *asking*. We use this ending with the word *is* or *are*. Let's add another word to the chart: *jump*. Work with students to fill in the verb forms for *jump*. Ask students to suggest additional examples.

PRACTICE Have students draw a T-chart with the headings Yesterday and Today. Write the following words on the board: *play, help, paint, talk*. Have students use each word in three sentences so that one tells about yesterday and two tell about today. (He played. He plays. He is playing.) Tell students to write their sentences in the correct column on their T-charts.

Verb Endings: Change Spelling

INTRODUCE Write the following sentence on the board: *I smile*. Read the sentence and smile. Find a student who is smiling back at you. Say and write: [Name of student] smiles. Below that, say and write: We are smiling. Then end by saying and writing: We smiled. Underline the *-s*, *-ing*, and *-ed* in the words. Remind students that they know these word endings. Today they will learn about using these endings when they need to make spelling changes.

TEACH/MODEL Explain the process of dropping the final *e* and doubling consonants before adding inflected endings. Create the chart below for display. Leave space for the example words *(smile* and *shop)*, which you will fill in as you teach.

	Add *-s*	Add *-ed*	Add *-ing*
Word Ends with *e* smile	✓ smiles	First drop the *e*. smiled	First drop the *e*. smiling
Short Vowel, Ends with Consonant shop	✓ shops	Double the consonant. shopped	Double the consonant. shopping

Refer to the sentences you wrote on the board. Circle the *e* in *smile.* Say: This word ends in e. The e is dropped when you add -ed or -ing. Write *smile* in all four places on the chart. Then talk about adding the endings. I want to add -s. The check mark means I can just add it without changing anything. I want to add -ed. The rule is to drop the e. Erase the *e* in *smile,* and then add the ending. Repeat to record *smiling* on the chart. Follow the same teaching pattern for the word *shop.*

PRACTICE Have students draw a T-chart with the headings Yesterday and Today. Write the following words on the board: *nap, grin, mope, race.* Have students use each word in three sentences so that one tells about yesterday and two tell about today. (She napped. She naps. She is napping.) Tell students to write their sentences in the correct column on their T-charts.

Compound Words

INTRODUCE Write the word *sun* on the board and draw a picture of the sun above it. Say: The word *sun* is found in many longer words, like *sunshine*. Write *shine* after *sun*. Then write *sun* again and elicit from students other compound words that start with *sun* (examples: *sunrise, sunset, sunlight, sunburn, sunbeam, sunblock*). Write each word on the board. Underline *sun* in each one and read the words together.

TEACH/MODEL Tell students that you have been writing compound words. Write information about compound words as simple equations:

Compound Word = 2 words

Compound Word = 1 small word + 1 small word

backpack = back + pack

Below the right side of the last equation, write separately the words of several common compounds and ask students to blend the words, saying a compound word for you to write. Some words you might use are: *sand + box, snow + ball, rain + drop*. Some Spanish examples are: *abre + latas = abrelatas, rasca + cielos = rascacielos, para + sol = parasol*.

PRACTICE Write two sets of words on the board. Set 1: *cup, flash, team, out, neck, bed, bath, tea*. Set 2: *cake, light, work, side, tub, tie, pot, room*. Have students write compound words, using the words on the board.

ENGLISH LANGUAGE LEARNERS

Compound words exist in many languages, including Spanish, Vietnamese, Haitian Creole, German, and Russian. Students may readily understand the concept of compound words but may need additional help with decoding to break English compound words into their parts. Provide extra practice as needed.

Contractions

INTRODUCE Say: I'm so happy to be at school today! Aren't you? It's a great day. We'll have fun today! Write *I'm*, *aren't*, *it's*, and *we'll* on the board. Say: Some of the words I just used are called contractions. A contraction is one word that is made from two words put together and made shorter, such as when I say "I'm" instead of "I am."

TEACH/MODEL Display this chart, which shows how a contraction is formed. Talk through each row so students can actually see how four common contractions are made.

Start with two words.	Drop one or more letters.	Add ' and close up the word.
it is	it is	it's
you will	you will	you'll
I am	I am	I'm
has not	has not	hasn't

PRACTICE Write three columns of words on the board. Column 1: *hadn't, wasn't, didn't, I'll, we'll, you'll, it's, she's, he's*. Column 2: *I, we, had, it, did, was, you, he, she*. Column 3: *not, will, is*. Have students come to the board and draw a line from the contraction to the words that make up the contraction. For example, students should draw a line from *hadn't* to *had* and from *had* to *not*.

ENGLISH LANGUAGE LEARNERS

Some languages such as the Romance languages include contractions, but English language learners may need help recognizing them in English and using apostrophes correctly. Provide extra practice as needed.

Prefixes: *un-*, *re-*

INTRODUCE Take a ribbon, string, or piece of yarn, and tie a bow. Say: I tie a bow. Then untie it, saying: I untie the bow. Tie the bow again and say: Now, I retie the bow. Write *tie, untie,* and *retie* on the board. Underline *un-* and *re-*. Repeat the tying demonstration and elicit from students what *untie* and *retie* mean.

TEACH/MODEL Present the prefixes *un-* and *re-*. Explain how they change the meaning of a word, using the chart below.

Prefix	+ Base Word	= New Word
un- (not)	fold lock wind	unfold unlock unwind
re- (again)	fold read play	refold reread replay

Explain that *un-* also can be used in words that describe feelings or ways of being. Give the examples of *unhappy, unkind,* and *unsafe.* Spanish examples include *infeliz, incompleto, recontar,* and *rehacer.*

PRACTICE Create word cards with these prefixes and base words: *un-, re-, like, heat, play, use, lucky.* Have students use the cards in different combinations to make words that have prefixes. Then have students show you a base word without a prefix, add a prefix, say the new word, and tell you what it means.

ENGLISH LANGUAGE LEARNERS

Some English prefixes have equivalent forms in the Romance languages. For example, the prefix *im-* in English (*impossible*) corresponds to the French *im-* (*impossible*) and the Spanish *im-* (*imposible*). Students who are literate in these languages may be able to transfer their understanding of prefixes by using parallel examples in their home language and in English.

Prefixes: *pre-, dis-*

INTRODUCE Hold up a storybook and ask students: What do we usually do before we read a new book? Yes, we talk about the title and the cover. We look at the pictures. We think about what the story might be about. This is called prereading. We do these things before we read. Write *preread* on the board and underline *pre-*. Say: The prefix *pre-* means "before." So, we preread before we read.

TEACH/MODEL Present this chart to review *pre-* and to introduce *dis-*.

Prefix	+ Base Word	= New Word
pre- (before)	read made	preread premade
dis- (not)	like agree	dislike disagree

Point out that if students know what the base word means, they should be able to figure out what the new word means.

PRACTICE Create word cards with these prefixes and base words: *pre-, dis-, cook, made, like, trust*. Have students use the cards in different combinations to make words that have prefixes. As an additional challenge, have students show you a base word without a prefix, add a prefix, say the new word, and tell you what it means.

Prefixes: *mis-*, *mid-*, *non-*

INTRODUCE Write the word *dog* on the board, but misspell it so that it reads *dag*. Point to the word and say: This should spell *dog*. Did I spell the word correctly? No, I did not spell the word correctly. I misspelled the word. What do you think the word *misspelled* means? Repeat the misspelling demonstration until you are sure that students understand that *misspell* means "to spell something incorrectly." Conduct further demonstrations with the words *midair* (throw an eraser or pen in the air) and *nonstop* (say: without stopping).

TEACH/MODEL Present the prefixes *mis-*, *mid-*, and *non-*. Using the chart below, explain how prefixes change the meaning of a word.

Prefix	+ Base Word	= New Word
mis- (not or wrong)	place	misplace
mid- (in the middle of)	day	midday
non- (not or without)	stick	nonstick

PRACTICE Create word cards with these prefixes and base words: *mis-, mid-, non-, stop, spell, point, day, fiction, place*. Have students use the cards in different combinations to make words that have prefixes. As an additional challenge, have students show you a base word without a prefix, add a prefix, say the new word, and tell you what it means.

ENGLISH LANGUAGE LEARNERS

Point out to Spanish speakers that the prefix *mid-* is related to the Spanish word *medio*, which means "half" or "middle." Use cognates such as *midnight/medianoche* and *midday/mediodía* as examples.

Suffixes: *-ly, -ful*

INTRODUCE Write *cheerful* on the board. Say the word, and ask if anyone feels cheerful today. Underline *-ful* and explain that it means "full of." Say: So, if I feel full of hope, what word could I use to say how I feel? Write *hopeful* on the board, underlining *-ful*. Explain that *-ful* is a suffix. A suffix is added to the end of a word to change the meaning.

TEACH/MODEL Present this chart to review *-ful* and to introduce *-ly*.

Suffix	What It Means	Examples	Spanish Suffixes and Examples
-ful	full of; tell what something is like	joyful, careful	-oso cuidadoso
-ly	tell how something is done	softly, neatly	-mente suavemente

PRACTICE Prepare word cards. On one side, write a base word. On the other side, write a phrase that will tell students which suffix to add. Have students read the two sides and then tell you the new word. Ideas for cards:

safe/tell how it is done (safely)

peace/tell what it is like (peaceful)

kind/tell how it is done (kindly)

play/tell what it is like (playful)

Suffixes: *-less, -ness*

INTRODUCE Show students the trashcan. Say: Everything in here is useless to me. I do not use it. Write *useless* on the board, and underline *-less*. Say: This suffix changes the base word to mean "it does not have." So *useless* means "it does not have a use."

TEACH/MODEL Present this chart to review *-less* and to introduce *-ness*.

Suffix	What It Means	Examples
-less	does not have	fearless (does not have fear)
-ness	has	goodness (has good)

PRACTICE Create word strips with meanings of words that have suffixes. Have students read the strips, or read the strips aloud to students. If you read the strips aloud, show the phrases so students can see the underlined target base words. Then have students say the word that is described. Suggested strips:

does not have <u>fear</u> (fearless)

has only <u>dark</u> (darkness)

does not make <u>sense</u> (senseless)

has swift speed (swiftness).

Suffixes: *-able, -ible*

INTRODUCE Write *likeable* on the board. Say the word and ask students if they think puppies are likeable. Underline *-able* and explain that it means "able to." Say: So, if we are able to read a sentence, what word could we use to describe that sentence? Write *readable* on the board, underlining *-able*. Explain that *-able* is a suffix. Remind students that a suffix is added to the end of a word to change the meaning.

TEACH/MODEL Present this chart to review *-able* and to introduce *-ible*.

Suffix	What It Means	Examples
-able	able to; can be	enjoyable, useable, readable
-ible	has the quality of	collectible, reversible

PRACTICE Make word cards. On one side, write a base word. On the other side, write a phrase that will tell students which suffix to add. Have students read the two sides, and then tell you the new word. Make sentences together using the words to check understanding, or have students pantomime a word and have the others guess the *-able/-ible* word. Ideas for cards:

use/able to (useable)

read/able to (readable)

reverse/has the quality of (reversible)

collect/has the quality of (collectible)

Suffixes: *-er, -or*

INTRODUCE Write *ballplayer* on the board. Say the word, and ask students if any of them play ball. Underline *-er* and explain that it means "a person or thing that ____." Then say: If a man acts in a movie, what is he? Yes, an actor. Write *actor* on the board, underlining *-or*. Tell students that *-or* also means "a person or thing that ____." Explain that *-er* and *-or* are suffixes. Remind students that a suffix is added to the end of a word to change the meaning.

TEACH/MODEL Present this chart to review *-er* and *-or*.

Suffix	What It Means	Examples
-er, -or	a person or thing that ____.	*teacher, opener, sailor, collector*

PRACTICE Create word strips with meanings of words that have suffixes. Have students read the strips silently, or read the strips aloud to students. If you read the strips aloud, show the phrases so students can see the underlined target base words. Then have students say the word that is described. Ideas for strips:

a person who teaches (teacher)

a person who paints (painter)

something that opens things (opener)

a person who sails (sailor)

something that beeps (beeper)

Syllable Patterns: VCCV, VCV

INTRODUCE Write the word *basket* on the board. Ask: How many vowel sounds do you hear in the word *basket*? Say and clap it with me: bas/kit, basket. That's right, there are two vowel sounds /a/ and /i/. Now write the word *tulip* on the board. Ask: How many vowel sounds do you hear in the word *tulip*? Let's clap together. Listen: tü/lip, tulip. Yes, there are two vowel sounds, so there are two syllables. Repeat this drill with the word *cabin*.

TEACH/MODEL Point to the word *basket* on the board. Draw a line between the two syllables and say: When a word has more than one vowel sound, divide it into parts. Explain that when there are two consonants between two vowels, you divide the word between the consonants. Now point to the word *tulip* on the board. Draw a line between the *u* and the *l*. Say: This word has one consonant between two vowels. In the word *tulip,* the consonant goes with the second vowel, making the first vowel long. Say it with me: tulip, tü/lip. Then point to the word *cabin* on the board. Draw a line between the *b* and the *i* and say: This word also has one consonant between two vowels. But in the word *cabin*, the consonant goes with the first vowel, making the first vowel short. Say it with me: cabin, kab/ən.

PRACTICE Write the following words on the board: *better, ladder, shadow, window, robot, sofa, robin, wagon, zebra, pony, candle.* Clap as you read each word aloud to emphasize the syllable break in the word. Model drawing a line between the first and second syllable in *better*. Then have students come to the board and draw a line between the two syllables in each word. Next, have students create a T-chart with the following headings: Words with Long Vowels, Words with Short Vowels. Have students record the words on the board in the correct column.

ENGLISH LANGUAGE LEARNERS

Speakers of monosyllabic languages, such as Cantonese, Hmong, Khmer, Korean, and Vietnamese, may pronounce a two-syllable word as two separate words. Have students practice saying multisyllabic words.

Syllables: *-tion, -ture, -ion*

INTRODUCE Write the word *onion* on the board. Say: This word is *onion,* un/yən. How many vowel sounds do you hear in the word *onion*? Say it with me, un/yən, onion. That's right, there are two vowel sounds. Now write the word *lotion* on the board. Ask: How many vowel sounds do you hear in the word *lotion*? Listen: lō/shən, lotion. Yes, there are two vowel sounds, so there are two syllables. Repeat this drill with the word *picture.*

TEACH/MODEL Explain that the spelling patterns *-tion, -ture,* and *-ion* form their own syllables. Display the following chart:

-tion	-ture	-ion
mo/tion, motion	pic/ture, picture	on/ion, onion
ac/tion, action	na/ture, nature	stal/lion, stallion

PRACTICE Write these words on the board: *fiction, nature, mixture, station, motion.* Clap as you read each word aloud to emphasize the syllable break in the word. Model drawing a line between the first and second syllable in *fiction.* Then have students come to the board and draw a line between the two syllables in each word.

ENGLISH LANGUAGE LEARNERS

The suffix *-tion* has similar forms in other languages, such as French (*-tion*), Spanish (*-ción, -sión*), and Portuguese (*-çäo*). Students can look for cognates for *-tion* words in their home languages. For example, the English word *direction* is *direction* in French, *dirección* in Spanish, and *direçäo* in Portuguese.

PREPARE TO READ

Word Associations

Choose three selection vocabulary words and write them on the board. Discuss each word's meaning and give examples. Use the words in sentences and invite students to ask questions about each word. Then challenge students to associate one of the chosen vocabulary words with a presented word or phrase. For example, you might ask:

- Which word goes with protecting and obeying? (officer)
- Which word goes with seeing and exploring? (flashlight)
- Which word goes with eating or sharing? (portion)

See It, Learn It, Own It

Write the vocabulary words for a selection or module on the board or on large sheets of paper. Display the words. Ask students to rate their knowledge of the words. Students should indicate whether they do not know the word at all; whether they have heard of the word; whether they know something about the word; or whether they know the word well. Ask volunteers to share word meanings as well as other information or associations about the words. Clarify meanings as necessary, and then invite other volunteers to use each word in a sentence. Record sentences and discuss.

Use Visuals

Write the vocabulary words for a selection or module on the board. Point to each in turn and provide a student-friendly definition. Then display pictures that evoke the words' meanings. For example, for the word *portion,* you might show a picture of several orange slices, a piece of pie, or a helping from a bowl of rice or vegetables. Challenge students to name as quickly as possible other items they might have a portion of. Discuss students' responses.

Possible Sentences (Part 1)

Identify a list of four key concepts, terms, or words from the selections students will read. The terms might be familiar or unfamiliar. Write them on the board and discuss their meanings. Then ask student volunteers to choose two of the four words and use them in a sentence that they think might possibly appear in their reading. Record sentences as students suggest them.

INTERACT WITH TEXT

Possible Sentences (Part 2)

As students encounter the selected words from Possible Sentences Part 1 during reading, have them return to their possible sentences and, with a partner, compare these sentences with words as used in the selection context. Ask pairs to discuss their understandings of the concepts, terms, or words and indicate whether their understandings changed as they read. Invite students to recraft the original possible sentences based on new understandings and share them with the class. Record alternative sentences as students continue to read.

Your Turn!

Review the meaning of each word as it is used in the selection. Then ask students to connect the word with their own knowledge and experience. So, for the word *stomping,* ask students to name and describe a time when they found themselves stomping or to imagine and explain an appropriate time in the future when they might need or want to stomp.

Vocabulary Vote

Have the class choose four selection vocabulary words from the module. Write them on the board. Using selection context, discuss the words' meanings, clarifying and elaborating as needed. Then have student pairs choose one of the words and come up with two sentences, one in which the word is used correctly and one in which an incorrect meaning is suggested. Invite pairs to share their sentences with the class, and have the class vote on which of the two sentences uses the word correctly.

What It Is/What It Isn't

This activity works best with concepts/terms that are nouns. To deepen students' understanding of a key concept in one of the selections from the module, create a What It Is/What It Isn't notecard. Divide a large notecard in half, both vertically and horizontally. Write the word or concept you'll explore at the top of the card. Label the box on the top left-hand side, What It Is. On the bottom left-hand side, write Examples. The top right-hand box is labeled, What It Isn't. The bottom right-hand side is labeled, Nonexamples. As a class, populate the card, discussing students' responses as they are offered. For example, a card for the word *vegetable* might look like this:

VEGETABLE	
What It Is something you eat nutritious part of a plant	**What It Isn't** a color a school supply a fruit
Examples beans peas carrots	**Nonexamples** the color black a pencil an apple, a pear, a cherry

Multiple Meanings

Select words from the module that have multiple meanings. Write these words on the board. Discuss with the class alternate meanings for each word and add those meanings next to the words. As students discover the words in context, ask them to indicate by raising their hand which meaning works best in the selection. Students should explain why they chose the meanings they did.

Word Sorts

Provide students with index cards on which vocabulary words are written, one word per card. Ask students to sort the words in categories you provide, such as Words that Show Action, Words that Name Things, Words that Connect to the Unit Theme, and so on. Or have students create categories and explain the rationale behind their sorting.

EXPRESS AND EXTEND

Word of the Day

Choose one of the vocabulary words from the module to be the word of the day. Write it on the board, along with clues about the word. So, for the word *fresh,* you might provide the following clues:

1. This word is an adjective, or describing word.

2. It can be used to describe something new.

3. It is often used to describe water.

4. People like to buy this kind of fruits and vegetables.

5. It means the opposite of *stale.*

Provide an envelope for students to enclose their guesses in. Remind them to include their names with their guesses. At the end of the day, the student who provides the first correct guess you draw from the envelope is the winner for the day.

Name That Word!

Explain to students that you will read aloud five words from a selection. Then you will give clues about one of these words, and the first student to guess the correct word will win the game. For example, you might provide the following clues for the word *certain:* This word is a describing word. This word describes what you are when you are very sure of something. Repeat for the remaining words.

Pantomime

Identify words from the module that lend themselves to pantomime, such as *gnaw, fold, fell,* and *jab.* Say the words aloud and review their meanings as a group. Then, assign pairs one of the words and ask them to think of a way they could act out or pantomime the meaning of the word for the rest of the class. Provide assistance and feedback as needed. Invite each pair to come to the front of the class or circle to perform while the rest of the class tries to guess the correct vocabulary word.

Memory Game

Prepare a maximum of 25 cards: 12 word cards with vocabulary words from the module; 12 match cards with definitions or pictures; and 1 wild card. Shuffle the cards and place them facedown in a 5 x 5 grid. Explain that, for each turn, a student will turn over and read two cards. If the cards are a match (for example, the word *enormous* and a picture of an elephant), the student will take the cards. If they are not a match (for example, the word *dim* and a picture of a bright sun), the student will turn the cards back over and leave them in the same place. Play continues in turn until only a single card remains. Students may use the wild card only if they can provide an appropriate match. For example, if a student draws the elephant picture and the wild card, he or she can say the word *enormous* aloud. This can be checked at the end of the game by looking at the remaining card, which should match the answer supplied earlier. The student with the most cards wins.

Bingo

Help students arrange word/picture cards in a 5 x 5 grid, placing a free card in the middle. Explain that you will select definitions from the definition pile and read them aloud. Students will place markers on the word/picture cards in their grids that match the definitions. The first student to mark an entire row, column, or diagonal wins the game.

Yes/No and True/False

Prepare a list of yes/no questions and true/false statements for the vocabulary words in a particular selection or module. For example, for the words *grand* and *island,* you might prepare the following questions or statements:

- Yes or no: Is a t-shirt grand?
- True or false: An island is surrounded by land.

Divide the class into two teams. Have one player from each team come up and sit in chairs in front of the class. Say each question or statement aloud, and the first student to correctly answer *yes, no, true,* or *false* has 10 seconds to explain his or her answer. If the player successfully explains, his or her team gains a point. If the player answers incorrectly or cannot provide an adequate explanation within the time limit, his or her team loses a point. The team with the most points at the end wins the game.

Making Connections

Identify words in the module that go together, such as nouns, verbs, adjectives, or words that describe a topic. Ask students to tell which two of the three words you will say aloud go together. For example: Which two of the following words are location words: *around, aunt, beside?*

Extra Examples

Identify vocabulary words in the module that are verbs. Say each word (for example, *glow*), review its meaning with the class ("to give off a bright light"), and provide an example (*The digital numbers on my clock glow in the darkness of my room*). Challenge students to write down as many other examples of the word as they can within a certain time frame (a firefly, a light bulb, the moon, and so on). Ask students to count how many examples they came up with. The student with the highest number of appropriate examples wins the game, but invite all students to share their examples with the class.

Decorate Your Word!

Have students choose their favorite word from a selection or module. Explain that they will write and then decorate their word in order to show what it means. For example, for the word *whisper,* they might write the word in very small letters and draw a picture of a person whispering in someone's ear. Help students as necessary to write their word in the center of a piece of paper. Then provide art supplies as well as scissors and magazines. You may choose to play a word-guessing game with students' pictures and then display them around the room.

Same and Different

Identify pairs of words from the module that are similar (such as *sparkling* and *glistening*) and pairs that are different (such as *rises* and *sets*). Say the two words aloud and ask students to tell if they are similar or different and explain why.

Either/Or

Review with students the vocabulary words learned in a selection. Then have them answer the following either/or questions: Which word means "a living thing with roots in the soil," *plant* or *seed*? Which word means "a little object that is placed in the soil to grow," *plant* or *seed*?

Card Games

Prepare a deck of 40 word cards, using the words students explored in a particular module or unit. Then prepare match cards for each word card, which might include a definition, a synonym, an antonym, a cloze sentence in which the word makes sense, a picture symbolizing the word's meaning, an English translation, or some other appropriate match. For example, a student might pair a word card labeled *defend* with a match card on which its definition appears, "to protect." Students can play a variety of games with these cards.

For Fish, all the cards are dealt and players pick one card from the player on their left in turn, placing any pairs they make on the table. The first player to pair all cards wins. For Old Teacher (a variation of Old Maid), an extra card is prepared with a generic drawing of a teacher. The game is played like Fish, except the student who is left with this card is the "old teacher."

In all card games, students must read their pairs aloud. Other players can challenge a student's pairs, in which case a dictionary would be used to settle the dispute. Either the challenger or the player may get an extra turn, depending upon who is correct.

COGNATE ACTIVITIES

Cognate Sort

Create word/picture cards for words in English that have numerous cognates, such as *music, computer, park,* and *family.* Then create word cards with cognates for these words, such as *música, musique; computador, komputer; parque, parc; familia, famiglia.* Have students sort the cognates under the correct word/picture cards. Be sure to ask students if they know of other cognates you might add to the list. Afterward, conduct a discussion with students about what similarities and differences they notice between the words and how cognates can be helpful to them as they explore new languages.

Cognate Match

Make a list of words in English and their Spanish cognates, such as *bank, banco; university, universidad; museum, museo.* Give each student in the class either a word in English or a Spanish cognate. If there are an odd number of students, take one of the cards yourself. Challenge the students to move about the room until they find the person who is a match for their card. Then invite each matched pair to write the word and its Spanish cognate on the board and circle letters that are different. Repeat the activity with cognates from other languages.

Cognate Find

Create picture cards for words in English that have numerous cognates, such as *bank,* *train,* and *telephone.* Give pairs of students one of the picture cards and have them identify as many cognates for the word as they can, either by conducting research on the Internet or consulting multilingual speakers in the classroom or community. Have them share their findings with the class.

True or False?

Organize students in groups and give each group a different list of pairs between English words and true or false Spanish cognates for these words. Have students identify whether the words in each pair are true cognates or false cognates. For example, *class* and *clase* are true cognates, but *rope* and *ropa* are false cognates. Suggest that students consult multilingual speakers in their group or in other groups, use dictionaries, or conduct research on the Internet in order to identify whether each pair is true or false. Have groups share and explain their answers with the class. Repeat with cognates from other languages.

Unlock Language Learning

Part 4 Unlock Language Learning

Trouble at the Sandbox

Reproduce and distribute copies of the *Being Polite* student page on page 398. Explain that one important theme, or message, in *Trouble at the Sandbox* is that people in a community should care about one another's feelings and needs. One way people can do this is by being polite to others. Confirm that students understand what it means to be polite. Then help them understand how to read the chart. Point to the column that lists polite actions. Point to the column that lists polite words.

Discuss what the friends in the illustration are doing. Then read aloud the polite actions and polite words in the chart. The friends in the picture are acting politely and using polite words as they work in the sandbox. To help a friend is a polite action. You can use the polite words, "May I help you?"

With partners, have students use actions and words from the chart to describe what they think the friends in the picture are saying and doing. Scaffold with sentence frames such as: *The girl wants to _____. She says _____. The boy says _____.*

Then have students share with a partner one polite thing they can say and do for a friend. Scaffold with additional sentence frames: *One polite thing I can say is _____. I can say _____ to show _____.*

TALK ABOUT SENTENCES

For students who need support in accessing key ideas and key language in *Trouble at the Sandbox,* use the Sentence Talk Routine on pages 476–477 to draw students' attention to the relationship between meaning and the words, phrases, and clauses in the text.

Lesson	Sentence(s) to Deconstruct
1	(p 5) As they were doing this, a long shadow blocked out the light.
2	(p 7) One of the big boy's friends got the truck from Josh.
3	(p 9) "Ms. Lee, Ms. Lee, there are these boys and they've…" Theo began.
4	(p 13) "Awesome!" said Izzy. "Let's get straight to work."
5	(p 16) When she came back out, she didn't look angry anymore.
6	(p 21) "Sorry," he said, lifting his head and looking Theo in the eye.
7	(p 24) "We need some sand moved over there," Theo said, pointing to a corner.

SPEAK AND WRITE ABOUT THE TEXT

Use the Text-based Writing Routine on pages 478–479 to model how to speak and write about key ideas and details in *Trouble at the Sandbox*.

Lesson	Text-based Writing	Scaffolded Frames
1	What do the words at the top of page 5 help you understand about the boy who stands over Theo and his friends?	• The words say a "_____ blocked out the light." This tells me that the boy is _____ than Theo and his friends. • The words _____ tell me that the boy is _____. • The words help me understand _____.
2	On pages 6 and 7, why are the big boys at the sandbox?	• The big boys want to take Theo, Izzy, and Josh's _____. • One of the big boy's friends _____. • The big boys _____.
3	On page 9, how does Theo show that he is upset about what happened to the trucks?	• Theo says Ms. Lee's name _____ times. He starts to tell her about what the _____ did, but doesn't finish what he is saying. • Theo says, _____ but _____.
4	On page 13, how do you know that Theo and his friends are happy to have the trucks back?	• Izzy says _____. • The picture shows Izzy, Theo, and Josh_____. • I know they are happy because _____.
5	How does the picture on page 17 help you understand why Ms. Lee doesn't look angry when she comes back from the staff room?	• The picture shows a _____. Ms. Lee knew the big boys took the trucks so that they could make _____. • The picture shows _____, so Ms. Lee knew _____.
6	On page 21, what does the big boy do to show that he is really sorry about taking the trucks?	• The big boy says _____. He lifts his _____. He looks Theo in the _____. • The big boy says _____ and _____. • The big boy _____.
7	On page 24, what does Theo say and do to show he is willing to have Ben help build the volcano?	• Theo picks up _____. He hands it to _____. He tells _____ what he can _____. • Theo _____ and says _____. • Theo shows he is willing to have Ben help when he _____.

EXPAND UNDERSTANDING OF VOCABULARY

Use the Dig Deeper Vocabulary Routine on pages 474–475 to continue to develop conceptual understanding of the following past tense verbs: *searched, shrugged, tipped, mumbled*, and *nodded*. Review the past tense of regular verbs. Display and read aloud the following sentence: *Yesterday, Theo **searched** for the truck.*

Point out that -ed is added to many verbs to tell about actions that happened in the past. Explain that *searched* is a past-tense verb because it ends in -ed. In addition, many sentences have words that signal that the action happened in the past, such as the word *yesterday.*

Name _____

Being Polite

The friends know how to be polite.

Polite Actions	Polite Words
Help	May I help you?
Share	Yes, you may use the pail.
Thank	Thank you for helping me.
Care	I'm sorry you lost your pail.

Share one polite thing you can say to a friend.

I can say _____.

Share one polite thing you can do for a friend.

I can _____.

Snowshoe Hare's Winter Home

BUILD BACKGROUND FOR *SNOWSHOE HARE'S WINTER HOME*

Reproduce and distribute copies of the *Animals in the Winter* student page on page 400. Explain that to better understand the animals' actions in *Snowshoe Hare's Winter Home*, it helps to know what different animals do during the winter. Read aloud the chart categories and confirm students' understanding of the action described in each. Then read aloud the information in the chart as students follow along.

Invite partners to talk about the animals in the chart. Scaffold with sentence frames: *A _____ is an animal that _____ in the winter. Two animals that _____ in the winter are _____ and _____.* Then have partners share two things they learned about animals in the winter. Scaffold with additional sentence frames: *One thing I learned about _____ is that they _____ in the winter. I also learned that _____.*

TALK ABOUT SENTENCES

For students who need support in accessing key ideas and key language in *Snowshoe Hare's Winter Home*, use the Sentence Talk Routine on pages 476–477 to draw students' attention to the relationship between meaning and the words, phrases, and clauses in the text.

Lesson	Sentence(s) to Deconstruct
8	(p 6) He hopped a few steps and grinned at his own tracks on the snowy ground.
9	(p 8) Snowshoe Hare dipped a paw, then shook off the chilly drops.
10	(p 12) Bit by bit, his brown fur had changed when cold days signaled the coming winter.

SPEAK AND WRITE ABOUT THE TEXT

Use the Text-based Writing Routine on pages 478–479 to model how to speak and write about key ideas and details in *Snowshoe Hare's Winter Home*.

Lesson	Text-based Writing	Scaffolded Frames
8	On page 6, how do you know that Snowshoe Hare enjoys being in the snow?	• He _____ and _____ at his tracks in the snow. • I know he enjoys the snow because _____.
9	On page 8, how does Hare feel about spending winter in the water?	• Hare thinks the water is _____. • I learned that _____.
10	On page 12, how do you know that Hare adapts in the winter?	• His fur _____ when _____, so I know he adapts. • I know he adapts because _____.

Animals in the Winter

What do animals do in the winter?
Which animals do the same thing?

Hibernate (go into deep sleep)	Stay in Home and Rest	Migrate (go to another place)	Adapt (change)
bear	beaver	duck	hare
turtle	trout	monarch butterfly	fox

TeamTalk

Share two facts about animals in the winter.
In the winter, some animals _____.
Other animals _____.

Friends Around the World

BUILD BACKGROUND FOR *FRIENDS AROUND THE WORLD*

Reproduce and distribute copies of the *City and Country* student page on page 403. Explain that to understand the details in *Friends Around the World,* it may help to know how living in a city is different from living in the country. Begin by confirming students' understanding of the words *community, city,* and *country.* Then help students read the chart. Point to where we will learn about the city. A city is a large community. Now, point to where we will learn about the country. Small communities are found in the country.

Read aloud the chart categories. To check students' understanding, have them discuss what they see, hear, and smell in the classroom. Scaffold with sentence frames: *I see_____ in the classroom. I hear_____.* Then read the chart aloud as students follow along. Clarify terms such as *garbage, fumes, mountains, crickets,* and *fresh.*

Then invite students to talk with a partner about the different sights, sounds, and smells in each place. Scaffold with sentence frames such as: *I see _____ in a city, but I do not see _____ in the country. I hear _____ in _____. But I hear _____ in_____.*

Then have partners share what they think would be fun about living in a city and living in the country. Scaffold with additional sentence frames: *It would be fun to live in a city because _____. It would be fun to _____ if I lived in the country.*

TALK ABOUT SENTENCES

For students who need support in accessing key ideas and key language in *Friends Around the World,* use the Sentence Talk Routine on pages 476–477 to draw students' attention to the relationship between meaning and the words, phrases, and clauses in the text.

Lesson	Sentence(s) to Deconstruct
1	(p 6) I live in New York City, in the United States of America.
2	(p 10) I walk to school in a heavy parka, boots, and a warm hat.
3	(p 16) There are street vendors selling food on almost every corner.
4	(p 18) The lake was frozen, so we drilled a hole in the ice.
5	(p 22) In the winter, I like to go ice skating in Central Park.
6	(p 28) The doctor arrived by airplane in just one hour.
7	(p 30) There are exciting things to do in all four places.
11	(p 20) We ride our horses behind the cows to bring them home.
12	(p 20) On weekends I like to play backyard cricket with my sister.

Use the Text-based Writing Routine on pages 478–479 to model how to speak and write about key ideas and details in *Friends Around the World*.

Lesson	Text-based Writing	Scaffolded Frames
1	What do the pictures on pages 6 and 7 tell you about New York City?	• The pictures tell me that there are ____ and ____ in New York City. • From the pictures, I can tell _____.
2	On page 10, what do Akiak's clothes tell you about the weather where he lives?	• Akiak wears clothes that are _____. This tells me that the weather is _____. • I know that the weather _____ because Akiak ____.
3	On page 16, what does Hau see on the streets of Ho Chi Minh City?	• Hau sees ____. They are selling _____. • Hau sees ____.
4	On page 18, why does Akiak's family drill holes in the ice?	• Akiak's family drills holes in the ice so they can ____. • Akiak's family ____.
5	On page 22, what is something Isabel says she likes about the winter?	• Isabel likes to _____ in the winter. • In the winter, ____.
6	On page 28, what happens when Dan needs to see a doctor?	• Dan's mother calls _____. A doctor comes to Dan's farm by _____. • When Dan needs to see a doctor, ____.
7	What do you think is the most exciting thing to do in all of the places?	• The most exciting thing to do is ____ because ____. • I think ____.
11	On page 20, what detail helps you understand what the words *round up* mean?	• The words *round up* mean "____." I know this because Dan says he likes ____. • I know that the words *round up* mean ____ because____.
12	On page 20, what does Dan like to do in his backyard?	• Dan likes to play ____ with his ____ in his backyard. • Dan enjoys ____.

Use the Dig Deeper Vocabulary Routine on pages 474–475 to continue to develop a conceptual understanding of the following common nouns: *subway, caribou, uniform, blizzard, barbecue, museum,* and *skeleton*. Review the role of common nouns in sentences. Then display and read aloud the following sentence: *There was a **thunderstorm** last week.*

Point out that *thunderstorm* is a common noun because it names a kind of storm. Then point out that the common noun *thunderstorm* is preceded by the article *a* in the sentence. Explain that the words *a, an,* and *the* in a sentence often signal that a common noun will follow.

Unit 1 Module B

Name _____

City and Country

What is it like to live in a city?
What is it like to live in the country?

Community	I see . . .	I hear . . .	I smell . . .
City	• buildings • cars, trucks, and buses • people • streets and sidewalks	• car horns • trucks • music • people	• food • garbage • car and truck fumes
Country	• mountains and woods • trees and grass • houses • farms	• birds • wind • crickets	• fresh air • grass • flowers

Team *Talk*

What might be fun about living in a city?
In a city, I can _____.
What might be fun about living in the country?
In the country, I can _____.

403

The House on Maple Street

Reproduce and distribute copies of the *How Communities Grow* student page on page 405. Confirm students' understanding of *community*. Then explain that the chart shows how communities begin small and become larger as years go by. A community begins with one person or family. The community grows bigger when people build homes nearby. Then read aloud each sentence in the chart as students follow along. Have students discuss the actions in each step: *Someone builds _____. As a community grows, _____.* Then have students share with a partner why communities change and the ways they change.

TALK ABOUT SENTENCES

For students who need support in accessing key ideas and key language in *The House on Maple Street,* use the Sentence Talk Routine on pages 476–477 to draw students' attention to the relationship between meaning and the words, phrases, and clauses in the text.

Lesson	Sentence(s) to Deconstruct
8	(p 16) There was only a forest and a bubbling spring where the animals came to drink.
9	(p 26) But they dreamed of gold and places far away and were gone the next morning.
10	(p 37) Automobiles drove on the road, along with carts and wagons, and there were many new houses.

SPEAK AND WRITE ABOUT THE TEXT

Use the Text-based Writing Routine on pages 478–479 to model how to speak and write about key ideas and details in *The House on Maple Street*.

Lesson	Text-based Writing	Scaffolded Frames
8	What does the picture on pages 16 and 17 tell you about the forest?	• The picture tells that there was a _____ in the forest. • I see _____.
9	On page 26, why did the settlers come to the forest?	• The settlers came to the forest to _____. • On their way to California, _____.
10	What details in the picture on page 37 tell how the farm has changed?	• The farm now has _____ and _____. • The illustration shows _____.

Name _____

How Communities Grow

How does a place become a community?

| A person builds a house or a farm. |

| People build homes nearby. |

| People build stores, schools, and roads. |

| More people come to live and work in the community. |

Why do communities change over time?
Communities change because _____.
What is one way a community changes?
One way a community changes _____.

Name _____

Title _____

A Big Sandcastle

It was a hot, summer day. Izzy, Theo, and Josh went to the beach.

"Let's build a big sandcastle," Izzy said. Theo and Josh thought that would be fun. "What should we do first?" Theo asked.

"First, I'll put water in the pail," Josh said. "Then we can wet the sand."

After the sand was wet, Izzy began to pile the sand. "We can use this pile of sand for our castle," she said. Theo and Josh liked that idea.

Next, Theo made shapes in the pile using the shovel. Josh got more water to wet the sand.

At last, the sandcastle was done. "Our sandcastle is huge!" said Theo. The children felt proud.

Name _____

Title _____

Two Communities

Akiak and Dan live in different communities. A community is a place where people live. Akiak lives in a small city near the Arctic Circle, and Dan lives with his family on a farm in Australia. The people in Akiak's community use animals to do work and to travel. Dan's family also uses animals to work on the farm and to go places. It's snowy and cold where Akiak lives, but Dan's home looks dry and hot. There are things that are the same and things that are different in both Akiak's and Dan's community.

Performance-Based Assessment
Unit 1 Module A

Reproduce and distribute copies of the student model on page 406. After completing the Prepare to Write activities on pages 188–189 in Unlock the Writing in Part 2, use the student model to illustrate the elements of narrative writing.

Remind students that a story has a beginning, middle, and end. Explain that the beginning of the story tells when and where the story takes place. Also remind students that characters are the people or animals in a story. Read aloud the first paragraph of the student model and discuss the text with students. Point to the words *hot, summer day.* Why do you think the writer begins the story with these words?

Continue discussing the middle and end of the story. Have students point to the words as you read them aloud. Ask: Why does the writer use the word *first* in this sentence? Remind students that words such as *first, next, then,* and *at last* help show the sequence of events in a story. Then have students work with a partner to discuss the end of the story. Scaffold with sentence frames such as: *Theo says _____. The children feel _____ because _____.*

Unit 1 Module B

Reproduce and distribute copies of the student model on page 407. After completing the Prepare to Write activities on pages 193–194 in Unlock the Writing in Part 2, use the student model to illustrate the features of an explanatory paragraph that compares and contrasts two places.

Read aloud the first sentence and discuss it with students. How does the writer introduce the topic in the first sentence? If students have difficulty responding, ask: What two things does the author say are different in the first sentence? Explain that as they read the paragraph, they should look for words that compare such as *both, but, same,* and *different.*

Then have students point to and read aloud the sentences that show how the two communities are alike. Have them do the same for the sentence that shows how the two communities are different. Finally, discuss the closing sentence. Remind students that closing sentences leave the reader with a feeling that the paragraph is complete. How does the writer end this paragraph? Point out that this writer wrapped up ideas in the paragraph by summing up the idea that there are things that are the same and different in both communities.

Alexander, Who Used to Be Rich Last Sunday

Reproduce and distribute copies of the *Needs and Wants* student page on page 411. Explain that to understand the story events in *Alexander, Who Used to Be Rich Last Sunday,* it helps to know the difference between needs and wants. Explain that a need is something a person must have to live, and a want is something a person would like to have but doesn't need to live. Then help students understand how to read the chart. Point to the column that lists things that people need. Now point to the column that lists things that people want.

Read aloud the chart. If necessary, confirm students' understanding by having them discuss items they want and need. Scaffold with sentence frames: *I want _____. Something I need is _____ because _____.*

Then have students share with partners how needs and wants are different and discuss why they should think about what they need before buying something they want.

TALK ABOUT SENTENCES

For students who need support in accessing key ideas and key language in *Alexander, Who Used to Be Rich Last Sunday,* use the Sentence Talk Routine on pages 476–477 to draw students' attention to the relationship between meaning and the words, phrases, and clauses in the text.

Lesson	Sentence(s) to Deconstruct
1	(p 7) It isn't fair because what I've got is…bus tokens.
2	(p 13) Anthony told me to use the dollar to go downtown to a store and buy a new face.
3	(p 24) My father said that there are certain things a boy can never kick, no matter how ratty and mean his brothers are being.
7	(p 16) And even though I told my friend David I'd sell him all the gum in my mouth for a nickel, he still wouldn't buy it.
8	(p 21) I tried to get my nickel out with a butter knife and also my mother's scissors.
9	(p 30) I told my grandma and grandpa to come back soon.
11	(p 14) Nicky said to take the dollar and bury it in the garden and in a week a dollar tree would grow.
12	(p15) Mom said if I really want to buy a walkie-talkie, save my money.

Use the Text-based Writing Routine on pages 478–479 to model how to speak and write about key ideas and details in *Alexander, Who Used to Be Rich Last Sunday.*

Lesson	Text-based Writing	Scaffolded Frames
1	On page 7, why is Alexander upset that he only has bus tokens?	• Alexander's brothers have _____. • Alexander is upset because _____.
2	On page 13, what does Anthony tell Alexander to spend his money on?	• Anthony says that Alexander should buy _____. • Anthony _____.
3	On page 24, how does Alexander show that he is unhappy?	• Alexander _____ his _____. • To show that he is unhappy _____.
7	How does the picture on page 16 help you understand how David feels about buying Alexander's used gum?	• David looks _____. He feels _____ about Alexander's used gum. • David is _____.
8	On page 21, how did Alexander loose eight cents?	• Alexander flushed _____ down the toilet. Then he dropped _____ through a crack. • First, Alexander _____. Then, _____. • Alexander _____.
9	On page 30, why did Alexander tell his grandparents to come back soon?	• His grandparents give him _____. • Alexander wants _____.
11	On page 11, what advice does Nicky give Alexander?	• Nicky tells Alexander he should _____ so that a dollar tree will grow. • Nicky says _____.
12	What does Alexander really want to spend his money on?	• Alexander wants to buy a _____. • The thing Alexander really wants _____. • Alexander _____.

Use the Dig Deeper Vocabulary Routine on pages 474–475 to continue to develop conceptual understanding of the following nouns: *walkie-talkie, lox, college, downtown,* and *accident*. Begin by reviewing that nouns are words for people, places, and things. Display and read aloud the following sentence: *Alexander wanted to buy a **walkie-talkie**.*

Confirm students' understanding of the noun *walkie-talkie*. Explain that *walkie-talkie* is a compound word made up of two smaller words that are separated by a hyphen. Then point out the role of the noun *walkie-talkie* in the sentence by explaining that the noun functions as the object of the verb *buy*. Have students write sentences using the nouns.

Unit 2 Module A

Name _____

Needs and Wants

Needs are the things you must have to live.
Wants are things you would like to have.
You do not need wants to live.

Needs	Wants
food	candy
water	toys
clothes	books
home	bike

How is a need different from a want?
Needs are different from wants because _____.

Why should you think about what you need before buying something you want?

I should think about my needs before buying something
I want because _____.

A Chair for My Mother

Reproduce and distribute copies of the *Earning, Saving, and Spending* student page on page 413. Assess students' understanding of the words *earn, save,* and *spend*. Then explain that the chart shows how people get money and use it responsibly. Read aloud the chart. Then invite partners to share how they can earn, save, and spend money.

TALK ABOUT SENTENCES

For students who need support in accessing key ideas and key language in *A Chair for My Mother,* use the Sentence Talk Routine on pages 476–477 to draw students' attention to the relationship between meaning and the words, phrases, and clauses in the text.

Lesson	Sentence(s) to Deconstruct
4	(p 53) Then her boss, Josephine, gives me a job too.
5	(p 67) "You are all the kindest people," she said, "and we thank you very, very much."
6	(p 69) So that is how come Mama brought home the biggest jar she could find at the diner and all the coins started to go into the jar.
10	(p 63) But everything else in our whole house was spoiled.
13	(p 77) But they let me sit in it while they carried it up to the door.

SPEAK AND WRITE ABOUT THE TEXT

Use the Text-based Writing Routine on pages 478–479 to model how to speak and write about key ideas and details in *A Chair for My Mother.*

Lesson	Text-based Writing	Scaffolded Frames
4	On page 53, when does the girl help her mother?	• The girl goes to the restaurant to_____. • The girl helps _____.
5	On page 67, how does Grandmother feel?	• Grandmother is _____ and _____. • The neighbors make Grandmother feel _____.
6	On page 69, how will the family use the large jar?	• The family will _____ in the jar. • The jar will _____.
10	What does the picture on page 64 help you understand?	• I understand that the girl's family is _____. • From the picture _____.
13	On page 77, how can you tell that the girl is happy about getting the chair?	• The girl sits in the chair while her family _____ to the door. • I can tell the girl is happy because _____.

Unit 2 Module A

Name _____

Earning, Saving, and Spending

How do people earn money?
How do people save money?

People do a job to **earn** money.

$\downarrow$

They **save** the money they earn in a bank.

$\downarrow$

They **spend** the money they saved on something they need or want.

What can you do to earn money?
I can earn money by _____.
Where can you save money?
I can save money _____.
How would you spend the money you save?
I would spend my money on _____.

Money Matters!

Reproduce and distribute copies of the *Ways to Pay* student page on page 416. Explain that to understand the information in *Money Matters!* it helps to know the difference between a credit card and a debit card. Begin by confirming students' understanding of the words *money, pay, buy, bank,* and *bank account.* Discuss that when a person buys an item, they may use a credit card or a debit card as a form of payment. Briefly explain that both cards store information about how much money a person has available to spend. By using the cards, the buyer does not need to carry a lot of bills and coins to the store. Then help students understand how to read the chart. Point to the row where we will learn about credit cards. Now, point to the row where we will learn about debit cards.

Read aloud the chart as students follow along. Then discuss what students have learned about credit cards and debit cards, scaffolding with sentence frames such as: *The money on ____ belongs to ____. A debit card can be used ____.*

After discussing the information in each row, have students share with a partner when they think the different forms of money should be used. Scaffold with sentence frames such as: *A good time to use _____ is _____.*

Then have students discuss with their partner the difference between a credit card and a debit card. Scaffold with additional sentence frames: *A credit card lets a person ____ from the bank. A debit card ____.*

TALK ABOUT SENTENCES

For students who need support in accessing key ideas and key language in *Money Matters!,* use the Sentence Talk Routine on pages 476–477 to draw students' attention to the relationship between meaning and the words, phrases, and clauses in the text.

Lesson	Sentence(s) to Deconstruct
1	(p 4) We can save money or we can spend it.
2	(p 9) It is still used today for special transactions such as land sales.
3	(p 13) A gold rush happens when people hear gold has been found.
4	(p 17) Today, most people use cash only for small purchases.
5	(p 23) A big salary might be good, but you might not like your job.
6	(p 29) Housing and food are common items in family budgets.
11	(p 15) Why is it a crime to make fake money?
12	(p 29) It may not seem like much, but in one year you would have $65.00.

Use the Text-based Writing Routine on pages 478–479 to model how to speak and write about key ideas and details in *Money Matters!*

Lesson	Text-based Writing	Scaffolded Frames
1	On page 4, what are some ways people can use money?	• People can ____ with money. • People use money to ____. • Money can ____.
2	On page 9, what did you learn about how the Yap people use money?	• I learned that the Yap use ____ as money. • The picture shows that Yap money ____. • Since the money ____, the Yap people ____.
3	On page 13, how does the author use the word *rush* to explain what a "gold rush" is?	• The text says "people rush to ____" when they hear that gold has been found. • The people rush or ____ to ____.
4	On page 17, how does the author compare the different ways people pay for things?	• People use cash to ____. • People use ____ for ____.
5	Use information from page 23 to explain how a salary can relate to happiness.	• A big salary can ____ if you ____. • A small salary can ____ because ____. • Your happiness and your salary relate because ____.
6	According to page 31, what are some things most families include in their budgets?	• Most families include ____ and ____ in their budgets. • Most families include ____.
11	According to page 15, how do people react to fake money?	• People do not ____ cash when there is too much fake money around. • Fake money causes ____.
12	According to page 29, how does a budget help you save your money?	• A budget let's you make a plan for how much money you ____. Then you can ____ the money you have left over. • When you set up a budget ____.

Use the Dig Deeper Vocabulary Routine on pages 474–475 to continue to develop conceptual understanding of the following action verbs: *exchange, earn, refuse, bought, sold,* and *borrow*. Review the role of action verbs in sentences. Display and read aloud the following sentence: *I can **buy** that toy with my money.*

Point out that the verb *buy* is preceded by the name of who or what is performing the action. Also point out that *toy* is the direct object that receives the action.

Name _____

Ways to Pay

What is a credit card?
What is a debit card?

Card	How It Is Used
 **Credit Card**	The money on the card belongs to the bank. People use the card to buy things. They are using the bank's money. They pay the bank back later.
Debit Card	People put money in the bank. They use the card to pay. The money comes out of their own bank account when they pay.

How are a credit card and a debit card different?
A credit card _____.
A debit card _____.

I Wanna Iguana

Reproduce and distribute copies of the *Pet Needs* student page on page 418. Help students understand how to read the web. The words in the middle tell us that the web is about what pets need. Each box around the middle tells us one thing a pet needs. Then read each box aloud. If necessary, confirm students' understanding of words on the web. Then have partners share ways a person can take care of a pet. Scaffold with sentence frames: *A person can _____ their pet. To make sure their pet _____, a person can _____.* Then have partners share something they should think about before getting a pet and one thing a pet needs.

TALK ABOUT SENTENCES

For students who need support in accessing key ideas and key language in *I Wanna Iguana,* use the Sentence Talk Routine on pages 476–477 to draw students' attention to the relationship between meaning and the words, phrases, and clauses in the text.

Lesson	Sentence(s) to Deconstruct
7	(p 83) Nice try, though. Love, Mom
8	(p 82) Signed, Your sensitive son, Alex
9	(p 92) And I would clean his cage when it got messy.
10	(p 91) If I knew the fish was going to jump into the spaghetti sauce, I never would have taken the cover off the jar!

SPEAK AND WRITE ABOUT THE TEXT

Use the Text-based Writing Routine on pages 478–479 to model how to speak and write about key ideas and details in *I Wanna Iguana.*

Lesson	Text-based Writing	Scaffolded Frames
7	On page 83, what tells you who wrote this letter?	• The writer uses the word _____ to show _____. • I know _____.
8	On page 82, how does Alex try to convince his mother?	• Alex signs the letter with the words _____. • Alex uses _____.
9	On page 92, what does Alex say he will do to take care of the iguana?	• Alex says he _____ when it got messy. • He tells Mom _____.
10	What does Alex explain on page 91?	• Alex says he didn't _____the fish would _____. • Alex explains _____.

Name _____

Pet Needs

What things do pets need?

food and water

the right kind of
place to live

A Pet Needs . . .

excercise

baths

What should you think about before getting a pet?
I should think about _____.
What is one thing a pet needs?
A pet needs _____ because _____.

Name _____

Money for Blocks

Emma loved to play with blocks. She wanted to buy more blocks, but she didn't have money. Emma had an idea. She would earn money to buy more blocks.

She asked her mother for jobs to do. "First, you can clean your room," her mother said. Emma's room was too messy. So she didn't want to clean it.

Next, Mother told Emma to put the dishes away. "I hate putting the dishes away," Emma thought. She did not do the job.

Then, Emma's mother told her to walk the dog. "It is too hot to walk outside," Emma thought. So she stayed inside.

In the end, Emma did not earn money. She could not buy more blocks. Emma had another idea. "I can wait until my birthday to get more blocks!"

Name _____

I Need a Bicycle

I think it is important for every kid to have a
bicycle. That is why I would like to have a bicycle. If
I had a bicycle, I would be able to get exercise. It is
important for kids to get exercise, and I think that
riding a bike would be a fun way to stay fit. To stay
safe, I would wear a helmet. I could also ride my
bicycle with Dad. Another reason it would be good for
me to have a bicycle is that I would be able to get to
school faster. I could ride with my older sister to be
safe. That's another thing. . . my sister has a bicycle,
so why shouldn't I have one, too? I know that a
bicycle costs a lot of money. That is why I have saved
up my money to pay for it. For all of these reasons, it
is important that I have a bicycle.

Performance-Based Assessment
Unit 2 Module A

Reproduce and distribute copies of the student model on page 419. After completing the Prepare to Write activities on pages 200–201 in Unlock the Writing in Part 2, use the student model to illustrate the features of narrative writing.

Read aloud the first paragraph and discuss it with students. Who is the character in this story? What is her problem? If students have difficulty responding, have them reread the title and first few pages in *Alexander, Who Used to Be Rich Last Sunday* that tell who the character is and his problem. Then read the second paragraph with students. Point to the word in the second sentence that gives a clue about when the story event happened. Why do you think the writer began the sentence with the word *First*?

Continue reading to the end of the model. Pause as you read to ask questions about the sequence of events and about details that tell how Emma feels and what she thinks. Then invite partners to discuss how the sentences tell about Emma's struggle to earn money. Scaffold with sentence frames: *Emma wants to buy _____. She can _____ to earn money. She can also _____ and _____ to earn money. Emma does not want to _____. She thinks _____.*

Unit 2 Module B

Reproduce and distribute copies of the student model on page 420. After completing the Prepare to Write activities on pages 206–207 in Unlock the Writing in Part 2, use the student model to illustrate the features of opinion writing.

Read aloud the first sentence and discuss it with students. How does this sentence introduce the writer's opinion? What is the writer going to try to prove? If students have difficulty identifying the opinion, underline the words *I think*. How do these words help you figure out the writer's opinion?

Next, have students identify the first reason the writer gives to support his or her opinion. Point to the part of the paragraph that gives evidence to support this reason. Have students work with a partner to discuss what other reasons the writer gives to support his or her opinion. Scaffold with sentence frames such as: *The writer needs a bicycle because _____. With a bicycle, the writer could _____.* Have students think about how the writer addresses concerns that the audience might have, such as safety and how expensive a bicycle would be.

Finally, discuss the conclusion. How does the writer conclude this opinion piece? Point out how the writer restates his or her opinion in a different way.

Theodore Roosevelt: The Adventurous President

Reproduce and distribute copies of the student page *Conserving Nature* on page 424. Explain that in order to better understand events in *Theodore Roosevelt: The Adventurous President,* it is important to know what it means to conserve, or to protect nature. Confirm students' understanding of the terms *nature* and *conserve.* Then help students read the web. The middle circle tells us what information we will find in the web. Point to the circle with the picture of the boy and the girl planting a tree. This circle tells us a detail about how people conserve nature. Then read aloud the details in each circle on the web. Have students follow along, pointing to the words and picture as you read.

Next, have students share with a partner and explain what it means to conserve nature using the information they learned in the web. Scaffold with sentence frames such as: *To conserve nature means to _____. When a person _____, they _____.*

Then have students share with a partner two things that they will do to help conserve nature. Scaffold with an additional sentence frame such as: *It is important for me to _____ to conserve nature because _____.*

TALK ABOUT SENTENCES

For students who need support in accessing key ideas and key language in *Theodore Roosevelt: The Adventurous President,* use the Sentence Talk Routine on pages 476–477 to draw students' attention to the relationship between meaning and the words, phrases, and clauses in the text.

Lesson	Sentence(s) to Deconstruct
1	(p 2) He was the perfect man for the job—a new kind of president for a new century.
2	(p 22) About that time, trouble started brewing in Cuba—a small island in the Atlantic Ocean, ninety miles from Florida.
3	(p 27) The leaders had an idea: In the next election, Teddy should be President McKinley's running mate for vice president.
4	(p 39) Once they began to explore the river, they had no idea where it would lead them.
5	(p 42) He set aside 230 million acres of land for national parks, wildlife lands, and forests.
6	(p 33) Teddy had a favorite saying based on an African proverb: "Speak softly and carry a big stick. You will go far."
12	(p 31) Teddy wasn't trying to favor the workers over the owners.
13	(p 28) They would have to compete against one another for customers or he would make sure they were brought to trial.

SPEAK AND WRITE ABOUT THE TEXT

Use the Text-Based Writing Routine on pages 478–479 to model how to speak and write about key ideas and details in *Theodore Roosevelt: The Adventurous President*.

Lesson	Text-based Writing	Scaffolded Frames
1	On page 2, why is Teddy called the perfect man for the job of president in the early 1900s?	• Times were _____ and Teddy wanted the country to be a _____. • Teddy was perfect because _____.
2	On page 22, what does the text say Teddy thought about Spain being in control of Cuba?	• Teddy thought Spain should _____ because he wanted _____. • Teddy thought _____ because _____.
3	On page 27, why did the Republicans think that Teddy should run as vice president instead of governor?	• Republican leaders believed that Teddy might _____ to other Republican leaders if he were vice president. • The Republican leaders were afraid _____ because _____.
4	What does the first paragraph on page 39 help you understand about Teddy when he was older?	• Teddy was still _____ and he showed it by _____. • Even when Teddy was older he _____.
5	On page 42, what do you learn about Teddy's role as a conservationist?	• Teddy set aside millions of acres of land for _____, _____, and _____. • Teddy is known as a conservationist because _____.
6	In the sidebar on page 33, what was the "Big Stick" policy that Teddy used?	• The "Big Stick" policy meant that Teddy could tell others _____. • The "Big Stick" policy _____.
12	On page 31, how did Teddy improve the working conditions of miners?	• Teddy got the mine owners to agree to better _____ for the miners and an _____ work day. • Teddy worked to _____.
13	According to page 28, what did Teddy do to keep railroad ticket prices low?	• Teddy told the railroads that he would bring them to _____ if they did not follow the law. • Teddy enforced the law by _____.

EXPAND UNDERSTANDING OF VOCABULARY

Use the Dig Deeper Vocabulary Routine on pages 474–475 to continue to develop a conceptual understanding of the following adjectives: *unusual, popular, extinct,* and *grateful*. Begin by reviewing the function of an adjective. Display and read aloud the following sentence: *Theodore Roosevelt was a **lively** politician.*

Remind students that an adjective describes a noun or a pronoun. Point out that the word *lively* is used as an adjective in the sentence. It tells what kind of a politician Roosevelt was—a lively politician.

Name _____

Conserving Nature

How do people conserve nature?

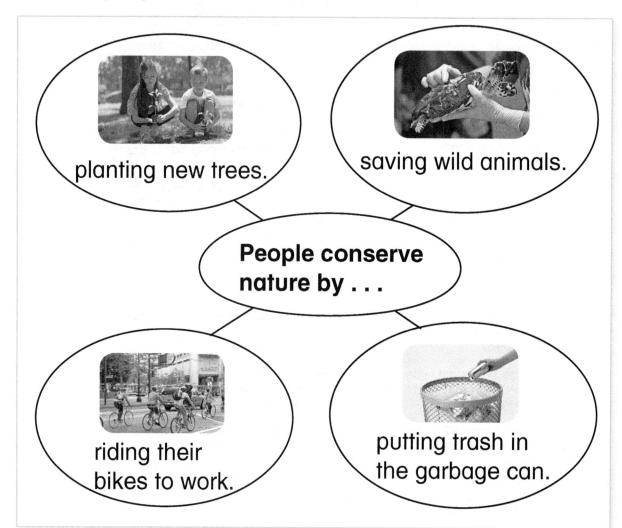

planting new trees.

saving wild animals.

People conserve nature by . . .

riding their bikes to work.

putting trash in the garbage can.

What are two things you will do to help conserve nature?

I will _____ to help conserve nature.

I will also _____.

Marching with Aunt Susan

Reproduce and distribute copies of the student page *All About Voting* on page 426. Explain that in order to understand *Marching with Aunt Susan,* it helps to know about voting in the United States. Begin by clarifying students' understanding of the verb *vote.* Then read aloud the chart. Pause to clarify difficult terms. Then have students share two things that they learned about voting in the United States.

TALK ABOUT SENTENCES

For students who need support in accessing key ideas and key language in *Marching with Aunt Susan,* use the Sentence Talk Routine on pages 476–477 to draw students' attention to the relationship between meaning and the words, phrases, and clauses in the text.

Lesson	Sentence(s) to Deconstruct
8	(p 118) "We can work to pass laws that will help adults *and* children."
9	(p 122) "What do you want to be—a man?" he yelled.
10	(p 134) At a celebration of her eighty-sixth birthday at the 1906 meeting of the National American Women's Suffrage Association, Susan proclaimed her famous rallying cry, "Failure is impossible."
11	(p 115) "I get to spend my allowance any way I want."

SPEAK AND WRITE ABOUT THE TEXT

Use the Text-based Writing Routine on pages 478–479 to model how to speak and write about key ideas and details in *Marching with Aunt Susan.*

Lesson	Text-based Writing	Scaffolded Frames
8	On page 118, how do you know Aunt Susan wants more than voting rights for women?	• Aunt Susan says that if _____, then _____. • Aunt Susan _____.
9	On page 22, what do the boy's words tell you about how men felt about women voting?	• The boy's words tell me that in the late 1800s, _____. • I know that _____ because _____.
10	On page 134, how do you know that Aunt Susan never gave up her fight?	• At _____ when she was 86, Susan _____. • I know Susan never gave up because _____.
11	On page 115, how is what Bessie says about her allowance different from what she hears the women say?	• The women say the _____ how they can spend their money. But Bessie can spend her money on_____. • It is up to the _____, but Bessie can _____.

Name _____

All About Voting

Voting lets Americans make choices about their community and country.

Who can vote?	Americans 18 years old and older
What do they vote for?	• Leaders such as president, governor, and mayor • Solutions to problems affecting a community
When do they vote?	On Election Day, a Tuesday in early November
How do they vote?	Inside a booth where they press buttons to vote

Share two things that you learned about voting.

In the United States, _____.

I also learned that _____.

Change Makers

Reproduce and distribute copies of the *Ideas and Actions* student page on page 429. Explain that to understand the details in *Change Makers,* it helps to understand how people's ideas and actions combine to solve problems. Begin by confirming understanding of the words *problem, idea, action,* and *solve.* Then help students understand the progression in the charts using the chart on the left. Point to the problem. Confirm students' understanding of *hungry.* What does the boy do first to solve the problem? *He has an _____ about how to solve his problem. He has the idea to _____.* Point to the action that solves that problem.

Continue to read aloud the chart on the right. Have students point to each box as you read its contents. Clarify terms such as *sneakers* and *money* as needed. If necessary, confirm students' understanding by having them discuss how they would solve two similar problems. Scaffold with sentence frames such as: *When I am thirsty, I _____. If I wanted to buy _____, I could _____.*

After reading the chart, pose additional problems such as "I'm sleepy" or "I need more milk." Have students share with partners the ideas and actions they would take to solve each problem. Scaffold with sentence frames such as: *If I am sleepy, first I _____. Then I _____. If I need more milk I can _____.*

Then have partners discuss what they learned about how people solve problems. Ask them to share with each other a problem they had in the past and the idea and action they used to solve it.

For students who need support in accessing key ideas and key language in *Change Makers,* use the Sentence Talk Routine on pages 476–477 to draw students' attention to the relationship between meaning and the words, phrases, and clauses in the text.

Lesson	Sentence(s) to Deconstruct
1	(p 8) He started collecting electronic parts that people had thrown away.
2	(p 15) They wanted the cookies to be made without harming the rain forest.
3	(p 22) In 2014, he helped collect more than 50,000 pounds of food.
4	(p 26) Kids learn about healthy eating and growing food in this garden.
5	(p 29) The group links people to projects that need help.
6	(p 25) Adults need kids to help plant seeds and water the gardens.
12	(p 8) Now Kelvin's batteries power lights all over his neighborhood!

Use the Text-based Writing Routine on pages 478–479 to model how to speak and write about key ideas and details in *Change Makers.*

Lesson	Text-based Writing	Scaffolded Frames
1	On page 8, why did Kelvin start collecting electronic parts that people had thrown away?	• Kelvin collected electronic parts so that he could make a _____. • Kelvin wanted _____.
2	On page 15, why were the orangutans' trees being chopped down?	• The trees were chopped down to make way for _____ to be grown. • People chopped down the trees because _____.
3	On page 22, how did Zach help families in need?	• Zach collected more than _____ to help families in need. • Zach _____.
4	On page 26, what does the phrase *healthy eating* mean?	• *Healthy eating* means "_____." You can stay healthy by eating _____. • By eating healthy, _____.
5	On page 29, what does the community group Lion's Heart do?	• Lion's Heart _____ to _____ that need help. • People can join Lion's Heart to _____.
6	On page 25, how can kids help out in community gardens?	• Kids can help community gardens by _____ and _____ plants. • Community gardens need kids _____.
12	According to page 8, how did Kelvin solve a problem in his community?	• The people in Kelvin's community had no _____. So Kelvin made _____. • Kelvin's community had _____. Kelvin solved this problem by _____.

Use the Dig Deeper Vocabulary Routine on pages 474–475 to continue to develop a conceptual understanding of the following verbs from the text: *invent, create, destroy, endanger, harm, harvest,* and *link.* Begin by reviewing the role of verbs in sentences. Display and read aloud the following sentence: *Kelvin keeps **working** on ideas.*

Point out that the verb *working* contains the suffix *–ing.* Explain that adding *–ing* to verbs creates actions that continue to happen over time. Ask students to add *–ing* to the verbs to make *inventing, creating, destroying, endangering, harming, harvesting,* and *linking.* Students can then write sentences with the verbs using the *-ing* ending.

Name _____

Ideas and Actions

How do people solve problems?

PROBLEM:	PROBLEM:
I'm hungry.	I want new sneakers.

↓ ↓

IDEA:	IDEA:
I'll have a snack.	I'll do a job to get money.

↓ ↓

ACTION:

ACTION:

Team *Talk*

How do people solve problems?
People solve problems by _____.
What is a problem you had? How did you solve it?
My problem _____. An idea
I had_____. I solved it by_____.

City Green

Reproduce and distribute copies of the *Planting Seeds* student page on page 431. Explain that to understand *City Green,* it helps to understand what a seed needs to grow. Discuss that the word *plant* can be used as a noun and as a verb. Then read aloud the chart, clarifying terms as necessary. Confirm students' understanding by asking questions such as: Where does the girl plant the seeds? What is the second thing the girl does?

Then have partners share what they know about planting seeds and what they would plant in their own gardens.

TALK ABOUT SENTENCES

For students who need support in accessing key ideas and key language in *City Green,* use the Sentence Talk Routine on pages 476–477 to draw students' attention to the relationship between meaning and the words, phrases, and clauses in the text.

Lesson	Sentence(s) to Deconstruct
7	(p 137) It was three floors up and down, an empty building nailed up shut for as long as I could remember.
8	(p 140) Now this block looks like a big smile with one tooth missing.
9	(p 153) Then Mr. Rocco from two houses down comes, carrying two cans of paint.
10	(p 165) And way in the back, taller than anything else, is a beautiful patch of yellow sunflowers.

SPEAK AND WRITE ABOUT THE TEXT

Use the Text-based Writing Routine on pages 478–479 to model how to speak and write about key ideas and details in *City Green.*

Lesson	Text-based Writing	Scaffolded Frames
7	On page 137, why would an empty building be nailed shut?	• A person would nail an empty building shut because _____. • A building that is empty _____.
8	How does the illustration on page 140 help you understand the description of the block?	• The illustration shows that the block _____. • It shows that _____.
9	On page 153, why does Mr. Rocco bring cans of paint?	• Mr. Rocco brings paint so the neighbors can _____. • He brings cans of paint _____.
10	On page 165, who planted the sunflowers in the garden?	• The sunflowers grew because _____ planted them in the garden at _____. • The sunflowers are _____.

Name _____

Planting Seeds

How does a seed grow?

1.  Plant the seeds in soil in a sunny area.	2. Water the seeds.
3.  Soon the seeds will sprout.	4.  The sprouts will grow into plants.

What does a seed need to grow?

A seed needs _____, _____, and _____
to grow.

What would you plant in a garden?

I would plant _____ in a garden.

Name _____

Title _____

Eleanor Roosevelt

Who was Eleanor Roosevelt?

Eleanor Roosevelt was first lady of the United States from 1933 to 1945. She is the longest serving first lady in American history. She was married to President Franklin D. Roosevelt.

What did Eleanor Roosevelt do while she was first lady?

Eleanor went on tours of America. She found out how people lived. She found out what they thought. Then she told the president. She also wrote a daily column. She gave radio talks. Eleanor helped the president stay in touch with Americans.

What big ideas did Eleanor Roosevelt support?

Eleanor thought women should be paid as much as men. She was very interested in child welfare. She wanted equal rights and good housing for everyone. After her husband died, Eleanor joined the United Nations. She worked hard for human rights. Eleanor wanted to make life better for people everywhere.

Name _____

Title _____

My Park

My new park will be a nice place for everyone in my community. Every kid and adult will have something fun to do in my park. The park will also be a place where people can come to relax.

My park will have a big playground with swings and a long slide. Tall trees will surround the park. The trees will give people lots of shade. Also, the trees will be home to many birds and squirrels.

A long, winding path will go through the park. On the path, people can run, walk, or ride their bikes. Benches will line the path so people can sit and enjoy the nice weather.

I think my park will be a fun and relaxing place for people in my community to gather.

Performance-Based Assessment
Unit 3 Module A

Reproduce and distribute copies of the student model on page 432. After completing the Prepare to Write activities on pages 212–213 in Unlock the Writing in Part 2, use the student model to illustrate the elements of informative writing.

Point to the title and explain that the model answers questions about Eleanor Roosevelt, an important American. Then read aloud the first question. Ask: Which word begins this question? *The word _____ begins this question.* Which punctuation mark ends it? *The question ends with a _____.* Read aloud the answer to the first question. Point out that the answer is one paragraph and it appears right below the question. Ask: What did you learn in the first answer? *I learned _____.* Remind students that a good answer includes accurate facts and details and thoroughly answers the question.

Continue reading the student model aloud and discussing the remaining questions and answers. Then have students discuss with a partner how the question and answer format of the student model helps them better understand information about Eleanor Roosevelt. Scaffold responses with sentence frames such as: *When I see the question word _____, I know that the next paragraph will give information about _____. The question asks _____. The answer tells about _____.*

Unit 3 Module B

Reproduce and distribute copies of the student model on page 433. After completing the Prepare to Write activities on pages 218–219 in Unlock the Writing in Part 2, use the student model to illustrate the features of an informative/explanatory text.

Discuss the first paragraph and point out how the writer tells what the text will be about. Then have students point to the second paragraph as you read it aloud. Explain that this paragraph discusses one thing the park will have. Point out adjectives that the writer uses to describe things in the playground. Confirm students' understanding by asking: How does the writer explain what the slide looks like? *The writer says the slide is _____.*

Continue reading aloud and discussing the main topics of each paragraph and adjectives the writer uses. Then have students focus on the illustration. Point out that the parts of the park the writer mentions are also shown in the illustration. Then have students discuss with a partner how the illustration helps them better understand the text. Scaffold with sentence frames: *The illustration helps me _____. The _____ in the illustration helps me understand what the _____ looks like.*

The Earth Dragon Awakes

Reproduce and distribute copies of the *Big Earthquakes* student page on page 437. Explain that to understand the story events in *The Earth Dragon Awakes,* it helps to know more about the causes and effects of earthquakes. Point out that earthquakes are natural disasters, then have students share what they already know about earthquakes. Then help students understand how to read the chart. A *cause* is what makes something happen. The *effect* is the thing that happens.

Read aloud the chart as students follow along. To confirm students' understanding, ask: What causes earthquakes to happen? *Earthquakes are caused by _____.* What is one thing that happens when there is a big earthquake? *One thing that happens when there is a big earthquake is _____.*

After discussing the information in the chart, have partners talk about the cause and the effects of earthquakes. Scaffold with sentence frames such as: *The ground _____ because rocks _____. When rocks _____.* Then have partners discuss what they learned about earthquakes.

TALK ABOUT SENTENCES

For students who need support in accessing key ideas and key language in *The Earth Dragon Awakes,* use the Sentence Talk Routine on pages 476–477 to draw students' attention to the relationship between meaning and the words, phrases, and clauses in the text.

Lesson	Sentence(s) to Deconstruct
1	(p 14) "If I were a chicken and saw your knife, I'd be scared, too," Ah Sing says.
2	(p 22) "The Earth Dragon must be scratching," he laughs.
3	(p 43) A few steps ahead, a heavy sack thumps against the cobblestones.
4	(p 63) Next to him is a woman wearing so many layers of clothing that she can barely walk.
5	(p 102) By Saturday, April 21, twenty thousand people have fled San Francisco by boat.
6	(p 111) However, we couldn't see the wreckage because we had no electricity, so our television didn't work.
7	(p 104) A few days ago, they used to read books just like that one.
13	(p 103) He could commute from Oakland on the ferry, but he decided to camp out in the tents that have been set up in Golden Gate Park.

Use the Text-based Writing Routine on pages 478–479 to model how to speak and write about key ideas and details in *The Earth Dragon Awakes*.

Lesson	Text-based Writing	Scaffolded Frames
1	On page 14, how can you tell Ah Sing doesn't believe animals can feel an earthquake coming?	• Ah Sing thinks that the chickens _____ of Ah Quon's _____. • Ah Sing says _____.
2	On page 22, how does Ah Sing react to the shaking earth?	• Ah Sing jokes that the Earth Dragon _____. • Ah Sing _____ and says _____.
3	On page 43, why are heavy sacks falling onto the streets?	• People are _____ to save their _____. • People want to _____.
4	On page 63, why is the woman that Henry sees barely able to walk?	• The woman is _____ all of her _____ because _____. • The woman _____.
5	On page 102, what does the author include that helps you understand that the story is based on actual events?	• The author includes a _____. He says that _____ people had fled San Francisco by boat. • The author includes _____.
6	On page 111, how does the author describe his own experience with earthquakes?	• The author's _____ went out and he had _____. • Because the author's _____, he _____.
7	On page 104, why are Chin and Henry no longer interested in the "penny dreadfuls"?	• Chin and Henry had enough _____ because of the earthquake. • The boys feel _____.
13	On pages 102–103, the author says thousands of people fled San Francisco after the earthquake. According to the text, what were the conditions like for the people who decided to stay?	• There were _____ in Golden Gate Park for people to stay in after the Earthquake. • People who stayed in the city lived in _____ or _____.

Use the Dig Deeper Vocabulary Routine on pages 474–475 to continue to develop a conceptual understanding of the following plural nouns: *plates, missiles, ferries,* and *ruins*. Begin by reviewing the role of plural nouns in sentences. Then display and read aloud the following sentence: *People from the **cities** nearby came to help clean up after the earthquake.*

Point out that the noun *cities* is preceded by the article *the*. Explain that the words *a, an,* and *the* often signal that a noun will follow. Point out the *–ies* ending and explain that *cities* is a word that names more than one place. Introduce the singular form, *city,* and show students how the *y* is dropped and replaced with *i* before adding the *–es* ending. Then have students work with a partner to write sentences using the singular and plural form of each noun.

Name _____

Unit 4 Module A

Big Earthquakes

What causes a big earthquake?
What happens when there is a big earthquake?

Cause
Rocks under Earth's surface bump into each other.

Effects			
The ground shakes.	Buildings fall down.	Roads crack in half.	People get hurt.

What can happen when rocks move under Earth's surface?
An _____ can happen when rocks move under Earth's surface.

What is something you learned about earthquakes?
I learned that _____.

Seek the Sun

Reproduce and distribute copies of the *Sunshine and Shade* student page on page 439. Explain that to understand *Seek the Sun*, it helps to understand the difference between sunshine and shade. Read the chart aloud as students follow along. Discuss the similarities and differences between sunshine and shade. Scaffold with a sentence frame such as: *Sunshine helps _____, but shade _____.* Then have partners share what they have learned about sunshine and shade.

TALK ABOUT SENTENCES

For students who need support in accessing key ideas and key language in *Seek the Sun*, use the Sentence Talk Routine on pages 476–477 to draw students' attention to the relationship between meaning and the words, phrases, and clauses in the text.

Lesson	Sentence(s) to Deconstruct
8	(p 6) When the sandalmaker and his wife rolled up the bed quilts in the morning, even on a sunny morning, it was still dark and cold in their house.
9	(p 7) "How can we seek the sun each day here in the shadow of a tall building?"
10	(p 11) Today in Japan, when tall buildings are constructed, the amount of shadow that can fall on nearby buildings is limited by law.
12	(p 5) For fifty years, husband and wife prayed at the great temple nearby.

SPEAK AND WRITE ABOUT THE TEXT

Use the Text-based Writing Routine on pages 478–479 to model how to speak and write about key ideas and details in *Seek the Sun.*

Lesson	Text-based Writing	Scaffolded Frames
8	On page 6, what affect did the tall building have on the husband and wife?	• The tall building made their home _____ and _____. • There was no longer any _____, so _____.
9	On page 7, how can you tell that the tall building upsets the husband?	• The man wonders how he and his wife can _____ each day in the building's shadow. • The man is upset because _____.
10	On page 11, what was the effect of the judge's rule?	• Because of the judge's rule, today in Japan, tall buildings _____. • The judge ruled _____ so _____.
12	On page 5, what is something the husband and wife do every day?	• The husband and wife go to the _____ to _____. • Every day _____.

Unit 4 Module A

Name _____

Sunshine and Shade

Sunshine	Shade
gives places light	makes places dark
helps all plants grow	helps only some plants grow
makes things warm	makes things cold

Share one fact about sunshine.

Sunshine _____

Share one fact about shade.

Shade _____

Disaster Alert!

Reproduce and distribute copies of the *What Is a Disaster?* student page on page 442. Explain that to understand the information in *Disaster Alert!*, it helps to understand the difference between a normal weather event and a disaster. Also explain that a disaster is any event that happens suddenly and creates a lot of damage.

Point to the first picture, read the label, then review the information below the image. Clarify difficult terms such as *harm* and *predicted*. Discuss that a typical rainstorm does not have a negative impact on human life. Scaffold with a sentence frame such as: *Rain does not _____ humans*. Then read aloud the rest of the chart as students follow along, clarifying terms as necessary. Confirm students' understanding of the severity of the events by having them compare rain, thunderstorms, and tornadoes. Scaffold with sentence frames such as: *People know when _____ and _____ are coming. But they do not know when a _____ is coming. Rain is not a _____, but a tornado is a _____.*

After discussing the information in the chart, have partners talk about what they learned about the different storms. Scaffold with sentence frames such as: *Both a _____ and a _____*. Then have students talk with their partner about which of the three storms they think is a disaster.

TALK ABOUT SENTENCES

For students who need support in accessing key ideas and key language in *Disaster Alert!*, use the Sentence Talk Routine on pages 476–477 to draw students' attention to the relationship between meaning and the words, phrases, and clauses in the text.

Lesson	Sentence(s) to Deconstruct
1	(p 8) After a tornado, emergency workers look for survivors.
2	(p 10) In coastal areas, strong winds and high tides can cause floods.
3	(p 19) There is no way to know if the hole will get bigger while they work.
4	(p 24) Eruptions also contain hot clouds of ash and poisonous gas.
5	(p 30) They dig trenches and clear trees that could become fuel.
11	(p 6) Parts of roofs are peeled off; windows are broken; some tree trunks are snapped.
12	(p 27) The information they collect is used to predict when a volcano will erupt.

Use the Text-based Writing Routine on pages 478–479 to model how to speak and write about key ideas and details in *Disaster Alert!*

Lesson	Text-based Writing	Scaffolded Frames
1	On page 8, what are some things people might do after a tornado?	• After a tornado, emergency workers ____. • People might _____.
2	On page 10, what did you learn about how floods are caused in different places?	• On the coast, _____ can cause a flood. In cities, _____ can cause a flood. • Floods happen when _____.
3	On page 19, what happens during a sinkhole rescue?	• Rescue workers use ____ to _____. • Other people should _____ because _____.
4	On page 24, what are some reasons the writer gives to explain why volcanoes are dangerous?	• Sometimes volcanoes _____. • Eruptions can _____, which _____.
5	What do you learn on page 28 about how workers try to stop bushfires?	• I learned that firefighters _____ and ____ to help stop a bushfire. • I learned that bushfires _____.
11	According to the chart on page 6, what is an example of moderate damage that an EF1 tornado can cause?	• An EF1 tornado can cause parts of roofs to _____. • An example of the moderate damage an EF1 tornado can cause is _____.
12	According to page 27, what does a volcanologist do?	• A volcanologist _____ a volcano's temperature and _____ samples. • The job of a volcanologist is to _____.

Use the Dig Deeper Vocabulary Routine on pages 474–475 to continue to develop conceptual understanding of the following vivid adjectives: *violent, rotating, coastal, battery-powered, electrical, active, faulty,* and *extreme*. Begin by reviewing the role vivid adjectives play in a sentence. Display and read aloud the following sentences: *There was a storm. There was a **bad** storm. There was a **violent** storm.*

Point out how the second sentence adds an adjective—*bad*—to provide more information about the storm. Then discuss how the third sentence uses a more vivid adjective—*violent*—to provide more specific information that tells exactly what kind of storm there was.

Name _____

What Is a Disaster?

When is weather a disaster?

Rain	Thunderstorm

• can be light or heavy • does not cause harm • can be predicted	• can bring heavy rain, thunder, lightning, and wind • can cause lights to go out • can be predicted
Tornado 	• very strong, fast winds • can blow buildings and trees down • can hurt people and animals • usually cannot be predicted

Which storm is a disaster?

A _____ is a disaster because _____.

Danger! Earthquakes

BUILD BACKGROUND FOR *DANGER! EARTHQUAKES*

Reproduce and distribute copies of the *What Are Earth's Parts?* student page on page 444. Review the cross-section diagram of Earth by reading the labels aloud as students point to each part of Earth. If necessary, pause during reading to confirm students' understanding of terms such as *liquid* and *melted*. After discussing the diagram, have students discuss details about Earth's three parts. Scaffold with sentence frames such as: *The ____ is the ____ layer. Earth's ____ is_____.* Then have partners discuss two facts they learned about Earth.

TALK ABOUT SENTENCES

For students who need support in accessing key ideas and key language in *Danger! Earthquakes,* use the Sentence Talk Routine on pages 476–477 to draw students' attention to the relationship between meaning and the words, phrases, and clauses in the text.

Lesson	Sentence(s) to Deconstruct
6	(p 19) A magnitude 7 or higher can destroy a city.
7	(p 15) Earthquakes can knock down buildings and wreck highways.
8	(p 32) Cracks in the earth up to 30 feet wide opened like giant jaws.
9	(p 35) Since then, stronger buildings have been erected.

SPEAK AND WRITE ABOUT THE TEXT

Use the Text-based Writing Routine on pages 478–479 to model how to speak and write about key ideas and details in *Danger! Earthquakes.*

Lesson	Text-based Writing	Scaffolded Frames
6	According to page 19, what is a magnitude 7 or higher earthquake able to do?	• A magnitude 7 or higher earthquake can ____. • At magnitude 7 or higher, _____.
7	According to page 15, what is an effect of an earthquake?	• An earthquake can ____ buildings. • An earthquake can ____.
8	On page 32, what words help you understand what the Anchorage earthquake was like?	• The writer uses the comparison of ____ to ____. • The writer describes ____ by ____.
9	On page 35, what change does the writer describe?	• The new buildings are ____ because ____. • After many buildings were destroyed, ____.

Name _____

What Are Earth's Parts?

Earth has three layers.

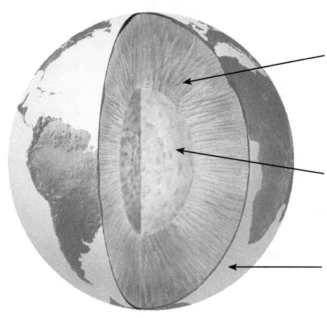

Earth's **mantle** is made up of melted rock.

Earth's **core** is very hot. It is made up of liquid and rock.

Earth's **crust** is the rock that is under the land and oceans.

Team**Talk**

Share two things you learned about Earth.

I learned _____.

I also learned _____.

Unit 4 Module A

Name _____

Title _____

A Surprising Find

9:00 A.M.
April 21, 1906
San Francisco, California

"Over here, Chin!," I heard Henry shout.

I ran to Henry. In the middle of broken bricks and rubble, I saw a tiny ball of fur. "Is it alive?"

"I think we should tell your dad," Henry said.

At that moment, I noticed Dad nearby. He was helping some men.

"Father, we found a puppy! Come quick!" I said, out of breath.

I rushed Father over to the puppy.

"It is alive, but it is hurt," my father said. "I think there is a doctor nearby. Let's see if she can help."

After a short walk, we found the doctor. She looked at the puppy. "It just needs some medicine, water, and rest," she said.

We thanked the doctor. I'm so happy that we were able to save the hurt puppy.

Name _____

Title _____

Too Much Water!
The Dangers of a Flood

We need water to live, but too much water can be a bad thing. When too much water fills an area, there is a flood. Normally, the ground can absorb or soak up water. However, in a flood, water flows through streets and into buildings.

Floods can hurt people. If power lines are knocked down, people won't have electricity. If tap water is contaminated or made dirty, people won't have good water to drink or use. If roads are destroyed, people won't be able to travel safely.

Eventually, the waters of a flood move away. Then people must rebuild. They must fix power lines and broken buildings. It is hard work, but they must start a new life after this dangerous natural event has passed.

Performance-Based Assessment
Unit 4 Module A

DISCUSS THE STUDENT MODEL

Reproduce and distribute copies of the student model on page 445. After completing the Prepare to Write activities on pages 224–225 in Unlock the Writing in Part 2, use the student model to illustrate the features of narrative writing.

Read aloud the heading and first three paragraphs, then discuss what is happening at the beginning of the story. What is the setting? What is the problem? Who is telling the story? If students have difficulty responding, review story elements such as setting, narrator, and problem and solution. Point to a word in the heading that tells when the story takes place. What do the words *I said* tell you about who is telling the story? How can you tell that Chin is worried?

Read aloud to the end of the story. Pause during reading to discuss different parts of the story. What words does Chin say? What does Chin's father think they should do? Why does the writer use the words *after a short walk* in this sentence? Remind students that words such as *after* help show the sequence of events in a story. Then have students work with a partner to discuss the end of the story. Scaffold with a sentence frame such as: *The boys are _____ because _____.*

Unit 4 Module B

DISCUSS THE STUDENT MODEL

Reproduce and distribute copies of the student model on page 446. After completing the Prepare to Write activities on pages 229–230 in Unlock the Writing in Part 2, use the student model to illustrate the features of a magazine article.

Read aloud the headline and discuss how it introduces the topic of the magazine article. Then read the first sentences of the piece. How does this introduce the writer's main idea about this natural event? If students have difficulty identifying the main idea, underline the word *but* and discuss the contrast the writer is presenting.

Next, have students read the rest of the first paragraph. Circle the words *normally* and *however* and discuss how they work together to explain what life is like before and during the natural event described in this magazine article. Show me the details the writer provides to explain what a flood is like.

Then point out the parallel sentence structure the writer uses in the second, third, and fourth sentences of the middle paragraph. Have students work with a partner to explain how each of these sentences supports the point the writer makes in the first sentence. Scaffold with sentence frames such as: *The writer says ____ can hurt people because ____. Another bad effect of a flood is ____.*

Finally, discuss the conclusion. How does the writer refer back to the main point? Note how the writer draws a conclusion about this natural event.

John Chapman: Planter and Pioneer

Reproduce and distribute copies of the *Wilderness and Community* student page on page 450. Explain that to understand the events in *John Chapman: Planter and Pioneer,* it helps to know a little about how a wilderness area is different from an area that has been settled, such as a community. Confirm students' understanding of the terms *wilderness* and *community.* Then help students understand how to read the chart. Point to the row that will tell us what the wilderness is like. Now, point to the row that will tell us what a community is like.

Read the chart aloud as students follow along. If necessary, pause during reading to confirm students' understanding of terms such as *wild, quiet, loud,* and *buildings.* Scaffold using sentence frames such as: *A _____ is an animal that is wild. I may cover my ____ when I hear a _____ noise.*

After discussing the chart, invite students to talk about what they might see if they were to go into the wilderness. Scaffold with sentence frames such as: *I may see _____ in the wilderness. I would see _____.*

Then have students share with a partner one way the wilderness is different from a community. Scaffold with additional sentence frames such as: *In the wilderness, _____, but in a community, _____. The wilderness is different from a community because_____.*

TALK ABOUT SENTENCES

For students who need support in accessing key ideas and key language in *John Chapman: Planter and Pioneer,* use the Sentence Talk Routine on pages 476–477 to draw students' attention to the relationship between meaning and the words, phrases, and clauses in the text.

Lesson	Sentence(s) to Deconstruct
1	(p 4) He loved the way the plants grew so thick and tangled.
2	(p 7) One night he slept in a hollowed-out tree stump.
3	(p 11) Besides water, there was hardly anything else to drink out on the wild frontier.
4	(p 21) A meal of honey, fruit, berries, and cornmeal mush cooked in his tin pot was plenty.
5	(p 24) But the wild wolf in the story stayed at Johnny's side to protect him from danger.
6	(p 15) If he could find the right spots to plant his trees, people would come to those places.
12	(p 4) He planted so many apple trees that people stopped calling him John Chapman.
13	(p 28) So they told stories that made him sound like a superman.

SPEAK AND WRITE ABOUT THE TEXT

Use the Text-based Writing Routine on pages 478–479 to model how to speak and write about key ideas and details in *John Chapman: Planter and Pioneer*.

Lesson	Text-based Writing	Scaffolded Frames
1	On page 4, what did John love about the wilderness?	• John loved the way the plants grew _____ and _____. • The thing John loved about the wilderness _____.
2	On page 7, what words tell you where John slept?	• The words "_____" tell me where John slept. • John slept in _____ one night and in _____.
3	According to page 11, why did people on the frontier love apple cider?	• People loved apple cider because there was only _____ to drink. • People on the frontier _____.
4	According to page 21, how was John Chapman a simple man?	• John Chapman ate _____ cooked in his _____. • John Chapman was a simple man because _____.
5	How does the picture on page 24 help you understand that the wild wolf protected John?	• In the picture, the wolf is standing at _____ while John gets close to the _____. This shows me that the wolf is _____ for John. • I understand _____.
6	According to page 15, how did John help build the frontier?	• John _____ so that the _____. • John helped _____.
12	According to page 12, why did people start calling John "Johnny Appleseed"?	• People started calling John "Johnny Appleseed" because he _____. • People started _____.
13	On page 28, for what reason did people begin telling legends about Johnny Appleseed?	• People told _____ about Johnny Appleseed because _____. • People wanted _____.

EXPAND UNDERSTANDING OF VOCABULARY

Use the Dig Deeper Vocabulary Routine on pages 474–475 to continue to develop conceptual understanding of the following adjectives: *tangled, wild, clever, tattered, thankful, drowsy,* and *venomous*. Begin by reviewing the role of adjectives in a sentence. Display and read aloud the following sentence: *John was **cold** because his clothes were **thin***.

Explain that adjectives are used in sentences to describe nouns. Point out that the adjectives *cold* and *thin* describe John and his clothes. Tell students that adjectives can help readers understand what something or someone looks like, acts like, smells like, feels like, or sounds like. Have students work with partners to write sentences using the adjectives.

Name _____

Wilderness and Community

What is the wilderness?

How is the wilderness different from a community?

 Wilderness	• has many trees and wild animals • is quiet • has no people • has no buildings or roads
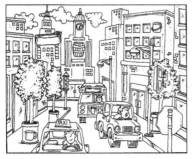 Community	• has some trees and some animals • may be loud • there are many people • there are houses, stores, and roads

Team *Talk*

Share one way the wilderness and a community are different.

In the wilderness, _____.

In a community, _____.

Johnny Appleseed

BUILD BACKGROUND FOR *JOHNNY APPLESEED*

Reproduce and distribute copies of the *Who Were the Settlers?* student page on page 452. Explain that long ago, Americans moved from the East to make new homes in the West. If available, trace a path on a map from the eastern United States to western states such as Indiana or Oklahoma to confirm students' understanding of what it means to travel from east to west. Then read aloud the web as students follow along. You may wish to clarify terms and discuss in more detail some facts on the web. After discussing the web, invite partners to talk about two facts they learned about the settlers.

TALK ABOUT SENTENCES

For students who need support in accessing key ideas and key language in *Johnny Appleseed,* use the Sentence Talk Routine on pages 476–477 to draw students' attention to the relationship between meaning and the words, phrases, and clauses in the text.

Lesson	Sentence(s) to Deconstruct
7	(p 65) Johnny Appleseed (on floor) reading to settlers
8	(p 55) John wanted to see the frontier and help the settlers.
9	(p 63) He sold or gave apple seeds and trees to many settlers there.
10	(p 69) John shared apple seeds, apple trees, and stories.

SPEAK AND WRITE ABOUT THE TEXT

Use the Text-based Writing Routine on pages 478–479 to model how to speak and write about key ideas and details in *Johnny Appleseed*.

Lesson	Text-based Writing	Scaffolded Frames
7	Look at the caption on page 65. What does the caption tell about the picture on page 64?	• The caption tells me that Johnny Appleseed is the man _____ in the picture. • From reading the caption _____.
8	According to page 55, why did John start walking west?	• John wanted to _____ and _____. • John started walking west because _____.
9	Why do you think the settlers called John Chapman "Johnny Appleseed"?	• The settlers called him Johnny Appleseed because he gave or sold _____ and _____ to them. • Settlers gave him the name because _____.
10	According to page 69, why do people today remember Johnny Appleseed?	• Johnny Appleseed helped _____. He shared _____. • People remember Johnny Appleseed because _____.

Name _____

Who Were the Settlers?

Long ago, people called *settlers* moved across the
United States.
They wanted to make new homes in the West.

Settlers moved across the country by horse and wagon.	Some settlers were farmers. Others were people looking for adventure.
Settler Facts	
Settlers were men, women, and children.	Settlers worked hard to build farms and towns.

Share two things you learned about settlers.
I learned that settlers _____.
I also learned _____.

Pioneers to The West

BUILD BACKGROUND FOR *PIONEERS TO THE WEST*

Reproduce and distribute copies of the *What Is a Prairie?* student page on page 455. Explain that to understand the story events in *Pioneers to the West*, it helps to know a little about a landform called a prairie. Begin by explaining that land on Earth is shaped in several different ways. For example, a piece of sloping land that looks as if it touches the sky is a landform called a mountain. Explain that this web will tell about a landform called a prairie. Then help students understand how to read the web. The middle box tells us that the prairie landform is the subject of the web. Each circle surrounding the box tells us one detail about the prairie.

Read the web aloud as students follow along. Clarify terms such as *flat, open, rich,* and *dry.* To confirm students' understanding, you may wish to have them compare details they learn from the web about the prairie with another familiar landform such as a hill or mountain. Scaffold using sentence frames such as: *A mountain is _____, but a prairie is _____. A prairie is better for growing plants than a _____ is because _____.*

After discussing the web, have students share with partners how prairies can differ. Scaffold using sentence frames such as: *Some prairies are _____ and other prairies are _____. Prairies can be _____.* Then have partners share two facts they learned about prairies. You may wish to scaffold with an additional sentence frame: *The _____ on a prairie is _____.*

TALK ABOUT SENTENCES

For students who need support in accessing key ideas and key language in *Pioneers to the West,* use the Sentence Talk Routine on pages 476–477 to draw students' attention to the relationship between meaning and the words, phrases, and clauses in the text.

Lesson	Sentence(s) to Deconstruct
1	(p 9) George never forgot his Sioux mother, and he visited her often.
2	(p 12) John was a quick learner, and he found $100 worth of gold in one day.
3	(p 16) This was a house that was actually "dug out" of the earth.
4	(p 20) A homestead was a piece of land a person could own simply by living on it for five years.
5	(p 27) Throughout the 1800s, thousands of American Indians were forced off the land that their people had lived on for hundreds of years.
6	(p 28) Traveling a well-know path made the trip safer.
11	(p 4) These settlers, or pioneers, left their homes for many reasons.
12	(p 17) The many blizzards, or snowstorms, cut off all supplies.

Use the Text-based Writing Routine on pages 478–479 to model how to speak and write about key ideas and details in *Pioneers to the West*.

Lesson	Text-based Writing	Scaffolded Frames
1	On page 9, how do you know that George Staples was thankful to the Sioux tribe?	• I know that George was thankful because he _____. • George showed thanks by _____.
2	According to page 12, what did John McWilliams learn quickly?	• John quickly learned to _____. • John _____.
3	What does the photograph on page 16 help you better understand about a dugout house?	• The photograph helps me understand how a dugout house was made _____. • I can understand _____.
4	According to page 20, what is a homestead?	• A homestead is a piece of _____ that the _____ allows people to _____ after having lived on it for _____. • A homestead is _____.
5	What does the picture on page 27 show?	• The picture shows Native Americans who had been _____ by the United States government. • The picture shows _____.
6	According to page 28, why did pioneers follow the trails shown on the map?	• The pioneers followed these trails because they were _____ and _____. • The trails were _____.
11	According to page 4, what is a pioneer?	• *Pioneer* is another name for a _____. The pioneers were people who _____ for many reasons. • The word *pioneer* _____.
12	According to page 17, what problem did blizzards cause the Ingalls family?	• Blizzards _____ all the _____ to the Ingalls family. • The blizzards caused _____.

Use the Dig Deeper Vocabulary Routine on pages 474–475 to continue to develop a conceptual understanding of the following abstract nouns from the text: *conflict, fortune, opportunities, destiny,* and *progress*. Then display and read aloud this sentence: *Matt told the **truth** when asked if he took the cookie.*

Point out that in this sentence, the word *truth* comes after the article *the*. Explain that articles such as *a, an,* and *the* in a sentence signal that the word that follows is a noun. Point out that *truth* is an abstract noun. Explain: Some nouns name ideas that may be hard to picture. You cannot see, hear, taste, smell, or touch the things they name. These nouns are hard to define. For example, the noun *truth* names "an agreement with facts or something that is real." You might point out that other nouns, such as *cookie*, are concrete nouns because you can see, hear, taste, smell, or touch the things they name. Then have students work with partners to write sentences using the abstract nouns.

Unit 5 Module B

Name _____

What Is a Prairie?

A prairie is a landform.
Landforms are the different shapes of land on Earth.

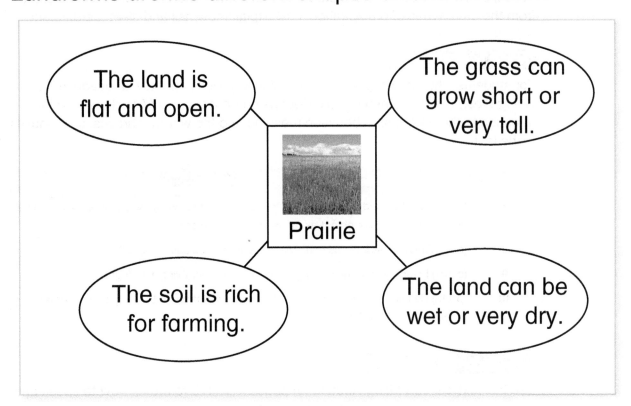

Share two facts you learned about prairie land.

The prairie _____.

Also, _____.

Going West

BUILD BACKGROUND FOR *GOING WEST*

Reproduce and distribute copies of the *Types of Precipitation* student page on page 457. Explain that to understand the story events in *Going West,* it helps to know about the different ways water can fall from the sky. Read aloud the chart. As you read, confirm students' understanding of terms such as *ice, thunderstorms, frozen,* and *air.* Afterward, have students share with a partner how rain is different from the other types of precipitation, and explain how hail and sleet are different.

TALK ABOUT SENTENCES

For students who need support in accessing key ideas and key language in *Going West,* use the Sentence Talk Routine on pages 476–477 to draw students' attention to the relationship between meaning and the words, phrases, and clauses in the text.

Lesson	Sentence(s) to Deconstruct
7	(p 75) But Papa said we were going to a place where anything you planted would grow and a farm could stretch out as far as the eye could see.
8	(p 98) When the storm was over, Mama's garden was squashed flat.
9	(p 101) I crept behind the rocking chair, my knees trembling with fright.
10	(p 113) He hitched our horse to the plow and broke through the tough prairie grass to the dark, rich soil beneath.

SPEAK AND WRITE ABOUT THE TEXT

Use the Text-based Writing Routine on pages 478–479 to model how to speak and write about key ideas and details in *Going West.*

Lesson	Text-based Writing	Scaffolded Frames
7	According to page 75, why did Papa take his family west?	• Papa thought that in the West _____ and _____. • Papa wanted to _____.
8	On page 98, what happens to Mama's garden?	• Mama's garden was _____ because of the storm. • A storm _____.
9	On page 101, why did Hannah hide behind the rocking chair?	• Hannah was _____ of the Indians. • Hannah hid behind it because _____.
10	On page 113, what did Papa do to prepare the land for planting?	• Papa hitched the horse to the _____ and _____ the tough prairie grass. • First, Papa _____. Then he _____.

Unit 5 Module B

Name _____

Types of Precipitation

What are the different kinds of precipitation?

Rain is water that falls from clouds. It rains when the air is warm. 	**Hail** is ice that is made by strong thunderstorms. It hails when the air is hot. 
Sleet is a type of frozen rain. It falls as small balls of ice. Sleet happens when the air is cold. 	**Snow** is soft ice that falls from clouds. It snows when the air is very cold. 

Team *Talk*

How is rain different from hail, sleet, and snow?
Rain is different because _____.
How are sleet and hail different?
Sleet _____, but hail_____.

Name _____

Title _____

I think a lesson that people can learn from Johnny Appleseed is sharing. This is an important lesson because it shows how people can help others live and be happy.

Johnny Appleseed shared the things he owned. For example, he collected apple seeds and apple trees. Then he sold the seeds and trees to settlers. Also, he sometimes even gave the seeds and trees to the settlers without taking money. Then the settlers planted apple orchards so that they could have food for their families. Because Johnny shared, everyone had apples to eat.

What Johnny Appleseed did to help settlers teaches us that it's important to share what we have with others. This is a good lesson because when you share, you will make others happy. And you will be happy, too!

Name _____

Title _____

Prairie Storm

Mia became scared as she saw the sky darken over her sod house. She had not lived on the prairie long, but she already knew how harsh the wind would blow and how heavy the rain would fall.

As Mia ran home, what had been a gentle breeze quickly became a strong wind. Next, she saw a flash of lightning. Then thunder rumbled in the clouds. Finally, the rain began to fall in sheets. All of a sudden, Mia heard a few loud bangs. "That doesn't sound like thunder," she thought. The noise was coming from behind the house.

Mia raced around back. She saw the barn door was wide open and swinging in the wind. "All the animals will get loose!" Mia said. She ran into the wind and rain toward the barn. She used all her strength to push the door closed in the heavy wind. She didn't want the frightened cattle to run away.

She was dripping wet and panting when she finally entered the dark, cool house. "You are a very brave girl," her mother said. Mia felt proud . . . and cold.

Performance-Based Assessment
Unit 5 Module A

Reproduce and distribute copies of the student model on page 458. After completing the Prepare to Write activities on pages 236–237 in Unlock the Writing in Part 2, use the student model to illustrate the features of opinion writing.

Read aloud the first paragraph and discuss its purpose. What lesson did this student write about? Why do you think the writer began the response with the words *I think?* If necessary, remind students that using the words *I think* makes it clear to readers that you are stating your opinion. What is the writer's opinion about the lesson?

Explain that a writer uses reasons and examples to support his or her opinion and as a way to persuade or convince readers to agree with the opinion. Read aloud the second paragraph. What reasons and example does the writer use to explain how Johnny Appleseed teaches people about sharing? How do these reasons and examples support the writer's opinion?

Read aloud the last paragraph. Point out that the writer concludes by restating his or her opinion. Which sentence restates the writer's opinion? Then have students work with a partner to discuss the writer's opinion and share one reason the writer gives to support his or her opinion. Scaffold with sentence frames such as: *The writer thinks _____. The writer thinks this because _____.*

Unit 5 Module B

Reproduce and distribute copies of the student model on page 459. After completing the Prepare to Write activities on pages 242–243 in Unlock the Writing in Part 2, use the student model to illustrate the features of a narrative.

Read aloud the first paragraph and discuss it with students. From what we know about life on the prairie, we can tell the story takes place long ago because the character, Mia, lives in a sod house. Who can tell us what the problem in this story is? *The problem is _____.*

Read the story aloud as students follow along. Pause to discuss details the writer uses to tell about the character's thoughts, feelings, and actions as you read the story. Also, point out words and phrases the writer uses to sequence the events. Why does the writer begin the sentences in paragraph 2 with the words *next, then,* and *finally?*

Point to the last paragraph as you read it aloud. This paragraph ends the story. It is called a conclusion. This conclusion shows how Mia felt at the end of the story. It is a good conclusion because it shows that Mia solved her problem.

68 Ways to Save the Planet Before Bedtime

Reproduce and distribute copies of the student page *Fossil Fuels* on page 463. Explain to students that in order to better understand *68 Ways to Save the Planet Before Bedtime,* it is important to know about fossil fuels. Name the three fossil fuels and explain that they were formed deep within the earth over a very long time from plants and animals that died over 300 million years ago. Point out the importance of fossil fuels in energy production and the negative impact that burning fossil fuels has on Earth's environment. Go on to briefly explain that the fossil fuels are nonrenewable resources, meaning that once people use them up, it will take millions of years for Earth to produce more.

Then help students read the chart. Point to the row that will tell us about coal. Now, point to the column that will tell us where each fossil fuel is found. Then read aloud the information in the chart as students follow along. Pause to clarify challenging terms. Then have students discuss with partners why fossil fuels are important. Scaffold with sentence frames such as: *All three fuels _____. _____ is important because _____.*

Then have partners share a similarity between how all three fossil fuels are used and one fact they learned about fossil fuels.

For students who need support in accessing key ideas and key language in *68 Ways to Save the Planet Before Bedtime,* use the Sentence Talk Routine on pages 476–477 to draw students' attention to the relationship between meaning and the words, phrases, and clauses in the text.

Lesson	Sentence(s) to Deconstruct
1	(p 2) That might *sound* like a good thing, but even the smallest rise in temperature can have *big* effects on our planet.
2	(p 4) Without them there would be too many flies, and that would mean plants would not grow as well.
3	(p 8) The heating in many buildings uses electricity, which is usually made with fossil fuels, or gas, which *is* a fossil fuel.
4	(p 14) Quite a lot of what we throw away is actually stuff that could be reused or turned into something else.
5	(p 16) The next time you plan to go somewhere, think "Can I go by bike?"
6	(p 21) Do a sponsored walk, swim, or cycle for an environmental charity.
12	(p 6) You know what that means: longer journeys = more greenhouse gases.
13	(p 22) Great news: you've already started to think differently by reading this book!

Use the Text-based Writing Routine on pages 478–479 to model how to speak and write about key ideas and details in *68 Ways to Save the Planet Before Bedtime*.

Lesson	Text-based Writing	Scaffolded Frames
1	According to page 2, why is global warming not a good thing?	• Global warming is not a good thing because even the _____ in temperature has _____ on the planet. • Global warming _____.
2	According to page 4, why are spiders important?	• Spiders are an important part of the _____. • Without spiders, there would be _____ and _____. • Spiders are important because _____.
3	On page 8, what is made using a fossil fuel?	• Fossil fuels are used to make _____. • Usually, _____.
4	On page 14, what do the text and pictures tell us about reusing?	• We can reuse _____ by _____. • The text and pictures show us how to _____.
5	How does the illustration on page 16 explain why bikes are better than cars?	• The illustration shows _____. This tells me that _____. • I can tell by the illustration that _____.
6	According to page 21, what can you do to raise money for an environmental charity?	• I can do a sponsored _____, _____, or _____ for an environmental charity. • To raise money, _____.
12	According to page 6, what effect does the shipping of clothing have on the environment?	• When clothes have to travel _____ they cause more _____ to be released. • When a person buys clothes _____.
13	According to page 22, what affect does the author hope you have after reading this book?	• The author wants us to _____ about Earth. • The author wants _____.

Use the Dig Deeper Routine on pages 474–475 to continue to develop a conceptual understanding of the following nouns: *resources, litter, waste, passenger, packaging, charity,* and *pollution*. Begin by reviewing that a noun names a person, place, or thing. Display and read aloud the following sentence: *I can trade my* **clothes** *with a* **friend***.*

Point out the nouns in the sentence: *clothes* and *friend*. Explain that the word *clothes* names a thing and *friend* names a person. Explain that a noun can be the object of a verb in a sentence. Point out that in this sentence, *clothes* is the object of the verb *trade*. Also explain that the object of a preposition is always a noun. Then point out that *friend* is the object of the preposition *with* in the sentence. Have students work with partners to write sentences using the nouns.

Unit 6 Module A

Name _____

Fossil Fuels

What are the fossil fuels?

Fossil Fuel	Where It Is Found	What It Looks Like	How It Is Used
Coal	in the ground	black rock or brown dirt	• to make electricity • to make soaps and medicine
Oil	in the ground between rocks	black, thick liquid	• to make electricity • to heat homes • to fuel cars
Natural Gas	in the ground near oil	cannot be seen	• to make electricity • to heat homes • to cook food

What do people use all three fossil fuels for?

People use all the fossil fuels _____.

Share one fact you learned about fossil fuels.

I learned _____.

On Meadowview Street

BUILD BACKGROUND FOR *ON MEADOWVIEW STREET*

Reproduce and distribute copies of the *Animal Homes* student page on page 465. Explain that to understand *On Meadowview Street,* it helps to know where animals live. Review the meaning of *backyard*, then explain that there are animals people may see in their backyards. Explain that the chart shows these animals and where they make their homes. Read aloud the chart as students follow along. Then invite students to discuss with a partner an animal they might see in their backyard or near their home and where they think that animal might live. Scaffold with additional sentence frames such as: *A (n) _____ is in my backyard. A (n) _____ lives in_____.*

TALK ABOUT SENTENCES

For students who need support in accessing key ideas and key language in *On Meadowview Street,* use the Sentence Talk Routine on pages 476–477 to draw students' attention to the relationship between meaning and the words, phrases, and clauses in the text.

Lesson	Sentence(s) to Deconstruct
7	(p 12) As the grass grew taller, more flowers popped up all over the yard.
8	(p 4) Caroline was about to explore the new street to see if there *was* a meadow on Meadowview Street when she noticed a small blossom.
9	(p 20) In no time there were birds and insects everywhere, around the tree and zipping among the flowers.
10	(p 23) She lugged large rocks to the edge, making ledges and little caverns for creatures to live in.

SPEAK AND WRITE ABOUT THE TEXT

Use the Text-based Writing Routine on pages 478–479 to model how to speak and write about key ideas and details in *On Meadowview Street.*

Lesson	Text-based Writing	Scaffolded Frames
7	On page 12, what happens as the grass in Caroline's yard grows taller?	• As the grass grows taller, _____ popped up in the yard. • As the grass grew _____.
8	On page 4, what does Caroline notice in the grass?	• Caroline notices a _____ in the grass. • Caroline _____.
9	According to page 20, what was Caroline's yard like?	• There were _____ and _____ everywhere. • In Caroline's yard, _____ and _____.
10	In what way does the illustration on page 23 tell more about the text?	• I can tell by the illustration _____ and _____. • The illustration shows _____.

Name _____

Animal Homes

You may see animals in your backyard.
Where do these animals make their homes?

Animal	Where it Lives
bird	in a nest in a tree
frog	near a pond
rabbit	in a burrow

What other animal might you see in your backyard?
In my backyard, I might see _____.
Where does this animal make its home?
The animal makes its home _____.

Alfred Nobel: The Man Behind the Peace Prize

Reproduce and distribute copies of the *Why Dynamite?* student page on page 468. Explain that to understand the information in *Alfred Nobel: The Man Behind the Peace Prize,* it helps to know how people used dynamite to do important jobs. Review that dynamite is a kind of explosive that can be burned to make holes in rock or blow large rocks into smaller pieces. Then help students understand how to read the chart. Read aloud the heading for the first column. Discuss how each entry in this column describes one way people used dynamite by naming an action. Then, read aloud the heading for the second column and explain that this column names what dynamite helped people build. Next, read the chart with students. If necessary, scaffold to confirm students' understanding: *You can use dynamite to _____. People can make _____ with dynamite.*

After discussing the chart, invite partners to talk about an action and result of using dynamite. Scaffold with a sentence frame such as: *People used dynamite to _____ so that they could _____.* Then, have partners share one way people used dynamite.

TALK ABOUT SENTENCES

For students who need support in accessing key ideas and key language in *Alfred Nobel: The Man Behind the Peace Prize,* use the Sentence Talk Routine on pages 476–477 to draw students' attention to the relationship between meaning and the words, phrases, and clauses in the text.

Lesson	Sentence(s) to Deconstruct
1	(p 125) Upon the anvil was a drop of liquid nitroglycerin.
2	(p 126) Most often, gunpowder was used for these purposes, but it wasn't very safe.
3	(p 141) He thought that if people were afraid of the harm that explosions could cause, perhaps they would settle things peacefully first.
4	(p 142) People everywhere were shocked by the news, but nobody was more shocked than Alfred Nobel.
5	(p 138) But to the world, Alfred Nobel had invented something called dynamite.
6	(p 146) The entire estate of Alfred Nobel, one of the richest men in all of Europe, would be used to create yearly prizes for those who have rendered the greatest services to humankind.
11	(p 136) The rods would ignite only if they had a blasting cap, making them unlikely to explode on their own.
12	(p 141) In many countries, people began to use dynamite to solve problems by hurting others.

SPEAK AND WRITE ABOUT THE TEXT

Use the Text-based Writing Routine on pages 478–479 to model how to speak and write about key ideas and details in *Alfred Nobel: The Man Behind the Peace Prize*.

Lesson	Text-based Writing	Scaffolded Frames
1	On page 125, what event is the writer describing?	• A _____ of nitroglycerin fell on the anvil. This made Alfred think about the ____ of the liquid. • Alfred Nobel began to think about _____ when _____.
2	Use information from page 126 to compare and contrast the uses of nitroglycerin and gunpowder.	• Nitroglycerin _____, while gunpowder _____. • Both nitroglycerin and gunpowder _____.
3	On page 141, how does Alfred think people will feel about his new invention?	• Because his invention _____, Alfred thinks _____. • Alfred thinks people will _____.
4	On page 142, how does the reason why people were shocked compare to the reason why Alfred was shocked?	• People were shocked because _____, but Alfred was shocked because _____. • The people _____, but Alfred _____.
5	On page 138, what did you learn about the name for dynamite?	• I learned that Alfred _____. • I learned that to the world, _____.
6	On page 146, what words does the writer use to explain why Alfred could create these prizes?	• The writer uses the words "_____" to explain why Alfred could create these prizes. • The words "_____" tell the reader that _____.
11	On page 136, what was the purpose of the blasting cap?	• The blasting cap would keep the dynamite from _____. • The purpose of the blasting cap _____.
12	On page 141, why was Alfred sad about his new invention?	• Alfred had hoped dynamite would bring _____. Instead, people were using dynamite to _____. • Alfred was sad because _____.

EXPAND UNDERSTANDING OF VOCABULARY

Use the Dig Deeper Routine on pages 474–475 to continue to develop conceptual understanding of the following specific nouns: *anvil, plug, blasting cap, ports, dynamite, obituary, will, estate, humankind,* and *legacy.* Begin by reviewing the role specific nouns play in a sentence. Display and read aloud the following sentences:

*Put the **piece** in the drain to save the water.*
*Put the **plug** in the drain to save the water.*

Point out that a *plug* is a piece of material that can be placed in the drain of a tub to keep the water from emptying out. Then, discuss how the word *plug* provides the reader with more specific information about the type of piece being used in this sentence. Then, invite students to write sentences using the nouns.

Name _____

Why Dynamite?

What were the uses of dynamite?

Action	Result
to make large holes in mountains	Tunnels were built for cars and trains.
to break large rocks into smaller pieces	Miners could move rock more easily.
to take down large buildings	Land was cleared to build new things.

Team *Talk*

Share one way people used dynamite.

People used dynamite to _____.

A Picture Book of Eleanor Roosevelt

Reproduce and distribute copies of the *The First Lady* student page on page 470. Explain that to understand *A Picture Book of Eleanor Roosevelt,* it helps to know what a first lady is. You may wish to explain that the first lady is married to the President of the United States. You may also wish to clarify that not all first ladies do all the jobs listed on the web. Read the web aloud as students follow along, confirming their understanding of terms as you read. Next, have students discuss the web with partners. Scaffold with sentence frames such as: *The first lady is _____. A job that a first lady does is _____.* Then have partners share two things they learned about the job of first lady.

TALK ABOUT SENTENCES

For students who need support in accessing key ideas and key language in *A Picture Book of Eleanor Roosevelt,* use the Sentence Talk Routine on pages 476–477 to draw students' attention to the relationship between meaning and the words, phrases, and clauses in the text.

Lesson	Sentence(s) to Deconstruct
7	(p 158) She felt she was starting a new life.
8	(p 160) While Eleanor was in England, her uncle, Theodore Roosevelt, became the president of the United States.
9	(p 169) She brought back detailed reports on what she heard and saw.
10	(p 176) When she came home, she brought messages from the soldiers to their families.

SPEAK AND WRITE ABOUT THE TEXT

Use the Text-based Writing Routine on pages 478–479 to model how to speak and write about key ideas and details in *A Picture Book of Eleanor Roosevelt.*

Lesson	Text-based Writing	Scaffolded Frames
7	Use information on page 158 to explain why this moment of Eleanor's life was important.	• Before, Eleanor felt like _____. Now Eleanor felt like _____. • This was an important moment for Eleanor because _____.
8	On page 160, what important event happened?	• Eleanor's uncle Theodore became _____. • While Eleanor _____, her _____.
9	What does the text on page 169 help you understand about Eleanor?	• Eleanor felt it was important for her to _____ the president. • I can understand that Eleanor _____ because _____.
10	What details on page 176 give you more clues about Eleanor's character?	• I learned that Eleanor was _____ first lady. • From the details, I can tell that Eleanor _____.

Name _____

The First Lady

What might a first lady do?

welcomes and hosts visitors to the White House	goes to important events with the president

First Lady

supports important causes and issues	helps the president make decisions

Share two things you learned about the job of the first lady.

A first lady _____.

Another thing a first lady may do is _____.

Name _____

Title _____

My Book Review

I think that anyone who reads On Meadowview Street will want to do something to preserve nature. This story teaches us that it's easy to preserve nature in our own backyards.

In the book, Caroline turns her backyard into a nature preserve. She does this by planting trees and letting wildflowers grow. Soon animals and insects come to live in her backyard.

The book also shows us how we can build homes for animals. Caroline built a birdhouse for a wren and a pond for small creatures.

The illustrations helped me understand how Caroline changed their plain backyard into a beautiful nature preserve. The illustrations would make any reader want to do this, too.

We think that preserving nature is hard, but this book shows readers it's easy to make changes to preserve nature.

Name _____

Title _____

Eleanor Roosevelt

In A Picture Book of Eleanor Roosevelt, David A. Adler argues that Eleanor brought hope to many people. I think he is right because Eleanor used words and actions to help others during hard times.

The author says that Eleanor had a radio program and wrote a newspaper column. In these ways, Eleanor could share her thoughts and ideas about many issues. Therefore, her words could bring hope to the American people.

The author also says that Eleanor visited soliders who were fighting in World War II. When she returned, she brought messages from the soldiers to their families.

Through her words and actions, Eleanor gave Americans hope about the future.

Performance-Based Assessment
Unit 6 Module A

DISCUSS THE STUDENT MODEL

Reproduce and distribute copies of the student model on page 471. After completing the Prepare to Write activities on pages 248–249 in Unlock the Writing in Part 2, use the student model to illustrate the features of a book review and its benefits for helping people choose books to read.

Read aloud the first paragraph and then discuss the paragraph with students. Notice how the writer grabs the readers attention in the first paragraph by stating his or her opinion about why people should read the book. You can tell that this sentence states the writer's opinion because it begins with the words *I think*.

Continue reading to the end of the book review. As you read, pause to discuss reasons and evidence that the writer has provided to support his or her opinion that the book will encourage readers to preserve nature. Have students point to transition words as you read them aloud. When you use the word *also*, the reader knows that you are connecting your ideas together.

Point to the conclusion. Say: See how the writer ends the review by restating his or her opinion?

Unit 6 Module B

DISCUSS THE STUDENT MODEL

Reproduce and distribute copies of the student model on page 472. After completing the Prepare to Write activities on pages 254–255 in Unlock the Writing in Part 2, use the student model to illustrate the features of opinion writing.

Read aloud the first sentence and discuss how it introduces the opinion David A. Adler includes about Eleanor Roosevelt. Then read the second sentence of the first paragraph. How does this sentence introduce the writer's opinion about Adler's opinion of Eleanor? If students have difficulty identifying the writer's opinion about Adler's opinion, underline the phrase *I think he is right,* circle *because,* and discuss what reason the writer then provides to support this opinion.

Next, have students read the first body paragraph. What is the first reason the writer discusses? Show me the details the writer provides to tell more about this reason. What linking words does the writer use to connect the reasons to the opinion? Repeat with the second body paragraph.

Finally, discuss the conclusion. Note how the writer restates the opinion to provide a sense of closure.

Dig Deeper Vocabulary

Use this routine to help students acquire a more in-depth understanding for select academic vocabulary. Through discussion using multimodal methods, students will unlock the meaning of vocabulary so they can use the words and learn elements of syntax.

1. Display the words listed in the Expand Understanding of Vocabulary section of the current Unit/Module Part 4 Unlock Language Learning lesson. Explain to students that these words appear in the text they are reading and that they are all similar in some way. For example, all words are verbs.

2. Model reading the words. Then have students practice reading the words aloud with you. Poll students about their familiarity with each word in order to gauge understanding.

3. Convey the meaning of the words using different modalities such as showing a picture from a magazine or the Internet, drawing a picture, acting out or gesturing, or using realia. Describe each word in context to guide students to associate the new words with familiar vocabulary. For example, act out the meaning of *shrugged* for students. I can act out the meaning of this word by shrugging my shoulders. Shrug your shoulders and then say: I shrugged my shoulders. Now you act out how to shrug.

4. Enrich students with a deeper understanding of each word by creating a list of synonyms. Provide students with one or two examples of synonyms for each word, then proceed to generate a list of additional synonyms with students.

5. Have students turn to a partner and take turns telling a sentence for each word. Use sentence frames as needed. For example: *I ___ when I ____. When I don't know ___, I shrug.*

6. Help students understand how different types of words function in a sentence. For example, share a sentence in which you signal out a specific kind of word or phrase using different colors to write each part of the sentence. Then explain the parts of the sentence and ask students to identify specific words or phrases in the sentence. Look at this example for using action words:

The boy shrugged when he didn't know the answer.

Explain that the first part of the sentence names a person, place, or thing. What is the person, place, or thing in the sentence? (The boy) The action word comes next. What is the action word? (shrugged) The rest of the sentence tells us more about what is happening. When did the boy shrug? (when he didn't know the answer)

TEACHING TIPS

- Have students use different modalities to figure out the meaning of words. Doing this aids their understanding, since they are using different formats to gain meaning.

- Have students write each vocabulary word on separate index cards and add a simple drawing or photograph from the Internet or a magazine that exemplifies the word on the back. Students can work in pairs to look at the picture and then name the word.

EXTEND

Have students create a word web relating the vocabulary words to other words they know. For example, words can be the same part of speech or have similar affixes, sounds, or meanings. Have students discuss how understanding word meanings helps them better understand the meaning of stories they read.

Sentence Talk

PURPOSE

Use this routine to deconstruct complex sentences from the texts that students are reading. Through instructional conversations students analyze key ideas, vocabulary, and sentence structures.

PROCEDURE

1. Identify a complex sentence from the current text. Recommended sentences can be found in the **Talk About Sentence**s section of the Part 4 Unlock Language Learning lessons for each Unit/Module. Sentences should include key details or explain a key concept, important vocabulary, and phrases and clauses that merit attention. They may also include figurative language.

2. Decide how to break up the sentence for discussion, focusing on identifying meaning-based phrases and clauses. For example, you could break the sentence below into three parts.

    In the winter, I like to go ice skating in Central Park.

3. Display the sentence, writing each sentence part in a different color. Prepare conversation starters to focus students' attention on each sentence part. As you discuss each part of the sentence, record students' comments.

    - What season does the first part of the sentence tell about?
    - Why is the word *skating* an important word? Turn and talk to a partner about what you know about *skating*.
    - Suppose the author was telling about an activity you do in the summer. What words might replace *ice* and *skating*?

4. Identify key words that may need to be defined in context or have structural significance.

    - What words does the author use to tell about winter? Yes, *ice* and *skating*. In the winter, the water in ponds turns to ice that people can skate on.
    - Now let's read the entire sentence together. The word *like* tells me that the author is going to talk about things that he or she likes.

5. Initiate the activity with students by reading together the page or paragraph in which the sentence appears. Have students turn and talk to a partner about key ideas and details in the text.

6. Then draw attention to the color-coded sentence on display. Use the conversation starters you prepared to focus students' attention on each part of the sentence. Students should take an active role and should be speaking as much or more than you do in this conversation. Periodically, also have students turn and talk to a partner or a small group of peers. Record students' responses during the conversation and reread them at the end of the conversation.

7. Reread the entire sentence and have students discuss or write about what it means. Provide scaffolds as necessary.

- The season is _____.
- Isabel goes ice skating in _____.
- That means that ice skating _____.

TEACHING TIPS

- When recording students comments, write each comment in the same color as the sentence part it refers to.
- Create and display a list of key words and phrases from the Sentence Talk Instructional conversations and encourage students to use the vocabulary when they speak and write about the text.

EXTEND

Have students discuss how understanding the meaning of the sentence helps them better understand the overall meaning of the text. Ask: What was the most important thing you learned? What will you keep in mind as you continue to read?

Text-Based Writing

Use this routine to explore linguistic and rhetorical patterns and registers in writing. Model how to include evidence from text in a written response.

From the section of the text that was read closely that day, present students with a question for guided/shared writing. See the **Text-Based Writing** column in the Speak and Write About the Text section of the English Language Learners Support lesson for recommended questions.

1. Write the question on the board and read it aloud with students. For example: *On page 8, why did Kelvin start collecting electronic parts that people had thrown away?* Identify key words in the question and check understanding. Help students determine what the question is asking and what information they need to respond to it. The question asks why Kelvin started to collect electronic parts. What are electronic parts? Electronic parts are parts of plastic and metal from larger machines. I can tell from the question that Kelvin must need those electronic parts for something. How can we find out why Kelvin needs the electronic parts? *We can ____to find evidence in the text about ____.*

2. Locate and read aloud the sentence/sentences in the text that the question refers to. If appropriate, also read the text that comes before/after the sentence. Lead students in a discussion of the text, checking comprehension and explaining key vocabulary and concepts as needed.

   To answer this question, first we need to think about the problem that Kelvin's family had. What is the main problem in this part of the selection? *Kelvin's family does not have ____.* Batteries are needed to make lights work. Why will collecting electronic parts help solve the problem? *Electronic parts can be used ____.* Which words show that to have light, you need batteries? *"The lights needed_____ to work."* Kelvin could help his family if he could give them batteries. Which words show what Kelvin does? *"Kelvin used the parts to ____.'* Kelvin started collecting electronic parts so he could build batteries to provide light for his family.

3. Guide students to answer the question orally, using the scaffolded sentence frames as needed. Check that students use a rhetorical pattern appropriate to the question. For example, a question that asks *why* something occurred should elicit a response that identifies a cause and effect.

4. Read aloud the question again for students: *On page 8, why did Kelvin start collecting electronic parts that people had thrown away?* Then model writing a response, talking through the process as you write.

   Kelvin started collecting electronic parts so he could build batteries to provide light for his family.

I will start my sentence with a capital letter. The verb *colleting* tells what Kelvin does. What does he do? He collects old electronic parts. Now I will use text evidence to tell why he does this. He does this so that he can build batteries because his family cannot afford to buy batteries. I will add those words to my sentence. I will put a period here to show that this is the end of the sentence.

5. Have students write their answers. For shared writing, have students work with a partner.

6. Give students the opportunity to share their writing with the group. Have students read their answers aloud or write them on the board. Check that students have used appropriate linguistic and rhetorical patterns and included text evidence as needed.

TEACHING TIPS

- Use graphic organizers, such as idea webs and cause/effect charts, to help students organize the text evidence needed to answer the questions.
- As you evaluate students' writing, identify sentences that can be expanded by adding details.
- Encourage students to write in complete sentences to reflect the more formal register of written English.

EXTEND

Ask a second question about the day's close read section and have students work with a partner or independently to discuss and write a response.

Clarifying Key Details

Use this routine to provide frames for conducting accountable conversations that require clarification.

PROCEDURE

1. Explain: Sometimes I don't understand what someone says. Maybe the speaker talks very softly. Maybe the speaker uses words I do not know. Maybe the speaker needs to give key details to explain an idea. When this happens, I need to ask questions so I will understand. This is called *clarifying*.

2. Explain that sometimes others might have questions about what students say. Remind students that they should answer other students' questions clearly and help them understand.

3. Remind students that when they ask questions in a group, they should be polite and not interrupt. Wait until the person finishes speaking. Then say, "excuse me," and ask your question.

4. Share the worksheet on the following page with students. Read the questions aloud, then talk about situations in which they might use the questions. Model completing the sentence frames using a topic that is familiar to students.

5. Have students use the questions and frames in a discussion about a selection you have recently read.

TEACHING TIPS

- Have students role-play discussions in which they ask questions for clarification.
- Create a classroom poster listing useful clarifying questions for students to refer to as needed.

EXTEND

Have students think of more clarifying questions and add them to the worksheet. Have them practice asking the questions with a partner or in a group.

Clarifying Key Details

Look at the examples of questions.
Use them when you don't understand what the speaker says.

When you did not hear what the speaker said:
I did not hear you. Can you please say that again?

When you do not understand what the speaker means:
You said _____. What does that mean?

I do not understand _____. Can you please explain?

Can you give me more details?

When someone says something you think is wrong:
I think you made a mistake. Can you show me in the book?

When you answer someone's question:
What I mean is _____.
I will explain _____.

Clarifying Information

PURPOSE

Use this routine to provide frames for conducting accountable conversations that require elaboration.

PROCEDURE

1. **Explain:** Sometimes I need more information to understand what a speaker means. I can ask the speaker for more details. I can ask the speaker to explain. This is called elaborating.

2. **Point out that sometimes students might want to add to a group discussion.** I can give more information in a discussion, too. I can explain my ideas. I can give information and evidence from the text.

3. **Remind students that when they want to say something in a group discussion, they should be polite and not interrupt.** Wait until the person finishes speaking. Then say, "excuse me" and speak.

4. **Share the worksheet on the following page with students. Talk about situations in which they might use the questions and statements. Model completing the sentence frames using a topic that is familiar to students.**

5. **Have students work with a partner to write an elaborating question and answer in the conversation at the bottom of the worksheet.**

TEACHING TIPS

- Have students role-play discussions in which they ask for and give more information.
- Create a classroom poster listing useful elaboration questions for students to refer to as needed.

EXTEND

Have students role-play another conversation between Pat and Dan, using the frames to ask for and give more information about another topic, such as a favorite sport.

Clarifying Information

Look at the examples of questions and statements.
Use them when you want to clarify information.

When you want more information from the speaker:

I want to know more about _____.

Can you give more details about _____?

When you want to give more information:

This makes me think _____.

I believe this is true because _____.

Pat and Dan are talking. Dan needs to ask for more information. Pat needs to give more information. Write a question and an answer.

Jan: Can you give more details about _____?

Pat: I believe _____ is important because _____.

Reach an Agreement

PURPOSE

Use this routine to provide frames for conducting accountable conversations that require reaching an agreement.

PROCEDURE

1. **Explain:** Sometimes when I work with a group, my group has to decide something together. We all have to agree on something or make a decision. This is called reaching agreement.

2. **Explain that sometimes when they are in a group, students must tell what they think.** Tell others what you think. Give reasons and evidence to explain your ideas and feelings.

3. **Point out that all the members of the group should have a chance to tell what they think.** Ask what others think. Listen carefully. If you need more information to understand what they think, ask for more information. **Remind students to use the frames they practiced on the other worksheets.**

4. **Explain that group members may agree or disagree.** Maybe you have the same idea as someone else. This is called agreeing. Maybe you have a different idea. Maybe you think someone's ideas are incorrect. This is called disagreeing. You can say if you agree or disagree. Give reasons and evidence.

5. **Remind students that it is important to be polite when they disagree.** If you disagree, be polite. Explain why in a friendly way.

6. **Explain that to reach an agreement, most of the group members must agree.** If some group members do not agree, you can vote. Count how many people agree. Count how many disagree.

7. **Read the worksheet on the following page aloud to the students. Talk about situations in which they might use the questions and statements. Model completing the sentence frames using a topic that is familiar to students.**

TEACHING TIPS

- Have students have discussions in which they express ideas and build agreement.
- Create a classroom poster listing useful frames for students to refer to as needed.

EXTEND

Have students work with a group to choose the best activity for a rainy day. Remind them to use the frames on the worksheet to express their ideas and agree or disagree. Encourage them to reach an agreement. Have groups present their conclusions. Suggest this frame: *My group thinks _____ because _____.*

Reach an Agreement

Look at the examples of questions and statements.
Use them when your group must decide something.

When you say what you think:

I think _____.

When you ask what others think:

What do you think, [name]?

When you agree:

I agree with [name] because _____.

When you disagree:

I disagree with [name] because _____.

When you both disagree and agree:

I think you are right about _____, but I do not agree that _____.

When you want to vote:

How many people think _____?

Scaffolded Reading/Writing Goals

UNIT 1: MODULE A

Reading Goal: Readers will use dialogue and actions to identify the points of view of characters in stories.

Emerging	Expanding	Bridging
Readers use what characters do and say to tell about the characters' thoughts.	Readers use the words of the characters and describe how characters act to tell about the characters' thoughts.	Readers show understanding that characters have unique points of view.

Writing Goal: Writers will write a narrative story in which they recount one or more sequenced events.

Emerging	Expanding	Bridging
Writers illustrate a short sequence of events about characters.	Writers use a writing model to help them write and illustrate a narrative that has a beginning, middle, and end.	Writers write a narrative that has a beginning, middle, and end and uses signal words.

UNIT 1: MODULE B

Reading Goal: Readers will identify main topics and key details in informational texts.

Emerging	Expanding	Bridging
Readers describe topics and details in informational texts.	Readers make connections between topics and details in informational texts.	Readers explain how details support topics and ideas in informational texts.

Writing Goal: Writers will write a compare-and-contrast paragraph that introduces a topic and includes facts.

Emerging	Expanding	Bridging
Writers use language to introduce communities and restate facts about each. Writers also write a closing sentence.	Writers use language to compare and contrast communities. Writers include introductory and closing sentences.	Writers introduce communities, then make comparisons and contrasts about each. They include specific and relevant details and close with a concluding sentence.

UNIT 2: MODULE A

Reading Goal: Readers will describe the structure of a story by identifying its beginning, middle, and end.

Emerging	Expanding	Bridging
Readers use illustrations and language to identify what happens first, next, and last in a story.	Readers describe what happens in the beginning, middle, and end of a story.	Readers use transitions words when describing the beginning, middle, and end of a story.

Writing Goal: Writers will compose a narrative with details that describe characters' actions, thoughts, and feelings.

Emerging	Expanding	Bridging
Writers illustrate a narrative about a child who struggles to earn and save money.	Writers use sentence frames to describe a narrative about a girl's struggle with earning and saving money.	Writers fully describe, in narrative form, a girl's struggle with earning and saving money.

UNIT 2: MODULE B

Reading Goal: Readers will ask and answer questions about details and information in a text.

Emerging	Expanding	Bridging
Readers explain details in the text.	Readers ask questions about details and information in the text.	Readers ask and answer questions about details and information in the text.

Writing Goal: Writers will compose an opinion paragraph that uses reasons to support their opinion.

Emerging	Expanding	Bridging
Writers introduce an opinion about something they want and provide one reason.	Writers use sentence frames to detail an opinion about something they want.	Writers introduce a clear, persuasive, and interesting opinion about something they want, providing reasons. They finish with a concluding sentence.

UNIT 3: MODULE A

Reading Goal: Readers will explain how illustrations and text features help them make better sense of what they read.

Emerging	Expanding	Bridging
Readers use illustrations and language frames to retell key ideas and details.	Readers use illustrations and language frames to make connections between key ideas and details.	Readers use illustrations and language frames to explain key ideas and important details.

Writing Goal: Writers will create a biographical sketch using multiple sources.

Emerging	Expanding	Bridging
Writers learn about a famous American.	Writers research and write questions about a famous American.	Writers research and write detailed questions and answers about a famous American.

UNIT 3: MODULE B

Reading Goal: Readers will explain how asking and answering questions leads them to understand key details in texts.

Emerging	Expanding	Bridging
Readers about informational texts.	Readers ask and answer questions about informational texts.	Readers explain how asking and answering questions can help them understand informational texts.

Writing Goal: Writers will create an explanatory text that introduces a topic and develops it with facts and details.

Emerging	Expanding	Bridging
Writers draw pictures of a new park.	Writers use language and a detailed illustration to describe a new park.	Writers use language and details to describe a new park in their community.

UNIT 4: MODULE A

Reading Goal: Readers will recount and describe characters' challenges in stories.

Emerging	Expanding	Bridging
Readers use illustrations and language to tell about characters in the story.	Readers use illustrations and language to tell about problems that characters in the story face.	Readers explain the challenges that characters in the story face.

Writing Goal: Writers will create narrative texts that include challenges and characters' responses to those challenges.

Emerging	Expanding	Bridging
Writers to briefly tell a short narrative about an adventure.	Writers tell a short narrative about an adventure. Writers provide a short sequence of events and include temporal words.	Writers tell a short narrative about an adventure with a sequence of events. Writers include temporal words and use vivid details to describe characters' thoughts, actions, and feelings. They conclude with a clear resolution.

UNIT 4: MODULE B

Reading Goal: Readers will identify multiple main topics in an informational text.

Emerging	Expanding	Bridging
Readers use visuals and language frames to describe main topics in informational texts.	Readers use language frames to describe main topics and then connect these topics with relevant details.	Readers describe main topics and then explain how details support the topics and ideas.

Writing Goal: Writers will compose an informative/explanatory text with facts, definitions, and a conclusion.

Emerging	Expanding	Bridging
Writers illustrate facts about a main idea.	Writers use illustrations and sentence frames to tell facts about a main idea and then provide a conclusion.	Writers write an informative text about a main idea. They include details, definitions, and a conclusion.

UNIT 5: MODULE A

Reading Goal: Readers will compare and contrast main ideas from two texts on the same topic.

Emerging	Expanding	Bridging
Readers use language frames to discuss similarities and differences between two informational selections on the same topic.	Readers discuss and explain how key ideas and details are the same and different in two informational selections on the same topic.	Readers compare and contrast key ideas and details in two informational selections on the same topic.

Writing Goal: Writers will state an opinion and support it with reasons.

Emerging	Expanding	Bridging
Writers use language frames to state an opinion.	Writers use language frames to state and support an opinion with reasons.	Writers state an opinion and support it with reasons and examples using linking words.

UNIT 5: MODULE B

Reading Goal: Readers will identify and use story structure and text features to understand texts.

Emerging	Expanding	Bridging
Readers use illustrations in a text to understand writing.	Readers use illustrations and language to explain a text.	Readers explain using story structure and text features can help them.

Writing Goal: Writers will support an opinion with reasons and evidence from the text they have read.

Emerging	Expanding	Bridging
Writers introduce an opinion.	Writers use language to tell about an opinion. They include several supporting details.	Writers use language to introduce their opinion. They include many specific supporting sentences. They also write concluding sentences.

UNIT 6: MODULE A

Reading Goal: Readers will identify and use story structure and text features to understand texts.

Emerging	Expanding	Bridging
Readers use illustrations and simple text to understand writing.	Readers use illustrations and language to explain how writers identify and use story structure.	Readers use illustrations and language to explain how story structure and text features can help them understand informational texts.

Writing Goal: Writers will support an opinion with reasons and evidence from the text they have read.

Emerging	Expanding	Bridging
Writers introduce an opinion. They include at least one supporting detail.	Writers use language to tell about an opinion. They include several supporting details.	Writers use language to introduce their opinion. They include evidence from the text to support the opinion.

UNIT 6: MODULE B

Reading Goal: Readers will identify the author's purpose using details from the text.

Emerging	Expanding	Bridging
Readers use language frames to describe at least two details from a text that identify the author's purpose.	Readers use language frames to describe clearly several details from a text that identify the author's purpose.	Readers describe in great depth many details from a text that identify the author's purpose.

Writing Goal: Writers will support an opinion with clearly stated facts, details, and conclusion.

Emerging	Expanding	Bridging
Writers write an opinion.	Writers state an opinion and include several facts and details that support their opinion.	Writers begin by stating an interesting opinion, include many relevant facts that provide strong support for this opinion, and finish with a conclusion.

Linguistic Contrastive Analysis Chart

THE CONSONANTS OF ENGLISH				
IPA*	English	Spanish	Vietnamese	Cantonese
p	*pit* Aspirated at the start of a word or stressed syllable	*pato* (duck) Never aspirated	*pin* (battery)	*pʰa (to lie prone)* Always aspirated
b	*bit*	*barco* (boat) Substitute voiced bilabial fricative /ɤ/ in between vowels	*ba* (three) Implosive (air moves into the mouth during articulation)	**NO EQUIVALENT** Substitute /p/
m	*man*	*mundo* (world)	*mot* (one)	*ma* (mother)
w	*win*	*agua* (water)	**NO EQUIVALENT** Substitute word-initial /u/	*wa* (frog)
f	*fun*	*flor* (flower)	*phuʼoʼng* (phoenix) Substitute sound made with both lips, rather than with the lower lip and the teeth like English /f/	*fa* (flower) Only occurs at the beginning of syllables
v	*very*	**NO EQUIVALENT** Learners can use correct sound	*Việt Nam* (Vietnam)	**NO EQUIVALENT** Substitute /f/
ɵ	*thing* Rare in other languages. When done correctly, the tongue will stick out between the teeth.	**NO EQUIVALENT** Learners can use correct sound	**NO EQUIVALENT** Substitute /tʰ/ or /f/	**NO EQUIVALENT** Substitute /tʰ/ or /f/
ð	*there* Rare in other languages. When done correctly, the tongue will stick out between the teeth.	*cada* (every) Sound exists in Spanish only between vowels; sometimes substitute voiceless ɵ.	**NO EQUIVALENT** Substitute /d/	**NO EQUIVALENT** Substitute /t/ or /f/
t	*time* Aspirated at the start of a word or stressed syllable English tongue-touch. Is a little farther back in the mouth than the other languages.	*tocar* (touch) Never aspirated	*tám* (eight) Distinguishes aspirated and non-aspirated	*tʰa* (he/she) Distinguishes aspirated and non-aspirated
d	*dime* English tongue-touch is a little farther back in the mouth than the other languages.	*dos* (two)	*Đōng* (Dong = unit of currency) Vietnamese /d/ is implosive (air moves into the mouth during articulation)	**NO EQUIVALENT** Substitute /t/
n	*name* English tongue-touch is a little farther back in the mouth than the other languages.	*nube* (cloud)	*nam* (south)	*na* (take)
s	*soy*	*seco* (dry)	*xem* (to see)	*sa* (sand) Substitute *sh–* sound before /u/ Difficult at ends of syllables and words
z	*zeal*	**NO EQUIVALENT** Learners can use correct sound	*ròi* (already) In northern dialect only Southern dialect, substitute /y/	**NO EQUIVALENT** Substitute /s/
ɾ	*butter* Written 't' and 'd' are pronounced with a quick tongue-tip tap.	*rana* (toad) Written as single *r* and thought of as an /r/ sound.	**NO EQUIVALENT** Substitute /t/	**NO EQUIVALENT** Substitute /t/
l	*loop* English tongue-touch is a little farther back in the mouth than the other languages. At the ends of syllables, the /l/ bunches up the back of the tongue, becoming velarized /ɫ/ or dark-l as in the word *ball*.	*libro* (book)	*cú lao* (island) /l/ does not occur at the ends of syllables	*lau* (angry) /l/ does not occur at the ends of syllables

* International Phonetic Alphabet

THE CONSONANTS OF ENGLISH

IPA*	Hmong	Filipino	Korean	Mandarin
p	*peb* (we/us/our) Distinguishes aspirated and non-aspirated	*paalam* (goodbye) Never aspirated	*pal* (sucking)	*pʰei* (cape) Always aspirated
b	**NO EQUIVALENT** Substitute /p/	*baka* (beef)	**NO EQUIVALENT** /b/ said between vowels Substitute /p/ elsewhere	**NO EQUIVALENT**
m	*mus* (to go)	*mabuti* (good)	*mal* (horse)	*mei* (rose)
w	**NO EQUIVALENT** Substitute word-initial /*u*/	*walo (eight)*	*gwe* (box)	*wen* (mosquito)
f	*faib* (to divide)	**NO EQUIVALENT** Substitute /p/	**NO EQUIVALENT** Substitute /p/	*fa* (issue)
v	*Vaj* ('Vang' clan name)	**NO EQUIVALENT** Substitute /b/	**NO EQUIVALENT** Substitute /b/	**NO EQUIVALENT** Substitute /w/ or /f/
θ	**NO EQUIVALENT** Substitute /tʰ/ or /f/	**NO EQUIVALENT** Learners can use correct sound, but sometimes mispronounce voiced /ð/.	**NO EQUIVALENT** Substitute /t/	**NO EQUIVALENT** Substitute /t/ or /s/
ð	**NO EQUIVALENT** Substitute /d/	**NO EQUIVALENT** Learners can use correct sound	**NO EQUIVALENT** Substitute /d/	**NO EQUIVALENT** Substitute /t/ or /s/
t	*them* (to pay) Distinguishes aspirated and non-aspirated	*takbo* (run) Never aspirated	*tal* (daughter)	*ta* (wet) Distinguishes aspirated and non-aspirated
d	*dev* (dog)	*deretso* (straight)	**NO EQUIVALENT** Substitute /d/ when said between vowels and /t/ elsewhere.	**NO EQUIVALENT** Substitute /t/
n	*noj* (to eat)	*naman* (too)	*nal* (day)	*ni* (you) May be confused with /l/
s	*xa* (to send)	*sila* (they)	*sal* (rice) Substitute *shi*– sound before /i/ and /z/ after a nasal consonant	*san (three)*
z	**NO EQUIVALENT** Learners can use correct sound	**NO EQUIVALENT** Learners can use correct sound	**NO EQUIVALENT** Learners can use correct sound	**NO EQUIVALENT** Substitute /ts/ or /tsʰ/
ɾ	**NO EQUIVALENT** Substitute /t/	*rin/din* (too) Variant of the /d/ sound	Only occurs between two vowels Considered an /l/ sound	**NO EQUIVALENT**
l	*los* (to come) /l/ does not occur at the ends of syllables	*salamat* (thank you)	*balam* (wind)	*lan* (blue) Can be confused and substituted with /r/

* International Phonetic Alphabet

IPA*	English	Spanish	Vietnamese	Cantonese
THE CONSONANTS OF ENGLISH				
ɹ	*red* Rare sound in the world Includes lip-rounding	**NO EQUIVALENT** Substitute /r/ sound such as the tap /ɾ/ or the trilled /r/	**NO EQUIVALENT** Substitute /l/	**NO EQUIVALENT** Substitute /l/
ʃ	*shallow* Often said with lip-rounding	**NO EQUIVALENT** Substitute /s/ or /tʃ/	*sieu thị* (supermarket) Southern dialect only	**NO EQUIVALENT** Substitute /s/
ʒ	*vision* Rare sound in English	**NO EQUIVALENT** Substitute /z/ or /dʒ/	**NO EQUIVALENT** Substitute /s/	**NO EQUIVALENT** Substitute /s/
tʃ	*chirp*	*chico* (boy)	*chính phủ* (government) Pronounced harder than English *ch*	**NO EQUIVALENT** Substitute /ts/
dʒ	*joy*	**NO EQUIVALENT** Sometimes substituted with /ʃ/ sound Some dialects have this sound for the *ll* spelling as in *llamar*	**NO EQUIVALENT** Substitute /c/, the equivalent sound, but voiceless	**NO EQUIVALENT** Substitute /ts/ Only occurs at beginnings of syllables
j	*you*	*cielo* (sky) Often substitute /dʒ/	*yeu* (to love)	*jau* (worry)
k	*kite* Aspirated at the start of a word or stressed syllable	*casa* (house) Never aspirated	*com* (rice) Never aspirated	*kʰa* (family) Distinguishes aspirated and non-aspirated
g	*goat*	*gato* (cat)	**NO EQUIVALENT** Substitute /k/	**NO EQUIVALENT** Substitute /k/
ŋ	*king*	*mango* (mango)	*Ngũyen* (proper last name)	*phaŋ* (to cook)
h	*hope*	*gente* (people) Sometimes substitute sound with friction higher in the vocal tract as velar /x/ or uvular /χ/	*hoa* (flower)	*ha* (shrimp)

* International Phonetic Alphabet

THE CONSONANTS OF ENGLISH				
IPA*	Hmong	Filipino	Korean	Mandarin
ɹ	**NO EQUIVALENT** Substitute /l/	**NO EQUIVALENT** Substitute the tap /r/	**NO EQUIVALENT** Substitute the tap or /l/ confused with /l/	*r*an (caterpillar) Tongue tip curled further backward than for English /r/
ʃ	*s*au (to write)	*si*ya (s/he)	Only occurs before /i/; Considered an /s/ sound	*sh*i (wet)
ʒ	*z*os village)	**NO EQUIVALENT** Learners can use correct sound	**NO EQUIVALENT**	**NO EQUIVALENT** Substitute palatal affricate /tɕ/
tʃ	*ch*eb (to sweep)	*ts*a (tea)	*cʰ*al (kicking)	*ch*eng (red)
dʒ	**NO EQUIVALENT** Substitute *ch* sound	*D*ios (God)	**NO EQUIVALENT** Substitute *ch* sound	**NO EQUIVALENT** Substitute /ts/
j	*Y*aj (Yang, clan name)	ta*y*o (we)	*j*e:zan (budget)	*y*an (eye)
k	*K*oo (Kong, clan name) Distinguishes aspirated and non-aspirated	*k*alian (when) Never aspirated	*k*al (spreading)	*k*e (nest) Distinguishes aspirated and non-aspirated
g	**NO EQUIVALENT** Substitute /k/	*g*ulay (vegetable)	**NO EQUIVALENT** Substitute /k/ Learners use correct sound between two vowels	**NO EQUIVALENT** Substitute /k/
ŋ	*g*us (goose)	a*ng*aw (one million)	ba*ŋ* (room)	ta*ng* (gong) Sometimes add /k/ sound to the end
h	*h*ais (to speak)	*h*indi (no)	*h*al (doing)	**NO EQUIVALENT** Substitute velar fricative /x/

International Phonetic Alphabet

THE VOWELS OF ENGLISH

IPA*	English	Spanish	Vietnamese	Cantonese
i	*beat*	*hijo* (son)	*di* (to go)	*si* (silk)
ɪ	*bit* Rare in other languages Usually confused with /i/ (*meat* vs. *mit*)	**NO EQUIVALENT** Substitute /ē/	**NO EQUIVALENT** Substitute /ē/	*sik* (color) Only occurs before velars Substitute /ē/
e	*bait* End of vowel diphthongized—tongue moves up to /ē/ or short *e* position	*eco* (echo)	*kê* (millet)	*se* (to lend)
ɛ	*bet* Rare in other languages Learners may have difficulty distinguishing /ā/ and /e/ (short *e*): *pain* vs. *pen*	**NO EQUIVALENT** Substitute /ā/	**NO EQUIVALENT** Substitute /ā/	*seŋ* (sound) Only occurs before velars; difficult to distinguish from /ā/ in all positions
æ	*bat* Rare in other languages Learners may have trouble getting the tongue farther forward in the mouth	**NO EQUIVALENT** Substitute mid central /u/ (short *u*) or low front tense /o/ (short *o*)	*ghe* (boat)	**NO EQUIVALENT** Hard to distinguish between /æ/ and /ā/
u	*boot*	*uva* (grape)	*mua* (to buy)	*fu* (husband)
ʊ	*could* Rare in other languages Learners may have difficulty distinguishing the vowel sounds in *wooed* vs. *wood*	**NO EQUIVALENT** Substitute long *u*	**NO EQUIVALENT** Substitute long *u* (high back unrounded)	*suk* (uncle) Only occurs before velars Difficult to distinguish from long *u* in all positions
o	*boat* End of vowel diphthongized—tongue moves up to long *u* or ʊ position	*ojo* (eye)	*cô* (aunt)	*so* (comb)
ɔ	*law*	**NO EQUIVALENT** Substitute long *o* or short *o* Substituting long *o* will cause confusion (*low* vs. *law*); substituting short *o* will not	*cá* (fish)	*hok* (shell) Only occurs before velars Difficult to distinguish from long *o* in all positions
ɑ	*hot*	*mal* (bad)	*con* (child)	*sa* (sand)
ɑ ʊ	*house* Diphthong	*pauta*	*dao* (knife)	*sau* (basket)
ɔ ɪ	*boy* Diphthong	*hoy* (today)	*ròi* (already)	*soi* (grill)
ɑ ɪ	*bite* Diphthong	*baile* (dance)	*hai* (two)	*sai* (to waste)
ə	*about* Most common vowel in English; only in unstressed syllables Learners may have difficulty keeping it very short	**NO EQUIVALENT** Substitute short *u* or the full vowel from the word's spelling	*mua* (to buy)	**NO EQUIVALENT**
ʌ	*cut* Similar to schwa /ə/	**NO EQUIVALENT** Substitute short *o*	*giò'* (time)	*san* (new)
ɝ	*bird* Difficult articulation, unusual in the world but common in American English Learners must bunch the tongue and constrict the throat	**NO EQUIVALENT** Substitute short *u* or /er/ with trill	**NO EQUIVALENT** Substitute /i/	*hæ* (boot)

* International Phonetic Alphabet

THE VOWELS OF ENGLISH

IPA*	Hmong	Filipino	Korean	Mandarin
i	*ib* (one)	*ikaw* (you) This vowel is interchangeable with /ɪ/; hard for speakers to distinguish these	zɪːʃaŋ (market)	*ti* (ladder) Sometimes English /i/ can be produced shorter
ɪ	**NO EQUIVALENT** Substitute /ē/	*limampu* (fifty) This vowel is interchangeable with /ē/; hard for speakers to distinguish these	**NO EQUIVALENT** Substitute /ē/	**NO EQUIVALENT**
e	*tes* (hand)	*sero* (zero)	*be:da* (to cut)	*te* (nervous) Sometimes substitute English schwa /ə/
ɛ	**NO EQUIVALENT** Substitute /ā/	*sero* (zero) This vowel interchanges with /ā/ like *bait*; not difficult for speakers to learn	*thɛ:do* (attitude)	**NO EQUIVALENT**
æ	**NO EQUIVALENT** Substitute short *e*	**NO EQUIVALENT** Substitute short *o* as in *hot*	**NO EQUIVALENT**	**NO EQUIVALENT** Substitute /ə/ or short *u*
u	*kub* (hot or gold)	*tunay* (actual) This vowel interchanges with vowel in *could*; not difficult for speakers to learn	*zu:bag* (watermelon)	*lu* (hut) Sometimes English long *u* can be produced shorter
ʊ	**NO EQUIVALENT** Substitute a sound like long *e* (mid central with lips slightly rounded)	*gumawa* (act) This vowel interchanges with long *u* like *boot*; not difficult for speakers to learn	**NO EQUIVALENT**	**NO EQUIVALENT**
o	**NO EQUIVALENT**	*ubo* (cough)	*bo:zu* (salary)	*mo* (sword) This vowel is a little lower than English vowel
ɔ	*Yaj* (Yang clan name)	**NO EQUIVALENT** Spoken as short *o*, as in *hot*	**NO EQUIVALENT**	**NO EQUIVALENT** Substitute long *o*
ɑ	*mov* (cooked rice)	*talim* (blade)	*ma:l* (speech)	*ta* (he/she) Sometimes substitute back long *o* or *u*
ɑʊ	*plaub* (four)	*ikaw* (you)	**NO EQUIVALENT**	**NO EQUIVALENT**
ɔɪ	**NO EQUIVALENT**	*apoy* (fire)	**NO EQUIVALENT**	**NO EQUIVALENT**
ɑɪ	*qaib* (chicken)	*himatay* (faint)	**NO EQUIVALENT**	**NO EQUIVALENT**
ə	**NO EQUIVALENT**	**NO EQUIVALENT** Spoken as short *o*, as in *hot*	**NO EQUIVALENT** Difficult sound for learners	**NO EQUIVALENT**
ʌ	**NO EQUIVALENT**	**NO EQUIVALENT** Spoken as short *o*, as in *hot*	**NO EQUIVALENT**	**NO EQUIVALENT**
ɝ	**NO EQUIVALENT** Substitute diphthong /əɨ/	**NO EQUIVALENT** Spoken as many different vowels (depending on English spelling) plus tongue tap /ɾ/	**NO EQUIVALENT**	**NO EQUIVALENT**

* International Phonetic Alphabet

Acknowledgments

Photographs

Photo locators denoted as follows: Top (T), Center (C), Bottom (B), Left (L), Right (R), Background (Bkgd)

4 Ambient Images, Inc./Alamy Images; **34** ©Blend Images/Alamy; **35(TL), 38, 40, 42** Simon & Schuster; **64** ©Blend Images/Alamy; **65(TL), 68, 70, 72** HarperCollins Publishers; **94** Zacarias Pereira da Mata/Shutterstock; **95(TL), 98, 100, 102** HarperCollins Publishers; **124** © amana images inc./Alamy; **125(BL), 142, 144, 146** Capstone Press; **154** © Blend Images/Alamy; **155(TR), 164, 166, 168** Greenwillow Books.